MORE PRAISE FOR *NAVIGATING THE COMMON LANGUAGE LEARNERS*

"Ferlazzo and Hull Sypnieski's book artfully combines a strong theoretical framework with highly practical and accessible ideas for lessons, units of study, and classroom organization and structure. Their teaching strategies and lesson ideas build on an assets-approach to teaching English learners that is refreshing, empowering, and imperative for student success. The authors acknowledge all that ELs bring to school—in terms of dispositions, prior learning, life experiences, and academic knowledge—showing us how to translate those skills, dispositions, and experiences into a useful foundation for academic learning in English. Teachers will find many useful and compelling resources in this book!"

—*Pia Wong, professor of education, Sacramento State University*

"*Navigating the Common Core with English Language Learners* is the best resource I've seen connecting Common Core and ELLs; in fact, it is just as valuable for my work with English proficient students."

—*Lara Hoekstra, classroom teacher with over 15 years of experience working with ELLs*

Navigating the Common Core with English Language Learners

Practical Strategies to Develop Higher-Order Thinking Skills

LARRY FERLAZZO AND KATIE HULL SYPNIESKI

JOSSEY-BASS™
A Wiley Brand

Published by Jossey-Bass
A Wiley Brand
One Montgomery Street, Suite 1000, San Francisco, CA 94104-4594—www.josseybass.com

Jossey-Bass books and products are available through most bookstores. To contact Jossey-Bass directly call our Customer Care Department within the U.S. at 800-956-7739, outside the U.S. at 317-572-3986, or fax 317-572-4002.

Wiley publishes in a variety of print and electronic formats and by print-on-demand. Some material included with standard print versions of this book may not be included in e-books or in print-on-demand. If this book refers to media such as a CD or DVD that is not included in the version you purchased, you may download this material at http://booksupport.wiley.com. For more information about Wiley products, visit www.wiley.com.

Library of Congress Cataloging-in-Publication Data
ISBN 978-1-119-02300-5 (Paperback) ISBN 978-1-119-02302-9 (ePDF)
ISBN 978-1-119-02301-2 (epub)

Cover image: © archideaphoto/iStockphoto
Cover design: Wiley

Printed in the United States of America

FIRST EDITION
PB Printing 10 9 8 7 6 5 4 3 2 1.

About the Authors

arry Ferlazzo has taught English and social studies to English language learners and mainstream students at Luther Burbank High School in Sacramento, California, for 11 years. He has written seven previous books, *The ESL/ELL Teacher's Survival Guide* (with coauthor Katie Hull Sypnieski); *Building a Community of Self-Motivated Learners: Strategies to Help Students Thrive in School and Beyond*; *Classroom Management Q&As: Expert Strategies for Teaching*; *Self-Driven Learning: Teaching Strategies for Student Motivation*; *Helping Students Motivate Themselves: Practical Answers to Classroom Challenges*; *English Language Learners: Teaching Strategies That Work*; and *Building Parent Engagement in Schools* (with coauthor Lorie Hammond).

He has won numerous awards, including the Leadership for a Changing World Award from the Ford Foundation, and was the grand prize winner of the International Reading Association Award for Technology and Reading.

He writes a popular education blog at http://larryferlazzo.edublogs.org/; a weekly teacher advice column for *Education Week Teacher*, and a weekly post for the *New York Times* on teaching English language learners. Larry is an Adjunct Faculty member at the Department of Education, California State University, Sacramento, teaching credential candidates how to work with English Language Learners at the secondary level. His articles on education also regularly appear in the *Washington Post* and *ASCD Educational Leadership*.

Larry was a community organizer for 19 years prior to becoming a public school teacher. He is married and has three children and two grandchildren.

Katie Hull Sypnieski has worked with English language learners at the secondary level for 20 years and has taught English and ELD at Luther Burbank High School in Sacramento, California, for the past 13 years.

She is a teaching consultant with the Area 3 Writing Project at the University of California, Davis, and has led professional development for teachers of ELLs at the district and site level.

She is the coauthor (with Larry Ferlazzo) of *The ESL/ELL Teacher's Survival Guide* and has written articles for the *Washington Post, ASCD Educational Leadership*, and *Edutopia*.

Katie lives in Sacramento with her husband and their three children.

About the Contributors

*C*aleb Cheung is the Science Manager and previously a science teacher in the Oakland Unified School District for the past 20 years. His work focuses on developing extensive districtwide structures and regional partnerships for improving science education and implementing the Next Generation Science Standards (NGSS). He has a background in biology and is National Board Certified in Early Adolescent Science. In 2005, Caleb won the Presidential Award for Excellence in Math and Science Teaching, and from 2006–2009 he served as a Commissioner and the Chair of the California Commission on Teacher Credentialing. He currently serves on the Science Curriculum Framework and Evaluation Criteria Committee to align California's Science Framework to NGSS.

Wendy Jennings has been a mathematics educator in Sacramento City Unified School District for the past 13 years. She has degrees in anthropology (BA), mathematics (BS), and human behavior (MA). Wendy also works with the UC Davis C-STEM center on the integration of computer programming and robotics into mathematics curriculum.

Elisabeth Johnson is a National Board Certified Social Studies teacher who has been at Luther Burbank High School for nine years. She is a teaching consultant for the Area 3 Writing Project at the University of California, Davis.

Laura Prival coordinates the elementary science program of the Oakland Unified School District (OUSD) in Oakland, California. Laura has coached many elementary teachers in OUSD as they increase the quantity and quality of science instruction in their classrooms and developed curriculum to help teachers and students transition to the Next Generation Science Standards. Laura has designed and led numerous workshops for teachers focusing on hands-on science, strategies for developing language and literacy through science, watershed awareness, climate change, and outdoor education. She has taught science in both urban and rural settings and was previously a fifth-grade multiple-subject teacher in OUSD. Laura has also worked as a service learning specialist, a curriculum writer, and an education consultant for nonprofit organizations. She is a doctoral candidate in Educational Leadership at Mills College with a focus on equity in elementary science instruction.

Claudio Vargas is the Coordinator of Elementary Science at the Oakland Unified School District (OUSD). He oversees and supports the implementation of the science program at the 54 district elementary schools. Before joining OUSD, Mr. Vargas served as the director of the Bay Area Science Project (BASP) at UC Berkeley's Lawrence Hall of Science (LHS). Mr. Vargas has led numerous professional development programs throughout the Bay Area, Los Angeles, Texas, and Central America. He has designed and implemented K–8 professional development programs that focus on developing teachers' science content knowledge and expanding their teaching strategies, with particular emphasis on strategies that provide English language learners with access to the core curriculum and accelerated language learning. Prior to joining LHS, Mr. Vargas worked for 10 years as a bilingual K–5 teacher and a science coach in the Oakland Unified School District.

Diana Vélez is a professional development specialist and curriculum developer at the Lawrence Hall of Science at the University of California, Berkeley. She currently works with various science education projects in the area of English Language Development and the integration of literacy, as well as classroom and districtwide implementation of the Next Generation Science Standards. Before coming to the Lawrence Hall of Science, Ms. Vélez was a science and math coach for an elementary school in Oakland, California and taught in a Spanish dual immersion program at the primary level.

Contents

    Wendy Jennings

Acknowledgments

Larry Ferlazzo: I'd like to thank my family—Stacia, Rich, Shea, Ava, Nik, Karli, and especially my wife, Jan—for their support. In addition, I need to express appreciation to my coauthor, Katie Hull Sypnieski, who has been a friend, classroom neighbor and coteacher for 11 years. I would also like to thank Kelly Young at Pebble Creek Labs and my many colleagues at Luther Burbank High School, including former principal Ted Appel and present principal Jim Peterson, for their assistance over the years. And, probably most important, I'd like to thank the many English language learner students who have made me a better teacher—and a better person. I must also thank David Powell, who has done an extraordinary job in making presentable manuscripts for all of my books, including this one. Finally, I must offer a big "Thank you" to Marjorie McAneny, Shauna Robinson, and Victoria Garrity at Jossey-Bass for their patience and guidance in preparing this book.

Katie Hull Sypnieski: I would like to thank all of my family members, especially David, Drew, Ryan, and Rachel, for their love and support. I'd also like to thank my dear friend Hannah, my neighbor Nancy, and my father-in-law, Douglas, who made it possible for me to work on this book during the summer when my kids were at home! Thank you to my amazing colleagues at Luther Burbank, especially Pam Buric, Dana Dusbiber, and Lara Hoekstra, for their collaboration and support over the years. Thanks to my coauthor, Larry Ferlazzo, whom I'm proud to call my colleague and my friend. Thank you also to the many educators at the California Writing Project who have taught me so much over the years. I must also thank Marjorie McAneny, Shauna Robinson, and Victoria Garrity at Jossey-Bass for all of the help they've provided to us. Finally, to the many students whom I've had the honor of teaching—thank you for all the love, laughter, and learning you've brought into my life.

Both of us want to give a special thanks to the extraordinary educators who have contributed lesson plans and chapters to this book and to supplemental online content: Wendy Jennings, Elisabeth Johnson, Caleb Cheung, Laura Prival, Claudio Vargas, Diana Vélez, John Doolittle, Laura Gibbs, and Leticia Gallardo.

Introduction

The Common Core Standards, and the standardized tests tied to them, are now being implemented in most states. And the few states that have not adopted them have created their own very similar ones.[1]

This transition offers school districts, schools, and teachers an opportunity to pause and reflect on their practices and consider how to ensure that students, including English language learners, are developing the skills necessary to thrive in our changing world. Transitions are often breeding grounds for anxiety and fear of the unknown. However, they can also be a doorway leading to growth and new possibilities.

We know many parents, teachers, and students are feeling anxious, especially around the new Common Core assessments. We share those concerns, especially since we think there are more pressing issues facing our schools and students than a need for new Standards, such as the need for increased school funding, family services, institutional commitment to—and advocacy for—ELL students, and time for teacher collaboration, to name just a few. Nevertheless, we live in the world as it is, not as we'd like it to be. Therefore, we are committed to facing change in ways that create the most positive outcomes for our students. *Navigating the Common Core with English Language Learners* is written in this spirit of adaptation and openness.

We have taken the four years since the publication of our previous book, *The ESL/ELL Teacher's Survival Guide*,[2] to reflect on, and review, our practice in light of the Common Core and apply what we consider to be its positive elements—particularly its emphasis on higher-order thinking—to improve our teaching. Though most of the content in our first book is certainly compatible with the Standards, and we still apply the practices described there in our classrooms, we have also developed new and refined older ones to make them even more effective for our students and more aligned to the new Standards.

Readers will find that at least 90% of the content in this book is new material not found in our previous one. Even though the word count of this book has strained the outer limits of our publisher's guidelines, it is by no means exhaustive. Each domain—reading writing, speaking/listening, language—and each subject—math, social studies, science—deserves its own book. However, we don't have the time to write them and we know few teachers who would have the time to read them!

You will also find that, though many of the lessons we discuss in these chapters are applicable to Beginning English language learners, more are written with Intermediate and Advanced ELLs in mind.

We believe that teachers of ELLs and non-ELLS alike will find our Social Emotional Learning lessons, our clear analyses of the Standards, and our classroom recommendations helpful.

Our students, their families, and we as educators face some very big challenges ahead. We hope that this book can help make those challenges a little more manageable for all of us.

For downloadable versions of all lesson plans and student hand-outs found in this book, go to the "Downloads" section of this book's web page at www.wiley.com/go/navccss. In addition, you will find two "bonus" book chapters on that page: One is on using Art with English Language Learners while meeting Common Core Standards, and is written by high school English and Art teacher John Doolittle. The second chapter is on how school counselors can assist both English Language Learners and their teachers as they work to meet Common Core Standards. This second chapter is written by Leticia Gallardo, a high school counselor.

CHAPTER ONE

English Language Learners and the Common Core: An Overview

Change is the law of life. And those who look only to the past or present are certain to miss the future.

—*John F. Kennedy*[1]

Change is a constant in life, and this is especially true in education. When faced with change some people cling strongly to the past, others dive in headfirst without question, and some take a more measured approach by evaluating both past and present as they move forward.

In terms of education, it is important to look to past research on effective teaching and learning, but not to cling to outdated, ineffective practices. It is also important to be in the present, the era of "Common Core," and to try new strategies, while not ignoring what we already know about good teaching practice.

When teaching English Language Learners, we need to evaluate current standards and consider how to teach them in light of what has already been learned about language acquisition. In our classrooms, we acknowledge our students for who they are in the present—getting to know their interests, assessing their current proficiency levels, and identifying their academic strengths and challenges. But, we also look to their past—inviting them to share the prior knowledge and rich experiences they bring with them.

It is this balance—looking at both past and present in order to shape the best future—that we hope will be apparent in this book, and particularly in this chapter. We start with an overview of general information related to teaching ELLs. While many of the topics in the first few pages are similar to those in our first book, *The ESL/ELL Teacher's Survival Guide*,[2] the information has been updated with recent research and demographics. Of course, the biggest change since we wrote our first book 4 years ago is the implementation of the national Common Core standards and new state English Language Proficiency standards occurring throughout the country. While many of the strategies outlined in our last book are compatible with Common Core, we've learned a lot in the past 4 years.

In this book, we will explain how we've used the Common Core standards to improve some of the ideas from our last book while also laying out new strategies we are using to help our students meet the challenges of Common Core. Obviously, it is not realistic for early Beginners to meet grade-level Common Core standards. However, the strategies for Beginning ELLs described in our first book and further developed in this book, lay the groundwork for them to do so as quickly as possible. For example, the pattern-seeking strategies in the Picture Word Inductive model[3] help prepare them for the pattern-seeking needed in the close reading required by Common Core. The use of Text Data Sets helps students develop preliminary essay writing skills as they organize and summarize categories. In addition, the dialogues we use with Beginners prepare students for the communicative tasks in the Speaking and Listening Common Core Standards, and the many vocabulary activities described for Beginners in our first book set the stage for the acquisition of the academic vocabulary required in the Language standards.

ELL Population Growth

It is hard to find a school or district in this country that doesn't have an English Language Learner population, and in many states, it is hard to find a classroom without any ELLs. English Language Learners represented nearly 10% of the total K–12 student population with 4.85 million ELL students enrolled in public schools during the 2012–2013 school year.[4]

California has the highest percentage of ELLs at 24% of enrollment in public schools, about 1.1 million students, followed by Texas with 832,000 ELLs comprising 17% of public school students.[5] In Nevada and New Mexico, ELLs represent nearly one in five students (18% and 17%, respectively). ELL students account for 17% of the student population in Colorado, 10% in Florida, and 9% in both New York and the District of Columbia.[6]

It is clear that the number of ELL students across the nation continues to steadily grow. However, some states, including South Carolina, Kentucky, Nevada, Delaware, Arkansas, Kansas, Mississippi, Alabama, Virginia, and North Carolina, have experienced huge increases in their ELL populations. According to the Annenberg Institute, "while the U.S. ELL population has grown 18% from 2000–2001 to 2011–2012, which is a significant increase, these states have experienced ELL growth ranging from 135% in North Carolina to an astonishing 610% in South Carolina."[7]

Languages Spoken by ELLs

While English language learners in the United States speak roughly 400 languages, the majority (approximately 80%) are Spanish-speakers.[8] In 2011, Latinos represented 24% of public school enrollment and are projected to be 30% by 2023.[9]

As of 2013, more than two-thirds of ELL students in 45 states and the District of Columbia spoke Spanish. In 19 states, including Texas and California, more than three-quarters of all ELL students spoke Spanish. Other states, like West Virginia, Minnesota, and Ohio among others, were less homogeneous and their ELL populations spoke a diverse set of languages such as Vietnamese, Chinese, Somali, Hmong, and Arabic.[10]

How Are English Language Learners Described?

ELLs are a diverse, dynamic group, which is evident in the large number of "labels" used to describe them. Here are some of the most common:

ELL, or English language learner: ELL (or EL) is the most current term used in the United States to describe students who are in various stages of acquiring English. The U.S. Department of Education defines an ELL (or EL) as:

> An individual who, due to any of the reasons listed below, has sufficient difficulty speaking, reading, writing, or understanding the English language to be denied the opportunity to learn successfully in classrooms where the language of instruction is English or to participate fully in the larger U.S. society. Such an individual (1) was not born in the United States or has a native language other than English; (2) comes from environments where a language other than English is dominant; or (3) is an American Indian or Alaska Native and comes from environments where a language other than English has had a significant impact on the individual's level of English language proficiency.[11]

LEP, or limited English proficiency: LEP is still used by the U.S. Department of Education for ELLs, age 3–21, who have not yet demonstrated proficiency in English, and for whom this affects their ability to perform on state standards and assessments, to access classroom content, and/or to participate fully in society.[12]

DLL, or dual language learner: A child between the ages of 0 and 8 who is in the process of learning English in addition to his or her home language(s). These children may or may not also be considered ELLs by their schools, depending on their performance on English language proficiency assessments.[13]

ESL, or English as a second language: The term *ESL* was formerly used as a designation for ELL students, but is more commonly used now to refer to "a program of instruction designed to support ELL students" and is often still used at the postsecondary level to refer to multilingual students (National Council of Teachers of English,[14] 2008).

ELD, or English language development: ELD is often used to describe instruction and programs for ELL students that focus on developing English language proficiency in the domains of reading, writing, listening, and speaking.[15]

TESOL, or teaching English to speakers of other languages: TESOL is widely used to describe both TEFL (teaching English as a foreign language) and TESL (teaching English as a second language). In general, "TEFL emphasizes aspects of teaching English in countries where English is not widely used in daily life and the term TESL tends to emphasize the needs of learners who will use English in their daily lives, in addition to their mother-tongue. TESOL encompasses both."[16]

Along with many educators and researchers, we prefer to use the term ELL because it emphasizes students as *active learners* of English, rather than as being limited or deficient in some way.

Adolescent English Language Learners and Long-term ELLs

The adolescent English learner population in this country is growing fast and contains students from a variety of linguistic, cultural, and educational backgrounds.[17]

Newcomer or refugee students represent a small, but highly vulnerable subgroup of the adolescent English learner population.[18] While some of these students come with high literacy skills and content knowledge, many have had interrupted formal education in their home countries. These students enter U.S. schools with limited educational experiences and lower levels of literacy in their home languages.

A larger number of adolescent ELLs were born in the United States, are second- or even third-generation immigrants, and have been enrolled in U.S. schools since kindergarten.[19]

One out of every four children in the United States is an immigrant or the U.S.-born child of immigrants.[20]

Nationwide 82% of current ELL students in grades K–5 are native-born, and 55% of ELLs in grades 6–12 were born in the United States.[21]

Researchers have identified secondary ELL students who have attended school in the United States for 6 years or more,[22] but who continue to require language support services in school as long-term English language learners, LTELs, or LTELLs.[23] Many of these students have developed high levels of oral proficiency, but lack academic language and literacy skills needed to master subject matter.

They often remain "stuck" at the intermediate level of proficiency and face dispro-portionately high dropout rates.[24] LTELs comprise approximately one third of all secondary ELLs in both New York City public schools and Chicago Public Schools. In Colorado, 23% of secondary ELLs are LTELs, and 59% in 40 school districts in California are considered LTELs.[25] However, despite the large number of these students in many schools and districts across the country, LTELs often represent an "invisible population" because of a lack of research on their particular experiences and a lack of programs in schools designed to meet their specific needs.[26]

California researchers, educators, and legislators have been in the forefront of calling attention to the needs of LTELs, particularly the organization Californians Together, led by Dr. Laurie Olsen (http://www.californianstogether.org). According to Californians Together, three out of four (74%) English learner students in grades 6–12 have been in California schools for 7 years or more and have still not attained proficiency in English. Of this group, 19% of secondary ELLs meet the state's mul-tiple criteria that designate them as Long-term English Learners (7 years or more in California schools, scoring Far Below Basic or Below Basic on the state academic exams in English Language Arts and failing to progress on the state's English lan-guage proficiency exam).[27]

In 2010, Californians Together published *Reparable Harm: Fulfilling the Unkept Promise of Educational Opportunity for California's Long Term English Learners,* which contains a wealth of research, recommendations, and resources on LTELs.[28]

As a result of new legislation passed in 2012,[29] California is making an effort to identify students who are currently long-term ELs and those who are "at risk" of becoming LTELs in order to provide them with the educational support they need. The law also requires that the Department of Education provides school and district level data annually on those students who are, or are at risk of becoming long-term ELLs.[30]

ELL Research Basics

Just as the number of ELLs has continued to grow, so does the research base on how ELLs acquire language and how this affects instructional practices and policy. While we will cite current ELL research throughout this book, in this section, we will first highlight a few foundational concepts of language development research.

BICS AND CALP

Jim Cummins, a professor at the University of Toronto, first introduced the distinction between BICS (basic interpersonal communicative skills) and CALP

Table 1.1 BICS and CALP

BICS	CALP
Listening and speaking skills that are acquired quickly in a new language in order to communicate in social situations	The academic language and more cognitively demanding skills required for academic success
Usually acquired within the first couple of years	Often takes longer to develop, between 5 and 7 years, or longer for students with less proficiency in their native language
Context-embedded (meaning is accomplished with the assistance of contextual cues such as pictures, body language or intonation)	Context-reduced (meaning must be constructed without the benefit of contextual cues and literacy demands are high)
Example: Asking someone for directions or talking with friends on the soccer field	Example: Responding to an essay prompt or summarizing a chapter in a textbook

(cognitive academic language proficiency). His research has had a major impact on policy and practices in second language education.[31] Table 1.1 summarizes Cummins's distinctions.

In more recent research, CALP has been expanded to include three dimensions of academic English: Linguistic (knowledge of word forms, functions, grammatical elements, and discourse patterns used in academic settings), Cognitive (higher-order thinking involved in academic settings), and Sociocultural-psychological (knowledge of social practices involved in academic settings).[32]

Instruction based on CALP is still widely accepted as best practice. Many researchers agree upon the need to focus on academic language proficiency in order for ELLs to be successful in school.

ACQUISITION VERSUS LEARNING

There is general agreement among researchers that there is a distinction between acquiring a language and learning a language.[33] Acquisition involves being able to easily and naturally use the language to communicate in a variety of situations, both academic and social. Language learning requires a more conscious approach and

Table 1.2 English Proficiency Level "Labels"

Traditional Labels	Beginning	Early Intermediate	Intermediate	Early Advanced	Advanced
WIDA	Entering	Emerging	Developing	Expanding	Bridging
ELPA 21	Level 1	Level 2	Level 3	Level 4	Level 5
California	Emerging — — — — — →Expanding — — — — — →Bridging				
New York	Entering ——→ Emerging ——→ Transitioning ——→ Expanding				

might include being able to correctly complete a grammar worksheet. However, this does not mean the two are mutually exclusive.

Much debate over the place of explicit grammar study has occurred throughout the years. Recent research points to a balanced approach—that second language instruction can provide a combination of both explicit teaching of language features such as grammar, vocabulary, and pronunciation, and implicit learning stemming from meaningful communication in the second language.[34]

This type of language instruction—using meaningful input and contexts to help students develop proficiency while also teaching specific language features and functions in context—is critical in helping ELLs meet the Common Core standards.

ENGLISH LANGUAGE PROFICIENCY LEVELS

Researchers agree that ELLs progress through general stages of language acquisition. These stages have traditionally been divided into five levels of English proficiency: Beginning, Early Intermediate, Intermediate, Early Advanced, and Advanced. More recently, consortiums made up of states and organizations, who are working on new ELD standards and assessments aligned to Common Core, use different descriptors for each level. We will be discussing these groups and their work later in this chapter.

Table 1.2 illustrates how these different proficiency level labels correspond. In this book, we will use Beginning–Advanced because that is how our school district classifies ELL students.

Of course, students' language acquisition often doesn't progress in a linear fashion within and across these proficiency levels. Students may demonstrate higher levels of proficiency in one domain versus another (e.g., listening versus writing) and may demonstrate different levels of proficiency within a domain depending upon the task. It is important to remember that a label of "Level 1" or "Beginner" *doesn't identify the student*, but identifies what a student knows and can do at any stage of English Language Development.

Common Core and English Language Learners: A Summary

In 2009, an effort to develop the Common Core State Standards was launched by state education leaders in 48 states, two territories, and the District of Columbia, through their membership in the National Governors Association Center for Best Practices (NGA Center) and the Council of Chief State School Officers (CCSSO).[35] The Common Core State Standards were released in June 2010 with the intention of establishing what students at each grade level need to know and be able to do in math and English Language Arts in order to graduate from high school ready to succeed "in college, career, and life, regardless of where they live."[36]

Upon their release, states began their own processes of reviewing and adopting the new standards. Public controversy over the development and implementation of the Common Core emerged, and many questions, particularly about how to effectively implement and assess the standards, were brought to the forefront by parents, students, teachers, researchers, and policy makers. Many educators worried that the national standards were being touted as a silver bullet. They questioned whether the resources to train teachers in the new standards would be there or if the training would result in any value for their students. Other concerns were raised about how these standards would be assessed and the links to big profits that publishers and testing companies were sure to make. At the same time, other educators, including the leadership of major teacher unions, voiced their support for the new standards. They supported Common Core's focus on critical thinking and deeper learning instead of drills and memorization, and felt that the standards provided room for teachers to use professional judgment in implementing them.[37, 38]

Despite the controversy, 43 states and the District of Columbia have adopted the CCSS.[39]

The remaining states are developing their own set of "college and career ready" standards that seem to be very similar in intent to Common Core, but with different wording.[40] They are also similar to international college and career readiness standards, and the authors of the CCSS state that the standards are "informed by other top-performing countries to prepare all students for success in our global economy and society."[41]

For us, based on our years of teaching, we would have identified many other problems facing our students and schools as higher priorities over the lack of national standards. We are all for having our students be "college and career ready," but we're not sure that the socioeconomic infrastructure is there yet to support students, teachers, and schools in meeting the Common Core standard's definition of that state of readiness. But, we live in the world as it is, not as we would like it to be, and therefore we feel the need to develop strategies to make Common Core standards work for our students, their families, and our schools.

COMMON CORE ASSESSMENTS

In 2010, the U.S. Department of Education awarded grants to two consortia of states to develop new assessments aligned to the CCSS. PARCC—Partnership for Assessment of Readiness for College and Careers (http://www.parcconline.org) and SBAC—Smarter Balanced Assessment Consortium (http://www.smarterbalanced .org) both received four-year grants to develop new content assessments that follow the guidelines below:

- Be valid and reliable
- Support and inform instruction
- Provide accurate information about what students know and can do
- Measure student achievement against standards designed to ensure that all students gain the knowledge and skills needed to succeed in college and the workplace.[42]

Federal law requires that ELLs participate in these state assessments annually in English language proficiency, reading/language arts, and mathematics.[43]

ELL students in their first 12 months of attending school in the United States are entitled to a one-time exemption from the state's English/language arts assessment, but not the math or science assessments.[44] However, a number of states have sought waivers that would extend the "test-free" period to two years.[45] At the time of this book's publication, Florida and Connecticut were the only states whose waivers were approved.[46, 47] In December, 2015, Congress passed The Every Student Succeeds Act to replace No Child Left Behind. At the time of this book's publication, the new law's impact on these regulations was still unclear. Updated information will be available at Larry's blog under *The Best Resources for Learning about the Next Generation of State Testing*.[48]

No matter what exemptions may or may not be granted, the reality is that the vast majority of English Language Learners in this country have already taken or soon will be taking these new assessments. An important requirement of the grants to create these assessments was to include testing accommodation policies for ELLs and students with disabilities. The new assessments from both PARCC and SBAC, which were operational for the 2014–2015 school year, were mostly administered by computer and did contain technology-based accommodations, such as pop-up glossaries, audio captions, and text-to-speech and speech-to-text options. Other, nonembedded accommodations include the use of bilingual, word-to-word dictionaries, test directions being read aloud or in a student's native language, smaller testing environments, and extended time.[49, 50]

As teachers, we know in real life that even with testing accommodations these assessments can be a source of frustration and anxiety for our ELL students. It is important for both teachers and students to remember the "end game"—that acquiring language and content in meaningful ways is the goal, not learning how to score higher on a state test.

ENGLISH LANGUAGE PROFICIENCY STANDARDS

Common Core standards lay out the academic concepts and content that students need to know in different academic subjects. Teachers and students use language to teach and learn these subjects. In order for teachers to effectively provide scaffolds for ELLs so they can learn the academic content specified in Common Core, they must know how language develops across proficiency levels and be aware of the specific language practices students need in order to access this content. English Language Proficiency standards are one resource teachers can use to gain that knowledge.

Several major efforts have been undertaken across the United States in the past few years to develop these types of English Language Proficiency standards that align to Common Core. In terms of helping English Learners to meet the Common Core, very little guidance was provided in the original publication of the standards. Basically, it was left up to each state to determine how to best align their English Language Proficiency Standards with the Common Core.[51] What follows is a good faith and nonexhaustive summary of some of these major efforts with links to more information about each one.

CCSSO

To address the lack of guidance on how to support English Language Learners meeting the Common Core standards, the Council of Chief State School Officers (CCSSO) published the *English Language Proficiency Development Framework*, to support states with the process of aligning their ELP standards to CCSS and the Next Generation of Science Standards that were published in April 2013.[52] This framework was developed by leading ELL researchers and educators and was published in September 2012.[53] Many states, along with educational organizations, have looked to this document to inform their creation or revision of English Language Proficiency standards that align to Common Core.

WIDA

WIDA formerly stood for World-Class Instructional Design and Assessment, but no longer uses this as an acronym. It still uses the name WIDA, and is a nonprofit cooperative group whose purpose is to develop equitable standards and assessments for English Language Learners. In 2012, WIDA published a revised version of their ELD standards titled *The WIDA English Language Development (ELD) Standards*. This new edition of amplified ELD standards are aligned to Common Core and represent "the social, instructional, and academic language that students need to engage with peers, educators, and the curriculum in schools."[54] Currently, 36 states belong to WIDA (see https://www.wida.us/membership/states/ for a list) and have adopted the WIDA standards. Educators in other states and around the world find the WIDA standards—along with WIDA's Can-Do Descriptors (specific descriptions of the language students should be able to understand and produce at various levels of proficiency)—to be helpful resources (https://www.wida.us/standards/CAN_DOs/).

ELPA21

The Council of Chief State School Officers (CCSSO), the Understanding Language Initiative at Stanford University, and the 10 states who are part of the ELPA21 consortium (see http://www.elpa21.org/standards-initiatives/ells-elpa21 for a list) worked with WestEd, an education research and consulting organization, to develop a set of *English Language Proficiency (ELP) Standards* in April 2014.

These ELP Standards focus on what students *do* with language to accomplish content specific tasks (language functions) and on the vocabulary, grammar, and discourse specific to a particular content area or discipline (language forms) as they work to meet college and career ready standards.[55]

CALIFORNIA ELA/ELD FRAMEWORK

In 2012, California adopted ELD standards that align with Common Core.[56] These standards recognize that ELLs have a linguistic challenge, not a cognitive challenge. The ELD standards are designed to help teachers, students, and their families evaluate ELLs' language growth as they simultaneously develop the skills set forth in Common Core.

In 2014, California released the ELA/ELD Framework,[57] which provides guidance for both ELD and content-area teachers on how to integrate the ELD and Common Core standards and how to maximize the opportunities for ELLs to develop language within content practices. It is considered by many to be an innovative document that lays out a considerable amount of current research and instructional theory along with vignettes providing "glimpses of instruction" in ELA and ELD.[58]

NEW YORK STATE BILINGUAL COMMON CORE INITIATIVE

In 2012, New York, under its Bilingual Common Core Initiative,[59] began developing new English as a Second Language and Native Language Arts Standards aligned to the Common Core. While the development process continues, they have released "language progressions" for their Common Core learning standards at each grade level. The "New Language Arts Progressions" are for students learning a new language (e.g., students in English as a Second Language or Language Other than English classes) and the "Home Language Arts Progressions" are for students developing a home language (e.g., students in Native Language Arts or language classes for speakers of that language).[60]

There's some debate about how useful all of these new English Language Proficiency standards are to teachers working day-to-day in their classrooms. However, teachers will need to familiarize themselves with the ELP standards that their students will be assessed by. These standards also offer a "shared language" that ELD and content teachers can use to collaborate on effectively meeting the needs of ELLs in all classes.

ENGLISH LANGUAGE PROFICIENCY ASSESSMENTS

English Language Proficiency assessments are being developed based on these new ELP standards. These tests are separate from the Common Core assessments given in each state. They will replace older versions of both diagnostic and summative assessments currently being used by states for placement, monitoring, and reclassification of ELLs. The U.S. Department of Education provided grants to two state-led consortia to develop these "next generation of ELPD assessments."

One assessment system, ASSETS—Assessment Services Supporting ELs through Technology Systems (http://www.assets.wceruw.org)—is being developed in collaboration with WIDA and several organizations, including WestEd, the Center for Applied Linguistics, and the University of California, Los Angeles, along with 30 states. This assessment system builds on WIDA's task assessments and will include diagnostic, summative and formative assessment tools. It should be fully operational in 2015–2016.[61]

Another grant was awarded to ELPA21—English Language Proficiency Assessment for the 21st Century (http://www.elpa21.org), a consortium of states led by Oregon and in collaboration with CCSSO and Stanford University. As a first step in the assessment development process, ELPA21 developed new ELP standards that we described in the previous section. Subsequently they have designed assessments aligned to these standards. Their diagnostic/screener and summative assessments are intended to be fully operational in the 2015–2016 school year.[62]

In addition to being "valid, fair, and reliable," these new assessments must meet the following additional criteria:

- Be based on a common definition of English language learner adopted by all consortium states
- Include diagnostic (e.g., screener, placement) and summative assessments

- Assess English language proficiency across the four language domains (reading, writing, speaking, and listening) for each grade level from kindergarten through Grade 12

- Produce results that indicate whether individual students have attained a level and complexity of English language proficiency that is necessary to participate fully in academic instruction in English

- Be accessible to all ELLs with the exception of those who are eligible for alternate assessments based on alternate academic standards

- Use technology to the maximum extent appropriate to develop, administer, and score assessments[63]

Other states, including California,[64] New York,[65] and Texas,[66] are not participating in either consortium and are developing their own ELP assessments.

Clearly these ELP assessments, as well as the Common Core assessments, will be challenging for our ELL students, especially if they are administered on a computer. We hope that the next generation of ELP assessments will deliver equitable assessments that teachers can use to inform their instruction.

Key Shifts in Common Core

The Common Core State Standards place heightened content and language demands on all students. ELLs must meet these demands while also developing proficiency in English. Ensuring that students are able to accomplish this goal is a huge task for teachers. The Common Core State Standards document doesn't provide a curriculum or prescribe how teachers should teach; it lays out what students need to be able to do at each grade level.

There is a focus throughout the new standards on extensive language use, not just in English Language Arts, but also in math, history/social studies, and science. Thus, many researchers and educators are calling for a paradigm shift. In the past, ELA teachers have traditionally been charged with literacy instruction. However, teachers in all disciplines must be "language teachers" in order to help students meet the standards in each content area. This new reality makes collaboration among teachers a crucial piece in implementing the Common Core. In later chapters of our book, content area teachers share key Common Core shifts in math, Social Studies, and science and how to address these shifts in their subject areas.

KEY SHIFTS IN ELA

In English Language Arts, the standards call for three key shifts that support college and career readiness, according to the Common Core State Standards Initiative.[67]

These "shifts" represent important differences from previous standards and have an impact on instructional, curricular, and assessment practices. We will begin by summarizing the Common Core shifts and then share four key shifts for ELLs.

Shift 1: Regular practice with complex texts and their academic language. The standards emphasize that students must read increasingly complex texts in order to be ready for the demands of college- and career-level reading. As they gain experience with a variety of complex texts they simultaneously build their reading comprehension skills and academic language. Academic language includes both general academic vocabulary that appears in a variety of content areas (such as "effect" or "correlation") and domain-specific vocabulary that is specific to a discipline (such as "molecule" or "decimal"). This academic vocabulary is not only critical to comprehension, but also allows students to participate in academic conversations (both oral and written) across content areas and to be able to read increasingly complex texts on their own.

In other words, students need to learn how to navigate the types of challenging texts they will see in college and beyond, and they need to acquire the academic language that will enable them to be successful readers, writers, and speakers.

Shift 2: Reading, writing, and speaking grounded in evidence from texts, both literary and informational. The reading standards focus on students being able to read and understand arguments, ideas, and information based on evidence in the text. Rather than answering questions based only on prior knowledge or experience, students must be able to answer text-dependent questions and make inferences supported by in-text evidence. In writing, there is a focus in the standards on evidence-based writing in order to inform or persuade.

In other words, students need to learn how to identify evidence in a variety of texts and be able to use evidence in their own writing and speaking to support their points.

Shift 3: Building knowledge through content-rich nonfiction. The standards emphasize the important role informational text plays in helping students develop content knowledge and vocabulary. The K–5 standards require a 50–50 balance between informational and literary reading. The 6–12 ELA standards place much more of an emphasis than in the past on informational texts, particularly literary nonfiction (nonfiction that contains literary elements like imagery or sensory details). The 6–12 literacy standards in history/social studies, science and technical subjects require students to learn how to build knowledge through reading and writing independently.

In other words, students need to read more informational text than they have in the past in order to build content knowledge and to inform their writing.

KEY SHIFTS FOR ELLs

In our state, California, the state board of education adopted the *ELA/ELD Framework* in 2014 designed to facilitate the teaching of ELLs in light of the CCSS and the new California ELD Standards.[68] The framework describes four shifts from previous notions of English Language Development and Instruction.[69] Though it comes from California, we believe these shifts apply to English Language Learners navigating "college and career ready" standards everywhere.

Language is seen as a resource for making meaning.

In other words, teachers of ELLs shouldn't teach language as a collection of grammar rules, but as a meaningful resource used to achieve various purposes (informing, persuading, expressing feelings, etc.).

When ELLs develop *language awareness* (conscious understandings about how language works to make meaning in different situations) they are in a better position to comprehend and produce language.

In other words, ELLs at all levels are capable of learning *how* language works and what kinds of choices they can make with language depending on their purpose, audience, etc.

For ELLs at all levels of English language proficiency, *meaningful interaction with others and with complex texts is essential* for learning language and learning content.

In other words, ELLs must engage in authentic and engaging conversations around complex ideas and texts. Teachers must provide the scaffolding for ELLs at all levels to build their knowledge of both language and content through these types of interactions.

ELLs learn language and content better through *intellectually challenging tasks and texts*.

In other words, supporting students in reading challenging texts doesn't mean giving them a watered-down version. ELLs must be given access to challenging concepts and texts, but they need to be supported through appropriate scaffolding.

In later chapters we describe practices we've found successful in addressing the shifts in both Common Core and for English Language Learners.

ELA Anchor Standards

In this section, we will summarize the key elements of the College and Career Readiness Anchor Standards for English Language Arts. The anchor standards represent broad standards in ELA for K–12 students. These standards "anchor" the whole document because they represent what students should ultimately be able to do upon graduation in order to successfully transition to college and beyond. The grade-specific ELA standards correspond to the CCR Anchor Standards by number, but also contain added specificity regarding end-of-year expectations. As explained in the standards document, "The CCR and grade-specific standards are necessary complements—the former providing broad standards, the latter providing additional specificity—that together define the skills and understandings that all students must demonstrate."[70]

The CCR Anchor Standards are divided into four domains: Reading, Writing, Speaking and Listening, and Language. Each domain is divided into smaller sections that we have listed below, along with an "everyday" translation in our own words. For each domain we will also present some general, and certainly not all-encompassing, "don'ts and do's" related to teaching these standards with English Language Learners in mind, which we elaborate on in later chapters. We've decided to lead with the "don'ts" and end with the "do's" to reflect our own learning process of making mistakes and learning from them. The actual Anchor Standards for each domain are reprinted in the appropriate chapters appearing later in the book. A more detailed description and analysis of these standards also appears in these chapters.

ANCHOR STANDARDS FOR READING

Key Ideas and Details: Determining what a text says, what it means, and what conclusions can be drawn from it supported by evidence from the text.

Craft and Structure: Focusing on what a text looks like and analyzing the way language and structure are used to shape its meaning.

Integration of Knowledge and Ideas: Looking at how a text connects to others, including visual/multimedia texts, and evaluating the validity and reasoning of the claims and evidence presented in the text.

Range of Reading and Level of Text Complexity: Being able to do all of the above independently with a wide variety of complex texts.

Reading Don'ts and Do's

Don't discourage students from tapping prior knowledge while reading. Don't do the reading and thinking *for* students by going line by line and explaining every word and concept. Don't simplify or translate complex texts for close reading.

Do help ELLs navigate difficult texts by accessing and building background knowledge, chunking the text, modeling, and using other appropriate scaffolds. Model the reading strategies you use to make sense of text so that these processes are made explicit to students. Choose texts that relate to the teaching goal and that are at an appropriate level of challenge for your students. Provide scaffolding to support students as they work both collaboratively and independently to comprehend, analyze, and evaluate texts.

ANCHOR STANDARDS FOR WRITING

Text Types and Purposes: Writing clear, well-reasoned arguments supported by evidence. Clearly and accurately presenting information and explaining complex ideas. Narrating real or imagined experiences in an interesting and coherent way. In other words, being able to produce good argumentative, informative/explanatory, and narrative writing.

Production and Distribution of Writing: Producing writing where the development, organization, and style are appropriate to the writer's task, purpose, and audience. Using a process (planning, revising, etc.) to improve one's writing and using technology to collaborate, produce, and publish writing.

Research to Build and Present Knowledge: Conducting both short and more extensive research projects. Finding information from multiple print and digital sources and assessing its relevance and credibility. Incorporating information without plagiarizing.

Range of Writing: Having practice with writing in both shorter time frames and extended ones and writing for a variety of tasks, purposes, and audiences.

Writing Don'ts and Do's

Don't simply "assign" writing to students and expect them to produce anything good. Don't teach writing in isolation from reading and speaking. Don't ask students to produce claims about unfamiliar topics or issues and come up with evidence to support them.

Do remind students of the argument, informative, and narrative skills they already use in their everyday lives. Give students multiple opportunities, collaboratively and independently, to practice the thinking and the academic language involved in building arguments. Provide students with the support they need in order to read several texts on a topic so they can build knowledge and formulate evidence-based claims. Use mentor texts (models of good writing) so students can identify the features of effective argument, informational, and narrative writing.

ANCHOR STANDARDS FOR SPEAKING AND LISTENING

Comprehension and Collaboration: Being a productive member of academic discussions (whether it be whole class, group, partner) means effectively communicating one's own ideas and being able to build upon, connect, and evaluate the ideas of others.

Presentation of Knowledge and Ideas: Presenting one's findings and supporting evidence in a logical way appropriate to task, purpose, and audience. Using digital media and visuals to enhance the presentation of one's ideas. Using formal English when appropriate.

Speaking and Listening Don'ts and Do's

Don't place a lower priority on the Speaking and Listening standards. Students need this type of practice daily!

Do give students lots of opportunities to share their ideas with one another. Provide structure and support for conversations so students can practice using academic language in an authentic, engaging way. Post sentence frames for academic discussions on the wall and circulate during group work to ensure students are using them. Help students incorporate digital media when presenting their ideas—this increases the engagement and mirrors the standards.

ANCHOR STANDARDS FOR LANGUAGE

Conventions of Standard English: Having a command of grammar and usage in writing and speaking, and of capitalization, punctuation, and spelling in writing.

Knowledge of Language: Using what one knows about the way language works in various contexts to communicate more effectively and to better comprehend when reading or listening.

Vocabulary Acquisition and Use: Being able to figure out new words and phrases on one's own by using context clues, looking at word parts, and consulting reference materials when appropriate. Being able to make sense of figurative language and words with multiple meanings. Acquiring and effectively using both academic and domain-specific words and phrases in a way that shows "college and career readiness" when reading, writing, speaking, and listening.

Language Don'ts and Do's

Don't assign students huge lists of isolated vocabulary words and expect them to learn to use them by simply looking up the meanings and copying them down. Don't teach grammar and conventions in isolation or out of context. Don't expect students to acquire grammatical structures and apply them in their own writing and speaking if they're only doing grammar drills and worksheets.

Do evaluate the text types that students will be reading and writing and teach them the academic words and structures they will need to access these tasks. Provide opportunities for students to practice this vocabulary through meaningful interactions with their peers and in authentic reading and writing situations. Teach students the grammatical structures associated with specific text types *in context*, identifying both "good" and "bad" examples to help students identify and then apply the desired structures in their own writing.

CHAPTER TWO

Creating the Conditions for English Language Learners to Be Successful in the Common Core Standards

Farmers and gardeners know you cannot make a plant grow ... What you do is provide the conditions for growth.

—Sir Ken Robinson[1]

If facts are the seeds that later produce knowledge and wisdom, then the emotions and the impressions of the senses are the fertile soil in which the seeds must grow.

—Scientist and author Rachel Carson[2]

These two opening quotations illustrate the important role that Social Emotional Skills (also known as noncognitive skills, along with many other labels[3]) can play in students learning the academic skills listed in the Common Core Standards. In this chapter, we discuss why students developing these Social Emotional Skills can improve their ability to master the knowledge described in the Standards and how teachers can support that process.

It's important to note that this notion is not one that is just coming out of our heads. In fact, it's being promoted by the originators of the Common Core Standards and education researchers.

The Council of Chief State School Officers (CCSSO), along with the National Governors Association and the school reform group Achieve, developed the Common Core Standards.[4] One of CCSSO's initiatives is the Innovation Lab Network, a group of 12 states that is focused on piloting what they consider particularly innovative school practices.

CCSSO issued a report from the Network in 2013 titled "Knowledge, Skills, and Dispositions: The Innovation Lab Network State Framework for College, Career, and Citizenship Readiness, and Implications for State Policy."[5] The report recommends that:

> Along with mastery and application of essential content as typically prescribed and monitored in state standards, assessments, and accountability systems, it is necessary that students cultivate higher-order cognitive and meta-cognitive skills that allow them to engage in meaningful interaction with the world around them. Further, members agreed that these knowledge and skills are not achieved in a vacuum but require the development of underlying dispositions or behavioral capacities (such as self-regulation, persistence, adaptability) that enable lifelong pursuit of learning. (p. 3)

The report goes on to state that these "Socio Emotional Skills," "higher-order cognitive and meta-cognitive skills," and "dispositions" are "mutually reinforcing"[6] with the academic knowledge in the Common Core Standards. In other words, all elements can be learned better when they are taught side-by-side.

Coincidentally (or not) these targeted "skills" and "dispositions" also appear to be the primary qualifications that employers are looking for in potential employees, according to multiple surveys.[7]

CCSSO is not alone in highlighting the role of "Socio Emotional Skills" (the report uses that term instead of the more common "Social Emotional Skills") in the Common Core.

The school reform group Achieve, another of the three CCSS originators, encourages that the Standards be used as a "platform" for educators to help students develop self-motivation, metacognition, and self-control.[8]

In addition, the American Institutes for Research concludes that "CCSS makes the assumption" that students have these kinds of Social Emotional skills.[9]

To sum it up, it is safe to say that those behind the Standards recognize, as teachers have long known, that if students do not feel motivated, confident, and curious, very little of the "knowledge" being taught is likely to engage them.

We are not placing this topic near the beginning of our book to suggest that that these "skills" and "dispositions" need to all be taught prior to the content of the Common Core Standards. Rather, we are including this chapter to emphasize that, as the Council of Chief State School Officers (CCSSO) and others suggest, they should be taught *alongside* Common Core content knowledge.

Without them, it's like teaching someone to sing by providing them with the words, but not the music.

CCSSO lists many "skills," which they define as "strategies," and "dispositions," which they define as "mindsets."[10] The CCSSO suggests that acquiring these skills and dispositions can facilitate students in learning the knowledge in the Common Core. We agree that all the skills and dispositions the CCSSO lists are important. However, we are only highlighting ones that, based on our teaching experience, we feel are especially useful to learning in the classroom. It's important to keep in mind that there is also a great deal of overlap between many of these skills and dispositions—for example, where might metacognition end and critical thinking begin?

The "skills" of goal-setting, metacognition, critical thinking, and creativity/ innovation, and the "dispositions" of agency, self-control, and persistence/resilience are the ones we review in this chapter. In addition to teaching CCSSO-recommended skills, the strategies and lessons we suggest incorporate the Standards at the same time. In other words, they are "three-fers":

1. They teach the Socio Emotional Skills and Dispositions that the CCSSO report says are critical for students to develop in order to be successful in mastering the Common Core Standards, even though many are not explicitly included in the Standards themselves.

2. They are all accessible to Intermediate and Advanced English Language Learners. *Some* may not be practical for very early ELL Beginners to complete in English. However, if the teacher or an aide speaks the home language of the student, then there is value in having him/her do these activities in that language to help them develop skills they can apply to learning English. We need to "keep our eyes on the prize," which is helping our students acquire English skills as quickly as possible. On more than one occasion, their use of a home language will likely be a very effective means to that end.

3. The strategies and lessons we'll be recommending also correspond to specific skills listed in the Common Core Standards themselves.

You will also find that many of the teaching ideas in this chapter and throughout the book emphasize what researchers have identified as four key qualities that encourage the development of intrinsic motivation:

1. *Autonomy:* Having some degree of control over what needs to happen and how it can be done

2. *Competence:* Feeling that one has the ability to be successful in doing it

3. *Relatedness*: Feeling connected to others, and feeling cared about by people whom they respect

4. *Relevance*: Seeing work as interesting and useful to their present lives and/or hopes for the future[11]

In our last book, *The ESL/ELL Teacher's Survival Guide*, we also shared specific lessons—on the advantages of being bilingual or multilingual and another on the qualities of a successful language learner—designed to help ELL students develop further intrinsic motivation for learning a new language.[12]

These "skills and dispositions," taught in the context of encouraging intrinsic motivation, are important for all learners. They are especially critical to apply in the ELL classroom because of the extra challenges most of our students face: They are adapting to a new culture, customs, and country; they are learning the content knowledge all the other students are learning while at the same time acquiring a new, difficult-to-learn language; some might be recovering from trauma they experienced in their home countries; and a number are coming from uneven and limited academic backgrounds. Many of our ELL students, because of their background, might very well have a number of these skills and dispositions—perseverance, for example—precisely because of the previous challenges they have faced. Yet, they may need help in learning how to channel those mindsets into an academic context.

We teach these same skills and dispositions to our mainstream students, as well. So even though these lessons and strategies are accessible to ELLs, please do not hesitate to use them with your non-ELL students, too—either as they are or in a modified form.

Skills

Goal-setting, metacognition, critical thinking, and creativity/innovation are the four skills considered most important for effective learning.

GOAL-SETTING

Extensive research has shown that a scaffolded and supported goal-setting process, particularly one where students choose their own goals, enhances student motivation and academic achievement[13] and specifically helps in developing second-language proficiency.[14]

Researchers typically divide goals into two types—learning goals (also known as mastery goals) and performance goals. Learning goals are motivated by a desire to increase one's skills and ability in an area or in accomplishing a task, while performance goals tend to be more motivated by a desire for recognition—from friends, teachers, or family—and a competitive desire to "be better" than others. Students have been found to persist more when they face obstacles if they are focusing on learning, rather than on performance goals.[15]

This heightened level of perseverance is generated because learning goals can often be more likely achieved by effort without a finite end point ("I want to be more focused in class" or "I want to speak English more clearly and with more confidence"). Performance goals are more easily attributed to innate ability with a more definitive ending—that is also based on an outsider recognizing it—so a student can give up on working toward achieving it more easily if it doesn't appear in reach at some point ("I want to get an 'A' this semester" or "I want to read 10 books this semester") or cease trying once it's assured.

Interestingly, those who make a higher priority of learning goals have been shown to achieve higher performance levels than those who actually emphasize performance goals.[16] When students are focused on a performance goal, they tend to pay less attention to "understanding" and more on "the score." For example, one of the formative assessment tools we regularly use with our students is having them read passages to us—individually—for a minute each and then count the number of words they read accurately, while at the same time noting their level of prosody (reading with feeling and intonation). A performance-goal-oriented student might try to rush through this evaluation of reading fluency to get the highest word count number possible, notwithstanding our cautions about accuracy and prosody, and may not care if they know the meaning of many the words they are reading. On the other hand, a student with a learning goal of improving their reading comprehension, fluency, and prosody is likely to have a much higher increase in their overall literacy level.

That is not to say that performance goals are evil. We live in the world as it is, not the world as we would like it to be. In the world as it is, most school cultures (and the culture outside the four walls of educational institutions) put a high value on performance goals—grades, test scores, and so forth. As you will see in the Goal Setting and Planning Sheet (see Exhibit 2.1), the form does include space for one performance goal, with several other spaces for learning ones. As with most things, it's not a question of either/or. Rather, it's more of a question of where we place an emphasis. Researchers suggest that including a performance goal is fine as long as the person "has the knowledge to attain it."[17] This is just one of many reasons we began this section discussing a "scaffolded and supported" goal-setting process. Teachers can play a key role in helping students choose challenging, yet realistic, goals. However, it's critical that *students* take the lead in setting their goals because of the effect it can have on increasing intrinsic motivation, its effectiveness in helping them more ably suppress distractions, and its impact on strengthening perseverance.[18]

Recent research suggests that self-perception also plays a major role in accomplishing goals, and that it might be valuable to say, "I am a writer, and will learn the skills needed to write better in English over the next two months" instead of just saying "I will learn the skills needed to be better in English over the next two months."[19]

The next "Goal-Setting Lesson Plan" provides step-by-step instructions on how to apply these points in the classroom. You can also find additional lesson plans and other resources about goals in our previous book, *The ESL/ELL Teacher's Survival Guide*[20] and in Larry's books, *Helping Students Motivate Themselves*,[21] *Self-Driven Learning*,[22] and *Building a Community of Self-Motivated Learners*.[23]

Goal-setting Lesson Plan

This lesson is designed for Early Intermediate ELLs and above, but can easily be modified for Beginners with even more simplified sentence frames.

Instructional Objectives

Students will:

1. Practice English reading, writing, speaking, and listening skills.
2. Write a list of personal learning goals.
3. Develop a system of self-assessing their progress toward those goals.

Duration

Forty minutes, plus 15 minutes each week or every other week for self-assessment of progress.

Common Core English Language Arts Standards

Writing

- Produce clear and coherent writing in which the development, organization, and style are appropriate to task, purpose, and audience.

Speaking and Listening

- Prepare for and participate effectively in a range of conversations and collaborations with diverse partners, building on others' ideas and expressing their own clearly and persuasively.

- Adapt speech to a variety of contexts and communicative tasks, demonstrating command of formal English when indicated or appropriate.

Language

- Demonstrate command of the conventions of standard English grammar and usage when writing or speaking.
- Demonstrate command of the conventions of standard English capitalization, punctuation, and spelling when writing.

Materials

- Access to the Internet and a computer projector to show a video from the Best Video Clips on Goal Setting (http://larryferlazzo.edublogs.org/2013/07/11/the-best-video-clips-on-goal-setting-help-me-find-more/).
- Student copies of the Goal Setting and Planning Sheet (Exhibit 2.1).
- Student copies of the Goals Feedback Form (Exhibit 2.2) when self-assessments are done weekly or biweekly.
- Individual notebooks or folders for each student.

Procedure

First Day

1. The teacher writes the word "goal" on the board and asks students to write down anything they know about the word or any similar or related words. Students share what they wrote with a partner, and the teacher invites some to share with the entire class. Once the definition is clear, the teacher tells students that scientists have found that people tend to be more successful—they accomplish more of what they want—by setting goals and regularly checking to see how they are doing in achieving them.
2. The teacher then shares an example from her life in which she set a goal and accomplished it, and how she felt that setting a goal helped her (for example, when she felt discouraged, remembering her goal kept her going).
3. Next, the teacher shows a video of the 2012 Volkswagen commercial titled "Dog Strikes Back" or another video of her choice at the Best Video Clips on Goal Setting (http://larryferlazzo.edublogs.org/2013/07/11/the-best-video-clips-on-goal-setting-help-me-find-more/).

4. The teacher then lists these questions on the overhead and asks students to work in pairs and write down the answers in complete sentences (the questions can be modified for different video clips):

   - What was the dog's goal?

   - What actions did the dog take to accomplish his goal?

   - How did the dog check to see if he was making progress in accomplishing his goal?

   - What obstacles (problems) do you think the dog had when trying to accomplish his goal?

   - Did he accomplish the goal?

   - Students share their answers with a partner and then the teacher reviews them with the entire class and collects the responses.

5. Then, the teacher explains that she's given an example of goal setting in her life, they've seen a commercial about goal setting, and that now it's time for students to set their own goals. She then distributes a copy of the Goal Setting and Planning Sheet (Exhibit 2.1). The teacher completes a model for the "Attitude" section for herself, and then students work on that section. She may need to explain the meanings of some words, and can ask more fluent English students to assist others. The whole class should go through the form together section by section.

6. Students can then share their completed forms in groups of three or four, and be told that they can make changes to their forms if they hear ideas they like from their classmates.

7. Students should have regular class notebooks or folders where they can tape or glue their Goal Sheets. The teacher will need to review the completed forms in order to follow up with each student in individual conversations. If the teacher does not have regular access to student folders/notebooks, she can collect the forms to photocopy. She can return them the next day and ask students to then glue them in their notebooks.

Weekly or Biweekly

1. Feedback, including self-feedback, is a critical component of successful goal-setting.[24] Therefore, each week or every 2 weeks, perhaps on Mondays, students can review their goals and complete the Goals Feedback Form (Exhibit 2.2). Students can be given the option to share with classmates before turning in their forms to the teacher. This kind of regular self-monitoring and

evaluating is also considered a hallmark of metacognition,[25] the ne
be discussing.

Assessment

- Collect and review video answers and completed goal forms.
- If the teacher feels a more involved assessment is necessary, you can develop a simple rubric appropriate for your class situation. Free online resources to both find premade rubrics and create your own can be found at the Best Rubric Sites and a Beginning Discussion about Their Use (http://larryferlazzo.edublogs.org/2010/09/18/the-best-rubric-sites-and-a-beginning-discussion-about-their-use/).

Possible Extensions and Modifications

- Students can make posters about their goals, which can be hung up around the classroom or on windows for others to see.
- The teacher can take a photo of student written goals or a poster and have students do an audio recording. See the next Tech Tools box for more information.
- Recent research suggests that intrinsic motivation can be increased further if students take another step after the three listed in Exhibit 2.1. In this fourth step, students could be asked "to write about the impact that achieving each goal would have on specific aspects of their lives and the lives of others."[26] As long as the teacher provides a model, this can be a useful extension activity.

Tech Tools

Voice Recording for Speaking Practice

If students create posters (or even any written work), turning them into a slideshow with audio narration of students saying their goals aloud provides great speaking practice for ELLs. There are many easy and free iPhone/iPad apps for making these presentations, including Shadow Puppet (http://get-puppet.co/education/), Fotobabble (http://www.fotobabble.com/) and VoiceThread (https://voicethread.com/). The slideshows can then be posted on a class blog for viewing (see Chapter 4 for a discussion of blogs).

EXHIBIT 2.1. Goal Setting and Planning Sheet

Name _____

ATTITUDE

Goal: I am a _____ (good learner, respectful person, helpful person, etc.) and I want to be even_____ (more positive, more respectful, more eager to learn, more eager to help others, etc.).

Action: I will _____ (remind myself each day that what I'm learning today will help me achieve my life dreams, offer to help another student each day, offer to help the teacher each day, etc.).

Obstacle: If _____ (I let boyfriend/girlfriend problems start affecting how I act in class, I feel sad in class about missing my family in Mexico, etc.), then I will _____ (ask to see the school counselor, write a letter to my sister, etc.).

ENGLISH

Goal: I am a _____ (writer, reader, good speaker, etc.) and I want to become a better _____ (writer, reader, speaker) in English.

Action: I will _____ (do Duolingo or another computer site one half hour a day at home, ask the teacher for more challenging work, attend seventh period, etc.).

Obstacle: If _____ (I get distracted by Facebook, I start feeling like I don't want to do my homework), then I will _____ (stop being online and read an English book instead, think about how learning English will help me become successful in my long-term goal of becoming a doctor/lawyer/restaurant owner/etc.).

BEHAVIOR

Goal: I am a _____ (serious student, a role model for my classmates, etc.) and I want to become _____ (more focused, less talkative in class, more prepared, more respectful, etc.).

Action: I will _____ (change my seat to sit farther away from a person I talk with too much, help other students more when I'm done with my work, ask the teacher how I can help, apologize when I do something wrong, etc.).

Obstacle: If _____ (I get distracted from my work, I don't feel like working, (talk to my friends too much in class), then I will _____ (ask to go outside for two minutes to collect my thoughts, ask to change seats, think about what a person I respect would do, etc.).

ACADEMIC

Goal: I am a _____ (scholar, serious student, etc.), and I want to get a(n) _____ (A, B, C) in class.

Action: I will _____ (do my best work all the time, do harder projects on the computer, ask for extra credit work, etc.).

Obstacle: If _____ (I get behind on doing my homework, I don't understand something in class , I don't feel like doing my best on an assignment, etc), then I will _____ (ask the teacher for a one-time extension on due date for homework, ask the teacher or a classmate about what I don't understand, remember how learning English will help me become successful in my long term goal of becoming a doctor/lawyer/restaurant owner/etc.).

EXHIBIT 2.2. Goals Feedback Form

Name _____

Date _____

ATTITUDE:

Copy your goal here:

Did you make progress toward achieving your goal in the past week?

What did you do to make progress toward achieving your goal?

What can you do this week to make progress toward achieving your goal?

ENGLISH:

Copy your goal here:

Did you make progress toward achieving your goal in the past week?

What did you do to make progress toward achieving your goal?

What can you do this week to make progress toward achieving your goal?

BEHAVIOR:

Copy your goal here:

Did you make progress toward achieving your goal in the past week?

What did you do to make progress toward achieving your goal?

What can you do this week to make progress toward achieving your goal?

ACADEMIC:

Copy your goal here:

Did you make progress toward achieving your goal in the past week?

What did you do to make progress toward achieving your goal?

What can you do this week to make progress toward achieving your goal?

Is there anything your teacher can do to help you achieve your goals?

Metacognition

Metacognition has the common definition of "thinking about thinking." In other words, it is the self-awareness to know what our strengths and weaknesses are, and how and when to apply the former and compensate for the latter. Broadly explained, learners applying metacognitive strategies plan in advance for effective learning, monitor and make adjustments during the lesson/activity to maximize their learning, and reflect afterwards about which learning strategies worked and which did not for them.[27] Explicit teaching of metacognitive strategies has been shown to lead to increased academic achievement for all students,[28] and specific research has demonstrated its benefit to English language learners.[29] In addition, students who become skilled at using these strategies have demonstrated higher levels of intrinsic motivation.[30] This increased motivation is understandable, since metacognitive skills directly contribute to two of the key qualities mentioned earlier in this chapter that need to be present for intrinsic motivation—autonomy and competence.

There is often a very fine line between what are labeled "metacognitive" strategies, "learning strategies," and "cognitive strategies." Here's a less-than-perfect, though illustrative, analogy that can be helpful for teacher understanding, though we wouldn't use it with our ELL students. It could be said that learning and cognitive strategies are tools in a toolbox, along with the *experience* the handyman/woman has in using them to create and fix things. Metacognition, on the other hand, is when the handyperson:

- Keeps the tools clean and organized
- Keeps an eye out for new ones at the hardware store
- Has a goal for how much work he wants and how to get it
- Determines what tools are needed for a particular job and obtains additional ones if needed
- Considers which of his skills and knowledge are needed to apply toward each particular project
- Afterwards thinks about what he did well in this particular job, as well as what he could have done better, so the next one goes more smoothly—maybe even with what he learned in this job, he can take on bigger ones in the future.

In other words, as explained earlier, metacognition focuses on planning, monitoring, problem-solving, and evaluation.[31]

As with most, if not all, learning activities, it is important to model what metacognition is and what students can do to help them develop it.[32] Here is a mini-lesson that shows how this can be done:

Metacognition Mini-Lesson

1. This exercise from Larry's book, *Self-Driven Learning*,[33] is a good one to do for introducing metacognition to students. After writing the word "metacognition" on the overhead and asking students to repeat it:

> The teacher crunches up a piece of paper, throws it, and intentionally misses a garbage can. The paper falls to the right (of course, students will love that the teacher misses it). The teacher tells the class, "Okay, now I know that I have to adjust my shot. I'm thinking about it, and maybe I need to adjust to the left. I've seen people shoot free throws underhand, so maybe I'll have a better chance if I throw it that way, too, because it would have a higher arc."
>
> The teacher crunches up another sheet of paper, throws it, and it lands just short, hitting the rim of the can (again, the teacher probably receives great cheers or catcalls from the class). He or she says, "It looks like I'm getting closer. I think I'll just have to throw it a little harder and it should go in."
>
> The teacher gets another piece of paper and throws it—bull's-eye! He or she says, "Now, the next time I want to try to make a basket here, I'll know to throw it underhand and aim better. That's the kind of thinking I go through on the basketball court, and how we improve in lots of ways. We take the time to think about why?"
>
> He or she then tells the class, "Let's see how I do shooting the ball without using metacognition." He quickly crumples up three pieces of paper and just throws them one by one in the direction of the can. None go in. The teacher tells the class, "I'm going to ask a question, and I don't want anyone to call out an answer. Why didn't those three balls go in? Tell a partner." The teacher calls on one student, who probably responds, "Because you didn't think about what you learned from trying it earlier."
>
> "Exactly," the teacher says. "If we don't 'think about our thinking,' we won't learn from our mistakes or from our successes. We'll always start from scratch when we face a problem. By using metacognition, we'll be able to more effectively apply what we learn now to the future. That's what metacognition is . . . ."[34]

2. Following that exercise, a teacher could tell students that, just like she did when she made changes to throwing the paper, there are things that students can do to help them learn better when they are having problems with English. The teacher gives an example of one—make a list of things you don't understand very well and ask the teacher or other people about them. She writes that on the overhead under the title "Ways To Help Learn." She then asks students to think for a minute—without saying anything—about other things they can do. Then, after a minute, she breaks students into pairs or threes to quickly share what they wrote. Next, she asks students to share and adds to the list, while asking students to copy them down.

3. Strategies on the list could include—but not be limited to (it would be valuable to verbally provide a student or teacher example to illustrate each strategy):

- Setting goals.

- Drawing pictures.

- Connect what I am learning to things I already know, perhaps through using a K-W-L chart.

- Ask classmates for help.

- Remember what has helped me in the past.

- After I'm done, double-check my work.

- Use Google Translate or a dictionary.

- Plan how I am going to work on a project before I start. For example, creating an outline or some other graphic organizer for an essay or project.

- Highlight or underline important words in a text.

- When I don't understand a word, I can use context clues, do a word analysis (prefix, root, suffix), and think if it's a cognate (similar to words in other languages).

- After I've finished an activity, take a minute to think about what things I did that helped me.

- Ask my teachers questions to clarify or confirm my thinking and not just to get the answer (does it look like I'm on the right track? I think this question means _____—is that right?).

- Take notes (see the "Tech Tools: Note-Taking Resources" box). (Some of these strategies are adapted from Larry's book, *Self-Driven Learning*.[35])

4. After the list has been completed, students can glue or tape it to their folders or in a notebook, and/or the list could be done on a piece of easel paper and hung on the classroom wall. The teacher can explain that students can refer to this list when they are having problems, and there will be times when the teacher will ask them to share which of the examples on the list they have recently used. Students should also think about which ones help them the best—different ones will work for different people. The teacher can explain that they will also be adding to the list in the future.

Tech Tools

Note-Taking Resources

There are a number of different popular note-taking techniques (one of the useful learning strategies we listed), including some that have been found to be particularly effective for English language learners. Descriptions and examples, including images and videos, are at the Best Resources for Effective Note-Taking Strategies (http://larryferlazzo.edublogs.org/2015/06/23/the-best-resources-on-effective-note-taking-strategies-help-me-find-more/) and can be used by teachers to demonstrate them in the classroom.

Here are other activities that can be done in the classroom to promote metacognition:

- **The goal-setting exercises** discussed earlier in this chapter are part of the planning section of metacognition.
- **"Wrappers"** are a tool for students to monitor their learning. It describes a strategy that "wraps around" a learning activity and is designed to promote metacognition. For example, prior to watching a video clip or reading a short informational text, the teacher tells students that while they are viewing or reading, they should identify the three most important points and why. After giving students a few minutes to write them down, the teacher explains what she believes are the three most important points and why. Students then compare the teacher's conclusions to their own notes. In an experiment, this form of modeling done only three times dramatically increased the similarity between student and teacher notes in subsequent lessons.[36]

- **At the end of a unit**, ask students to consider which activities they found particularly useful and why; which ones they found difficult, why they were challenged by them, and what strategies they applied to do them successfully or what they could have done differently to do them better.

- **In an interesting twist**, ESL teacher Lizzie Pinard suggests that students look at a textbook chapter *prior* to beginning it, to have them explore and discuss if the sequence looks useful and if there should be any deletions or additions.[37]

- **Many teachers have students keep "learning journals"** where students periodically keep track of *what* they learned. Psychologist Marilyn Price Mitchell recommends, instead, that they note *how* they learned. She recommends the following questions, which could easily be modified:[38]

  - *What was easiest for me to learn this week? Why?*

  - *What was most challenging for me to learn? Why?*

  - *What study strategies worked well as I prepared for my exam?*

  - *What strategies for exam preparation didn't work well? What will I do differently next time?*

  - *What study habits worked best for me? How?*

  - *What study habit will I try or improve upon next week?*

Other questions could include:

- Think of a time you "got stuck" answering a question, pronouncing a word, understanding a sentence, and so forth, and were able to figure it out. What was the situation and how were you able to solve it?

- What did I do this week in class that didn't help me learn? What should I change?

- When I didn't know what a word meant, did I always immediately go to Google Translate, or did I first try other strategies? Were there times when it was better to use Google Translate and other times when it was better to use other strategies?

- Have I tried my best most of the time this week in class? If there were times I didn't, why did that happen and what can I do to change it?

- What was the one thing I did this week that helped me learn best?

Depending on the English level of your students, questions may need to be simplified and sentence frames may be necessary for responses. For example, in response to the last question, teachers might want to put on the overhead:

"_____ helped me learn best this week because _____."

ELL Beginners could also draw images in response or even write it out in their home language. As we mentioned earlier, we want to "keep our eyes on the prize," which is to help students obtain as many tools in their toolbox as possible and develop the ability, confidence, and reflective discipline to know which ones they should use in different situations. If that means not every entry in a learning journal is in English, so be it. If you have a mixed-level class, having higher-proficiency ELLs helping less-advanced levels is always an option, too.

Obviously, teachers wouldn't want to ask all of these questions at once. One or two of them could be asked at the end of an individual activity or single class period. Some days they could be shared with a partner and the class, and on other days kept private or only given to the teacher. They can also be asked on a weekly or biweekly basis and teachers can alternate between asking these reflective questions and reviewing student goals (mentioned in the previous section).

Not only does this kind of reflective activity reinforce the use of metacognitive strategies in the future, but research also shows it improves understanding and retention of the content that has just been taught.[39]

Additional resources on metacognition, including lesson plans, can be found in two of Larry's previous books, *Self-Driven Learning*[40] and *English Language Learners: Teaching Strategies That Work*.[41]

Critical Thinking

Critical thinking, though universally hailed as an important skill for students to develop—in both the Common Core Standards (http://www.corestandards.org/ELA-Literacy/) and in numerous lists of Social Emotional Skills—doesn't appear to have a "universal" definition. We describe it as the ability to seek out, elicit, and consider different information and various perspectives of situations, fairly weigh the evidence on all sides, explore how it all connects to existing background knowledge, and then use that process to come to an independent conclusion.

Critical thinking skills have been found to help ELLs in language acquisition, particularly through increasing problem-solving abilities, oral communication skills, writing competence, and student motivation.[42, 43] However, teaching critical thinking skills is considered to be a major challenge by many ELL teachers because of a number of issues, including students' lack of vocabulary and, in some cases, students coming from prior school environments where that skill was not promoted.

However, there are ways to help ELLs, even at the Beginning Level, to begin developing critical thinking skills. Here are some ideas:

INDUCTIVE LEARNING

Inductive Learning is the process of providing examples and having students categorize them to identify patterns and concepts, and can be an exceptional instructional strategy for developing critical thinking skills. It contrasts with "deductive" learning, which is when the teacher starts with the concept, and then students are given examples to reinforce it.

In these types of inductive lessons, students can categorize words, text passages, images, and so forth, provide evidence to support their conclusions, and find additional examples to expand the content in their categories. This method can be used to teach grammar, text structures, phonics, and so on, as well as knowledge needed in content classes.

Researchers suggest that learning a second language is directly linked to a person's ability to discern patterns.[44] Concepts learned through pattern identification are more easily transferable to new situations by students than knowledge learned in other ways,[45] so inductive learning helps develop a critical thinking skill that is especially beneficial to ELLs.

Our last book, *The ESL/ELL Teacher's Survival Guide*,[46] shared numerous examples of inductive learning for all levels in the ELL classroom, and Larry has done the same in all his student motivation books. Throughout this book, too, you will find many additional suggestions incorporating the inductive method, including a lesson plan in this chapter on making mistakes that can be found under "Perseverance/Resilience."

GRAPHIC ORGANIZERS

Graphic organizers are a mainstay in ELL classrooms, and many lend themselves specifically to promoting critical thinking skills. Two of our favorites for this purpose are Word Webs and Venn Diagrams. In Word Webs, students draw a circle in the middle of a paper and write a word they are given or that they choose inside it. Then they have to add other words to "branches" that have connections to that word, and then draw branches to those words. Of course, they have to be able to support the connections they draw with evidence.

In Venn Diagrams, typically two or three interlocking circles are drawn and students have to write down attributes that are similar or different.

One reason we are partial to these two graphic organizers in particular is because they are both easily adaptable into classroom games. The class can be broken into groups of two to three students, and each group given a small whiteboard with eraser and marker. There are many variations of games using Word Web. In one, the teacher writes a word on the front whiteboard and each group writes a word connected to it on their small whiteboard and an explanation. For example, if the teacher wrote "blue" on the front board, a small group could write "red, because it is also a color." Groups receive one point for making a logical connection and then the teacher picks one of the student-generated words to connect to the first word, creating a Word Web to build upon as the game goes on.

Venn Diagrams can also be used in different game forms. In one, the teacher can draw and label the circles on the board and students could be given a list of the answers. The teacher can call out the name of the circle, and each group has to pick a correct answer from their list. In another variation, developed by teacher Russel Tarr,[47] students are given the Venn Diagram with the circles labeled. Then, the group works on their own to complete the diagram. As the teacher calls out the name of the circle and asks for answer possibilities, the groups press inexpensive "answer buzzers" that are easily purchased online. The first group to "buzz" has an opportunity to answer and will either gain or lose points depending upon their response. In this game form, critical thinking takes place in the collaborative group discussion, where students must provide evidence for their answers.

For example, in our Beginner's class we label the interlocking circles Winter and Summer. Then students work individually to develop answers (cold, hot, beach, snow, baseball, fun). Next, students meet in small groups to share and revise their answers using sentence frames like "Why do you think _____ goes in _____?" We circulate to support students in using the sentence frames. Then students are ready to play the Venn Diagram game.

Our favorite resource for other free graphic organizers for promoting critical thinking is Exploratree (http://www.exploratree.org.uk/). We will be discussing graphic organizer use later in this book, as well.

IMPORTANCE OF QUESTIONS

Developing question-asking skills is another way to cultivate students' critical thinking abilities.

For a class of Intermediate or Advanced ELLs, one simple first step would be to either give students a list of quotations about the importance of asking good questions or show them on the overhead (you can go to the "A More Beautiful Question" website—http://amorebeautifulquestion.com/question-quotes/—or just type in " quotes about the importance of asking good questions" in an Internet search) and then provide students with "The Importance of Asking Good Questions" (see Exhibit 2.3), which incorporates the "They Say, I Say" academic writing outline.[48]

EXHIBIT 2.3. The importance of Asking Questions

Choose one of the quotations on the importance of asking good questions and write a paragraph with three parts:

1. They Say

2. I Say

3. Why I Said It (Use your experiences, observations of others, something you have read)

_____ said, "_____
_____."

I think he/she means that _____
_____.

I agree/disagree with him/her. For example, I experienced/I saw/I read

_____

_____.

Adapted from *They Say / I Say* by Gerald Graff and Cathy Birkenstein

Introduction to Literal and Interpretive Questions

One way to emphasize the importance of asking good questions is to teach students the difference between "literal" (also called "Right There") questions and "interpretative" (also called "Think About") questions. The teacher could model these two types of questions by first asking "What color is my hair?" and then "How do you think I'm feeling today?" Then, provide students with this list:

Literal Question-Starters: Where . . . , When . . . , What is . . . , What happened . . . , Who . . . , How many . . . , Which . . .

Interpretive Question-Starters: Why . . ., How . . ., What if . . ., How would you compare . . ., What would you predict . . .

A teacher could have students practice writing different literal and interpretive questions about simple texts and emphasize the fact that interpretive questions will challenge you to think and learn more. If lessons on the impact of learning on the brain have already been taught (see the "Agency" section in this chapter), the teacher can explain that interpretive questions help the brain grow.

After we introduced our Intermediate students to the idea of interpretative questions, we did a simple activity with them as a unit project (covering several chapters in the textbook) in our History class to reinforce the concept and also as a formative assessment:

First, we gave students the Unit Project form (Exhibit 2.4), which asks them to list the name of a chapter, an interpretive question of their choice extending the content of the chapter (about a topic they were interested in and whose answer could not be found in the book), why they were interested in the question, and then left space for their answer. The form provided space for three different questions. We then went to the computer lab to search for answers online. While students were researching their answers, we approached a few of the students whose leadership skills were a little more advanced and asked if they would lead small groups the next day using the format in Group Leader Instructions (Exhibit 2.5). The next day, the class used the process outlined in the Group Leader Instructions Exhibit, which included peer feedback on the quality of the questions and answers, along with repeated opportunities to practice speaking and listening.

Teacher modeling, followed by practicing, leading to students developing their own high-interest questions for which they received peer feedback, all combined to a steadily climbing level of higher-order thinking questions.

Tests "in Reverse"

Another reinforcing, and more challenging, exercise applying literal and interpretive questions is to give students a test "in reverse." In other words, the test lists the answers, and they have to develop the questions using both literal and interpretive question-starters. An American History test on immigration and industrialization in the early 20th century that we used with ELLs can be seen in Exhibit 2.6. Of course, this activity could be used for any ELL level to practice asking questions.

EXHIBIT 2.4. Unit Project

Name _____

NAME OF CHAPTER:

MY QUESTION:

WHY I AM INTERESTED IN LEARNING THE ANSWER:

ANSWER IN MY OWN WORDS:

_____

NAME OF CHAPTER:

MY QUESTION:

WHY I AM INTERESTED IN LEARNING THE ANSWER:

ANSWER IN MY OWN WORDS:

_____

NAME OF CHAPTER:

MY QUESTION:

WHY I AM INTERESTED IN LEARNING THE ANSWER:

ANSWER IN MY OWN WORDS:

EXHIBIT 2.5. Group Leader Instructions

1. Choose one person to say each of their questions. After each question, ask the group:

- Is it an interpretive (think about) question? If not, have the group help the person make it a better related question that they can research on Friday when we go to the library.

Then have the next person share their questions and repeat the process. Then you share yours.

2. Choose one person to say the answer to each of their questions. After each answer, ask the group:

- Does the answer seem like the person put serious time and effort into finding it?

- Was the answer in their own words?

- Should the person look for more information to improve his or her answer when we go to the library on Friday?

3. Of all the questions and answers shared in the group, which was the best interpretative question and answer? Why was it the best question and answer?

4. What was the most important thing the group learned from their discussion?

You will stand and report to the entire class the answers to numbers three and four.

Bloom's Taxonomy

Bloom's Taxonomy and Revised Bloom's Taxonomy are, of course, the most well-known analyses of higher-order thinking and questioning. In our ELL classes, as students become more comfortable with the idea of interpretive questions, we simply and gradually introduce the higher levels one at a time using a similar process that we used to initially teach literal and interpretive ones. The question starters we use for literal and interpretative roughly correlate to the lower two levels of Bloom's, so it's then relatively easy to go up the pyramid. Lists of question starters for all the levels can be easily found online.

More extensive lesson plans for advanced ELLs and fluent English speakers can be found in two of Larry's previous books on student motivation—one on

EXHIBIT 2.6. U.S. History, Chapter 5–9

Name _____

U.S. History, Chapters 5–9

Here is a list of ANSWERS. Please write the QUESTION next to, or underneath, each. Some may be literal questions and some may be interpretive ones which might not have exact answers in the book. Please use the question-starters we've practiced.

1. filled with hope

2. Great Irish Famine, freedom of religion, to build railroads

3. This person focused on making money and the other person organized workers

4. John D. Rockefeller

5. anger

6. eight-hour work days, not allowing children to work, the right to strike

7. Mother Jones

8. They would have lived in poverty in their home countries

9. animals, forests, metals, and water

10. Because they had to earn money to help their families

Bloom's Taxonomy in *Helping Students Motivate Themselves*[49] and another on asking higher-order questions in *Self-Driven Learning*.[50]

- **Critical pedagogy** is a strategy developed by Paulo Freire to develop literacy skills and critical thinking, which we reviewed in our last book.[51] In Chapter 4, on writing, we discuss how we have expanded this Freirean process to further incorporate Common Core Standards.

- **Encouraging consideration of multiple perspectives** is a key part of critical thinking. There are obviously many opportunities for teachers to raise this point in multiple lessons. We've found that initially introducing the idea in three ways (that also function as language-learning opportunities) near the beginning of the year sets the stage for more formal uses of the concept later on in lessons.

The first way is a relatively common idea used in many International Baccalaureate Theory of Knowledge classes around the world (it's also a class that Larry teaches) to introduce the idea of different perspectives on the same issue. A student is a "model" in the middle of the classroom, students are given a sheet of paper and a pencil, and are asked to draw only the portion of the "model" that they see. After 5 or 10 minutes, different students bring their drawings to the front to show on the overhead (which generally leads to a great deal of laughter), and the teacher asks why they are all so different, since there is only one model. Students will answer that they are seated in different parts of the classroom and could see only part of the model. The teacher can explain that this is a concept we need to keep in mind when we consider and study many topics—that there are many different ways to see something, not only the way we look at it, and it's our challenge to look at things from different perspectives before we make a decision.

This simple lesson can be followed by showing a number of short videos.

- "The Guardian Commercial—Points of View" (http://bit.ly/navccss1), which shows the same incident from multiple points of views, and shows how incorrect interpretations of the event could result in major misunderstandings if we don't look at all perspectives.
- A series of short and funny commercials titled "Don't Judge Too Quickly" (http://larryferlazzo.edublogs.org/2015/06/26/dont-judge-too-quickly-is-a-great-series-of-videos-for-tok-ell-students/), which make a similar point. Note that a few of the commercials might not be appropriate for the classroom (depending upon students' ages), so teachers will definitely want to review them ahead of time.

In addition to asking students what the "message" is for each video, ELLs can be asked to write down what happens in each one, which can then also be shared verbally with partners and with the entire class. Students can even be asked to think about and share times when they jumped to conclusions without knowing all the facts.

This activity can be referred to regularly during the year to remind and reinforce the idea of looking at different issues from multiple perspectives.

Another exercise in this vein that could be used regularly during the year is called "Perceive (or See)—Believe—Care About," which comes from Project Zero at Harvard[52] (see "Visible Thinking Routines" later in this section). In this exercise, students (either on their own or in small groups), are asked to put themselves in the position of characters in a photo, video, story, or essay and have to answer these three questions:

What do you see?

What might you believe?

What might you care about?

- **Student reflection,** or "reflective thinking," has been described as the "processes of analyzing and making judgments about what has happened."[53] Learning journals, discussed in the metacognition section, can encourage this kind of reflective thinking. In addition to reflecting on the *how* of learning, considering the implications of *what* was learned can promote critical thinking and aid in comprehension and boost learning and retention of knowledge.[54–56]

"Daily Reflection Activity" (Exhibit 2.7) is a sheet that we periodically either distribute near the end of our classes or show on the overhead for use as an "Exit Slip." Sometimes we tell students which one of the listed questions we would like them to answer, and at other times they can freely choose. Of course, when we introduce this form near the beginning of the year we model answering the questions. Beginning ELLs can answer with drawings, as well as in their home language.

Doing the same thing can get "old" very quickly. Mixing-up reflective thinking activities between "how" and "what" journal questions; between answering teacher-directed questions and student-chosen ones; between sometimes sharing with partners and the class and sometimes just sharing privately with the teacher; and between some days doing it and some days not at all, can combine to maintain freshness and student interest in reflection.

- **"What if?" history projects and alternative endings to stories** can promote critical thinking,[57] though to maximize that value it's important to ensure that these alternatives are not just fanciful. Instead, they need to have some basis in evidence. Larry has shared a "What If?" history lesson in his book, *Self-Driven Learning*[58] that he uses with both ELLs and International Baccalaureate students where students have to choose a "point of divergence" in history and subsequent future events that are affected by it. However, those "future events" must be connected to evidence the student finds—if they suggest that Americans would have lost the Revolutionary War if George Washington had died from the harsh conditions at Valley Forge, then they must show evidence about his key role in keeping the army together as an effective fighting force.

EXHIBIT 2.7. Daily Reflection Acitivity

Please choose one of the questions below and respond to it on the bottom half of the sheet. Turn it in to your teacher before you leave.

1. What are two things you learned today?

2. What is the most interesting thing you've learned?

3. Imagine a simile or a metaphor about what we learned.

4. Think of one thing you have learned in class that you can apply in another class or another part of your life. What is it, and how can you apply it?

5. What was your favorite activity in class today? Why?

6. What was your least favorite activity in class? Why?

7. What would you tell your parents or guardians you did in class today?

8. How would you teach one thing you learned today to your little brother or sister (even if you don't have one)?

9. How does something you learned today connect to what you already knew?

10. What questions do you still have about what we did today?

11. How could the class have been better today?

STUDENT NAME _____

NUMBER OF QUESTION CHOSEN _____

STUDENT RESPONSE:

The same is true when imagining alternate endings to stories. For example, students might read a story about a boy and his dog and develop an alternate ending of a UFO coming and kidnapping them both. However, if there had been no prior allusion to UFO's in the story, this can be a fun activity and function as a language development exercise for ELLs (and we have used these kind of enjoyable alternate endings for that precise purpose), but it is unlikely to promote critical thinking.

- **"Visible Thinking Routines"** have been developed by Project Zero, a research group at the Harvard Graduate School of Education (http://www .visiblethinkingpz.org/VisibleThinking_html_files/03_ThinkingRoutines/ 03c_CoreRoutines.html). Some of their "routines" are particularly helpful for encouraging critical thinking. In addition to the Perceive-Believe-Care strategy that we referred to earlier, the ones that have worked the best with our ELL students have been:

  "See-Think-Wonder": Showing a photo and having students answer each of these questions: "What do you see? What do you think about that? What does it make you wonder?" (http://www.visiblethinkingpz.org/VisibleThinking_ html_files/03_ThinkingRoutines/03c_Core_routines/SeeThinkWonder/ SeeThinkWonder_Routine.html).

  "What Makes You Say That?": Again, showing a photo and asking these questions: What's going on? What do you see that makes you say that? (http://www.visiblethinkingpz.org/VisibleThinking_html_files/03_ ThinkingRoutines/03d_UnderstandingRoutines/WhatMakes/WhatMakes_ Routine.html).

  "I Used To Think . . . but Now I Think" can be used after a unit of study to reinforce our earlier point of not making assumptions or blanket claims since we are constantly evaluating new information that inform our changing judgments (http://www.visiblethinkingpz.org/VisibleThinking_html_files/ 03_ThinkingRoutines/03c_Core_routines/UsedToThink/UsedToThink_ Routine.htm).

Creativity and Innovation

Creative thinking, like critical thinking, has many definitions. We think a simple and sufficient way to describe it is as a proactive process that "uses information in unexpected ways to produce alternate or multiple answers to a problem."[59] It can be particularly countercultural in a school environment where students are often expected to be reactive to teacher questions, which often have only one correct answer.[60] One advantage of enhancing creative thinking is that it has been found to be particularly transferable to other academic content areas and beyond.[61]

Here are some specific suggestions on how teachers can help students develop creative thinking skills:

- **Explicitly teach the importance of creativity**. As with the other skills we've reviewed, specifically introducing the importance of creative thinking[62] can provide a strong background to help students begin to value and develop investment in the idea. The box offers a Mini-Lesson that teachers can use that we like because it looks at our ELL students through the lens of *assets* instead of *deficits*.

Creativity Mini-Lesson

1. First, place the Creativity Read Aloud (Exhibit 2.8), which highlights research showing that people with a multicultural background are more creative, on the overhead and give students their own copies. Read it to students while clarifying the meaning of new words.

2. Then follow with asking them to write responses to the two questions, which they then can share in pairs and with the entire class.

3. End by commenting that the class will be doing a number of activities throughout the year to help students increase their creative thinking, and then refer back to the lesson during the year when applying some of the other ideas listed in this section.

- **Modeling** most things we want to teach is perhaps the most important instructional strategy of all, and that holds true for helping students develop creativity, too.[63] We teachers need to use our imagination in developing lessons and not "get stuck in a rut." As neuroscience researchers have found, "The brain loves novelty and when new strategies are used to convey information, it is more receptive to learning."[64]

- **When preparing student assignments**, keep in mind the verbs often associated with the "Creating" Level of Bloom's Revised Taxonomy, including:

    assemble, create, devise, invent, design, construct, propose an alternative . . . , How else would you . . . , What changes would you make . . .

EXHIBIT 2.8. Creativity Read Aloud

A survey of 1,500 people who were the heads of companies in 60 countries and 33 different kinds of businesses found that creativity is the most important quality a person needs to have for success. Creative people tend to look at things from many different angles.

These two things are great news for English Language Learners. Researchers have found that people who have lived in more than one country tend to be more creative:

> *When you dive into a second culture . . . it increases your overall openness to new experiences. That kind of openness often leads to more creative ideas.*
>
> *A second thing that happens is that you . . . recognize that everything in the world can be viewed in many different ways.*
>
> *[Researchers] demonstrate that people who have spent time adapting to more than one culture are better able to generate new ideas.*
> — *Markman, 2015, http://www.fastcompany.com/3043220/why-people-with-multicultural-experience-are-more-creative*

There are still many things English Language Learners can do to increase their creativity, but they have a very good start!

WRITING PROMPT

1. What are some new experiences you have had since coming to the United States? Please list at least three.

2. What are at least three specific ways that the culture or customs in the United States are different from ones in your home country?

IBM 2010 global CEO study: Creativity selected as most crucial factor for future success. (2010, May 18). IBM. Retrieved from http://www-03.ibm.com/press/us/en/pressrelease/31670.wss.

Many more Bloom's Taxonomy verbs can be found by searching online. Of course, just using the words won't develop creative thinking—teacher modeling and support are needed.

- **A positive mood** and environment has been found to encourage creative thinking.[65] Maintaining a friendly classroom culture, developing solid teacher-student relationships and encouraging supportive student-student ones can help create this kind of atmosphere.

- **Asking the kind of "What if?" questions** discussed in the critical thinking section encourages creative thinking, as well.[66]

- **Recognizing failures and mistakes** as "opportunities to learn" and not only as points of negativity also encourages creative thinking.[67] We offer more specific ways to do this in the Agency and Persistence/Resilience sections.

- **Problem or project-based learning** (discussed more fully in Chapter 4 on writing when we discuss the skill of collaboration) is a particularly effective activity for promoting creative thinking among ELLs and other students. Problem and Project-Based Learning promotes active interaction with different perspectives, encourages flexibility, and challenges students to problem-solve (plus, of course, all the language-development opportunities that are present).[68]

- **Research shows that people** tend to be more creative if they are intrinsically motivated and have had autonomy in setting their own goals[69, 70]—two elements that have been discussed in other sections of this chapter. In fact, extrinsic motivation is related to *reducing* creative thinking skills.[71] Choice is a key part of this kind of self-motivation, so being clear on, for example, the goals of a reading assignment or homework, and then giving students options of exactly how to do them, can promote creativity.[72]

- **"Inside-out your mind"** is a term used by science writer Robert Krulwich to describe the notion of doing the opposite of a usual routine.[73] On occasion, have an "Inside-Out Day" for everyone (student changes should probably be approved by the teacher). A teacher could lead the class from the back instead of the front; a student could choose to take a very different route to get to school and write about his experience. Such a day could be a great excuse for some students to also sample different behaviors that they might not ordinarily do—a student who talks a lot during inappropriate times could choose to be quiet; another who procrastinates could commit to getting right to work. A fun introduction to this kind of exercise is showing a video clip from the Seinfeld television series where George decides to practice this exercise and do everything the opposite from his usual way (http://bit.ly/navccss2).

Larry has also applied this concept successfully outside of school. He was a community organizer for 19 years prior to becoming a teacher, and one year the organization he worked for was preparing a "Candidates Night" for those running for Mayor. They didn't want to do the usual routine of trotting the candidates out, asking them their positions on the organization's proposals, and then ending it there. Those were certainly productive, but they had already done quite a few of them.

So the organization's leaders considered what would be the opposite of what they usually did. They ended up bringing the candidates in and, instead of having them tell the community what they thought, the organization had people provide testimony on the issues that were important to them and how it affected their lives. Then, candidates had to share what they heard, and the crowd publicly graded them on their listening ability. It was a very successful action!

- **Applying the "constraints principle"** is a suggestion from an excellent free ebook from the British Council, *Creativity in the English Language Classroom*.[74] This strategy could include limiting words (story told in seven words), time (one minute to summarize lesson to partner), or materials (small groups are given six pieces of tape, six paper clips, and six pieces of paper to build the tallest tower—while speaking only English with each other or using gestures—and write a description of the process).[75]

- **The "random principle** ... putting two or more things together that do not belong together and finding connections" is another suggestion from the same authors.[76] One example of this strategy could be giving a few pictures of people, objects, and locations to a small group of students and asking them to use the images to compose a story connecting the images.

Tech Tools
Tools for Creativity

There are many free tools available for students to easily create content online, including videos, audio recordings, and multimedia stories. To start with, teachers might want to review Bloomin' Apps, a site designed by Kathy Schrock to correlate different tools with their appropriate levels of Bloom's Revised Taxonomy. Teachers can also explore these three regularly updated lists:

The "All-Time" Best 2.0 Tools for Beginning English Language Learners (http://larryferlazzo.edublogs.org/2015/04/16/the-all-time-best-2-0-tools-for-beginning-english-language-learners/)

The "All-Time" Best Ways to Create Online Content Easily and Quickly (http://larryferlazzo.edublogs.org/2014/02/23/the-all-time-ways-to-create-online-content-easily-quickly/)

The "All-Time" Best Web 2.0 Applications for Education (http://larryferlazzo.edublogs.org/2014/02/24/the-all-time-best-web-2-0-applications-for-education/)

Dispositions

We have described ways to teach what the CCSSO calls important "skills," such as goal-setting, metacognition, critical thinking and creativity/innovation.

Next, we will examine instructional strategies to promote what the CCSSO calls "dispositions," including agency, self-control, and persistence/resilience.

AGENCY

Agency is the ability to be proactive in determining one's life path and not just react to the surrounding circumstances.[77] Agency also recognizes that outside factors provide some limitations, and that people have some ability to influence and determine one's response to them.[78] Many of our English language learners face particularly large challenges in these outside factors—socioeconomically and linguistically. In addition, since many came to this country with little voice in the decision to do so, it may be an uphill battle to help them feel as though they do have control over what happens to them in life. Those issues make it even more important for teachers to encourage students to see these challenges not as limits to what they can do but, instead, obstacles that can be overcome.[79]

And our success in doing so will have a direct effect on our work in the classroom—multiple studies have found that a student's sense of agency strongly predicts their success in a language-learning context.[80]

Here are some strategies we can use in the classroom to assist our students develop a sense of agency:

- **Goal-setting and metacognitive reflection**: Both of these have been discussed at length earlier in this chapter, and both support the agency qualities of "These are my goals, and I can reach them" and "I know myself and what I need to do."[81]

- **Providing encouragement and feedback**: This is another action that can support student agency.[82] We are not talking about the "You're so smart! And such a great writer!" kind of encouragement, however. As Carol Dweck has documented in her work on a growth mindset, which we'll be discussing at length later in this section, it's important to provide encouragement that supports the idea that "the harder they work, the smarter they get."[83] That kind of feedback ("This is a great conclusion to your essay—look what happens when you take the time to revise!") supports looking at problems as obstacles to be overcome instead of having a fixed mindset, which views your present situation as destiny and does not prepare you well for coping when things don't go your way.

- **Self-talk** is a strategy students can use to encourage themselves. It's been called a form of "internal remodeling" and is a way to affect how you see yourself.[84] Research shows that when using this tool, it's better to use the pronoun "you" and/or say your name in the third person ("John, you can do this") instead of the "I" pronoun, because we have more of a tendency to use "You" for positive messages ("You can do this") and "I" for negative ones ("Boy, there is no way I can solve this problem"). With ELLs, we find that it is easier just to have them say their names—depending on their language level, explaining that "you" is them talking to themselves can get confusing. A short video of basketball superstar Stephen Curry winning a free-throw shooting contest and telling himself "Control your destiny!" (http://bit.ly/navccss3) could be a good one to show for demonstrating this point. Teachers, however, should ultimately use their best judgment about their classes—sometimes it might just be easier to have students, especially ELLs, say "I" in their positive self-talk and not worry about "you" or their name in the third person. The Growth Mindset lesson later in this section also includes suggestions for self-talk.

- **Contributing to others** helps students "gain self-confidence and come to see themselves as capable."[85]

  Here are two examples:

  - Working as a tutor: An ELL could help a family member at home (we included a form in our last book[86] that we have students use to document their reading to a younger sibling or cousin) or an Intermediate ELL could assist a Beginner. In our combined Beginner and Intermediate class, we periodically prepare Intermediate students to teach a lesson to a Beginner, or just have a Beginner read aloud a simple book to or with them (followed by their writing about why they liked or didn't like it). Research shows that this kind of interaction benefits both the tutor and the person doing the tutoring.[87]

  - Doing a class community project: Larry wrote in one of his previous books, *English Language Learners: Teaching Strategies That Work*,[88] about a lesson in critical pedagogy that led to students in his class organizing a job fair at the school for students and their families with different job-training providers.

Another year, when there was public concern about the disease known as SARS, his students developed flyers in English and their home language that provided clear and accurate information about it and distributed them to neighbors.

- **Students teaching others** develops agency in similar ways to tutoring. Not only does it enhance agency but, as researchers found, "simply telling learners that they would later teach another student changes their mindset enough so that they engage in more effective approaches to learning than did their peers, who simply expected a test."[89] Using the Jigsaw method, where students are provided different sections from the same text or different elements of a broader topic and then have to present to the entire class, is a particularly good strategy for ELLs because it creates an easy way teachers can differentiate (for example, an easier portion of the text can go to a student with lower-level English skills).

- **Providing students choice** whenever possible increases agency, engagement and motivation.[90] These could be "procedural" choices like where to sit or with whom students want to work in small groups. "Cognitive" choices are another option, which might be choosing which topics to explore in a project-based learning assignment or developing their own ideas for homework assignments. Both are good strategies, though researchers have found the latter to be more effective in promoting longer-lasting student autonomy and agency.[91]

- **Enhanced discovery learning**, such as the inductive method mentioned earlier and used often later in this book, promotes agency by having students construct more of their own understanding instead of giving it to them. A meta-analysis favorably reviewed by Robert Marzano found that a guided and scaffolded discovery process—which may very well include *some* direct instruction—is superior to lessons primarily relying on either direct instruction or "unassisted discovery" (in other words, lessons with little or no teacher guidance).[92] This kind of constructivist instructional strategy has been repeatedly found effective for non-ELL[93] and ELL students alike.[94]

- **Teaching students about their brains** and how learning a second language helps it grow can reinforce agency. Helping students see that the effort of their learning results in actual growth of their brain is another way for students to see that they do have control of their lives. This strategy builds on the work of Carol Dweck and is described extensively in Larry's book, *Helping Students Motivate Themselves*.[95] We typically teach this lesson at the beginning of the year, and periodically reinforce its points in the subsequent months. Students still talk about it when the school year ends.

Here is a simple lesson we do in our ELL classroom:

Learning and the Brain Lesson Plan

Instructional Objectives

Students will:

1. Learn the impact learning new skills has on the brain.
2. Practice using academic writing techniques.
3. Use collaboration to improve their writing and critical thinking abilities.

Duration

40 minutes

Common Core English Language Arts Standards
Reading

- Read closely to determine what the text says explicitly and to make logical inferences from it; cite specific textual evidence when writing or speaking to support conclusions drawn from the text.

Writing

- Write arguments to support claims in an analysis of substantive topics or texts using valid reasoning and relevant and sufficient evidence.
- Produce clear and coherent writing in which the development, organization, and style are appropriate to task, purpose, and audience.

Speaking and Listening

- Prepare for and participate effectively in a range of conversations and collaborations with diverse partners, building on others' ideas and expressing their own clearly and persuasively.
- Integrate and evaluate information presented in diverse media and formats, including visually, quantitatively, and orally.
- Present information, findings, and supporting evidence such that listeners can follow the line of reasoning and the organization, development, and style are appropriate to task, purpose, and audience.

- Adapt speech to a variety of contexts and communicative tasks, demonstrating command of formal English when indicated or appropriate.

Language

- Demonstrate command of the conventions of standard English grammar and usage when writing or speaking.
- Demonstrate command of the conventions of standard English capitalization, punctuation, and spelling when writing.

Materials

- Access to the Internet and a computer projector to show a video of the brain making neural connections (http://bit.ly/navccss4); brain scans (found here: http://news.psu.edu/story/334349/2014/11/12/research/learning-languages-workout-brains-both-young-and-old) and optional Jimmy Neutron video (http://bit.ly/navccss5).
- Student copies of the Learning and the Brain and Language Read Aloud (Exhibit 2.9) and Brain and Language Question/Response (Exhibit 2.10).

Procedure

1. The teacher tells students she is going to ask a question, and wants them to write or draw the answer to it on a sheet of paper during the next two minutes. She then asks, "What do you think happens to your brain when you learn something new, like a language?" The teacher writes this sentence frame on the overhead: "I think _____ because _____."

2. After two minutes, she announces that she wants students to get together in pairs to share what they wrote or drew, and that—if they want—they can make changes on their sheet based on what they learned. If students have been taught the sentence/question starters found in Exhibit 5.2 in Chapter 5, Speaking and Listening, the teacher can remind students to use them. If not, this could be an opportunity to teach a few of them, such as:
"What do you think?"
"I agree with you because_____"
"I wonder if it would be better if you _____"

"Sorry, I'm not quite clear on _____"

"What you wrote makes me think of _____"

3. The teacher asks a few students to share, including showing drawings on the overhead.

4. She then explains that she is going to show them a video of exactly what happens when they learn something new. She shows them the first minute of this video of actual connections forming in the brain when something new is learned (http://bit.ly/navccss4).

5. Next, she shows an image on the overhead of brain scans (found here: http://news.psu.edu/story/334349/2014/11/12/research/learning-languages-workout-brains-both-young-and-old) done by Penn State Professor Ping Li comparing the brain connections made by one group of people who didn't study a second language for six weeks; another group that didn't work very hard at learning new words in the second language during that period; and a third group that learned many of them. The teacher asks students to look at them and write down on their paper what differences they see. The teacher then asks students to repeat the pair/share/modify activity done previously, and asks some to share with the entire class. Students should say that there are many more new connections in the brains of people who learned the second language.

6. Then, the teacher puts the Brain and Language Read Aloud (Exhibit 2.9), on the overhead and gives copies to students. She says that she will read it and wants students to read along silently. She pauses to quickly explain any new words.

7. She then tells students she wants them to answer the same question they did earlier, though this time using the outline in Brain and Language Question/Response (Exhibit 2.10):

   What happens to our brains when we learn something new, like a second language?

8. She asks students to repeat the same sharing/revision process as earlier, but this time with a different person, followed by asking some to share with the entire class. Students can improve their writing based on the feedback they received from partners and then turn in their sheets to the teacher with eventually taping/gluing them into their learning journal.

9. The teacher asks students to remember this lesson as they learn new things—half-seriously, she can tell students that they will end up with bigger brains than everybody else who only speaks one language! If there's time, we like to end the lesson by telling students if they work hard in class, their brains will be so big that their heads will become the size of cartoon character Jimmy

Neutron and show a clip from that show—we are partial to one showing him getting ready for school (http://bit.ly/navccss5).

Assessment

- The teacher can collect and review the student writing assignment, as well as circulate throughout the room to assess how well students are using the academic sentence/question starters in conversation.

- If the teacher feels a more involved assessment is necessary, you can develop a simple rubric appropriate for your class situation. Free online resources to both find pre-made rubrics and create your own can be found at The Best Rubric Sites And A Beginning Discussion About Their Use (http://larryferlazzo.edublogs.org/2010/09/18/the-best-rubric-sites-and-a-beginning-discussion-about-their-use/).

Possible Extensions and Modifications

Intermediate or Advanced ELLs could also be given the article "You Can Grow Your Intelligence" (https://www.mindsetworks.com/websitemedia/youcangrowyour intelligence.pdf) to read and annotate using reading strategies, such as summarizing, asking questions, making connections and visualizing.

Tech Tool

Videos on Learning and the Brain

Depending on the English level of students, there are many additional videos and visuals about learning and the brain at The Best Resources For Showing Students That They Make Their Brain Stronger By Learning (http://larryferlazzo.edublogs .org/2011/11/26/the-best-resources-for-showing-students-that-they-make-their-brain-stronger-by-learning/). They could be added to this lesson plan or shown as a refresher at other times throughout the year, perhaps asking students to write down and share new learnings.

EXHIBIT 2.9. Brain and Language Read Aloud

"Learning and practicing something, for instance a second language, strengthens the brain," said [Professor Ping Li] "Like physical exercise, the more you use specific areas of your brain, the more it grows and gets stronger."[a]

But that is not all learning a second language does to the brain.

Scientists have also found that learning a second language actually makes your brain grow bigger.

Here is what *The Guardian*, a newspaper, wrote about it:

"Learning a foreign language can increase the size of your brain. This is what Swedish scientists discovered when they used brain scans to monitor what happens when someone learns a second language."[b]

NOTES

a. Indivero, V. M. (2014, November 12). Learning languages is a workout for brains, both young and old. *Penn State News*. Retrieved from http://news.psu.edu/story/334349/2014/11/12/research/learning-languages-workout-brains-both-young-and-old

b. Mackey, A. (2014, September 4). What happens in the brain when you learn a language? *The Guardian*. Retrieved from http://www.theguardian.com/education/2014/sep/04/what-happens-to-the-brain-language-learning?CMP=share_btn_tw

EXHIBIT 2.10. Brain and Language Question/Response

What happens to our brains when we learn something new, like a second language?

Use the A B C outline to write your answer:

ANSWER the question

BACK it up with evidence

make a COMMENT or CONNECTION

The brain _____ when we learn something new. (The Read Aloud said) or (The brain pictures showed) or (The video showed) _____ . This makes me feel _____ because

_____ .

- **Teaching with a growth mindset** orientation can provide students with another tool to enhance their sense of agency. As mentioned earlier in this chapter, the concept of a growth mindset is based primarily on the research of Carol Dweck.[96] Simply put, it means that success is based on effort and learning, not on "natural talent." No one is born "good" or "bad" at something—a belief that you are is considered having a "fixed mindset." Those with a growth mindset are more likely to view obstacles and mistakes as just common occurrences that are expected and that can be overcome. This mindset is exemplified by what a former colleague of Mahatma Gandhi told Larry years ago, "The key to Gandhi's success was that he looked at every problem as an opportunity, not as a pain in the butt."

On the other hand, those with a fixed mindset might have a long history of either being successful or unsuccessful at acquiring and developing a particular skill. Those who have been successful may have found it to be fairly easy and, once they encounter a roadblock—which we all do at some point—they may get discouraged more quickly and just stick to things that come easy. Those with a fixed mindset who have found it particularly difficult to learn something may eventually just give up and believe they are not capable of it ("I'm just not a good writer.").

Students with a growth mindset, however, have been found to be better learners and are more successful in school and in other areas as well.[97]

Teachers of ELLs may have an advantage when promoting a growth mindset to their students. Researchers have found that the experience of second-language learners in acquiring a new language makes them more likely to believe that it is what they learn, and not what they are born with, that makes a them the kind of person they are and who they want to be in the future.[98, 99]

So, how can we build a growth mindset in our classrooms?

Teacher Feedback

Teacher feedback, as discussed in the Agency section, should focus on praising effort and hard work ("I noticed that you were practicing pronouncing the words and asking your partner for advice before you read that passage to the class, and it really showed"). This type of feedback has also been called "process praise."[100] One important point that should be noted here is that, though praising effort should be a primary focus, we should also look for opportunities to praise students for their use of specific learning strategies. Just encouraging students to try harder can fall into the rut of "If the only tool you have is a hammer, then everything looks like a nail." Without the appropriate learning strategies (see the Metacognition section), even the hardest working student might not be successful. This kind of effective feedback does not have to be limited to teachers, however. Our upcoming Growth Mindset lesson discusses how students can do it, too.

As David Yeager, Gregory Walton and Geoffrey L. Cohen wrote in their article, "Addressing Achieving Gaps With Psychological Interventions": "Effective growth mindset interventions challenge the myth that raw ability matters most by teaching the fuller formula for success: effort + strategies + help from others."[101]

We have often read and heard students being told to just work harder in the name of Social Emotional Learning. We have seldom heard that admonition paired with the acknowledgement that outside support and help is a critical partner to that kind of hard work. We need to teach students ways to access outside support to ensure that their embrace of a growth mindset leads to success and not disillusionment.

Teaching about the Brain

Teaching about the brain, as described earlier, will help students view struggles in school not as a threat ("Am I dumb?") but as an opportunity to grow and learn ("This will make my brain stronger!")."[102]

Creating a Classroom Culture That Supports Making Mistakes

Creating a classroom culture that recognizes mistakes as learning opportunities on the natural road toward ultimate success, and not as a cause for punishment or ridicule, is another way to build a growth mindset. Related strategies and a lesson plan can be found in the section on Perseverance/Resilience.

Communicating High Expectations

Communicating high-expectations and confidence in student success also helps students develop a growth mindset. Research shows that students, particularly ones that might face a higher-degree of challenges, react better to difficult tasks that are combined with comments and actions communicating "This may be very challenging, but you've done great work in the past and I know you can do this, too." This kind of message increases student motivation and a growth mindset.[103]

Zaretta Hammond, author of the book "Culturally Responsive Teaching and the Brain,"[104] has refined this idea into a four-step process when working with individual students:

1. Communicate the high expectations and confidence in the student.

2. Point out what the student did right and what needs improvement.

3. Make specific suggestions about actions the student can take and/or elicit suggestions from the student.

4. Restate your confidence in the student's ability to succeed.[105]

Encouraging Perseverance

Encouraging perseverance, which has also been called "grit," also helps build a growth mindset. Angela Duckworth, a well-known researcher in this field, defines grit as "perseverance and passion for very long-term goals."[106] We discuss perseverance and grit more in the Persistence/Resilience section. Researchers suggest a strong connection between grit and a growth mindset—that each encourages the other.[107]

Explicitly Teaching Students about a Growth Mindset

Explicitly teaching students about a growth mindset can be an effective classroom strategy. As we've discussed, the concept of a growth mindset has many elements, including several for which we are have lesson plans in this chapter: how the brain learns, self-control, persistence, and the fact that mistakes are learning opportunities.

These lessons can be done over the course of weeks or months—we do them once a week over the course of a month. Though most are self-contained, we recommend that teachers begin with the Learning and the Brain lesson, followed by the upcoming one on the Growth Mindset. While teaching that lesson, be sure to make connections to the points previously learned about the brain. Follow this lesson with ones on self-control, persistence and mistakes (in any order) and make the point that they, too, are connected to a growth mindset.

It has been effective for our ELL students to devote time individually to each of these elements, providing time for the information to "sink-in," and tying them all together under the umbrella of the growth mindset.

Here is our growth mindset lesson:

Growth Mindset Lesson Plan

Instructional Objectives

Students will:

- Learn the concepts of Growth and Fixed Mindset and the differences between the two.
- Practice collaborative academic conversation.
- Acquire learning strategies that will help them in and outside of the school environment.

Duration

40 minutes, but it could take longer depending on which options the teacher uses to end the lesson.

Common Core English Language Arts Standards

Speaking and Listening

- Prepare for and participate effectively in a range of conversations and collaborations with diverse partners, building on others' ideas and expressing their own clearly and persuasively.
- Integrate and evaluate information presented in diverse media and formats, including visually, quantitatively, and orally.

Language

- Demonstrate command of the conventions of standard English grammar and usage when writing or speaking.
- Demonstrate command of the conventions of standard English capitalization, punctuation, and spelling when writing.
- Acquire and use accurately a range of general academic and domain-specific words and phrases sufficient for reading, writing, speaking, and listening at the college and career readiness level; demonstrate independence in gathering vocabulary knowledge when encountering an unknown term important to comprehension or expression.

Materials

- Access to the Internet and a computer projector to show videos from The Best Resources On Helping Our Students Develop A "Growth Mindset" (http://larryferlazzo.edublogs.org/2012/10/13/the-best-resources-on-helping-our-students-develop-a-growth-mindset/).
- Student copies of the Mindset Self-Talk (Exhibit 2.11).

Procedure

1. The teacher begins the lesson by having an overhead screen full of image results from an online search of the word "brain." He asks students to write on a sheet of paper what they remember from the lesson they had previously done on the brain—without looking at their notebook or folder. After a minute-or-two he tells students to share what they wrote with a partner and make changes to modify what they wrote to make it better, and then has some students share with the entire class.

2. The teacher then draws a long line like this on the board

People are born smart or not-so-smart and that's the way it stays.

People can become smarter by their actions.[108]

The teacher reads what the "continuum" says and tells students that based on what they learned about the brain, and other things they know, he wants them to think about it for a moment, and then come up, get a colored marker, and put an appropriate mark of their choosing that represents them on the line near what they think (the line should be long so many students can draw at the same time). The teacher should give an example ("If I think people are born smart and that's it, I would put a mark here"). He should tell students they should only draw for about thirty seconds before they return to their desks. This activity will probably be somewhat chaotic for a few minutes. This assumes that the teacher has already taught the Learning and The Brain lesson and, if so, most students will probably put a mark near the "People can become smarter by their actions." If the lesson has not been taught, students can do this activity individually and choose whether they want to share with the class or keep their opinion private.

3. The teacher explains another way some scientists look at this line is by calling the left side a "Fixed Mindset" and the right side a "Growth Mindset." The teacher writes those terms above the appropriate places on the line and asks students to repeat the terms chorally while using the gesture of a closed fist for a Fixed Mindset

and a gesture of opening their fist and raising it for a "Growth Mindset."[109] The teacher explains that scientists have found that people with a Growth Mindset are more successful in school and in other parts of life. In fact, the teacher can say that scientists have used machines to take pictures of people's brains and have seen that the brains of people who believe in a Growth Mindset worked harder and better than the brains of people who had a Fixed Mindset.[110]

4. Next, the teacher should show one or two short videos on a Growth Mindset and ask students to write down (or draw, depending on their English skills) one or two things they learn from each one. There are many options at The Best Resources On Helping Our Students Develop A "Growth Mindset" (http:// larryferlazzo.edublogs.org/2012/10/13/the-best-resources-on-helping-our-students-develop-a-growth-mindset/). We have found that the "Growth Mindset Video" (http://bit.ly/navccss6) and "Growth vs. Fixed Mindset" (http://bit .ly/navccss7) work best with our ELL students. After the videos, students can share what they wrote with a partner and then a few can share with the class. The teacher can teach a few academic sentence-starters for students to use with their partners if they have not been taught earlier:

"What answer did you write?"

"In my opinion, _____."

"It seems to me that _____."

"I agree with your opinion because _____."

5. Next, the teacher will show on the overhead and distribute Mindset Self-Talk (Exhibit 2.11). He explains that one side is what a person with a Fixed Mindset thinks and the other is what a person with a Growth Mindset would say to him/herself.

   The teacher explains that he will say each Fixed Mindset phrase, and then ask students to repeat it chorally. Then the teacher explains that he will repeat the Growth Mindset phrases, which have blanks. When students repeat it chorally, though, everyone should say their first name where there are blanks. If he has already taught Self-Talk as a learning strategy (see the earlier portion of this section), then students already know that when they talk to themselves they should use their name or the pronoun "you" (we find it easiest just to have students use their own name). However, as we explained when we first wrote about self-talk, it's up to teachers to use their best judgment—you might prefer to have your students say "I" instead of their names. The hand-out is designed for students to write and repeat their names, so it would have to be slightly modified in order to use "I," instead.

6. The teacher should ask students to think of times in the past when they have felt discouraged and add them to the left side, along with adding what they could have told themselves instead if they had a growth mindset.

7. The teacher should have students glue/tape the Mindset Self-Talk Figure in their notebooks/folders.

8. There are various options for ending the lesson:

   • The teacher could assign different Self-Talk sections to different students for them to quickly create posters of them to share and hang on the walls. Ideally, students could modify their posters to reflect times when they think they might experience particular challenges ("When I think 'I'll never speak English' after I get verb tenses confused, then I'll say, '(my name) will speak English with more practice.'" The teacher should provide a model or two for potential variations.

   • The teacher could have students break into partners and take turns repeating the different Self-Talk phrases.

   • The teacher could show one or more video clips from The Best TV/Movie Scenes Demonstrating A "Growth Mindset" (http://larryferlazzo.edublogs .org/2015/06/30/can-you-help-me-find-tvmovie-scenes-demonstrating-a- growth-mindset/) and ask students to write down and share how the characters demonstrated a growth mindset.

   • The teacher could ask students to write and/or draw about a time when they faced a challenge or problem where at one point or another they doubted they could do it, but eventually succeeded. Students could share what they wrote or drew with partners. The teacher should first provide an example from his life.

   • The teacher could write these sentence frames on the board and ask students to complete them:

     Having a _____ mindset will help me achieve my goals because _____.

     I would rather spend time with people who have a _____ mindset because _____.

     Students can share these with partners and also with the class. If the teacher doesn't do this exercise, it would be important for him to have brief individual conversations with each student in the near future to see if there is "buy-in" to the usefulness of the growth mindset. If so, then it provides a tool for the teacher to use regularly when he sees students falling into a fixed mindset (If a student complains about too much work, the teacher can say "You've said you want to have a growth mindset—remember what you can say to yourself"), as well as words to use when they are operating out of a growth mindset ("You showed a great growth mindset when you went back to revise that essay.").

Assessment

- The teacher can collect and review the student writing assignment, as well as circulate throughout the room to assess how well students are using the academic sentence/question starters in conversation.

- If the teacher feels a more involved assessment is necessary, you can develop a simple rubric appropriate for your class situation. Free online resources to both find pre-made rubrics and create your own can be found at the Best Rubric Sites and a Beginning Discussion about Their Use (http://larryferlazzo.edublogs.org/2010/09/18/the-best-rubric-sites-and-a-beginning-discussion-about-their-use/).

Possible Extensions and Modifications

See number 8 above for multiple options.

Another growth mindset lesson can be found in Larry's book, *Helping Students Motivate Themselves*.[111]

Tech Tool
Students Create Online Matching Games

Students can easily create online matching games or use an online site to create a paper version challenging their classmates to match-up the "If/Then" phrases on the Growth Mindset self-talk sheet. Ideally, of course, they would also include new phrases that they have added. Students can go to a site like Super Teacher Tools (http://www.superteachertools.us/) or others that can be found at SuperTeacherTools Looks Like a Great Site for Creating Online Learning Games (http://larryferlazzo.edublogs.org/2015/07/05/superteachertools-looks-like-a-great-site-for-creating-online-learning-games/). This kind of activity is also a great one for any language-learning classroom at just about any time, with phrases or words on the left and their meanings on the right.

EXHIBIT 2.11. Mindset Self-Talk

Put your name in the blank spaces

Fixed Mindset   **Growth Mindset**

If I think "I can't do this," then I'll say "_____ can't do this yet. _____will do it with practice."

If I think "I blew it!" then I'll say "_____ learns from mistakes."

If I think "It's good enough," then I'll say "_____ can do better."

If I think "I will never speak English!" then I'll say, "_____ will speak English with more practice."

If I think, "I'm dumb," then I'll say, "_____'s brain is getting bigger with every word he/she learns."

If I think, "English is too crazy!" then I'll say, "_____ will learn this language, even if it is crazy!"

If I think, "I give up!" then I'll say, "_____will look at the list of learning strategies and try another one."

If I think, "It's too hard!" then I'll say, "_____ gets stronger when things get hard."

SELF-CONTROL

Self-control is considered to be the ability to resist and control short-term impulses in order to make longer-term goals a higher priority.[112] In other words, as stated in a sign that Larry adapted from a phrase found online:

Self-control is choosing between what you want NOW and what you want MOST.[113]

We should point out how a number of researchers make a distinction between self-control and grit (which we'll discuss in the next section), though the two support each other. Those researchers, including Professor Angela Duckworth, suggest that self-control is resisting an immediate distraction in order to focus on a task at hand that can help you achieve a short-term goal ("I'm not going to throw an eraser at Juan because it's more important that I do my English reading assignment"). That short-term goal, in turn, is a step toward a long-term objective (It's more important that I do my English assignment because it will ultimately help me graduate from high school). Grit, according to Professor Duckworth, is a series of many proactive actions over years (though our personal opinion is that, for teenagers, a period of months would also qualify)—showing self-control on a daily basis—that focus on a central long-term goal (such as becoming a doctor).[114]

The definitions we use in the classroom are simpler: Self-control is "*not doing* something that you're not supposed to do even though you want to do it" and grit is "*doing* something - even when you may not feel like doing it at that moment - because it will help you achieve the big goals you want most." There is extensive research documenting a connection between high self-control and academic performance,[115] along with long-term life indicators including income and physical health.[116, 117]

As any teacher knows, classroom management is one of our most important responsibilities and can be a linchpin to teaching and learning. But that doesn't mean students sitting all the time and never speaking unless we speak to them first! We want to have an engaged, thinking, talkative classroom—especially with English language learners.

We are not going to spend this section discussing a long list of classroom management techniques—we touched on them in *The ESL/ELL Teacher's Survival Guide*[118] and Larry has written about the issue extensively in his three student motivation books.[119-121] We will, however, share the two best pieces of advice we've ever heard on that topic:

> *Will what I am about to do or say bring me closer or will it push me away farther from the person with whom I am communicating?*
>
> —*Marvin Marshall*[122]

> *In every interaction, you have a choice: Do you want to lift people up or hold them down?*
>
> —*Christine Porath*[123]

We want to emphasize that neither of these recommendations means teachers have to accept inappropriate behavior. They do mean that we can control the attitude, tone, and perspective we communicate with our responses to those student actions.

In addition to the explicit teaching of self-control strategies, researchers suggest that cultivating all the elements of a growth mindset, including how the brain is strengthened by learning, persistence (grit), supporting mistakes as opportunities to learn, and actively using metacognitive thinking all can support students developing a greater capacity for self-control. Applying the four qualities integral to intrinsic motivation that were listed at the beginning of this chapter —autonomy, competence, relatedness, and relevance[124]—can do the same.

Here is a lesson that we have used successfully to help students develop the skills they can use to control their impulses when they can lead to negative consequences to the learning environment (and outside of school, as well):

Self-Control Lesson Plan

Instructional Objectives

Students will:

- Learn about one of the most famous psychological experiments in history, the Marshmallow Test, and how it applies to their lives today.
- Practice the skill of identifying the meaning of unknown words by using context clues.
- Develop self-help strategies to assist them develop a stronger academic mindset.

Duration

50 Minutes

Common Core English Language Arts Standards

Reading

- Read and comprehend complex literary and informational texts independently and proficiently.

Speaking and Listening

- Adapt speech to a variety of contexts and communicative tasks, demonstrating command of formal English when indicated or appropriate.

Language

- Demonstrate command of the conventions of standard English grammar and usage when writing or speaking.

- Demonstrate command of the conventions of standard English capitalization, punctuation, and spelling when writing.
- Determine or clarify the meaning of unknown and multiple-meaning words and phrases by using context clues, analyzing meaningful word parts, and consulting general and specialized reference materials, as appropriate.

Materials

- Access to the Internet and a computer projector to show the TED Talk, "Don't Eat the Marshmallow" (http://www.ted.com/talks/joachim_de_posada_says_don_t_eat_the_marshmallow_yet?language=en).
- Student copies of either the Marshmallow Test Cloze (Exhibit 2.12) or the Marshmallow Test Read Aloud (Exhibit 2.13); and Strategies to Help with Self-Control (Exhibit 2.14).
- Construction paper and markers for all students.

Procedure

1. The teacher writes the term "self-control" on the board, says it and asks students to repeat it. The teacher tells everyone to hold up his or her pen or pencil as she models holding on. The teacher then says, "Imagine that I did something that got you very angry, and you want to throw your pencil at me." As the teacher is modeling getting ready to throw her pencil, she stops herself with her other hand and pretends her throwing hand is straining against the other hand that is holding her back. She explains, "self-control is the other hand holding you back." She asks all the students to pick up a pencil and mimic the same motion. In her playacting, she can grunt and make sounds while encouraging students to do the same, "It's hard to hold it back, isn't it?!" Have fun with this little "theater"—students will be laughing. The teacher explains that self-control is stopping yourself from doing something you know is wrong.

2. The teacher then gives each student either the Marshmallow Test Cloze (Exhibit 2.12) or the Marshmallow Test Read Aloud (Exhibit 2.13).

   If the teacher chooses to use the cloze, and students have not done a cloze activity before, she will explain that she will read the passage saying "uhm" at the blanks (explaining that only she gets to say it). After she is done reading, students have to choose a word from the "word bank" at the bottom and put it in the correct blank. In addition, students have to circle a clue word from the text that they used to help them choose the word from the "bank." After the teacher is done reading, she will model her thinking by putting the word "children" in the first blank and circling children in the first sentence. The teacher explains that they can use this strategy of looking for context clues to determine the meanings of new words they encounter while reading any text. Then students can have a few minutes to complete it. Students can either then share in partners or the teacher can immediately review it with the entire class.

If the teacher chooses to use the Read Aloud, she explains she will read a passage and wants students to read along silently. She may, or may not, briefly interrupt to define words that are new to students. In addition, she can ask students to practice annotation skills by using a reading strategy (summarizing, visualizing, evaluating, or connecting).

3. The teacher then explains that she is going to show a short video of one of the marshmallow tests and shows the TED Talk, "Don't Eat the Marshmallow" (http://www.ted.com/talks/joachim_de_posada_says_don_t_eat_the_marshmallow_yet?language=en).

4. Next, the teacher explains that self-control is part of having a growth mindset, and reminds students of the recent lesson they did on the concept. She then explains that there are many ways to develop self-control, and shows Strategies to Help with Self-Control (Exhibit 2.14) on the overhead and gives copies to students. If you have a class of ELL Beginners, you can avoid using the exhibit and instead playact the three strategies (if you use the exhibit, it certainly can't hurt to playact them, too).

5. The teacher then writes this prompt on the overhead, along with the paragraph frame, and asks students to answer it:

What is self-control and why do scientists think it is important? Do you agree with them? Can you think of a time when you might feel like losing self-control in the future? What will you do instead?

Answer the question using this paragraph frame:

Self-control is _____.
Scientists think it is important because _____. I agree/disagree with them because _____. I might want to lose self-control when _____. Instead, I'll _____.

She can tell Beginners that they can instead draw a response, perhaps just a poster with one side showing a situation where they might lose self-control and on the other side showing what they would do instead.

6. Students can then share with partners and the entire class, perhaps in a "speed dating" routine where desks are moved and half the class is seated facing the other half. Students share their posters and then one side moves to the next desk when the teacher calls "Switch" until several people have gotten a chance to share. Students can be shown some sentence/question frames to use in the sharing activity, including:

"Could you be more specific about _____?"

"I don't understand what you said about _____?"

"I agree with you that _____."

"That's an interesting idea."

7. The teacher can collect the paragraphs for review and return them the next day so that students can glue/tape them into their notebooks/folders.

Assessment

- The teacher can collect and review the completed cloze or Read Aloud and the Self-Control paragraph, as well as circulate throughout the room to assess how well students are participating in the "speed-dating" procedure and using the academic sentence starters.

- If the teacher feels a more involved assessment is necessary, you can develop a simple rubric appropriate for your class situation. Free online resources to both find premade rubrics and create your own can be found at the Best Rubric Sites and a Beginning Discussion about Their Use (http://larryferlazzo.edublogs.org/2010/09/18/the-best-rubric-sites-and-a-beginning-discussion-about-their-use/).

Possible Extensions and Modifications

1. See the Tech Tools box titled Voice Recording for Speaking Practice earlier in this chapter for details on how teachers can take photos of posters and students can provide audio accompaniment for posting on a class blog.

2. Students could make a variety of posters summarizing what they learned and how they will apply their new knowledge. For example, one poster could be divided into four boxes—two at the top and two at the bottom. Students could

draw in the top left box a time when they showed self-control and complete the sentence "I wanted to _____, but didn't because . . ." In the top right box the student could draw why they didn't do it and write why ("I knew I would get in trouble with my Mother."). In the bottom left box students could draw and write about a time when they regularly have problems maintaining self-control ("If I feel like talking to my friend when the teacher is talking"). In the bottom right box students could draw and write about what they will do instead ("Then I'll ask to change seats or ask to go to the bathroom").

This lesson plan has been adapted from one in Larry's book, *Helping Students Motivate Themselves*,[125] which contains a lesson more appropriate for very advanced or English proficient students.

EXHIBIT 2.12. The Marshmallow Test Cloze

A scientist brought together a group of children and put each of them in a room alone. The scientist gave each child a marshmallow. He told the _____ that he would come back in 20 minutes. If the children did not eat the _____ before he came back, he would give them a second marshmallow.

Only about 30% of the children waited to get the _____ marshmallow.

Over the next 30 years, the children who showed self-control by not eating the marshmallow did better in school, had _____ jobs, and were more healthy than the children who did _____ the marshmallow.

This experiment has been repeated many times and has had the same results. People who show self-control can be very successful.

better   marshmallow   children   eat   second

Source: Stromberg, J. (2014, September 24). *7 things marshmallows teach us about self-control.* Vox Media. Retrieved from http://www.vox.com/2014/9/24/6833469/marshmallow-test-self-control Urist, J. (2014, September 24). What the marshmallow test really teaches about self-control. *The Atlantic.* Retrieved from http://www.theatlantic.com/health/archive/2014/09/what-the-marshmallow-test-really-teaches-about-self-control/380673/

EXHIBIT 2.13. The Marshmallow Test Read-Aloud

A scientist brought together a group of children and put each of them in a room alone. The scientist gave each child a marshmallow. He told the children that he would come back in 20 minutes. If the children did not eat the marshmallow before he came back, he would give them a second marshmallow.

Only about 30% of the children waited to get the second marshmallow.

Over the next 30 years, the children who showed self-control by not eating the marshmallow did better in school, had better jobs, and were more healthy than the children who did eat the marshmallow.

This experiment has been repeated many times and has had the same results. People who show self-control can be very successful.

EXHIBIT 2.14. Strategies to Help with Self-Control

1. Avoid what is tempting you. If it's a marshmallow, hide it or look away from it. If you want to talk to friend a lot in class, change your seat. If you want to use your phone all the time, put it in your backpack and zip it up.

2. Distract yourself. If you want to throw an eraser at someone, untie and tie your shoelaces, instead.

3. Prepare an "if-then" plan. Think about times when you often lose self-control. Make a plan about what you are going to do when you start feeling that way. For example:

   "If I feel like talking to my friend John when the teacher is talking, then I will think about the good job I can get when I learn English."

   "If I feel like hitting Ava, then I'll think about the nice things she's done for me in the past."

   "If I feel like making noises, then I'll ask the teacher if I can go outside for a minute."

Source: Stromberg, J. (2014, September 24). *7 things marshmallows teach us about self-control.* Vox Media. Retrieved from http://www.vox.com/2014/9/24/6833469/marshmallow-test-self-control

PERSISTENCE AND RESILIENCE

Two other related qualities highlighted by the CCSSO that students need in order to learn the academic knowledge in the Standards are persistence (perseverance) and resilience. They are both also key elements of a Growth Mindset. In fact, it's thought that having a growth mindset could be a critical prerequisite toward developing both.[126]

As we did in the Self-Control section, we will use the term popularized by Professor Angela Duckworth—*grit*—to describe persistence/perseverance—both because it is gaining popularity in the education world and for the practical reason that it's easier for ELLs to say. Professor Duckworth defines grit as having a passion for a goal that you can stick with for a long time. Also, as we said earlier, we define grit as "*doing* something - even when you may not feel like doing it at that moment - because it will help you achieve the big goals you want most." Resilience has a number of different definitions.[127] We're comfortable looking at it as the part of grit that means—"when things are hard, you bounce back."[128] In other words, it's a question of how you respond to setbacks.

Many of our students have demonstrated in the past, and continue to demonstrate, extraordinary amounts of grit and resilience in their lives—by the sacrifices they made in their often perilous journeys to the United States, by many of the extra responsibilities they take on at home to care for family members, and by the long hours they often work outside of school to contribute toward the household income.

So, when we talk about helping our students develop grit and resilience, we are talking about how to encourage our students to apply qualities that many already have—the difference is that we want to to help them develop intrinsic motivation to apply these attributes to academic pursuits.

Extensive research has shown higher qualities of grit has led to increased chances of high school graduation[129] and higher grades.[130]

Research has also shown that encouraging resilience by helping students understand that mistakes are opportunities to learn and not indicators of disaster or a comment on their intelligence also leads to improved academic performance.[131]

Encouraging the use of metacognition, learning strategies, and the positive attitude of a growth mindset (particularly teacher feedback focused on effort instead of intelligence or ability)[132] are key ways teachers can support students using grit and resilience in the classroom.[133]

Research has been inconclusive about the effectiveness of explicitly teaching about grit and resilience as a strategy to help students apply it in the classroom.[134] However, we have found it useful to do so, particularly with ELLs, in order to help develop a common language about all the aspects of a growth mindset. Also, when students are experiencing challenges in the classroom, it provides an opportunity to have a different kind of conversation instead of a one-way talk about "getting back to work."

Here are two simple lessons—one on grit and the other on resilience. The grit lesson plan was inspired by Daniel Pink's "One-Sentence Project," which you can read more about in Larry's book, *Building a Community of Self-Motivated Learners*;[135] the resilience lesson focuses on how to embrace making mistakes.

We also want to clarify that, yes, these lesson plans and the ideas listed earlier in this "Persistence and Resilience" section will help our students apply academic grit in the context of what we quoted earlier: "the fuller formula for success: effort + strategies + help from others." At the same time, we want to re-emphasize what we discussed in the section on Agency - that it's also important to help our students learn what the formula means outside of the classroom. Let's assist our students to recognize the socio-economic challenges that they might face and help them acquire the active citizenship skills they might need to meet them. Then, they can also effectively use their grit to combat *those* challenges.

Grit Lesson Plan

Instructional Objectives

Students will:

1. Learn about the concept of perseverance (grit) and how it applies to their lives.
2. Practice academic language.

Duration

50 minutes

Common Core English Language Arts Standards

Reading

- Read closely to determine what the text says explicitly and to make logical inferences from it; cite specific textual evidence when writing or speaking to support conclusions drawn from the text.

Writing

- Write informative/explanatory texts to examine and convey complex ideas and information clearly and accurately through the effective selection, organization, and analysis of content.

Speaking and Listening

- Prepare for and participate effectively in a range of conversations and collaborations with diverse partners, building on others' ideas and expressing their own clearly and persuasively.

Language

- Demonstrate command of the conventions of standard English grammar and usage when writing or speaking.

- Demonstrate command of the conventions of standard English capitalization, punctuation, and spelling when writing.

- Apply knowledge of language to understand how language functions in different contexts, to make effective choices for meaning or style, and to comprehend more fully when reading or listening.

Materials

- Access to the Internet and a computer projector to show videos from the Best Video Clips Demonstrating "Grit" (http://larryferlazzo.edublogs.org/2013/07/15/the-best-video-clips-demonstrating-grit-help-me-find-more/).

- Student copies of Grit Read Aloud (Exhibit 2.15).

- Construction paper and markers for all students if the teacher decides that students should create posters.

Procedure

1. The teacher explains that students have done a goal-setting lesson already (see the first lesson plan in this chapter) and that those represent more short-term goals. Now, the teacher continues, we want to spend some time thinking about long-term goals. The teacher says that she wants students to decide on three goals—1 year from now, 5 years from now, and 50 years from now. The teacher shows a model poster and explains that her last goal is not 50 years from now but, instead, before she dies. The goals are written differently from the short-term goals—they are written from someone else's perspective. In other words, what you want others to say about you.

   The model poster would be divided into three parts. The teacher writes a sentence frame for each section saying what the student did and how he or she did it. Here are examples for each one:

   - In 1 year, people will say, "John graduated from high school because he studied very hard."

- In 5 years, people will say, "John entered medical school because he learned a lot in college."
- In 50 years, people will say, "John was a great doctor because he cared about his patients."

The teacher can write sentence frames on the board. Beginners can draw a picture only, or just write their goal without writing how they accomplished it. The teacher can also have students write the three sentences without making a poster, in order to save time.

2. The teacher can have students share their goals with partners and have some share with the entire class. Their partner conversations are an opportunity to practice academic language, including:

- "Could you expand a bit on what you said about _____?"
- "Something else I'd like to know is _____."
- "Can you explain what you mean by _____?"

The teacher can model these frames on the overhead.

3. Next, the teacher places Grit Read Aloud (Exhibit 2.15) on the overhead and gives a copy to each student. She tells students she is going to read it and asks students to read along with her silently. After she is done, she writes a model of the writing assignment in the Read Aloud, and asks students to begin working on their own.

4. Students can share what they wrote with a partner and the teacher can have a few share with the entire class.

5. This step is important and should not be skipped by the teacher: The teacher points out that having grit doesn't mean that you can't change your mind on your long-term goals, or ask for help. And it doesn't mean you are focused on it all the time and never do other things. It just means you don't give up easily if you know doing something will help your long-term goals.

6. The teacher can end the lesson there or end with showing some videos from the Best Video Clips Demonstrating "Grit" (http://larryferlazzo.edublogs.org/2013/07/15/the-best-video-clips-demonstrating-grit-help-me-find-more/), especially "Training Day—Steve Nash" (http://bit.ly/navccss8) and "Trust Your Power—NFL's Derrick Coleman" (http://bit.ly/navccss9). Other videos on that list might be more accessible to ELLs, though. Students should write how each video demonstrated grit.

Assessment

- The teacher can collect and review the completed writing assignment and goal list or poster, as well as circulate throughout the room to assess how well students are using academic language in their partner conversations.

- If the teacher feels a more involved assessment is necessary, you can develop a simple rubric appropriate for your class situation. Free online resources to both find premade rubrics and to create your own can be found at the Best Rubric Sites and a Beginning Discussion about Their Use (http://larryferlazzo.edublogs.org/2010/09/18/the-best-rubric-sites-and-a-beginning-discussion-about-their-use/).

Possible Extensions and Modifications

Students can also record their goals using online audio tools described in the first Tech Tools box in this chapter.

Larry has more extensive lesson plans on grit in his books *Helping Students Motivate Themselves*[136] and *Building a Community of Self-Motivated Learners*.[137]

EXHIBIT 2.15. Grit Read Aloud

We have learned about self-control, which is *not* doing something that you know you're not supposed to do even though you want to do it. You show self-control when you want to throw an eraser at another student, but you stop yourself from doing it.

Scientists have also discovered something called grit. That is *doing* something - even when you may not feel like doing it at that moment - because it will help you achieve the big goals you want most. You show grit when you decide you really want to go to college in two years and then you work very hard in your high school classes in order to graduate — even though there are days you don't want to study or do your homework, you still do it because you want to go to college. You show grit when you work towards achieving the one-, five-, and 50-year goals you just wrote.

WRITING PROMPT

All of us have shown that we have grit. In your own words, what is grit? Think of at least one or two times when you had a goal that was months or years in the future and you achieved it. Use this frame to write about it:

Grit is _____. I wanted _____.

After _____ months/years, I was successful. I was successful because

_____.

Resilience Lesson Plan

Instructional Objectives

Students will:

Duration

30 minutes on the first day, 50 minutes on the second day, and 10 minutes every Friday

Common Core English Language Arts Standards

Reading

- Determine central ideas or themes of a text and analyze their development; summarize the key supporting details and ideas.

Writing

- Produce clear and coherent writing in which the development, organization, and style are appropriate to task, purpose, and audience.
- Develop and strengthen writing as needed by planning, revising, editing, rewriting, or trying a new approach.

Speaking and Listening

- Prepare for and participate effectively in a range of conversations and collaborations with diverse partners, building on others' ideas and expressing their own clearly and persuasively.
- Adapt speech to a variety of contexts and communicative tasks, demonstrating command of formal English when indicated or appropriate.

Language

- Demonstrate command of the conventions of standard English grammar and usage when writing or speaking.
- Demonstrate command of the conventions of standard English capitalization, punctuation, and spelling when writing.

Materials

- Access to the Internet and a computer projector to show the video clip from the movie "Meet the Robinsons" titled "You Failed!" (http://bit.ly/navccss10)

or another clip from the Best Posts, Articles and Videos about Learning from Mistakes and Failures (http://larryferlazzo.edublogs.org/2011/07/28/the-best-posts-articles-videos-about-learning-from-mistakes-failures/).

- Student copies of a Mistakes Data Set (*not* the data set in Exhibit 2.16—that is just an example).

- Large paper and glue sticks for all students.

Procedure

First Day

1. The teacher shows the video clip from the movie "Meet the Robinsons" titled "You Failed!" (http://bit.ly/navccss10) or another clip from the Best Posts, Articles, and Videos about Learning from Mistakes and Failures (http://larryferlazzo.edublogs.org/2011/07/28/the-best-posts-articles-videos-about-learning-from-mistakes-failures/). The teacher asks students to write down what happened in the video. Students then share with a partner and a few share with the entire class.

2. The teacher emphasizes the message of the video—failing, or making mistakes, is okay because we learn from them. If we don't make any, then we're not taking risks and we're not trying hard enough. If the teacher has already taught the Growth Mindset lesson, he can remind students that this kind of attitude is part of having a growth mindset.

3. The teacher says he makes mistakes all the time and learns from them. Ideally, he can share an example of a mistake he made in class sometime and how and what he learned from it ("Last week I didn't have a good lesson plan prepared and things didn't go very well. I learned from how students reacted that I need to be better prepared when I come to class") and/or an experience he had learning a second language ("I was at a restaurant in Mexico and used the wrong Spanish word for waiter. The waiter was very nice about it and told me the correct word"). He should write the second example on the overhead.

4. The teacher explains that he would like each student to think about two common mistakes they have made when learning English—they could be in the domains of speaking/listening or writing/reading. The teacher writes another example on the overhead, "I said 'bottle' the wrong way and people couldn't understand me. My friend helped me learn the correct way to say it." The teacher tells students to try to identify mistakes while speaking or listening to

English and/or when writing or reading English, if possible. The teacher invites Beginners who might not know enough English yet to draw their mistakes.

5. Students share what they wrote with a partner (using academic language sentence starters like "So you are saying _____? and "Can you explain that again?" that are modeled by the teacher), modify them if desired, and turn them in to the teacher. The teacher explains the class will do something with them the next day. That night, the teacher will review what students wrote, revise them so that the grammar and spelling is relatively correct, and turn them into an inductive data set. We discuss inductive learning in upcoming chapters, as well. It should look something like the Mistakes Data Set (Exhibit 2.16) example.

Second Day

6. The next day, the teacher will give copies of the data set to all students. Depending on the English level of students, the teacher can read them one-by-one from the overhead or, after a teacher model, students can read them in partners. The teacher explains that students will read each one, circle a "clue" word that provides evidence about which of the two categories it belongs in, and then write the category next to it (students can write the entire name, or just initials, like "S/L" for "Speaking/Listening" and "W/R" for "Writing/Reading"). The teacher models the first example. After students have completed the data set, the teacher will review it with the entire class.

7. Then, the teacher provides poster paper, scissors, and glue to all students and tells them to cut and paste each of the items in the data set on the paper under the names of the appropriate categories. They should make sure there is a fair amount of space left at the bottom.

8. After the class is finished with cutting and gluing, the teacher tells students he wants each of them to add at least two more mistakes under each category (a total of four new ones) that they have made and learned from. Students write them down, share with a partner (again, using the academic sentence starters), modify them if desired, and then a few can be shared with the entire class.

9. The teacher asks students to hold up their categorized data sets with the new mistakes. The teacher says, "Look at all the things we learn from making mistakes! If you didn't make mistakes, you might not have learned all of these things! Every Friday, I would like each student to write and share in class a "Mistake of the Week"—a mistake you made and learned from. If you aren't making mistakes, you aren't learning! I'll also highlight a mistake I made."

10. At some point during this lesson plan or when "Mistakes of the Week" are recognized at a later date, it is important for the teacher to point out that there is a difference between making these kinds of learning mistakes and making mistakes when something very bad can happen—trying to drive on the wrong side of the road is not a good mistake to make. We celebrate the kinds of mistakes we make when we are trying to learn something, not the kinds of mistakes that we know could hurt others or ourselves.[138]

Assessment

- The teacher can collect and review the completed data sets, as well as circulate throughout the room to assess how well students are using academic language in their partner conversations.

- If the teacher feels a more involved assessment is necessary, you can develop a simple rubric appropriate for your class situation. Free online resources to both find premade rubrics and create your own can be found at the Best Rubric Sites and a Beginning Discussion about Their Use (http://larryferlazzo.edublogs.org/2010/09/18/the-best-rubric-sites-and-a-beginning-discussion-about-their-use/).

Possible Extensions and Modifications

- Students can choose one of their mistakes and make a poster depicting it and what they learned. The poster could then be shown on a video with the student narrating what happened, and then posted on a class blog.

- Highlight student and teacher Mistakes of the Week every Friday.

Another lesson on the value of making mistakes can be found in Larry's book, *Self-Driven Learning.*[139]

EXHIBIT 2.16. Example

MISTAKES DATA SET: Categories: **Speaking/Listening** and **Writing/Reading**

1. I said "bottle" wrong and Juan told me the right way to say it.

2. When I type my essay, I always make mistakes. When I type my English essay I always put the wrong helping verbs in the sentence. Ms. Ferlazzo told me if there is a green line under the sentence then click on the line and fix it.

3. When I went to the other school, I was talking to my teacher and then I said the wrong sentence that day. I learned how to say the sentence after she told me the right way.

4. Yesterday I spelled "orange" wrong and Felipe taught me how to spell it right.

5. Yesterday I spelled computer wrong and Lilia taught me how to spell it correctly.

6. Yesterday I said breakfast wrong and my friend corrected me on how to say the word correctly.

7. I was writing my calendar and I did a mistake with Wednesday; I wrote it like "Wenesday" the way I say it. I learned it when I used Google Translate.

8. Two weeks ago, I went to McDonalds and I did not understand the cashier. I learned how to order food through the computer. Then I went to the store and someone said, "How can I help you today." I told her I didn't understand and she got someone to help me who spoke Spanish and I learned what it meant.

9. Sometimes I don't know how to plan the words logically when I asked somebody a question. I learn how to ask some questions because I hear other people asking questions.

10. I said "hope" the wrong way and Ms. Johnson told me the right way to say it.

11. I said, "what did you go" and Mr. Ferlazzo said I must say, "where are you going?" That was when I knew the right way to say it.

12. Whenever I see Choua, I always say, "Who I am?" but he told me that it was wrong and he told me the right way to say it.

13. When I type in the computer, the computer helps me to understand the right thing to say.

For downloadable versions of the lesson plans and Tech Tools boxes found in this chapter, go to the "Downloads" section of this book's web page at www.wiley.com/go/navccss.

CHAPTER THREE

Reading

The more that you read, the more things you will know. The more that you learn, the more places you'll go.

—Dr. Seuss[1]

This chapter and the next three will be structured similarly. First, we will briefly summarize what Common Core says about the particular domain (reading, writing, speaking/listening, language). Next, we will examine each of the Common Core State Standards (CCSS) emphases in the domain more closely. Then, we will briefly summarize the key ways these standards might affect classroom practice for teachers of English language learners (ELLs). Finally, we will share specific instructional strategies for how teachers can meet those standards in the classroom in ways that are accessible to ELLs at both the lower and higher levels of proficiency.

We have structured these four chapters in the domains specified by the Standards (the reading anchor standards can be found in Exhibit 3.1). As most teachers know, however, life in the classroom is not separated into neat "silos." Just as every classroom activity has some of all the domains as part of it, so will these chapters.

What Does the Common Core Say about Reading?

The Common Core Standards call for students to "read closely"—which has commonly been reversed to "close reading"—and describes an in-depth text analysis often followed by written reflection based on evidence found in the readings, sometimes called "text-dependent questions." In addition, the Standards call for the reading that students do in grades 6–12 to be primarily nonfiction text (though that refers to all content classes and literature is still supported as "the core of the work" in the English classroom) that is *increasingly complex* in its use of vocabulary,

EXHIBIT 3.1. English Language Arts Standards » Anchor Standards » College and Career Readiness Anchor Standards for Reading

Key Ideas and Details

CCSS.ELA-LITERACY.CCRA.R.1

Read closely to determine what the text says explicitly and to make logical inferences from it; cite specific textual evidence when writing or speaking to support conclusions drawn from the text.

CCSS.ELA-LITERACY.CCRA.R.2

Determine central ideas or themes of a text and analyze their development; summarize the key supporting details and ideas.

CCSS.ELA-LITERACY.CCRA.R.3

Analyze how and why individuals, events, or ideas develop and interact over the course of a text.

Craft and Structure

CCSS.ELA-LITERACY.CCRA.R.4

Interpret words and phrases as they are used in a text, including determining technical, connotative, and figurative meanings, and analyze how specific word choices shape meaning or tone.

CCSS.ELA-LITERACY.CCRA.R.5

Analyze the structure of texts, including how specific sentences, paragraphs, and larger portions of the text (e.g., a section, chapter, scene, or stanza) relate to each other and the whole.

CCSS.ELA-LITERACY.CCRA.R.6

Assess how point of view or purpose shapes the content and style of a text.

Integration of Knowledge and Ideas

CCSS.ELA-LITERACY.CCRA.R.7

Integrate and evaluate content presented in diverse media and formats, including visually and quantitatively, as well as in words.

CCSS.ELA-LITERACY.CCRA.R.8

Delineate and evaluate the argument and specific claims in a text, including the validity of the reasoning as well as the relevance and sufficiency of the evidence.

CCSS.ELA-LITERACY.CCRA.R.9

Analyze how two or more texts address similar themes or topics in order to build knowledge or to compare the approaches the authors take.

Range of Reading and Level of Text Complexity

CCSS.ELA-LITERACY.CCRA.R.10

Read and comprehend complex literary and informational texts independently and proficiently.

(Common Core State Standards Initiative. (n.d.). English language arts standards. Anchor standards. College and career)

---

sentence structure, and organization. It is important to keep in mind that "text" does not mean only words on paper or on a screen[2,3]—it can also mean videos (closed-captioned ones are especially helpful for ELLs), infographics, charts, song lyrics, graphic novels, and so forth.

Two Key Elements of the Reading Standards

WHAT IS CLOSE READING?

We are going to introduce our definition of close reading with two analogies that help us and our students gain an understanding of "close reading."

Larry loves to play basketball—poor in quality, high in quantity. When he plays "pick-up" ball with his friends, they are loose on observing all the rules; they've played together often and know each other's moves, and are not too picky about the quality of the court or the actual basketball. Though they may practice some plays they'll use in a league contest, they are generally playing for the enjoyment of the game, while at the same time wanting to improve their overall skills and build their self-confidence. These games are the equivalent of our reading text messages, newspapers, and e-mails, along with books that we will often read for pleasure.

When it's time for league play, though, it's a different story—Larry and his friends need to remember and apply rules, they will slow the game down with time-outs to discuss what is working and what is not, and make adjustments during the game in offense and defense, depending on the conditions. They are enjoying it as much as their practice, but at a higher level—the sense of teamwork, the satisfaction of playing at their best, meeting challenges, and seeing the moves they've practiced work in a game played against an unfamiliar team. And the league games take place much less often than the pick-up ones. What goes on in these league games could be the equivalent of using close reading tools and strategies to gain an understanding of complex texts.

For nonsports fans, we think a metaphor that educator and author Amy Benjamin uses provides a helpful way to define close reading. She describes it as "driving in bad weather, at night, on unfamiliar roads."[4] In other words, you feel motivated to reach your destination, but you have to slow down and use "extra tools" like high beams and windshield wipers, along with minimizing distractions, like the radio. You remember "rules" that you've learned, like how to turn into a skid. And, most important, you have to "slow down."

It's different from when we might be on "automatic pilot" driving around town on a summer day.

This kind of "slowing down" often means students having opportunities for what our friend Kelly Young, a highly respected educator and consultant, calls "multiple touches" on the same text with different purposes for each one—perhaps one time to analyze its central idea, another for word choice and structure, another to find evidence in order to respond to an interpretative prompt, and so forth. Oftentimes, these "touches" include written annotation of the text—in the margins or on sticky notes if the text is in a schoolbook.

To reverse and modify an analogy suggested by psychologist Riccardo Manzotti,[5] we can look at texts as a house with a series of locked rooms, and every time we reread the text with a specific purpose, our mind creates a key to open a different door.

These re-readings of texts, of course, must be done within reason (close reading is done with short texts to teach strategies that students can then use periodically and independently in their reading of longer ones—a class should not "close-read" an entire novel) and with engaging lessons, which we will be shortly sharing. In addition, we will be reviewing the specific scaffolding required for ELLs to be successful in developing close reading skills.

Initial CCSS documents for publishers included recommendations against the use of prereading activities to activate student background knowledge, which the authors of the Standards felt might make readers less focused on the text. That admonition, though directed at publishers and not educators, spread among schools, but was quickly reversed by those behind the Standards.[6] In this chapter, we will be providing suggestions on how to encourage students to activate prior knowledge as a way to access texts and not as a "short-cut" to reduce the need for in-depth text analysis, which was an initial fear of the Standards's authors.

WHAT IS MEANT BY TEXT COMPLEXITY?

The Standards and their originators say that we must create a "staircase of text complexity"[7] in K–12 to prepare students for college and career demands.

According to the Standards,[8] a text's "complexity" is determined by three factors:

1. *Quantitative*, which it defines as an analysis of its sentence length, word use, and "text cohesion," which it says is best defined by a computer analysis. The Standards recommend specific tools to use that are free-of charge where text can be copied and pasted or specific books can be searched to determine their grade-level.[9]

2. *Qualitative*, which it describes as components that educators can judge, such as:

    a. *Structure*: Laying out events chronologically versus sophisticated use of devices like flashbacks, graphics that are supplemental or ones that are critical for understanding, sticking to the standard conventions of a particular genre or "mixing it up."

    b. *Language*: Is it conversational versus academic, does it include literary devices like figurative language?

    c. *Knowledge demands*: What kind of background knowledge is required for understanding the text?

    d. *Levels of meaning/purpose*: Are there multiple themes and purposes or a single one? Is the purpose clear, hidden, or vague?

3. *Reader and task considerations*, which emphasize teacher judgment in scaffolding, purpose of the learning task, and ways to build on student motivation. In other words, matching the *theory* of text complexity to the *reality* of your classroom.

And this passage from the Standards Appendix A is particularly important for teachers of ELLs:

> Teachers who have had success using particular texts that are easier than those required for a given grade band should feel free to continue to use them so long as the general movement during a given school year is toward texts of higher levels of complexity.

It goes on to say:

> . . . with the goal of students reading independently and proficiently within a given grade band by the end of the band's final year.[10]

We like the way 2010 National Teacher of the Year Sarah Brown Wessling summarizes what text complexity looks like in her classroom:

> The Three Bears Approach: Not too easy, Not too hard, Just right, but we want to make sure that as we're finding that just right kind of sweet spot for our students that we're always dialing it up just a tiny bit so that over the course of the year, over the course of the semester, over the course of the experience, students will be able to constantly grow in that way.[11]

Our interpretation of these guidelines is that we should do whatever we can to help students increase their reading proficiency. And our *goal* should be to help them reach their official grade-level by the end of the year. At the same time, we must be realistic—a Beginner or Intermediate in high school is unlikely to get there during their first year or two in the United States (remember—researchers have found that it takes 4–7 years for an ELL to reach academic English proficiency[12]). But the key indicator of success is if a student is reading increasingly complex texts while applying reading comprehension strategies in more sophisticated ways.

WHAT DOES THIS MEAN FOR READING INSTRUCTION IN MY CLASSROOM IN GENERAL?

When we combine all the elements of the reading strands in the Common Core Standards, then, what might it mean for teachers of ELLs?

We would suggest that it means to:

- Make sure that nonfiction text, *as well as fiction*, is well represented in the reading material you use with, and is available to, your students.

- Teach students to annotate text, no matter how simple or "complex" it might be, with key reading strategies like summarizing, asking questions, and identifying the main idea. Focus on only one or two reading strategies during each rereading of the text. In addition, teach students to use metacognition to self-monitor their comprehension so they know what strategies can help them in what situations. Remember: The end-goal of close reading is to prepare students to transfer their skills to situations in which you, the teacher, are not providing guidance.

- Recognize that the common teaching process of "I do, we do, you do" is probably not sufficient for ELLs and that additional scaffolding steps, which we discuss later in this chapter, will likely be required.

- Ask text-dependent questions that require students to look for evidence in what they are reading.

- Use the common, but not text-dependent, strategy known as "text-to-self" selectively. Asking students to connect the text to their own experiences can increase student motivation, but doesn't necessarily improve comprehension and understanding. However, if carefully constructed and monitored, text-to-self questions can provide one way to engage hesitant readers and writers as a prelude to answering more challenging text-dependent questions.

- Be strategic when spending time in prereading activities to provide background knowledge. In other words, make sure that it is a necessary tool for helping students access the text, and not for providing excess information and acting as a substitute for what could be learned from the text itself.

- Plan to gradually increase the complexity of texts you use with students during the year. This doesn't mean that it must be an uninterrupted incline. As Professor Timothy Shanahan writes:

> The idea is not to have students reading challenging texts exclusively. Students should have an array of reading experiences in the same way that a long-distance runner has a varied training schedule that intersperses different distances and speeds. These varied schedules enable the runner to build muscle, speed, and endurance.... This

means that students would, over the course of a school year (and even a school day), confront texts they could read easily with little teacher input as well as those in those upper bands specified by the standards.[13]

In other words, we are not alone[14] in being very careful and strategic in how often we have students close read a complex text. No matter how engrossing it is, or how creative we can make the close reading process appear, reading and rereading something multiple times holds the danger of causing student tedium, disengagement, or outright revolt.

As educator Laurie Elish-Piper has said, "Close reading is like broccoli. It's good for you, but only in moderation."[15]

An additional suggestion is that teachers should not do close reading of a text in isolation—it should be done in the context of a broader unit that includes numerous other learning activities.

Tech Tools
Online Free and Useful Resources

There are many free resources related to the Common Core available on the Internet. We think a small fraction of them are actually useful. You can find our collections, including large numbers of texts for close reading and mentor texts for writing suitable for classroom use at:

The Most Useful Resources for Implementing Common Core http://larryferlazzo .edublogs.org/2012/07/14/the-most-useful-resources-for-implementing-common-core-i-hope-youll-contribute-more/

The Best Resources for Learning about Common Core Standards and English Language Learners http://larryferlazzo.edublogs.org/2011/08/03/the-best-resources-for-learning-about-common-core-standards-english-language-learners/

A Collection of My "Best" Lists on the Common Core http://larryferlazzo.edublogs .org/2013/12/14/a-collection-of-my-best-lists-on-the-common-core/

HOW CAN READING INSTRUCTION IN MY CLASSROOM SUPPORT ELL STUDENTS IN MEETING COMMON CORE STANDARDS?

What follows below is a list of instructional methods that can be used in multiple types of reading activities with ELLs. Obviously, one key method in the Common Core context is close reading, which we will discuss at length. Many of the other teaching methods we describe can be enlisted in support of close reading or can be used independently of it.

Reading for Pleasure

In our last book,[16] we discussed the value of students reading books of their own choice for pleasure and shared how we make that happen in our own classrooms—and beyond. Our experience since then, along with more recent research,[17] has reinforced our belief in its effectiveness in helping ELLs develop literacy skills.

The Common Core Standards agree:

> Students need opportunities to stretch their reading abilities but also to experience the satisfaction and pleasure of easy, fluent reading within them, both of which the Standards allow for.[18]

Having a well-stocked classroom library is a critical asset in order to encourage reading for pleasure. Ours are "leveled" (Beginner, Intermediate, Advanced) and categorized (Fiction, Nonfiction, Bilingual) to assist, but not restrict, students' selection. Research shows that emphasizing "book leveling" can be constraining and destructive to students' growth as readers.[19] We believe, as has been said by many others in different ways, that the best book for a student is one the student wants to read. That being said, putting a Beginner in a situation where he or she has to wade through a bunch of Advanced books to find one that's accessible can also create needless frustration.

We have our students read a book of their choice for the first 10 minutes of class (and at least 20 minutes each night), with no related assignment or requirement most of the time (sometimes they might prepare a "book talk" for peers, respond to their daily reading in a "quick-write," or create a "book review" poster). Students can also use that time to search for a book in our classroom or at the school library. Though we discourage constantly changing titles, we also make sure that students know that there is no point in continuing to read a book that they don't like. We use this pleasure reading time to check in with individual students about their engagement, comprehension, and future interests. We make sure these conversations are "natural" and are not a formal assessment. We should also point out that during pleasure reading time—as well as during other class time—we allow students to use their cellphones to look up words that are new to them.

The books students read do not have to be written entirely in English; they also don't have to be print on paper and the reading of them doesn't always have to be done alone.

It's sometimes a challenge to find books for adolescent ELLs that are language-accessible and intellectually challenging—a children's or chapter book, understandably, is not always of great interest to these students and most commercially available bilingual books present the same problem. We've found that, particularly for Intermediates, purchasing both English and home-language copies of popular books that are at a higher English level is sometimes a good response to this dilemma. Students reading the English edition, with the home language copy available as a reference, can be engaged with the text and, especially if paired with an "assignment" of keeping an eye out for language similarities and differences,[20] this can have an added impact on language-learning. Of course, we can't monitor which copy they are reading outside of the classroom, but substantial research also shows that increased fluency in a home language assists second-language development,[21] and reinforcing a student's interest in reading is always a good thing. In our experience, this strategy has always been a winning one.

When a computer, tablet, or even a smartphone, is available, they, too, offer a wide range of opportunities for reading for pleasure—often including features that can dramatically boost literacy skills for ELLs. Many free tools provide audio support for the text, animations and other visuals, the ability to see the definition of a word with a click, and even the option of seeing various simplified and more complex versions of the same text. The Tech Tools box shares links to many of these sites, as well as sites that provide free printable books accessible to ELLs.

Reading in pairs is another option. Once a week in our combined Beginner and Intermediate class, students "pair up"—primarily, but not exclusively, with one Beginner and one Intermediate (we have found that pairing students up in this way is less frustrating for the Beginner and more confidence-boosting for the Intermediate). Students enter to see "Partner-Reading Instructions" (Exhibit 3.2) on the overhead. They are then given a few seconds to find a partner with whom they want to read and then 2 minutes to pick a book. We then explain that they will read to each other—a paragraph at a time—while both students are looking at the words.

At the end of those 10 minutes, they will pick three new words they saw, write them down on a piece of paper, and learn what they mean. They will also draw a picture representing the book, and write a sentence explaining why they like or don't like the book.

Students then either present to groups of other students and/or we take a photo of their poster and then they record their presentation with one of the many apps we discussed in Tech Tools boxes in Chapter 2.

Tech Tools

Online Resources for Reading for Pleasure

There are literally thousands of free sites that provide online high-interest reading for all levels of ELLs. We have collected our favorite choices in the following list.

The Best Websites to Help Beginning Readers http://larryferlazzo.edublogs.org/2008/01/22/the-best-websites-to-help-beginning-readers/

The Best Websites for Beginning Older Readers http://larryferlazzo.edublogs.org/2008/01/23/the-best-websites-for-beginning-older-readers/

The Best Websites for Intermediate Readers http://larryferlazzo.edublogs.org/2008/01/26/the-best-websites-for-intermediate-readers/

The Best Places to Get the "Same" Text Written for Different "Levels" http://larryferlazzo.edublogs.org/2014/11/16/the-best-places-to-get-the-same-text-written-for-different-levels/

The Best Sites Where Students Can Work Independently and Let Teachers Check on Progress http://larryferlazzo.edublogs.org/2008/05/21/the-best-sites-that-students-can-use-independently-and-let-teachers-check-on-progress/

There are also many free simple printable books available online that are accessible to ELLs. You can find a list of these resources at the Best Sources For Free and Accessible Printable Books http://larryferlazzo.edublogs.org/2009/07/31/the-best-sources-for-free-accessible-printable-books/

EXHIBIT 3.2. Partner-Reading Instructions

1. Find someone you want to read with and sit next to them — 30 Seconds

2. Pick a book you want to read together — 2 Minutes

3. Get one piece of paper for each pair of students — 30 Seconds

4. Read the book aloud to each other, taking turns. You will read together for 10 minutes.

5. On the piece of paper, write (for 10 minutes):

* Your names

* The title of your book

* Three words that are new to you in the book

* What those words mean, in your own words

* A picture representing the book

* Finish one of these sentences:

   "We liked this book because_____"

   "We didn't like this book because_____"

6. Practice presenting your poster, with each person saying about half of what you wrote.

7. You will present in small groups and/or record it for the class blog.

Pattern of Close Reading Instruction

Most teachers, and many writers about classroom management, are familiar with the concept of having procedures and *routines* to encourage student behavior—how to enter the classroom, how to leave, how materials are distributed, and so forth.

In this section, we would like to discuss the value of practicing *teaching routines*, specifically in applying the Common Core reading standards in our classrooms. The best definition for teaching routines is that they are "recurring patterned sequences of interaction that teachers and students jointly enact to organize opportunities for student learning in classrooms."[22] All teachers, including us, have these routines, ranging from how classroom discussions are conducted to, as we'll discuss in the next chapter, how we orchestrate a writing routine based on the work of Paolo Freire. These kinds of teaching routines can provide an effective planning and implementation framework for educators—almost like an education version of the "checklist" that physician and author Atul Gawande has written about that hospitals are using to ensure that critical steps are not missed in patient care.[23]

Their predictability can also provide a safe environment for students, particularly protecting "novices" from "overload"[24], which can certainly be a danger for students who are learning English at the same time they are learning all the other required conceptual and content knowledge.

"Teaching routines," though, do not have to mean doing the same thing time and time again. Novelty[25] and surprise[26] stimulates the brain and attracts student interest—they are essential qualities to regularly introduce in the classroom. A teaching routine for close reading provides numerous opportunities to add novelty to the equation through different types of "texts" (including videos, charts, and infographics); countless types of collaborative activities (including common ones like think/pair/share, jigsaws, and group projects); and a myriad of different purposes (asking/answering questions, comparing/contrasting, writing responses, using graphic organizers).

Larry spent 19 years as a community organizer prior to becoming a teacher, and learned that the "mantra" of a good organizer was "planning, action, evaluation." We feel that this three-step process works well for all lesson planning, and will model it here. The "action" part is the actual classroom teaching and contains its own teaching routines.

First, a note of caution—do we follow each step in this pattern of close reading instruction all of the time? No. Do we follow it most of the time? No. Do we apply many of the steps a fair amount of time? Yes. Are our lessons better when we do? Yes. There is never enough time in our personal or professional day to do everything the way it "should" be done, and we can only do our best under the circumstances that we inhabit.

Planning

First, the teacher must determine the *unit* the class will be working on for a period of time. Our criteria for a unit would be that it provides superior opportunities to meet Common Core Standards, maximize language learning, and generate student engagement. We've found that thematic units work well to meet these three goals, and researchers support our experience.[27]

Next, the teacher needs to decide the *purpose* of each close reading lesson (close reading a text is likely to occur over a period of days). In other words, what might be the primary language-learning purposes (e.g., applying three recently learned academic vocabulary words and learning one new word from use of context clues) and the Common Core Standard conceptual "takeaways" (e.g., identifying a use of figurative language and why it was used) he or she wants for students? As we discussed in the first chapter, the Standards contain the concepts students should learn, and, as teachers, we need to use our professional judgment (with help from our state's ELD Standards) to determine the language scaffolds our students need to acquire this knowledge.

Third, the teacher identifies a *text* or texts (remember, "text" can include a closed-captioned video, chart, infographic, etc.) appropriate for both the language-learning and Common Core objectives. We would recommend that the text selected for close reading be anywhere between one paragraph and two pages as long as it meets a criteria similar to the one we described earlier for unit selection. We tend to favor texts on the shorter end of that range for our ELLs, though they could be part of a longer text the class is reading. Once the text decision is made, then teachers must determine what background knowledge is required to comprehend the text and how to either elicit it from or provide it to students (see the next section). In addition, teachers should consider if any "text engineering"[28] might be required to make the text more accessible without reducing its complexity (adding images, breaking it up into smaller chunks of text, and adding headings).

The teacher then needs to decide the lesson sequence in the "Action" step of this three-step process, which could include many of the instructional strategies discussed later this chapter.

Action: The Lesson Itself (Prior to, during and after Close Reading)

Prior to Students' Close Reading

1. Facilitate background knowledge (see the next section in this chapter on this topic).
2. Explain the purpose of the lesson and reading.
3. Describe the process, or at least the first step in the process. We have found that explaining everything that students will be doing in the lesson can (a) be confusing, (b) could create a situation where some students might jump ahead,

and (c) make it more complicated to make changes to the original plan based on what is happening in the classroom.

4. Focus on metacognition—assuming that the metacognition lesson from Chapter 2 has been taught, remind students to keep those learning strategies in mind as they "self-monitor" their comprehension of the text as they read. In other words, be aware of what you don't understand so you can "fix it." Remind them of one or two of the strategies, if necessary.

During the Time Students Are Close Reading

Step One—Previewing the Text—*What the Text Might Say*

One process we've found helpful in this first step is to teach our students to ask a series of questions when they see a text for the first time. We use the analogy of being like a detective who is arriving at a crime scene. First, we need to survey the area, noticing what it looks like, who might be involved, and what might be happening and why. When students get a text for the first time, we teach them to similarly "survey" what it looks like and ask themselves questions such as the following (although not *all* of the questions in one lesson—use professional judgment to determine a match between the English level of your students, the complexity of the text, and the individual lesson plan design):

a. What type of text (a story, a newspaper article, a poem, etc.) is this? How do I know this? ("I think this text is _____ because _____.")

b. Who is the author? What do I know about him/her? How could I find out about the author if I don't know who he or she is? ("The author of the text is _____. I know _____. I don't know about the author, but I could find out more information by _____.")

c. When and where was this published? What might be important about this information? ("This text was published in _____ and _____. This information could be important because _____.")

d. What is the title of this text? What predictions can I make about the text based on the title? ("The title is _____. Based on this title, I predict _____ and _____.")

e. Who is this text written for (who is the audience)? What makes me think this? ("I believe this text is written for _____ because _____.")

f. What might be the purpose of this text? What makes me think this? ("I believe the purpose of this text is _____ because _____.")

Step Two—Basic Comprehension/Decoding—*What the Text Says*

(The short, italic headings in Steps Two, Three, and Four come from literacy expert Timothy Shanahan, n.d.):

1. Tell students the *purpose*—that during this ***first reading***, they should focus on developing a basic understanding of the text. To assist them in this purpose, we will provide some questions and we will encourage them to generate their own as we read the text together. The following list provides examples of these more literal-type questions along with sentence-frames for student responses (obviously, modifications can be made by teachers to make the questions more specific to the text being read). Depending on the English level of your students, determine a reasonable number of questions—don't overwhelm them with a huge list or the task of finding the definition of *every* word they don't know. After students have more experience with close reading, another option might be to provide copies of the Question and Answer Starter List in Exhibit 3.3 and give them the opportunity to select which questions they believe would be most helpful to them to figure out "what the text says." Note that many of the questions can be used for reading fiction and nonfiction texts, but others are more appropriate for one or the other. These are just examples and many more sentence frames can be developed by teachers or found online:

    a. What is the text about? ("I think the text is about _____ because _____." or "I think the text is about _____. The clues are _____ and _____.")

    b. What words are new to you?

    c. What are words you think you have difficulty pronouncing?

    d. Where does it take place? ("I think it takes place in _____ because _____.")

    e. When is it happening? ("I think it is happening _____ because _____.")

f. What is the setting of the text (setting means both place and time)? ("I think the text is set in _____ during _____. I think that because the author writes _____.")

g. What is a summary of the text? What is the plot? ("First _____. Second _____. Then _____.")

h. What do you predict is going to happen? ("I predict _____ because _____.")

i. What questions does the text make you wonder about? ("I wonder what/how/when/if/who _____because_____.")

j. Is there a conflict or problem in the text? ("I think a conflict/problem is _____ because the author writes _____.")

k. What is the theme? ("I think the theme is _____ because _____.")

Question k in particular might need more initial preteaching than other questions in this step. We teach theme by having students think of movies they have seen and having them identify the "message" (theme) instead of what happened (plot). We then build a "bank of themes"—a poster that contains a list of common ones that students can use as a reference.

2. Have students follow along silently on their own copy of the text or on the one displayed on the overhead as the teacher reads it aloud. Though there are cautions in the Common Core against using read alouds often as a substitute for students reading text independently (see the upcoming section on Read Alouds), we generally find the benefits of modeling pronunciation and prosody outweigh its drawbacks. And, with the need for rereading in the text when using close reading, students will still get plenty of opportunities to read it independently. We don't mean to suggest that the text always has to be read aloud, but we would suggest that the lower the English level of your students, the higher the number of times you should read the text aloud to them.

While the teacher is reading, he or she might want to pause to allow students time to annotate the text, perhaps with sticky notes if they can't write directly on it. These annotations can be used to help students to later answer the questions. For example, students might underline a few words that are new to them and then return later to identify which ones they think are most important and search for their meanings. Students might also write a question that pops into their mind about the text.

3. After the text has been read aloud, give students a few minutes to answer the teacher provided questions and identify evidence from the text to support their answers. Also encourage students to answer any questions they generated on their own while reading. Students should be given time to look up words and their pronunciation on Google Translate with the caution that they should use this learning strategy only after they have tried other word analysis strategies first like context clues and cognates.

4. Then, have students work in partners or small groups to share their answers to the teacher provided questions, including explaining what words might have been new to them but now they know what they mean. Students can also share the questions they might have generated and their answers to those questions. Remind students to use sentence starters like:

    a. "I think _____."

    b. "In my opinion, _____."

    c. "I disagree because _____."

    d. "I agree because _____."

    e. "While I agree with _____, I disagree with _____."

    The teacher should be circulating throughout the room during this 5-to-10-minute (depending on the number of questions) activity.

5. The teacher can call on individual students to respond to the questions, using her judgment based on what she heard while listening to the group discussions.

    Note: As stated earlier, it's easy to use this five-step sequence all the time and still maintain a sense of novelty. The text can be a video or a chart; the basic comprehension questions can be different; graphic organizers or posters can be used; small groups can be varied—ranging in number to how they are selected (student or teacher chosen; selection criteria can be serious—based on language level—or fun—based on the color of socks); and there can be multiple ways small groups report back (as individuals or as entire group; in writing or drawing; saying the meanings of new words or acting them out). In addition, the first reading and a subsequent rereading(s) sometimes can be on same day and other times can be spread out.

Step Three: More In-Depth Meaning—*Figure Out How the Text Works*

1. Tell students they will use the knowledge they gained from the first reading of the text to help them gain a greater understanding as they ***do a second reading of the text.*** They will work in partners taking turns reading every two sentences or every other paragraph of the same text to each other (or, they can read independently—remember, mix it up!). We do think that having students read to each other often during this rereading of the text works well as a scaffold. Explain that while they are reading and afterwards, they are going to "dig a little deeper" into the text, answering questions that could include some of the following (again, these will probably be teacher selected at first, but could be identified by students at times, also):

a. What is the mood of the text? ("I think the mood is _____ because of _____" or "I think the mood is _____. The clues are _____ and _____." or "The author said _____, so that makes me think that _____.")

b. A question about figurative language could be:

What did the author mean by _____? or Are there any words that you think might mean one thing but the author really meant it to mean something else? ("I think when the author wrote _____ he or she meant that _____ because _____.")

c. Is the author using sensory details (color, smell, physical descriptions, taste, etc.) to tell us something? ("The author says _____. I believe he or she is saying that because he or she wants us to think _____.")

d. Who is telling the story? ("I believe _____ is telling the story because _____." or "According to the text, _____, so _____.")

e. If you are highlighting a smaller portion of a lengthier text the class is reading, a question could be:

How does this portion relate to what came before and/or to what comes afterwards? ("I think this relates to what came before by _____ because_____.")

f. Who do you think the author is writing this text for—who is his/her audience? ("I think the author's audience is _____ because _____.")

g. What is a context clue to the meaning of _____? ("I think _____ means _____ because the author writes _____.")

h. Is there dialogue (people talking) in the text? If so, why do you think the author uses it? ("I think the author uses dialogue because he or she

wants to _____. For example, he or she wrote
_____.")

    i. Are there any kinds of patterns (something that is used more than once)? For example, are all the sentences long or short, or might the beginning sentences be short and the later ones long? Are words or punctuation repeated? ("The author appears to use a pattern of _____. For example, he or she _____. I think the author is using the pattern to _____.")

    j. Are there "loaded words" (words that elicit strong emotion) and, if so, how are they used by the author? ("I think _____ is a "loaded word" because _____. I think the author uses it to _____.")

    Again, don't overload your ELL students with too many questions!

2. If you have had partners read to each other and develop their responses, have each one go to a new partner to share their answers and see if they can develop better ones based on this discussion. Prepare students with question starters and sentence frames like:

    a. "What do you think is the answer to question _____?"

    b. "That could be true, but what could be another answer?"

    c. "What is your evidence?"

    The teacher, as usual, should be circulating during small-group discussions.

3. Students could then return to their original partners, or the teacher could call on students as they sit in their new groupings. Again, all sorts of options exist for novelty within this general pattern of a second reading.

Step Four—Picking It Apart: *Analyze and Compare the Text*

1. Tell students they will *read the text on their own* this time and answer one of these questions:

    a. Is the author pushing a particular position and, if so, what evidence does he or she give to support that position? ("I think the author believes _____. I think the evidence he or she uses to support his/her belief is _____. I think that evidence is valid/invalid because _____.")

    b. Do the pictures or charts contribute anything to the author's message? If so, what and how? ("The picture/chart seems to _____ because _____ " or "The picture doesn't seem to _____ _____ because _____ .")

c. Does this text remind you in some way of another text you have read? How? ("This text reminds me of _____ because that text also _____ .")

d. Is there any information you think the author might have intentionally left out of the text? Why? ("I think the author might have left out _____ because _____ .")

e. What do you think is the central message/idea of the text? ("I think the main message/idea of the text is _____ because _____ .")

We think this last question is a particularly important one. It's important to parse the details of any text, but the key to knowledge is understanding what it means as a whole. Writer Matthew Yglesias communicated this concept succinctly in his description of why Supreme Court Chief Justice John Roberts decided the key second Obamacare ruling—instead of concentrating on the details of a few words, he focused on what he viewed as the overall intent of the law. Yglesias summarized Roberts' justification in this way: "Meaning isn't built from the ground up by assembling individual word-bits. It's constructed holistically."[29]

2. Next, give students either another "text" from the same author, another one in the same genre, or a completely different kind of text providing information on the same topic. The text could be printed words, a closed-captioned video, a comic, an infographic, and so forth.

3. Then, have students repeat versions of Steps 2, 3, and the beginning of Step 4 with this second "text."

4. At that point, students can work alone and/or with partners to begin comparing the two texts, perhaps by using a graphic organizer like a Venn Diagram or the other multiple ones available online by searching "graphic organizers to compare and contrast." In addition to the questions already listed in previous steps, a key question to ask students at this time could be a variation of this one:

a. *Why do you think Text A contained certain information, text structures, or certain vocabulary while Text B did not?*

Converting the graphic organizer into a compare and contrast essay could be the culminating task if students are provided sufficient scaffolding.

Important Note to Teachers: You'll have noticed that our sentence-frames for student responses are not very lengthy. If desired, teachers can easily convert many of these answer frames, especially for Step Four, into culminating activities requiring paragraph-length or longer responses. However, apart from the Compare and Contrast example we discussed, we seldom incorporate lengthy student writing into close reading. Instead, since the close reading is part of a longer thematic unit, we have our ELLs apply what they have learned in responding to close reading to longer writing they do in other parts of that unit.

After Students' Close Reading

A key goal—if not *the* key goal—of close reading, and the reading strategies involved in it, is knowledge transfer. In other words, we want to assist our students to reach the point where they "transfer" use of these skills to other texts independently and where they can also apply them, as we often do, automatically and unconsciously.

In other words, we must add a fourth step to the traditional "I do, we do, you do" teaching formula, and that step is "You do it elsewhere." This can only happen through multiple uses of these strategies in multiple contexts.[30] Though, again, we caution against overuse of close reading.

In addition, we cannot overemphasize the value of metacognition and student reflection in promoting transfer. The more students recognize *for themselves* that they are becoming better readers through the use of these strategies, the more likely they will feel motivated to use them when we teachers aren't around telling them to do so.

Having students regularly reflect and share with their classmates about which questions help them most—and which help the least—to gain an understanding of the text is essential towards building this reading independence. The learning journals discussed in Chapter 2 can be a useful tool to encourage this kind of thinking.

Evaluation

The teacher taking time to reflect on how the lesson went is arguably the most important step in this pattern of instruction and is also the least likely one to happen in the hustle and bustle of a busy school and post-school day.

Taking a minute and asking ourselves simple questions can make a huge difference—not only for future lessons but also for how we feel that day. At lunchtimes and at the ends of many days, we also meet each other to discuss the day and commiserate. In other words, teacher evaluation and reflection does not have to be a solo activity.

To continue Larry's comparison to his organizing career, one of the lessons he learned was that a good evaluation can save a terrible action. The same is true here—a good evaluation where lessons are learned can make all the difference to how we feel when a lesson "goes south"—and it will. Consider questions like: What went well and what could have gone better? What did I do right and what could I have done differently? Were my goals achieved? How did students feel leaving the class?

EXHIBIT 3.3. Question and Answer Starter List

What the text might say:

1. What type of text (a story, a newspaper article, a poem, etc.) is this? How do I know this? ("I think this text is _____ because_____.")

2. Who is the author? What do I know about him/her? How could I find out about the author if I don't know who he/she is? ("The author of the text is _____. I know _____. I don't know about the author, but I could find out more information by _____.")

3. When and where was this published? What might be important about this information? ("This text was published in _____ and _____. This information could be important because _____.")

4. What is the title of this text? What predictions can I make about the text based on the title? ("The title is _____. Based on this title, I predict _____ and _____.")

5. Who is this text written for (who is the audience)? What makes me think this? ("I believe this text is written for _____ because _____.")

6. What might be the purpose of this text? What makes me think this? ("I believe the purpose of this text is _____ because _____.")

*What the text says** :

7. What is the text about? ("I think the text is about _____ because _____." or "I think the text is about _____. The clues are_____ and _____.")

8. What words are new to you?

9. What are words you think you have difficulty pronouncing?

10. Where does it take place? ("I think it takes place in _____ because _____.")

11. When is it happening? ("I think it is happening _____ because _____.")

12. What is the setting of the text (setting means both place and time)? ("I think the text is set in _____ during _____. I think that because the author writes _____.")

13. What is a summary of the text? What is the plot? ("First _____. Second_____. Then _____.")

14. What do you predict is going to happen? ("I predict _____ because_____.")

15. What questions does the text make you wonder about? ("I wonder what/how/when/if/who _____ because_____.")

16. Is there a conflict or problem in the text? ("I think a conflict/problem is _____ because the author writes _____.")

17. What is the theme? ("I think the theme is _____ because _____ _____.")

Figure out how the text works:

18. What is the mood of the text? ("I think the mood is _____ because of _____" or "I think the mood is _____. The clues are _____ and _____." or "The author said _____, so that makes me think that _____.")

19. A question about figurative language could be "What did the author mean by _____ ?" or "Are there any words that you think might mean one thing but the author really meant it to mean something else? ("I think when the author wrote _____ he/she meant that _____ because _____.")

20. Is the author using sensory details (color, smell, physical descriptions, taste, etc.) to tell us something? ("The author says _____. I believe he/she is saying that because he/she wants us to think _____ _____.")

21. Who is telling the story? ("I believe _____ is telling the story because _____." or "According to the text, _____, so _____.")

22. How does this portion relate to what came before and/or to what comes afterwards? ("I think this relates to what came before by _____ because_____.")

23. Who do you think the author is writing this text for — who is his/her audience? ("I think the author's audience is _____ because _____.")

24. What is a context clue to the meaning of _____? "(I think _____ means _____ because the author writes _____.")

25. Is there dialogue (people talking) in the text? If so, why do you think the author uses it? ("I think the author uses dialogue because he/she wants to _____. For example, he/she wrote _____ _____.")

26. Are there any kinds of patterns (something that is used more than once)? For example, are all the sentences long or short, or might the beginning sentences be short and the later ones long? Are words or punctuation repeated? ("The author appears to use a pattern of _____. For example, he/she _____. I think the author is using the pattern to _____.")

27. Are there "loaded words" (words that elicit strong emotion) and, if so, how are they used by the author? ("I think _____ is a "loaded word" because _____. I think the author uses it to _____.")

Analyze and compare the text:

28. Is the author pushing a particular position and, if so, what evidence does he/she give to support that position? ("I think the author believes _____. I think the evidence he/she uses to support his/her belief is _____. I think that evidence is valid/invalid because _____.")

29. Do the pictures or charts contribute anything to the author's message? If so, what and how? ("The picture/chart seems to _____ because _____" or "The picture doesn't seem to _____ because _____.")

30. Does this text remind you in some way of another text you have read? How? ("This text reminds me of _____ because that text also _____.")

31. Is there any information you think the author might have intentionally left out of the text? Why? ("I think the author might have left out _____ because _____.")

32. What do you think is the central message/idea of the text? ("I think the main message/idea of the text is _____ because _____.")

*The titles for the three headings came from Timothy Shanahan (http://www.scholastic.com/teachers/article/common-core-close-reading-0)

Activate and Build Student Prior Knowledge

Research overwhelmingly supports the idea that prior knowledge assists in close reading comprehension.[31] As literacy expert Timothy Shanahan summarizes: "Readers comprehend more when a text overlaps with their knowledge of the world, and they comprehend less when there is less such information in their minds."[32]

In the context of Common Core, however, teachers are challenged to find the "sweet spot" between providing/activating student prior knowledge to help with comprehension and making so much of it that it acts as a de facto replacement for the reading itself.

This is a challenge for all readers, and particularly for ELLs whose cultural context, and therefore life experience, may be substantially different from non-ELLs and texts that are often read in U.S. schools. On top of that problem, of course, comes the basic comprehension issue of lack of knowledge about the language itself.

Teaching can be another name for relationship building, and getting to know our students is a prerequisite to beginning to understand what background they bring to the classroom. With that knowledge, we can know if all that is required might be announcing the topic or title of the text ahead of time[33] or if more explanation is required.

If so, one simple alternative could be the old-standby of a "K-W-L" chart. Each student writes down a few pieces of information they think they know about the topic under "K" (for Know) and a few questions under "W" (for What I want to know). Students can then share in partners and perhaps share with the entire class for the possible creation of a classwide chart. Then students can add to the "L" column (for what I have Learned) as they read the text.

Another alternative is providing different and simplified texts/videos (or texts/videos in students' home language—you can find useful resources for them at the Best Multilingual and Bilingual Sites for Math, Social Studies, and Science[34]) giving background knowledge that can help ELLs understand a more complex reading, a strategy recommended by Stanford researchers working with states on Common Core implementation.[35]

In other words, simplifying a *preparatory text* to provide needed background knowledge is okay, but simplifying the *complex text* that is to be used in a close reading activity is not. The reason behind this guidance is that the same researchers suggest that simplifying complex texts—in other words, shortening sentences and changing vocabulary—does not promote better comprehension and may even have negative consequences for long-term language gain.[36] Other research has reached more positive conclusions, and particularly cites the increased sense of self-confidence that ELLs may gain providing a pay-off in an increased desire to read.[37]

Prior to the advent of Common Core, we found that simplified texts were a boon to our students, particularly our newer ELLs, and used them as a temporary "bridge" until their English level reached a higher level. Now, however, we generally use these simplified texts in preparation for more complex ones.

And it is easier than ever to find or create these kinds of accessible texts. There are now multiple free online resources that provide different leveled versions of the same text, including any teacher-chosen text that can be copied and pasted onto a form.

Tech Tools
Online Tools for Simplifying Texts

You can find a continually updated list of links to sites that will provide different "leveled" versions of the same text, different leveled texts for the same topic, or sites that will automatically edit your own text to a specific level, at the Best Places to Get the Same Text Written for Different Levels: http://larryferlazzo.edublogs.org/2014/11/16/the-best-places-to-get-the-same-text-written-for-different-levels/

Use of Graphic Organizers to Support Comprehension

Our last book contains examples of graphic organizers,[38] which help ELLs organize information and ideas after reading and in preparation for writing and speaking practice. In order to support our students as they tackle the types of complex texts required in Common Core, we have found it helpful to use graphic organizers to support the close reading process described above and/or any other learning activity.

Research shows that certain types of graphic organizers can improve reading comprehension and improve vocabulary knowledge.[39]

Because of the focus in Common Core on analyzing a text's structure and discourse patterns, using graphic organizers that represent these structures (such as compare-contrast, cause-effect, problem-solution, argument-reasoning) can help students to visually process how information in the text is organized and its interrelationships. Using graphic organizers can also increase engagement and active learning.

When creating and using graphic organizers to support reading comprehension, it is important for teachers to keep the research findings of Xiangying Jiang and William Grabe in mind:

- Using a graphic organizer that *reflects the text's structure* is likely to be more effective than using one that does not (for example, when reading an argumentative text, using an organizer to capture an author's claims and supporting evidence is more helpful than using a generic organizer that lists main ideas and supporting details)

- Students need to *actively* work to complete graphic organizers in order for them to be effective. Simply copying from a teacher model will not help students deepen their thinking and learning

- Graphic organizers created *by students themselves* can be more effective than those created by teachers.[40]

In the lesson plans found later in this chapter, we will describe how we use graphic organizers to support reading comprehension and to help students write effective summaries.

Tech Tools

Graphic Organizers

Links to many free online graphic organizers can be found at Not "The Best," but "A List" of Mindmapping, Flow Chart Tools, and Graphic Organizers (http://larryferlazzo.edublogs.org/2009/02/09/not-the-best-but-a-list-of-mindmapping-flow-chart-tools-graphic-organizers/). There is a section on that list specifically devoted to Common Core resources.

Read Alouds/Think Alouds

As we mentioned earlier, the Common Core cautions against using Read Alouds with secondary students as a substitute for students independent reading of text.[41] We aren't suggesting that Read Alouds replace the reading students do on their own. Instead, we use them often with our ELLs to support their literacy development and to spark their interest in reading. Our experience is supported by research that shows that the use of Read Alouds promotes critical thinking and language development while also encouraging metacognition.[42] Recent research on the brain also points to the benefits of reading text aloud. There is growing evidence to suggest that when we read text silently or aloud, our brains appear to process the words not according to what they mean, but instead based on how the words look and how they sound.[43]

When reading aloud to students, we select a short piece of text related to the unit of study and focus on modeling fluent reading with prosody (intonation, rhythm, and expression) while students follow along silently on their own copy of the text.

During a Read Aloud, we don't make a lot of comments or give lengthy explanations of word meanings. Instead, we might supply an easier synonym for a challenging word and then move on. We have found, especially with ELLs at less advanced proficiency levels, reading a text aloud is the best first step—whether we're using that text for close reading or any other reading activity. Read Alouds can be followed by any number of writing or speaking prompts that ask students to go back to the text and give evidence to support their inferences, a key skill highlighted throughout Common Core.

Students can also choose their own texts, create questions, and do a Read Aloud with a partner or in a small group. This kind of activity can increase engagement, critical thinking, and prosody.

In addition to conducting Read Alouds, we often turn them into "Think Alouds," also known as Interactive Read Alouds. During Think Alouds, the teacher models fluent oral reading, but also pauses at certain points in the text to share his or her thinking. This enables students to see how the teacher is employing various reading strategies to make sense of text. When doing a Think Aloud with our students we often model asking questions, using our background knowledge to make connections to the text, summarizing, visualizing, making inferences and looking for evidence in the text to support those inferences. In addition, we use other reading strategies, including using context clues to figure out the meaning of a word. Sharing our thinking processes with students helps them to become more aware of their own metacognition. It also helps them learn how to monitor their own comprehension and build a bigger "toolbox" of strategies they can use to understand texts, especially the types of complex texts called for in Common Core. As our colleague Kelly Young from Pebble Creek Labs likes to say, "Think Alouds make the unseen seen, the unconscious conscious."[44]

Think Alouds can also be followed by various speaking and writing prompts. One strategy we find particularly useful in helping ELLs formulate higher-level responses to a text is using the A-B-C format—or Answer, Back it Up, Comment/Connect—which was introduced to us by Kelly Young. Students are given a text-dependent question that they must answer, back up with evidence from the text, and then make a comment or connection about the evidence. Another format we teach students is P-Q-C—or make a Point; Quote from the text to support your point; make a Comment or Connection to your personal experience, another text, or some other knowledge. We will be discussing these strategies further in Chapter 4.

Students can also practice creating their own Think Alouds by writing their thoughts in the margins of a text and then conducting a Think Aloud with a partner (where they read the text aloud and pause to share these thoughts with their partner).

A key to making a Read Aloud or Think Aloud an effective strategy is teacher planning. The teacher should decide ahead of time where to break from the text during a Think Aloud and identify which reading strategies he or she wants to demonstrate.

Use of Visuals

Countless studies,[45] and the experience of millions of children and adult students, have found the use of visuals of incalculable value in learning a new language. In our last book, we discussed numerous ways to use them, and do so in other parts of this book as well. You can find even more ways by accessing the links in the next Tech Tools box.

Here, we are going to describe the use of visuals in two ways. First, using them in the Picture Word Inductive Model (PWIM) with Beginning ELLs as an entryway into the Common Core Standards and, second, using them as a "text" in close reading.

First, let's review the Picture Word Inductive Model (PWIM), which we explained in our last book in detail.[46] In this model, the teacher displays an enlarged image showing various objects and people in the classroom, surrounded by white space. Students and teacher together label objects in the picture. Working in language notebooks or on a poster board, students create categories (such as *furniture*) and sort words from the picture (and other words, which they add) into these categories. Eventually students use the words in fill-in-the-blank sentences, categorize and combine these sentences into paragraphs, and may ultimately work them into a longer piece of writing. This strategy begins to prepare students for the role of "detective" that is played by readers in the context of Common Core—looking for patterns, analyzing word meanings, and making inferences

Next, let's focus on using visuals, primarily photos, paintings, and video, in the context of close reading as defined by the Common Core. Interpreting and evaluating visual media is specifically called for in the Standards, and close reading—and the strategies that enable it—can be applied to visuals as well as to the printed word.

In fact, most, if not all, of the same steps described in the Patterns of Instruction section, including the listed questions, can be easily used with images—still and moving.

However, as we have repeatedly said, simply repeating the same process might increase the chances of close reading turning into a tedious process, so we have sometimes used alternative processes to close read a visual image.

We've found two tools that help ELLs examine visual images: Exhibit 3.4 is a widely used Photo Analysis Worksheet created by the Education Staff at the National Archives in Washington, DC, and Access Lenses (Figure 3.1) is a graphic created by educator Trevor Bryan and a group of educators called the 4 O'Clock Faculty.

EXHIBIT 3.4. Photo Analysis Worksheet

STEP 1. OBSERVATION

A. Study the photograph for 2 minutes. Form an overall impression of the photograph and then examine individual items. Next, divide the photo into quadrants and study each section to see what new details become visible.

_____

B. Use the chart below to list people, objects, and activities in the photograph.

People	Objects	Activities

STEP 2. INFERENCE

Based on what you have observed above, list three things you might infer from this photograph.

_____

_____

_____

STEP 3. QUESTIONS

A. What questions does this photograph raise in your mind?

_____

_____

B. Where could you find answers to them?

_____

_____

Created by The National Archives Education Staff, http://www.archives.gov/education/ Retrieved from http://www
.archives.gov/education/lessons/worksheets/photo.html

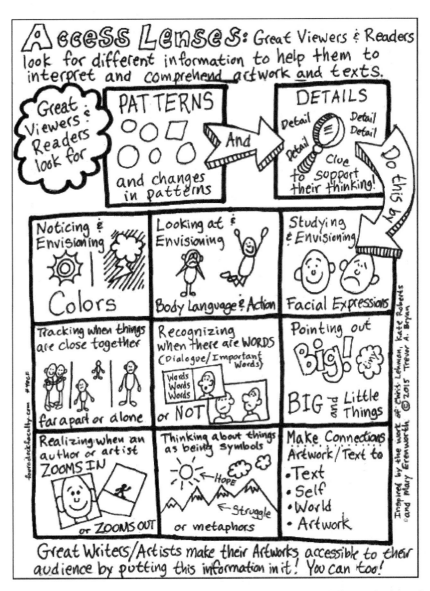

Figure 3.1 Access Lenses *Source:* Created by Trevor Bryan, http://fouroclockfaculty.com/2015/
05/visuals-access-lenses/, used with permission. Inspired by "Falling in Love with Close Reading,"
by Christopher Lehman and Kathleen Roberts. Retrieved from http://www.heinemann.com/products/
E05084.aspx

Here are other ways we have had students close read an image or images:

- After covering up a caption to a photo, we've sometimes used the three questions used by the Visual Thinking Strategies organization as a first step in a close reading/viewing process[47]:

  - *What's going on in this picture?*

  - *What do you see that makes you say that?*

  - *What more can you find?*

- We've borrowed a lesson idea in which a photo of a corner of a painting or photo is shown and students are asked to close read the photo for what it might reveal about the full image. Then, students can revise their analyses after viewing the complete image.[48]

- One of the questions we often ask students reading a text is:

  - *Is there any information you think the author might have intentionally left out of the text? Why?*

    We have found that this question can be modified for images in the following way:

  - *What is left outside the frame, and what makes you think that?*

Two excellent visuals we use to illustrate this question are a short video that shows an event that could be either a robbery or accident depending upon your perspective[49] and images from a video game with the theme "How you frame the story will change the story."[50]

Further resources to illustrate this point can be found at "How Framing Affects Our Understanding" by Frank Baker.[51]

Educator Frank Baker has done considerable work and writing about close reading of visuals (you can find links to his articles and website at the "Best" list link in the Tech Tools box). When presenting visuals to students, we've sometimes incorporated his list of the tools and techniques used "to imply or create meaning":

- Cameras (cinematography)

- Lighting

- Audio/sound (includes music)

- Set design

- Postproduction (editing, special effects)

- Actors (wardrobe; makeup; body language; expressions).[52]

Tech Tools

Resources for Close Reading Visual Images

There are plenty of free online resources available with ideas for close reading visual images. We've collected the best ones, and continue to add to them, at the Best Resources on Close Reading Paintings, Photos, and Videos (http://larryferlazzo .edublogs.org/2015/08/05/the-best-resources-on-close-reading-paintings-photos-videos/).

Teaching Reading Strategies

"Close Reading," a hallmark of Common Core, is not a strategy—it is a series of specific purposes, a combination of strategies designed to achieve them, and a student state of mind that cares enough about the first to want to apply the second in its pursuit. We can use our professional judgment to match—as best we can—the expectations from the Standards with the needs and abilities of our students to identify appropriate reading purposes. We can equip our students with reading strategies—practical tools they can use when we're around and when we're not—to achieve those goals. And we can help create a climate that helps students develop a motivated state of mind through the many lessons shared in the previous chapter.

As we teach these reading strategies, we need to remember these words from educator and author Jennifer Serravallo:

> . . . just as we offer strategies to students as ways for them to become independent while practicing a skill, we want them to eventually out-grow those strategies, too. Once the reader becomes skilled, the process, the strategy, becomes automatic and something to which the reader no longer needs to give conscious attention. Once the need for conscious use of a strategy fades away it will likely only resurface during times of real difficulty. . . . The strategy is a temporary scaffold, and like any scaffolding, there needs to be a plan for how it's removed.[53]

In other words, reading strategies have a life beyond close reading. Using them can enhance comprehension of any text—within or outside a close reading context. And, as we mentioned earlier in this chapter, using them in multiple contexts, including ones where students need to decide which strategy is most helpful to them, is necessary in order for them to develop automaticity and the ability to transfer their skills independently.

The National Reading Panel Report of 2000[54] identified several reading strategies as the most effective to assist comprehension. We've already discussed graphic organizers, as well as the importance of promoting metacognition so students can monitor their understanding and know which strategies will help them the most and when to apply them.

We will be reviewing some of their other recommendations, including summarizing, asking questions, and collaboration, in addition to one especially emphasized in the Common Core Standards: pattern seeking.

SUMMARIZATION

The Common Core standards for Language Arts, along with the Literacy standards for History/Social Studies and Science and Technical Subjects, call for students to summarize text objectively and accurately. And, as most of us can attest, the skill of summarizing—whether it be a news article, a conversation, a movie—is a critical component of daily communication and learning.

In the classroom, teaching our students summarizing strategies can help increase their understanding of academic content[55] and is one of the key strategies recommended by the National Reading Panel for assisting reading comprehension.[56] As education researcher Robert Marzano states, "Although the process of comprehension is complex, at its core, comprehension is based on summarizing—restating content in a succinct manner that highlights the most crucial information."[57]

The first step we use in helping our ELL students build their summarizing skills is to make connections to how they employ summarization on a daily basis—when they tell a friend about a movie they saw or when they give a friend the "highlights" of a long conversation they had with another friend. We ask students to think about the importance of "accuracy" when summarizing by asking them how they feel when their words haven't been accurately "summarized" by someone else. We can build on this type of prior knowledge and experience as we help students to apply summarizing skills to text.

As we discussed earlier in this chapter, graphic organizers assist students' comprehension of text by helping them visually process how ideas in the text are organized and relate to each other. We have found that having ELL students create visual summaries of complex texts increases their understanding and teaches them summarizing tools they can employ with different types of texts in other classes.

When doing a visual summary activity, the teacher can divide a complex text into numbered sections or chunks and then create a simple chart that contains the same number of boxes (i.e., if the text is broken up into six sections, then the chart would have six blank boxes numbered 1–6). After reading each section of text, students then draw an image (with pictures and symbols) to represent the key ideas in that section.

They can also include key words, phrases, or a one-sentence summary of the ideas in that section. The teacher should model this the first time students do it and as needed throughout the process. We've found this activity helps students to monitor their own comprehension as they work with a text and gives the teacher a way to quickly assess student comprehension. Students can later refer to their Visual Summary Charts when comparing different texts and in preparation for writing about the text (whether it be a summary or a longer essay). It is important to consider students' English proficiency levels when choosing and chunking a text. For students at less advanced levels, the overall text and the size of the chunks should be shorter than it would for students at higher English levels. See the Sample Visual Summary Chart (Figure 3.2) used in the Investigating a Text Lesson Plan at the end of this chapter.

Another strategy we use with our ELLs to practice summarization is called 3-2-1. We were introduced to this strategy by Ekuwah Moses in her online piece "3-2-1 and The Common Core Writing Book."[58] It involves reading a text and then identifying three important words, two phrases, and one full quote that summarizes the text. This can be modified in various ways, such as having students choose three important words, give evidence as to why they are important to the text as a whole, and/or do an illustration.

Teacher modeling can also be an effective way to help students employ summarizing skills while reading complex texts. As we discussed, teachers can make their own thinking visible to students by conducting a Think Aloud. We've found it helpful to do Think Alouds where we model our thinking as we work to generate summary statements for sections of a text. As we read a section of text aloud we might demonstrate looking for words/ideas that are repeated, prioritizing which details are most important and why, or identifying language structures that signify a writer's claim. We then give students lots of opportunities to practice summarizing on their own and to compare their summaries with classmates in order to improve accuracy.

ASKING QUESTIONS

Asking questions is a huge part of teaching and learning. There are two ways to look at it: student-generated questions and teacher-generated questions. The National Reading Panel Report cites both as ways to improve reading comprehension.[59]

As we discuss in Chapter 2, teaching ELL students about different levels of questions and how to develop their own (starting with the difference between literal and interpretive questions and then moving on to the different levels in Bloom's or Revised Bloom's) is key in building critical thinking skills. We've found, and researchers have reached similar conclusions, that teaching our students questioning strategies enhances personal involvement in the reading process and

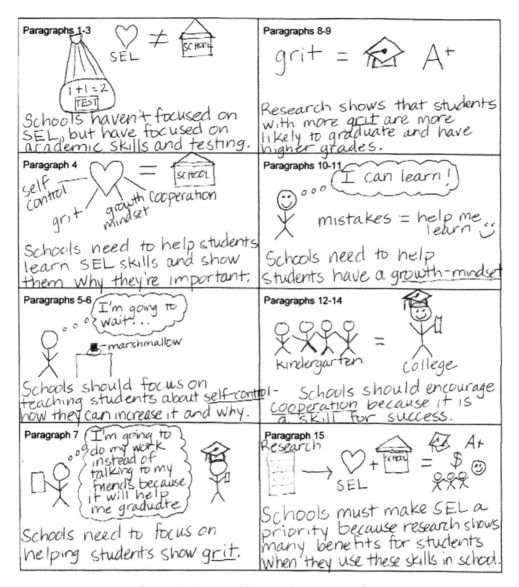

Figure 3.2 Sample Visual Summary Chart

increases motivation.[60] In addition, it results in "heightened self-awareness of their comprehension."[61] In other words, asking their own questions will likely increase students' use of self-monitoring and other metacognitive strategies.

As students read a text, we encourage them to continue the detective work we discussed earlier as they preview a text, by focusing more on the details of the crime scene—looking for clues to help them figure out what happened and what it all means. They will need to ask higher-level questions as they make theses inferences about the text and analyze its meaning and purpose. Teachers can help students in this process by giving students these types of higher-order questions to answer and by providing question stems that students can use to write their own questions, like the ones we listed earlier in the Pattern of Close Reading Instruction section. There are also many examples of question stems for the different levels of Bloom's available online. Of course, the ultimate goal is for students to develop automaticity in asking these higher levels of questions as they read increasingly complex texts on their own. And this goal can only be accomplished through regular practice.

For teachers, it is important to be strategic with the questions *we* are posing *to* students, especially ELLs. We don't want to make the mistake of assuming that a student at a lower level of English proficiency won't be able to comprehend or respond to higher order thinking questions. With appropriate scaffolds, even very early beginners can answer more challenging questions. Teachers can provide flexibility and support for students in the way they answer these questions – such as allowing students to answer in their home language or to communicate their answers using pictures or manipulatives. Aligning the questions we pose to our students' level of language acquisition *and* to the higher levels of thinking required by Common Core, "will allow ELLs to more fully engage in learning both language and content."[62]

Lastly, we'd like to bring attention to one particular questioning strategy where students ask questions about what comes next in a text—in other words, predicting. Making predictions can increase student curiosity and motivation for reading and can "prime the pump" for learning by activating prior knowledge. The act of making predictions before and while reading has been found not only to increase motivation, but also results in deeper levels of thinking as students are prompted by their predictions to "actively grapple with new concepts instead of passively receiving them."[63]

We teach our students that predicting can be a useful strategy when reading fiction and some nonfiction, and we model predicting strategies students can use for both.

COLLABORATION

The National Reading Panel identified students working together to learn reading strategies as one of the most effective ways for students to improve reading comprehension.[64] The Common Core Standards primarily highlight student collaboration in its speaking and listening, and in its writing, strands. However, since students are often writing about their reading, we feel safe in saying that, in addition to being a research-proven aid to comprehension, collaboration in reading is also a Common Core-supported learning activity. We included it several times in our "Pattern of Instruction" section, as we do in our classroom practice.

We think it's important to note that the Common Core Standards talk often about students working collaboratively. The Standards never mention working cooperatively. Though nothing in the Standards, or by the authors of the Standards, clarifies whether this distinction was made purposely,[65] we tend to believe it was a strategic decision. However, even if it was not, we believe that it is a strategically important pedagogical difference to make in the classroom in the best interest of our students.

While collaborative learning and cooperative learning are considered the same by a great many educators, they are, in fact, two different things.

The problem, however, is that if you type in the query "What is the difference between collaborative and cooperative learning?" into an online search box, you'll get many different responses, including quite a few that are contradictory.

We would suggest that collaboration—in the context of reading comprehension—means student discussions designed to help individuals improve their own intellectual and physical work.[66] In other words, it might mean students reading/analyzing a passage on their own in response to a prompt, discussing what they wrote in a group, and then revising their final product.[67] Or it could mean using the same process in a "think-pair-share" process not requiring writing or, as we discussed earlier, the same process could be used to develop a K-W-L chart to access and provide student background knowledge.

It would *not* mean posing a question to students and then having them meet to discuss what the answer should be without having them do some prior work—thinking, writing, and/or reading—on their own in order to be prepared to share and revise. And it would *not* mean assigning a project to a group of students that could easily be divided into separate tasks they would work on by themselves and then hastily put together—which is what projects in our own classrooms have looked like all-too-often in the name of *cooperative* learning.

As Connecticut teacher David Olio explains, in collaboration:

> Individual students need to feel empowered to examine an idea by testing it by other students, strengthening it, then leaving with a stronger idea.[68]

This is not to say that it's impossible for students to do common projects together while working *collaboratively*. We think it certainly is possible, and discuss them further in the writing and speaking/listening chapters.

As a preview to that discussion, we'd like to share the thoughts of another educator, project-based learning expert Suzie Boss:

> I encourage teachers to err on side of true collaboration. That's when a group or team, working together, produces something that exceeds what any 1 individual member of the team could accomplish solo

(because of complexity, time, multiple perspectives, innovation, etc.). Cooperation, on the other hand, could simply mean "getting along" or sharing resources or splitting up the work and never engaging with team members; [it] doesn't require [the] same mind-meld.[69]

It's also important to keep in mind that working with others has been shown to increase engagement, motivation and persistence[70] and no classroom can have too much of those qualities present.

We'll end this section with some lessons that Larry learned during his community organizing career. One of the key methodologies of organizing is first listening to people's stories. Then, you bring people together to share them with one another. Finally, real power is built by working together to develop a new interpretation of them.

For example, at our school, one year we made an important discovery after making many home visits to immigrant parents. We found that many were impressed with our use of technology in helping their children to learn English, and they all lamented the fact that they couldn't afford to have computers at their home so that their entire family could use them to improve their English. Then, at our invitation, the parents met together and shared their thoughts with each other and with our school's leadership. Everyone then made a decision to work together to create a program that provided free home computers and Internet access to immigrant families, which was ultimately recognized by the International Reading Association as one of the best programs in the world using technology to improve literacy.[71]

On a different level, collaboration in our classrooms can function in a similar way to promote literacy and other intellectual skills of our students. Too often, as educators, we don't include collaboration on our list of reading strategies to explicitly teach our students. Yet, its importance cannot be minimized and needs to be part and parcel of our literacy instruction.

SEEKING PATTERNS

The Common Core Standards talk about the importance of recognizing patterns in order to develop literacy—word patterns, patterns of syllables, patterns of events.

As we discuss in Chapter 2, research provides substantial backing for the value of pattern-seeking in learning just about anything, including literacy and a second-language. Earlier in this chapter, we described how we use the Picture Word Inductive Model with early Beginners to build English literacy skills through the use of pattern-seeking, which can also be also called inductive learning. The *inductive* process means students seek patterns and use them to identify their broader meanings and significance, while in the deductive process the teacher provides the meaning or "rules" and students then have to apply them.

We think "text data sets," which we discussed at length in our last book,[72] are excellent tools for helping students develop their "pattern-recognizing" abilities. Text data sets, like the one on mistakes in Chapter 2, the one in the upcoming Fables Lesson Plan, and others later in this book, are collections of numbered short texts ranging from one sentence to a paragraph (sometimes from the same longer text, other times from multiple texts on the same topic) that students read and, occasionally, close-read, and identify potential categories as a next step.

Once students place the text examples in categories (sometimes the categories are teacher-selected, other times they are developed by students), and support their placement with evidence (such as highlighted "clue" words or a justifying sentence), the teacher has various options for next steps—including having students research and add new examples to their categories and/or writing about them.

We have found that using this kind of inductive learning prepares students well to look for patterns on their own as they read other texts, along with providing them another useful way to think about organizing their research and reflections—into categories—when writing essays.

We'll close with Donalyn Miller's advice to students about seeking patterns that she shared in her Forward to the book, "Falling in Love with Close Reading":

> Look across all of the details you have collected and find patterns. As Dorothy Barnhouse and Vicki Vinton discuss in What Readers Really Do (2012), details alone do not mean much until you begin to see relationships across them...[Then] use the patterns to develop a new understanding of the text: Consider these patterns in light of what you have already learned from the text. Put these together to develop a new understanding of the text or a deeper, evidence-based interpretation.[73]

Lesson Plans

The following three lesson plans demonstrate how to scaffold close reading for Beginning, Intermediate, and Advanced ELLs.

"MINI" CLOSE READING LESSON FOR BEGINNERS USING SONG LYRICS

This simple mini-lesson, co-created by our colleague Alma Avalos, offers a template that can be used for just about any song. It utilizes close reading, student choice and, certainly, high student interest. The first part of the lesson could be done in one 55-minute class period and could even be stopped there, though the second half, where students apply close-reading to a song of their choice, is what we consider to be the lesson's key highlight. Our last book shares many other ways to use music in language-building lessons.

FABLES LESSON PLAN FOR HIGH BEGINNERS/INTERMEDIATE

The Fables Lesson Plan, focusing on Aesop's Fables, is designed for High Beginners and Intermediates, and we use it as part of a broader unit on the genre of "Stories." It includes most aspects of close reading, as well as multiple possible extension activities. It was co-authored by Laura Gibbs, a professor of folklore at the University of Oklahoma and inspired by a blog post written by Grant Wiggins.[74] Though it is designed as a four-to-five day lesson, there are many opportunities to shorten or lengthen it. Depending upon the grade level of your class, Aesop's Fables might or might not officially fit the definition of a "complex text" for your students. However, keep in mind Common Core's vision of text complexity as a "staircase" and our discussion of that concept earlier in this chapter. The fables, in this lesson plan, provide accessible texts that can be used for teaching and learning sophisticated reading comprehension strategies that can enable students to take the next "step" upward.

INVESTIGATING A TEXT LESSON PLAN FOR HIGH INTERMEDIATE/ADVANCED—PART ONE

The Investigating a Text Lesson Plan is designed for High Intermediate/Advanced ELL students and is the first of a two-part lesson sequence. The first part featured in this lesson focuses on close reading. The second part is the Argument Writing Lesson Plan, which can be found at the end of Chapter 4. Part Two shows how teachers and students can build on the knowledge and skills gained during this chapter's Part One close reading lesson and apply it to argument writing.

We have used both lessons as culminating activities after teaching the Social and Emotional Learning (SEL) lessons on growth mindset, self-control, and grit in Chapter 2. Because students will have worked with shorter texts in the lesson plans in Chapter 2, we purposely chose a longer text for this close reading lesson. However, you will see that we have "engineered" the text to make it more accessible by adding subheadings. Teachers could shorten this text if desired or use the lesson sequence with any text of the teacher's choosing—SEL related or not. Again, we want to emphasize the idea that students need to be progressively reading more challenging texts and that teachers of ELLs need to provide the scaffolding to help them do so.

Mini-Lesson: Song Lyrics Close Reading for ELL Beginners

Students are given the lyrics to the song "I Just Called to Say I Love You" by Stevie Wonder. Of course, teachers can pick any song that is accessible to ELLs and provides grammar or vocabulary learning opportunities. The song is played for the first time with students listening while they are reviewing the lyrics. Then the teacher reads the lyrics to the class, while asking them to underline any words that are new to them. The teacher gives students the Song Sheet (Exhibit 3.5), and asks them to complete just the first two questions (word definitions and theme). If the teacher has not already taught what "theme" means, he or she can do so at this time.

1. The teacher gives students time to complete the first two questions. Then students can share with a partner and then a few can share with the entire class.

2. Next, the teacher reads the lyrics and has the entire class repeat them. If a computer connected to an overhead project is available with online access, the teacher can go to a site like Lyrics Training (http://lyricstraining.com/) where a music video of the song is available, along with interactive comprehension questions designed to teach English. To play it as a class-wide game, students first have to put the lyrics someplace where they can't see them. The class could be divided into small groups with mini-whiteboards where they write their answers and hold them up when the teacher asks for answers. Each small group would receive a point for a correct response. Students could then do a class sing-along and the teacher can collect the Song Sheet.

3. The next day, the Song Sheet (Exhibit 3.5) is returned to each student to complete the rest of the questions on their own. Students can verbally share their answers with a partner, make needed changes to their form, and a few students can then share with the entire class.

4. Students can then be told that their assignment is to choose a song they like that is in English and is classroom appropriate, and then complete a copy of the Song Sheet for their song, which they can then share with another student.

5. Students can then turn the information on their Song Sheet into a poster. Depending on the number of students in class, they could present the poster to the entire class and play a classroom-appropriate music video of the song or just play an audio version.

EXHIBIT 3.5. Song Sheet

Name _____

SONG SHEET

1. **List three words from the song that are new to you and what each means. Please do not just copy the definition out of a dictionary—put it in your own words:**

   The word _____ means _____ .

   The word _____ means _____ .

   The word _____ means _____ .

2. **What is the theme of the song?**

   I think the theme of the song is _____ because _____ .

3. **What is the mood of the song?**

   I think the mood of the song is _____ because it
   has lines like _____ and _____ .
   Words like that mean that people feel _____ .

4. **Is the song-writer using any kind of pattern (something that is used more than once)? If so, why do you think the writer is using it?**

   The writer is using a pattern of _____ .
   For example, he/she repeats _____ .
   I think he/she is doing this because _____ .

5. What are your three favorite lines in the song, what do they mean and why do you like them so much?

One of my favorite lines in the song is _____.

It means _____. I like it

because _____.

Another favorite line in the song is_____.

It means _____. I like it

because _____.

My third favorite line in the song is _____.

It means _____. I like it

because _____.

Fables Lesson Plan for High Beginners/Intermediates

Instructional Objectives

Students will:

1. Learn new word meanings and the purpose of dialogue through a close reading.
2. Learn the definition of a "fable."
3. Develop pattern-seeking skills in examining themes from multiple fables.
4. Learn about the concept of inference and how to apply it.
5. Learn how to "mimic write" to improve writing skills.

Duration

Four and a half 55-minute class periods

Common Core English Language Arts Standards

Reading

1. Read closely to determine what the text says explicitly and to make logical inferences from it; cite specific textual evidence when writing or speaking to support conclusions drawn from the text.

2. Determine central ideas or themes of a text and analyze their development; summarize the key supporting details and ideas.

3. Interpret words and phrases as they are used in a text, including determining technical, connotative, and figurative meanings, and analyze how specific word choices shape meaning or tone.

4. Analyze how two or more texts address similar themes or topics in order to build knowledge or to compare the approaches the authors take.

Writing

1. Write narratives to develop real or imagined experiences or events using effective technique, well-chosen details, and well-structured event sequences.

2. Produce clear and coherent writing in which the development, organization, and style are appropriate to task, purpose, and audience.

Speaking and Listening

1. Prepare for and participate effectively in a range of conversations and collaborations with diverse partners, building on others' ideas and expressing their own clearly and persuasively.

2. Present information, findings, and supporting evidence such that listeners can follow the line of reasoning and the organization, development, and style are appropriate to task, purpose, and audience.

3. Adapt speech to a variety of contexts and communicative tasks, demonstrating command of formal English when indicated or appropriate.

Language

1. Demonstrate command of the conventions of standard English grammar and usage when writing or speaking.

2. Demonstrate command of the conventions of standard English capitalization, punctuation, and spelling when writing.

3. Determine or clarify the meaning of unknown and multiple-meaning words and phrases by using context clues, analyzing meaningful word parts, and consulting general and specialized reference materials, as appropriate.

4. Demonstrate understanding of figurative language, word relationships, and nuances in word meanings.

5. Acquire and use accurately a range of general academic and domain-specific words and phrases sufficient for reading, writing, speaking, and listening at the college and career readiness level; demonstrate independence in gathering

vocabulary knowledge when encountering an unknown term important to comprehension or expression.

Materials

- Overhead projector to display close reading texts: "The Peacock and the Crane" (Exhibit 3.6), "The Dog and the Rabbit" (Exhibit 3.7), the Fables Text Data Set (Exhibit 3.8), and the Fables Without Morals Sheet (Exhibit 3.9).
- Computer access and projector to display online images and the exhibits.
- Student copies of "The Peacock and the Crane," the Fables Text Data Set, and Fables Without Morals sheet

Procedure

First Day

1. The teacher explains that students are going to be reading very short stories over the next few days. They are called fables (the teacher writes "fables" on the board). The teacher says he is not going to tell students what a fable is yet, and asks any students who think they know to keep it a secret for now. The first fable, the teacher says, is about two birds—a crane and a peacock. The teacher then shows images on the overhead of each of the birds.

2. The teacher says he is going to pass out copies of a fable titled "The Peacock and the Crane" (Exhibit 3.6). He places a copy on the overhead and says he will read it aloud and wants students to read it silently with him. During this reading, he wants students to just get a basic understanding of the story. He instructs them to underline words that are new to them, but not to look them up while he is reading. Also, he wants students to think about what is happening in the story—first, second, and third.

3. After the teacher finishes reading the text, he tells students he wants them to look at the new words they underlined and put a star next to the two or three they think are the most important to understanding the story. Before they look up those words in the dictionary or in Google Translate, he asks students to first guess their meaning by looking at the words and phrases around them. The teacher writes these sentence frames on the overhead (this is a good opportunity to teach past tense, but the frames can also be modified in any way):

   I didn't know what _____ meant. I guessed it meant _____ because _____. Then I looked it up in Google Translate and learned that it meant _____.

The teacher can model it with a word in the text that students are likely to know already, like "fly":

I didn't know what "fly" meant. I guessed it meant going up in the sky because the story is about birds and that is what they do. Then I looked it up in Google Translate and learned that it meant what I had thought it meant.

He tells students that if they finish early he wants them to start answering the other question: *What happens in the story?* He writes this answer-frame on the overhead:

In the story, "The Peacock and the Crane," first _____. Second, _____. Third, _____.

The teacher gives students 5 minutes to complete two or three of the sentence frames and circulates around the room as students are working.

4. After a few minutes, he assigns each student a partner and tells them they should each read to the other the words they have chosen to learn. Then, the teacher calls on a few students (that he identified while he was walking around) to share what they wrote with the entire class.

    Note: During this part of the lesson and, in fact, during the entire lesson, teachers should be flexible about when students work alone and when they work with partners. Beginners might always work with a higher-level Intermediate, even when the lesson plan calls for students to work on their own.

5. Next, he asks students to return to their seats and complete the second answer frame about what happens in the story.

6. After a few minutes, he assigns a different partner to each student and asks students to share what they wrote with their new partner. He also explains that he wants each student to say "I think . . ." before they read their sentence and wants the other student to say either, "I agree because _____" or I disagree because _____." He tells students they can change what they wrote on their papers if they hear a better idea from their partner.

7. After students have shared, he asks one or two students he has identified while listening to the groups to bring their paper up to show on the overhead and read to the class.

8. The teacher then puts the story "The Dog and the Rabbit" on the overhead and tells students he wants them to look at it while he reads. But before he reads, he points to the word "Fables" on the board. He tells students that the story they have already read is a fable, and the story he is going to read now is not one. He

says that after he is done reading the story, he wants students to complete these sentence frames:

"The Peacock and the Crane" is a fable because _____.

"The Dog and the Rabbit" is not a fable because _____.

The teacher reads the story and gives students 3 minutes to complete the sentences.

9. The teacher assigns either the same or different partner to each student and they share their sentences, while the teacher is circulating around the room.

10. Some students, at least, should write that the first is a fable because it has a lesson at the end (or something similar—the teacher can also explain the word "moral") and that the second is not a fable because it doesn't have a lesson. The teacher asks one of the students who has this idea listed to come up and show and read their sentence.

11. The teacher explains that tomorrow the students are going to read "The Peacock and the Crane" again, along with several others written by a famous man named Aesop long, long ago.

    (If there is some time left prior to the end of this first class period, the teacher can start the second day activities early.)

Second Day

1. The teacher tells students to think for a minute about what they learned yesterday, without saying anything. Then, he asks students to tell a neighbor what they learned.

2. Next, the teacher asks students to take out "The Peacock and the Crane." The teacher also places his copy on the overhead. He tells students he wants them to read it to themselves silently and, as they are reading it, he wants them to notice the quotation marks. The teacher draws quotation marks on the board, along with the term *quotation marks.*

    He writes this question on the whiteboard:

    What are quotation marks? Why are they good to use in a story?

    He then writes this answer frame below the question:

    Quotation marks mean _____. *They are good to use in a story because* _____.

    He gives students 5 minutes to reread the fable and complete the answer frame.

3. Students then share their responses with a partner while the teacher is circulating throughout the room.

4. The teacher calls on one or two students he identified while walking around to bring their papers to the overhead and read them. Most will probably say something like quotation marks mean that someone is talking, and that they are used in a story because it makes it sound more interesting or because it moves the story along. The teacher can add other reasons for why it helps (including "I can see and imagine them talking in my head") and introduces the word "dialogue"—people or other characters talking to each other.

5. Next, the teacher gives students the first page of the Fables Text Data Set (Exhibit 3.8). He says they are going to be reading more fables by Aesop. He explains that on this page, he is going to read each story out loud one at a time. As he reads it, he wants students to read along silently and, as they did for "The Peacock and the Crane," underline words that are new to them. Then, like they did yesterday, they are going to pick two or three that they think are the most important and complete the same answer frames from yesterday. Then, they are going to use the second answer frame from the day before to tell what happens in each of the stories.

6. After the teacher reads each fable aloud, the student collaborative process from the day before is repeated.

7. After the class has reviewed three fables, the teacher then asks the students to pick one example of dialogue—two quotations from characters talking to each other—that they like and highlight it. The students should write why they like it next to the text. The teacher can provide a model (Note that most, though not all, of the fables in the data set have a dialogue):

I liked this dialogue because it showed they were arguing and it made the story more exciting.

8. The final class activity of the day is students lining up in two rows facing each other and doing a "speed-dating" routine of sharing which dialogue they liked and why to the person across from them. Then, when the teacher calls out "Switch" after 1 minute, the students in one row each move down one desk so that students are facing a new partner.

Third Day

1. The teacher puts the second page of the Data Set on the overhead and distributes it to students. The teacher says that students will work in partners on this sheet. They will take turns reading paragraphs to each other. At the end of each story, they can work together to complete the same three tasks from the previous day—listing two or three words that are new to them, saying what

happened in the story, and picking a favorite example of dialogue. The partners don't have to have all the same answers, though, and they should each have their own separate copies of the answers.

2. After 20 minutes, the teacher should have students change partners and each should share their answers. Afterwards, the teacher can call on individuals to share responses to some of the questions for a few of the text examples.

3. Next, the teacher should have students return to their regular seats and then give out the final page in the data set. The teacher explains that students will answer the same questions, and this time they will do it on their own, though, obviously, the teacher is there to help. The teacher circulates throughout the room while students are working on their own. While he is walking around, he has short individual conversations with several students and asks if they would be willing to lead small groups of three or four students and go through each of the three text examples and ask each student to share what they wrote.

4. After 15 or 30 minutes, the teacher divides students into small groups with the assigned leaders to share what everybody wrote. The class can end with the teacher calling on individuals to share with the entire class after the groups have completed their tasks.

Fourth Day

1. The teacher writes three category names on the board:
   - Unity (working together)
   - Hard work
   - Jealousy (the teacher may need to role-play the meaning of this word)

   The teacher explains that students will work on their own to highlight the clue words (evidence) they use to determine the correct category for each text example and then write the category name next to it. The teacher can model one or two examples. The teacher can explain that looking for patterns is a key learning strategy, and that this exercise will help students get better at that skill.

   Answers (Not to be shown to students. If students can reasonably justify a different category, however, then different answers are acceptable):
   - Unity (working together)—1, 5, 9
   - Hard work—3, 4, 6
   - Jealousy—2, 7, 8

2. After 15 minutes, the teacher can assign partners and students can share their categories and evidence (if some students are done early while others are still working, the teacher can ask them to pick one fable they agree or disagree with and explain their reasons). The teacher can then quickly review each one on the overhead.

3. The teacher reminds students that fables have a moral/lesson, which is often stated at the end. He then tells students that they are now going to read some fables that don't have the moral clearly written at the end, and they will have to discover the moral on their own. In other words, they will have to "infer" or make an "inference" to determine the moral. The teacher should write infer and inference on the board, and explain that one is a verb and the other is a noun. The teacher says that we make inferences by using clues based on things you already know. For example, the teacher could say, "If I came in here slumping a bit and sneezing, what would you *infer* about me?" Students might answer that you are sick, and the teacher can follow up by asking them how they know that those are clues to someone being sick. Students may answer that they know from their past experience and from their thinking.

4. The teacher puts one of the fables from Fables Without Morals (Exhibit 3.9) on the overhead and distributes the sheet to the class. He then reads it to students and models an answer to the question, "What is the moral of the story and why?" (Teachers can refer to the answer sheet, Exhibit 3.11, though other morals could also be reasonable answers, too):

    I think the moral of the fable is _____. *I think the clues are* _____ *and* _____.

5. Next, the teacher goes to another one of the fables without morals, reads it, and asks students to complete the answer frame on their own. The teacher asks students to share what they wrote with a neighbor, and invites some to share with the entire class. The teacher can then either move on to the next step in the lesson plan or have students complete the remaining fables on the sheet.

6. The teacher then tells students that they are going to write their own fables, and to include dialogue and a moral. He tells students that they should first decide what moral they want their fable to teach. They could use one of the morals from fables the class has read over the past few days or use another one. The teacher could share a list of additional morals for students who need more support. He tells students that when they read their fables to a classmate, they are not going to tell them what the moral is—their classmate will have to *infer* it based on clues in the fable and their past knowledge.

The teacher could share a simple fable that he wrote as a model on the overhead, covering up the moral with a piece of paper and asking students to share what they think it is and why.

7. Students begin writing their fables. If they cannot complete them by the end of the period, the teacher can assign its completion as homework.

Fifth Day

1. Students share their fable with a partner and the partner guesses the moral of the story. It is possible that the listener may need to ask the writer to read their fable a second time in order to determine the moral or clues to the moral. The teacher could have students share with more than one partner.

2. The lesson can end at this point, or move on to any of the Extension activities.

Assessment

- The teacher can collect and review the completed close reading text, data set, Fables without Morals sheet, and student-written fable, as well as circulate throughout the room to assess how well students are participating in the different group learning activities and using the answer frames.

- If the teacher feels a more involved assessment is necessary, you can develop a simple rubric appropriate for your class situation. Free online resources to both find premade rubrics and create your own can be found at the Best Rubric Sites and a Beginning Discussion about Their Use (http://larryferlazzo.edublogs.org/2010/09/18/the-best-rubric-sites-and-a-beginning-discussion-about-their-use/).

Possible Extensions and Modifications

- Students can make posters to illustrate their fables, and record themselves reading them with prosody using the tools listed in the first Tech Tools box in Chapter 2.

- Videos of Aesop's Fables (see the Tech Tools box) could be shown, either stopping prior to the morals being given and having students say what they think they are, or just showing a few for fun.

- The videos could be shown as models for students to create their own short videos illustrating their original fables (even if they are not recorded, students could perform them for the class).

Tech Tools

Aesop's Fables Videos

There are many freely available audio and video versions of Aesop's Fables, along with accompanying lesson ideas, that could be shown to students. You can find links to many of them at the Best Sites for Using Aesop's Fables in the Classroom (http://larryferlazzo.edublogs.org/2011/05/09/the-best-sites-for-using-aesops-fables-in-the-classroom/). In addition, you'll find a link titled "Supplemental resources for Aesop's Fables Lesson Plan." That link has images and background (collected by Laura Gibbs) related to all of the Aesop's Fables used in this lesson.

EXHIBIT 3.6. The Peacock and the Crane

A peacock, proud of his beautiful blue and green feathers, was making fun of the crane, whose feathers were gray.

"Look!" said the peacock. "My feathers are as beautiful as a rainbow, while your feathers are gray as the dust."

The crane then spread his wings and flew high in the air. As he looked down at the peacock, he called out to him. "Follow me up here if you can!"

The peacock could barely fly, so he was not able to rise up high in the sky like the crane.

"Let that be a lesson to you," shouted the crane. "Beauty is not everything!"

The moral of the story is that it's not good to brag.

EXHIBIT 3.7. The Dog and the Rabbit

The dog and the rabbit were home one day.
The dog told the rabbit, "I am hungry."
The rabbit told the dog, "I am hungry, too."
They were both hungry.

EXHIBIT 3.8. Fables Text Data Set

1. *The Farmer and His Sons*

A certain farmer saw that his sons were always arguing with each other, so he decided to teach them a lesson. He told them to each bring him a stick, and then he tied those sticks into a bundle.

"Sons," he said, "I want you to try to break this bundle of sticks."

Each of the sons tried to break the bundle, but it was impossible: even the strongest son could not break the bundle of sticks. Then the father untied the bundle and gave the sticks to his sons to break one by one, which they did easily.

"Let that be a lesson to you," he said. "If you stick together, you will be safe, but if you are divided, then anyone can break you. You are stronger together!"

There is strength in unity.

2. *Juno and the Peacock*

The peacock was proud of his beautiful feathers, but he was did not like the sound of his voice. He decided to pray to the goddess Juno for help. "Please give me a beautiful voice," he said. "I would like to have a beautiful voice like the nightingale has."

Juno smiled and replied, "Peacock, you are my favorite bird, but you cannot have everything. You have beautiful feathers, and the nightingale has a beautiful voice. All the creatures have their own gifts, each different from the other. Be happy with the special gift you have been given."

Be happy with the special gift you have been given.

3. *Hercules and the Farmer*

A farmer was driving his wagon along a country road, but the wheels of the wagon got stuck in the mud. The horses did their best, but they were not strong enough to free the wagon. The farmer then called on Hercules and all the other gods to get the wagon out of the mud.

Lo and behold, Hercules did appear, and he shouted loudly at the farmer, "Put your shoulder to the wheel, man, and urge on your horses! Do you think you can move the wagon by simply looking at it? Don't ask the gods to do your work for you. You need to make some effort yourself if you want the gods to help you."

Helping yourself is the best help.

4. The Tortoise and the Rabbit

The rabbit was making fun of the tortoise for being so slow. "I have never seen anybody as slow as you!" he said.

"Let's have a race to see just who is slow and who is fast," the tortoise replied. The rabbit laughed and agreed to a race, and all the animals came to watch.

At the start of the race, the rabbit ran quickly ahead, leaving the tortoise far behind. When the rabbit looked around, he could not even see the tortoise. "That tortoise can never catch me," he said. "I think I'll even take a little nap here, and then I will finish the race."

So the rabbit went to sleep by the side of the road, and the tortoise walked by slowly, not saying a word. The tortoise then kept on walking and walking until he reached the finish line. All the animals cheered for the tortoise, and the sound woke the rabbit. He looked up and saw that the tortoise had won the race.

"I may be slow," said the tortoise, "but I am steady."

Slow and steady wins the race."

5. The Stomach and the Body

Every day, the hands picked up food and gave the food to the mouth. The teeth chewed the food in the mouth, and the throat took the food to the stomach, and the stomach was very happy.

One day, though, the hands said, "We are tired of giving all the food to the stomach." The teeth said, "We are tired of having to chew all the food and then give it to the stomach." And then all the parts of the body started to complain: the feet and the legs and the eyes and the ears—all the parts of the body were angry at the stomach for eating all the food. So they decided to go on strike: the hands would not bring the food to the mouth, and the teeth would not chew, and the legs would not walk, and even the eyes and the ears refused to see and hear.

But after a day had gone by, all the parts of the body started to feel very weak, and the body could not move at all. Then the stomach explained, "Now you see that my job is important too! You give the food to me, and I give you the energy you need to do your jobs. We have to all work together for the body to be healthy!"

Everybody has a job to do.

6. The Thirsty Crow

It was a very hot day, and the crow was very thirsty. As she looked for water, she found a clay pitcher that had some water in it, but the pitcher was tall and narrow, and her beak could not reach down to where the water was. The crow sat there and thought about what to do, and then she had an idea. She picked up a small stone in her beak and dropped it into the pitcher. Then she picked up another stone and dropped it into the pitcher. It was not easy, but she kept on going, picking up and dropping another stone into the pitcher, and another . . . and another . . . until at last she had raised the level of the water in the pitcher. The crow flapped her wings happily, and then she took a good, long drink.

Hard work pays off.

7. The Dog and His Reflection

A dog had managed to steal a bone from the butcher and was proudly carrying his prize back home. On his way home, he had to cross over a stream, and as he crossed over the stream, he looked down and saw his reflection in the water, but he thought it was another dog.

"Hey," he thought to himself, "that dog has a bone, too!" He stopped and looked more closely. "And that dog's bone is bigger than my bone!" The greedy dog wanted to have the bigger bone, so he dropped his bone and jumped at the dog that he saw in the water. As a result, he almost drowned, and he lost his bone, too.

Be content with what you have instead of wanting what someone else has.

8. The Frog and the Bull

A little frog said to his father, "I have just seen the biggest monster in the world, with horns on his head that reach up into the sky!"

The father frog laughed and said, "That is just the farmer's bull. He really isn't all that big. Why, I am practically as big as he is!"

The little frog said, "I don't think so, Father! He was very, very big."

This made the frog feel jealous of the bull. He wanted to prove to his son that he was as big as the bull, so he puffed himself out and asked, "Am I as big as the bull now?"

The little frog said, "No, Father, the bull is bigger."

The father frog then puffed himself up bigger, and bigger, feeling more and more jealous, until finally he puffed himself up so big . . . that he burst into pieces.

Don't puff yourself up trying to imitate someone else.

9. The Ant and the Dove

A dove saw an ant fall into a stream. The ant struggled in vain to reach get out of the water, but she could not reach the land. The dove felt sorry for the ant, so she dropped a blade of grass into the water, making a bridge for the ant to walk on. Thanks to the dove, the ant was able to get out of the water.

The next day, the ant saw a hunter in the woods. He was hunting for doves! Just at the moment that the man was about to reach out his net to catch the dove, the ant bit the man on the ankle. "Ouch!" yelled the man. When the dove heard the man, she flew away to safety. Thanks to the ant, the dove was able to escape from the hunter.

When I help you and you help me, the story will end happily!

Source: Fables adapted from *The Aesop for Children*, with illustrations by Milo Winter, https://www.gutenberg.org/ebooks/19994; *The Fables of Aesop* by Joseph Jacobs, https://archive.org/details/fablesofsop00ae

EXHIBIT 3.9. Fables without Morals

1. *The Lion and the Mouse*

A lion lay sleeping the forest, and a mouse accidentally ran right into his nose. This woke the lion up, and he grabbed the mouse in his paw, planning to kill her.

"Have mercy!" cried the little mouse. "Please let me go and some day I will do you a favor."

The lion laughed. "What could a little mouse ever do for a big lion like me?" But he smiled and let the little mouse go.

A few days later, the lion was caught in a hunter's net. He roared so loudly that everyone in the forest could hear him, including the little mouse. She ran to the lion and gnawed at the net so that the lion could escape.

"Let that be a lesson to you," said the mouse:

____ (fill in the moral of the story) ____

2. *The Farmer's Daughter and the Bucket of Milk*

A farmer's daughter had milked the cows and was carrying the bucket of milk back home. As she walked along, she dreamed about what she would do with the milk. "I will use this milk to churn some butter. Then I will take the butter to market, and when I sell the butter, I will buy some eggs. I will hatch the eggs, and when the chicks grow up, I will sell the chickens. With that money I will buy a pretty new dress to wear at the fair. The young men will all want to dance with me, and when I dance, I will kick up my heels like this. . . !" And as she kicked up her heels, she lost her balance and spilled all the milk, and so she lost the milk, and the butter, and the eggs, and the chickens, and the pretty dress, too.

____ (fill in the moral of the story) ____

3. *The Tortoise and the Ducks*

Two ducks and a tortoise were friends, and one day the tortoise told the ducks that he would like to go flying with them and see the world. The ducks thought for a while and then came up with a plan. "We'll take this stick," said the ducks, "and hold it in our beaks. You will then grab the middle in your mouth and hang on. That way we can all go flying together."

The tortoise agreed, and then the ducks added this important instruction: "Whatever you do, hang on to the stick and don't open your mouth!" The tortoise agreed, and the plan worked perfectly: the tortoise was soon flying high with the ducks.

As the three friends were flying along, a crow noticed them and started to laugh. "I can't believe my eyes," said the crow. "It's a tortoise who thinks he's a bird!"

The tortoise was angry that the crow was making fun of him, so he started to reply, but as soon as he opened his mouth, he let go of the stick and fell all the way to the ground.

_____ (fill in the moral of the story) _____

4. *The Fox and the Crow*

A crow stole a piece of cheese and flew away with the cheese. A hungry fox followed the crow, hoping to steal the cheese and eat it. When the crow landed in a tree, the fox stood at the bottom of the tree and looked up.

"My lovely crow," said the fox, "I have never seen feathers so beautiful as your feathers. I have never seen a bird that could fly so fast or so high. You are truly the most amazing bird that I've ever seen."

The crow listened carefully to what the fox was saying. She liked what she heard.

"If only you could sing," the fox continued, "then surely you would be called the Queen of Birds!"

And the crow, without thinking, opened her beak and started to sing. The cheese then fell to the ground, and the fox quickly gobbled it up as the poor crow looked down. "Let that be a lesson to you," said the fox:

_____ (fill in the moral of the story) _____

5. *Three Bulls and a Lion*

A lion saw three bulls who lived together in a meadow. He tried to attack them, but they helped each other to drive him away. "As long as they are united," thought the lion, "I cannot defeat them. I need to find a way to drive them apart."

So the lion went to the first bull and said to him quietly, "Did you know the two other bulls think you are stupid? That's what I heard them saying this morning."

He then went to the second bull and said, "Did you know that the other two bulls say you have bad breath? That's what they told me this morning."

Finally, he went to the third bull and said, "I think you should know that the other two bulls are planning to chase you out of the meadow. I heard them whispering about it this morning."

The bulls began to stand in separate corners of the meadow and would not go near one another. It was an easy job for the lion to attack them now, one by one.

_____ **(fill in the moral of the story)** _____

Source: Fables adapted from *The Aesop for Children*, with illustrations by Milo Winter, https://www.gutenberg.org/ebooks/19994; *The Fables of Aesop* by Joseph Jacobs, https://archive.org/details/fablesofsop00ae

EXHIBIT 3.10. Answer Sheet for Fables without Morals

1. The Lion and the Mouse

The moral of this story is that even a little creature can help a big creature. It is also a positive example of gratitude: the lion did the mouse a favor, and the mouse returned that favor as promised.

2. The Farmer's Daughter and the Bucket of Milk

This is a fable from the Middle East that became part of the Aesop's fable tradition thanks to being included in La Fontaine's French Fables. The moral of this fable can be expressed with the English proverb: "Don't count your chickens before they're hatched." This type of folktale is referred to as the "Air Castle" type of fable, from the idea of building castles "in the air" — castles in your imagination, but not in reality.

3. The Tortoise and the Ducks

This is a fable from the Middle East that became part of the Aesop's fable tradition thanks to being included in La Fontaine's French Fables.

The moral of this fable is that you should not reply to people who insult you or make fun of you. Just stick to your plan and keep on going! If the tortoise had kept his mouth shut, this story could have been a great example of cooperation among friends, but instead it is a negative example of someone whose own words get him into trouble.

4. The Fox and the Crow

The moral of this story is that you should not trust in flattering words. The fox is often a trickster in Aesop's fables. The fox's tricks do not always succeed but in this case, because the crow is foolish, the tricky fox gets the cheese.

5. Three Bulls and a Lion

The moral of this story is that there is strength in unity, and you should be careful when your enemy is trying to destroy that unity. The lion is using a strategy called "divide and conquer." There is also a Biblical proverb that describes the situation of the bulls: "A house divided against itself cannot stand" (Gospel of Mark 3:25). The number of bulls varies from story to story: sometimes there are two bulls, sometimes three, sometimes four—but the moral works the same way no matter how many bulls there are.

Source: Fables adapted from *The Aesop for Children,* with illustrations by Milo Winter, https://www.gutenberg.org/ebooks/19994; *The Fables of Aesop* by Joseph Jacobs, https://archive.org/details/fablesofsop00ae

---

Investigating a Text Lesson Plan for High Intermediate/Advanced Students

Instructional Objectives

Students will:

1. Learn new word meanings through a close reading of a text.
2. Identify, summarize, and evaluate the claims and evidence in the text.
3. Make predictions and inferences about the text by answering higher-order questions in writing and speaking.

Duration

If this lesson is taught later in the school year after students have gained more experience with close reading, it will likely take three 55-minute class periods. However, if taught earlier in the year it could take five class periods.

Common Core English Language Arts Standards

Reading

1. Read closely to determine what the text says explicitly and to make logical inferences from it; cite specific textual evidence when writing or speaking to support conclusions drawn from the text.

2. Determine central ideas or themes of a text and analyze their development; summarize the key supporting details and ideas.

3. Interpret words and phrases as they are used in a text, including determining technical, connotative, and figurative meanings, and analyze how specific word choices shape meaning or tone.

4. Delineate and evaluate the argument and specific claims in a text, including the validity of the reasoning as well as the relevance and sufficiency of the evidence.

5. Read and comprehend complex literary and informational texts independently and proficiently.

Writing

1. Produce clear and coherent writing in which the development, organization, and style are appropriate to task, purpose, and audience.

2. Draw evidence from literary or informational texts to support analysis, reflection, and research.

Speaking and Listening

1. Prepare for and participate effectively in a range of conversations and collaborations with diverse partners, building on others' ideas and expressing their own clearly and persuasively.

2. Evaluate a speaker's point of view, reasoning, and use of evidence and rhetoric.

3. Present information, findings, and supporting evidence such that listeners can follow the line of reasoning and the organization, development, and style are appropriate to task, purpose, and audience.

4. Adapt speech to a variety of contexts and communicative tasks, demonstrating command of formal English when indicated or appropriate.

Language

1. Demonstrate command of the conventions of standard English grammar and usage when writing or speaking.

2. Demonstrate command of the conventions of standard English capitalization, punctuation, and spelling when writing.

3. Determine or clarify the meaning of unknown and multiple-meaning words and phrases by using context clues, analyzing meaningful word parts, and consulting general and specialized reference materials, as appropriate.

4. Acquire and use accurately a range of general academic and domain-specific words and phrases sufficient for reading, writing, speaking, and listening at

the college and career readiness level; demonstrate independence in gathering vocabulary knowledge when encountering an unknown term important to comprehension or expression.

Materials

- Overhead projector to display close reading text "'Intelligence Is Not Enough': Making the Case for Social and Emotional Learning in Schools" (Exhibit 3.11), "Investigating a Text Note-Taking Sheet" (Exhibit 3.12), "Visual Summary Chart" (Exhibit 3.13), "Sample Visual Summary Chart" (Figure 3.2).
- Computer access and projector to display video "5 Keys to Social and Emotional Learning" by Edutopia (http://bit.ly/navccss11) and the figures.
- Student copies of "'Intelligence Is Not Enough': Making the Case for Social and Emotional Learning in Schools" (Exhibit 3.11), "Investigating a Text Note-Taking Sheet" (Exhibit 3.12), and "Visual Summary Chart" (Exhibit 3.13).

Procedure

First day

1. The teacher tells students that they will be reading a text and working together like detectives to investigate, or figure out, what it says and what it means. The teacher asks students to think of two things that good readers do to help them understand a text and then has students share their ideas with a partner. The teacher can call on a few pairs to share out and reminds the class that they will be using these strategies as they read the upcoming text—they will start by making some predictions about the text.

2. The teacher passes out the text "'Intelligence Is Not Enough': Making the Case for Social and Emotional Learning in Schools" (Exhibit 3.11) and the Investigating a Text Note-Taking Sheet (Exhibit 3.12) She tells students they are going to be like detectives who are first arriving at a crime scene—they need to survey what the text looks like and look for any clues that stand out. She gives students a minute to scan the text and posts the following questions and answer frame on the overhead/document camera:

   - What type of text is this? How do I know this?

     I think this text is _____ because _____.

   Students can write their answers to this question on the note-taking sheet (Exhibit 3.12) in the section labeled "Step One." As the teacher circulates, she makes the determination whether she needs to prompt the class as a whole or individual students with a question like "Does this look like a short story or poem?" "Why not?" Then she asks students to share their answers with a partner and calls on a few pairs to share with the class. Students will likely say that the text looks like an article or essay because of the subheadings and the research references. The teacher confirms that this text is nonfiction and is a type of article called an "opinion piece" or "op-ed." If this is a new genre for students, the teacher can explain that these types of texts often appear in the opinion pages of newspapers, both in print or online.

   Note: Teachers also have the option of having students create this note-taking sheet on a larger piece of paper by folding it into four boxes and labeling them with the four steps listed on Exhibit 3.12. The teacher should be sure to tell students that they will be using this sheet to capture their thinking, questions, and learning about the text—it is okay if it looks messy and if they want to cross things out and add new ideas from others in the class. The teacher should also have a copy of the note-taking sheet to keep track of the ideas from the class and that students can use as a reference if they are absent.

3. Next, the teacher directs students' attention to the title of the text. She reads the title and posts the following question and answer frames on the overhead:

   • What is the title of this text? What predictions can I make about the text based on the title?

      The title is _____. Based on this title, I predict _____ and _____.

4. She gives students a few minutes to write their answers again under "Step One" on their note-taking sheet and circulates looking for a few helpful student examples and providing assistance to those students who might need more support. She then asks the students with the "helpful" answers to share out with the whole class. The teacher records the class predictions on her copy of the note-taking sheet and encourages students to add any new predictions they don't already have. If the teacher has taught the lessons on growth mindset, self-control, and grit from Chapter 2, this would be a good time to review the key ideas from those lessons, either by having students talk with each other or do a quick write to generate ideas.

   If the teacher feels more predicting is needed, she has the option of asking students to try and turn the title into a question. She explains that students can use this strategy with any text to come up with a question to focus their reading (this idea comes from the Expository Reading and Writing Course materials developed by California State University: https://www.calstate.edu/eap/englishcourse/). Some examples for this text might include:

- Why is intelligence not enough?
- Why make the case for social and emotional learning in schools?

5. The teacher tells students they are now ready to find out if their predictions are correct. She explains that for this *first reading*, they should focus on "what the text says" and on developing a general understanding of it. She tells students that they should follow along as she reads the text aloud and should use their pencil/pen to circle unfamiliar words (no more than two per paragraph).

6. The teacher reads the text aloud slowly and with prosody. As she reads, students circle unfamiliar words. The teacher can also pause periodically and give students time to write brief annotations (on sticky notes or on the text) like questions or reactions that pop into their mind as they are reading along. These pauses, however, should be brief in order to keep student engagement and focus at a high level. Remind students that good readers often read a text more than once and they don't need to understand every word or idea during a first reading.

7. When finished with this first reading, the teacher directs students to return to the text to identify three words per page that are either unfamiliar or less familiar and that they feel are most important for them to know. She asks students to share out, chooses one, and then models using context clues to guess the meaning. She tells students to use the same process for each of the three words per page and to check their guesses by looking up the meaning of the word (either on their phones or in a dictionary). The teacher asks several students to share their learning and records the new words and their meanings on the note-taking sheet under "Step Two." Another option is to have students write the meanings of the words in the margin of the text itself next to where the word appears.

8. The teacher then tells students to choose *one* of the following questions to answer in the "Step Two" section of their note-taking sheet:

- What is the text about?

     I think the text is about _____ because _____.
     or
     I think the text is about _____. The clues are _____ and _____.

- What questions does the text make you wonder about?

     I wonder what/how/why/if _____.

- Is there a conflict or problem in the text?

  I think a conflict/problem is _____because the author writes

  _____.

9. If there is time (it could also be done as the first activity for day two of the lesson), students can work in partners or small groups to share their answers. It can be helpful to post academic sentence frames similar to the ones below and remind students to use them in their discussions:

In my opinion, _____.

I'm wondering _____.

I agree/disagree because _____.

Second Day

1. The teacher asks students to think of something new they learned the day before (maybe a new word or an idea from the text) and then share with a partner.

2. The teacher then asks students to take out the article from the previous day (Exhibit 3.11) along with their note-taking sheet (Exhibit 3.12) and explains that now students will be doing a *second reading* of the text. She tells students that this time they will dig a little deeper into the text, focusing on "how the text works," and in particular looking for any claims the author is making and the evidence to support them.

3. The teacher quickly asks students to review the difference between a claim (an opinion, a point) and evidence (information and examples that support a claim) with a partner. The teacher asks pairs to discuss what kinds of clues they will be looking for to identify claims (i.e., use of the word "should" or "should not") and evidence (i.e., use of statistics or quotations from experts). *Note*: If students don't have a lot of experience with these concepts, they should be taught in more depth before this lesson. See Chapter 4's "Inductive" section for ideas on teaching students to identify, evaluate, and write effective claims and evidence.

4. The teacher explains to students that they will work in partners and take turns reading every few sentences or every other paragraph of the article. The teacher asks a student to pass out colored pencils or highlighters in two different colors and explains that one color (e.g., orange) will be used to highlight claims and another color (e.g., green) will be for evidence. The teacher tells students that as they read they are to pause at the end of each paragraph and discuss whether

they see any claims and/or evidence. The teacher then models the process on the overhead with the first few paragraphs or the first page.

5. As students are reading, discussing, and highlighting with their partners, the teacher circulates to provide assistance with pronunciation of challenging words and to check that students are on the right track identifying claims and evidence.

6. As students are finishing up, the teacher tells students to pick one example of a claim made by the author and the evidence to support it and to write this on their note-taking sheet under "Step Three."

7. The teacher then distributes the blank Visual Summary Chart (Exhibit 3.13) to each student. She explains that the class will be using their highlighting and the knowledge they've gained so far about "what the text says" and "how the text works" to help them summarize the article.

8. The teacher explains that she has divided the text into eight strategic "chunks" (introduction, similar topics, conclusion) and that each box on the chart represents one chunk. As stated earlier, it is fine to shorten this reading by deleting sections of the text. If the teacher does this, he or she will need to make sure to also change the Visual Summary Chart and will need to renumber the paragraphs. Using her copy of the article and the Visual Summary Chart, the teacher models on the overhead how to summarize the key ideas in the first chunk of text using her highlighter and the meanings of the words she has written in the margins. As she "thinks aloud," she says:

"When I look at the first three paragraphs and I have to decide where the most important information is in this chunk of text, I think paragraph 3 might be important because it has a lot of important words that we talked about. I see the phrase 'social and emotional skills' and I know that's important because the whole article is about the need for schools to teach them. I also see that it says 'education policy and practices haven't made them a focus' and we wrote that 'education policy' means 'laws about schools' and 'practices' means 'actions in schools.' I'm going to draw a heart to represent social and emotional skills. I'm going to draw a school next to the heart to represent education. I'm going to draw an equal sign between the heart and the school. However, because it is saying that schools haven't focused on social and emotional skills, I am going to cross out the equals sign.

I also see the word 'spotlight' and we wrote that it means 'getting a lot of attention,' so I think that's important. I'm going to draw a spotlight in my box. I'm wondering what the text says about the spotlight? It says here (points to the text) that the spotlight has been on teaching academic skills and on standardized tests. I'm going to draw a picture of a test and write 1 + 1 = 2 to represent the academic skills. Now, I'm going to write a summary statement at the bottom of this box to explain my pictures."

The teacher writes in the bottom of the box, "Schools haven't focused on social and emotional learning, but have focused on academic skills and testing." See Figure 3.2 for a sample of a completed Visual Summary Chart.

9. The teacher tells students they will be working with a partner to draw pictures and write summary statements for the next three boxes and then they will do the last four by themselves. The teacher can decide whether more modeling is needed or could alternate having students do a box and then the teacher modeling the next box.

10. When students are finished, the teacher collects the Visual Summary Charts to check for understanding and to determine which students may need more support the following day.

Third Day

1. The teacher passes back the Visual Summary Charts and explains that students will be using their charts and their note-taking sheets to do some even deeper thinking about the text and the claims made by the author.

2. The teacher tells students they will read the text on their own this time and when they are done, they will answer the following questions on their note-taking sheet under "Step Four"**:**

   - What do you think is the author's main claim?

     I think the author's main claim is _____ because _____.

   - Which evidence used by the author to support her claim is most convincing and why?

     I think that the most convincing evidence is _____ because _____.

3. The teacher gives students time to read and write their answers. She then assigns them to small groups of three to four and tells them they will share their answers. She posts and reminds them to use question starters such as:

   "What do you think is the answer to question _____?"

   "That could be true, but what could be another answer?"

   "Why do you believe that?"

   "What is your evidence?"

4. The teacher collects the note-taking sheets to review. She then passes out a sticky note or index card and tells students this will be their "exit ticket" out the door.

She posts the following reflection questions, tells students to choose one to answer, and gives them a few minutes to write their answers:

- What is one thing you learned from investigating this text?

- How did working with this text improve your reading skills?

- What is one thing you did well while working with this text and what is one thing you'd like to do better next time?

The teacher collects students' answers as they exit the class.

Assessment

- The teacher can collect and review the students' copies of the article, Visual Summary Chart, Note-Taking Sheet, and "exit ticket" writing, as well as circulate throughout the room to assess how well students are participating in the different group learning activities and using the answer frames.

- If the teacher feels a more involved assessment is necessary, you can develop a simple rubric appropriate for your class situation. Free online resources to both find premade rubrics and create your own can be found at the Best Rubric Sites and a Beginning Discussion about Their Use (http://larryferlazzo.edublogs.org/2010/09/18/the-best-rubric-sites-and-a-beginning-discussion-about-their-use/).

Possible Extensions and Modifications

1. Students can complete a similar lesson sequence (focusing on the four steps—What *might* the text say? What *does* the text say? How does the text work? What does the text mean and how does it compare to others?)—using a digital text such as the video "5 Keys to Social and Emotional Learning Success" by Edutopia (http://bit.ly/navccss11). During Step One students could make predictions based on the title of the video and examine who produced it. For Step Two, they could identify new words in the video and find out their meanings. During Step Three, they could complete a Visual Summary Chart with five boxes, one for each of the five keys to social and emotional learning presented in the video. During Step Four, students could use a graphic organizer, such as a Venn diagram, to compare the video to the "Intelligence Is Not Enough" article. Then they could convert their ideas into a compare and contrast essay.

2. The teacher can do the Argument Writing Lesson Plan in Chapter 4 that is designed to follow this one and shows how to scaffold argument writing.

Tech Tools
Additional Resources On Social Emotional Learning

Many additional resources, including accessible videos, on Social Emotional Learning can be found at the Best Social Emotional Learning (SEL) Resources (http://larryferlazzo.edublogs.org/2012/01/23/the-best-social-emotional-learning-sel-resources/). They could be used as student resources for further research, or additional close reading texts.

EXHIBIT 3.11. "Intelligence Is Not Enough": Making the Case for Social and Emotional Learning in Schools, by Katie Hull

1. Martin Luther King Jr. described the function of education as teaching students "to think intensively and to think critically" but he cautioned "that intelligence is not enough. Intelligence plus character–that is the goal of true education" [1].

2. Almost 70 years later, researchers and educators are urging a return to this ideal of providing an education that focuses not only on academic skills, but on teaching the social and emotional skills that enable young people to grow into successful people of "character."

3. Despite the fact that research suggests that students who possess these social and emotional skills are more successful in school and in life beyond, education policy and practices haven't made them a focus. Instead, the spotlight has largely been on teaching academic skills and increasing students' scores on standardized tests measuring these skills.

4. Of course, we need to teach students the academic skills they will need to succeed in college and in their careers. However, we must *also* help them develop and apply important social and emotional skills in schools. Some of these skills include the ability to show self-control, cooperate with others, have a "growth mindset", and demonstrate "grit." Many students show these qualities outside of the classroom — on the athletic field, with their families, and at part-time jobs. Schools need to create an environment where students learn how to apply, and see the benefits in applying, these skills in the classroom.

Self-Control

5. An important skill that schools need to assist students in developing is how to maintain self-control. Researchers suggest that self-control is the act of resisting an immediate distraction in order to focus on a task that can help you achieve a short term goal. Studies show that being able to control our impulses and delay gratification is a key predictor of success. There is extensive research documenting a connection between high self-control and academic performance, along with long-term positive effects on income and physical health [2].

6. Probably the most well-known of these studies on self-control was conducted by Dr. Walter Mischel and is known as the "Marshmallow Experiment." In this study, small children were placed in a room alone, and a marshmallow was put on a table in front of them. An adult told each child that he/she would remain in the room for 15 minutes and if he/she refrained from eating the marshmallow then he/she would get a second one. Children who demonstrated self-control — many used the strategy of distracting themselves — were found to be far more successful in high school and college, and were more financially, emotionally, and physically stable as adults. Subsequent research revealed that children could be taught strategies which helped them to wait longer before eating the marshmallow, in other words, to exercise more self-control. Students can and should be taught about self-control, how to increase it, and why it is important.

Grit

7. Having grit, or persistence/perseverance, is another skill which should be emphasized in schools. A number of researchers have described differences between self-control and grit, though the two support each other. As summarized above, many researchers, including well-known expert Angela Duckworth, suggest that self-control is resisting an immediate distraction in order to focus on a task that can help you achieve a shorter term goal ("I'm not going to throw an eraser at Juan because it's more important that I do my English reading assignment"). That short-term goal, in turn, is a step towards a long-term objective (It's more important that I do my English assignment because it will ultimately help me graduate from high school). Grit, according to Professor Duckworth, is showing self-control everyday for a longer period of time (months or years) while pursuing a long-term goal, such as becoming a doctor [3].

8. Extensive research has shown higher qualities of grit lead to increased chances of high school graduation [4] and higher grades [5]. In one study, Professor Duckworth developed a 12-item questionnaire to measure grit which she found to be remarkably predictive of success. Duckworth and her research team gave this grit questionnaire to more than 1,200 freshman cadets as they entered West Point Naval Academy. She found that the students who scored lower on the grit questionnaire were more likely to drop out than those who scored higher [6].

9. Many students already demonstrate an important part of grit called "resilience", or the ability to bounce back when obstacles come up, in their daily lives outside of school. Schools should build on this resiliency that students already have and help them apply it to their schoolwork.

Growth Mindset

10. Another trait related to grit is having a "growth mindset" and is also a key to success that schools must emphasize. The concept of a growth mindset is based primarily on the research of Carol Dweck, a Stanford professor and leading researcher in the field of motivation [7]. Simply put, it means that success is based on effort and learning, not on "natural talent." No one is born "good" or "bad" at something—a belief that you are is considered having a "fixed mindset." Those with a growth mindset are more likely to view obstacles and mistakes as just common occurrences that are expected and that can be overcome.

11. Research has shown that helping students understand that mistakes are opportunities to learn and not signs of disaster or a comment on their intelligence, also leads to improved academic performance. All students can benefit from learning about the difference between a "fixed" and a "growth" mindset and need to be taught ways to develop the latter.

Cooperation

12. Another invaluable social and emotional skill is cooperation. Students will be asked to work with others to accomplish tasks and goals throughout their education and in the world of work.

13. Recent research published in *the American Journal of Public Health* shows the link between cooperation and success. According to the study, 20 years ago kindergarten teachers rated children on several criteria including the ability to cooperate with peers, listen to others, share materials, and give suggestions and opinions without being bossy. Twenty years later, children who had been rated "well" in most categories were much more likely to have graduated high school, graduated from college, and have good jobs—among other measurements [8].

14. Unfortunately, some schools have created an environment of competition where students feel pressured to achieve the highest grade or test score. As one high school student lamented, "Sometimes our teachers tell us we can't work together because it is cheating. I understand not working together on a test, but sometimes I just need to talk things through and hear other people's ideas when I'm trying to solve a problem." Schools must recognize the value of cooperation if they want students to feel motivated to learn and to be prepared to succeed in the outside world.

15. With the growing body of research on the importance of teaching students these social and emotional skills, education policy makers and school districts must make them a *top priority* when considering how to best meet the needs of their students. For students in today's dynamic, global society, "intelligence is not enough."

EXHIBIT 3.12. Investigating a Text Note-Taking Sheet

Title of text:

Step One: What might the text say?

Step Two: What does the text say?

Step Three: How does the text work?

Step Four: What does the text mean and how does it compare to others?

EXHIBIT 3.13. Blank Visual Summary Chart

Paragraphs 1–3	Paragraphs 8–9
Paragraph 4	Paragraphs 10–11
Paragraphs 5–6	Paragraphs 12–14
Paragraph 7	Paragraph 15

For downloadable versions of the lesson plans and Tech Tools boxes found in this chapter, go to the "Downloads" section of this book's web page at www.wiley.com/go/navccss.

CHAPTER FOUR

Writing

The writer must believe that what he [or she] is doing is the most important thing in the world.

—John Steinbeck[1]

What Does the Common Core Say about Writing?

The Common Core writing standards (see Exhibit 4.1) call for students to focus on evidence-based writing—specifically argument and informative/explanatory texts in high school, with less time spent on writing "real or imagined" narratives (in elementary and middle school the Standards suggest that the split be *roughly* even between the three genres).[2] In reading the Standards and supporting documents[3] (and listening to their writers), though, one can easily get the idea that they *really* want teachers and students to focus on writing arguments that are, again, based on evidence from something that students are reading. In other words, students read a text or texts on a topic and develop a position (also called a claim) using the evidence in the text or texts to support their position. This process is different from the one used by many teachers, including us, in the past—first taking a position and then looking for evidence to support it, usually including substantial personal experience.

Our impression is that, as far as the focus on argument writing goes, the Standards' writers would love to be like the spouse who tells their partner on a Monday night that it doesn't matter where they go to dinner—he or she can choose whatever restaurant they like best—while knowing full well that the only one open is the favorite one of the spouse who is supposedly being magnanimous. We have nothing against argument, though we also think it's important to introduce our students to a variety of restaurants.

EXHIBIT 4.1. English Language Arts College and Career Readiness Anchor Standards for Writing

Text Types and Purposes

CCSS.ELA-LITERACY.CCRA.W.1

Write arguments to support claims in an analysis of substantive topics or texts using valid reasoning and relevant and sufficient evidence.

CCSS.ELA-LITERACY.CCRA.W.2

Write informative/explanatory texts to examine and convey complex ideas and information clearly and accurately through the effective selection, organization, and analysis of content.

CCSS.ELA-LITERACY.CCRA.W.3

Write narratives to develop real or imagined experiences or events using effective technique, well-chosen details and well-structured event sequences.

Production and Distribution of Writing

CCSS.ELA-LITERACY.CCRA.W.4

Produce clear and coherent writing in which the development, organization, and style are appropriate to task, purpose, and audience.

CCSS.ELA-LITERACY.CCRA.W.5

Develop and strengthen writing as needed by planning, revising, editing, rewriting, or trying a new approach.

CCSS.ELA-LITERACY.CCRA.W.6

Use technology, including the Internet, to produce and publish writing and to interact and collaborate with others.

Research to Build and Present Knowledge

CCSS.ELA-LITERACY.CCRA.W.7

Conduct short as well as more sustained research projects based on focused questions, demonstrating understanding of the subject under investigation.

CCSS.ELA-LITERACY.CCRA.W.8

Gather relevant information from multiple print and digital sources, assess the credibility and accuracy of each source, and integrate the information while avoiding plagiarism.

CCSS.ELA-LITERACY.CCRA.W.9

Draw evidence from literary or informational texts to support analysis, reflection, and research.

Range of Writing

CCSS.ELA-LITERACY.CCRA.W.10

Write routinely over extended time frames (time for research, reflection, and revision) and shorter time frames (a single sitting or a day or two) for a range of tasks, purposes, and audiences.

The Standards also call for writing to be well organized—with a particular audience in mind—and that revision is an actively used strategy. In addition, it calls for students to work collaboratively on online projects, develop judgment to evaluate the quality of sources found on the Internet and elsewhere, and gain an understanding of how to avoid plagiarism. Finally, the Standards call for a "range of writing" that could include anything from a "quickwrite" to a more lengthy research project.

Three Key Elements of the Writing Standards

This short review of the key components of the writing standards will focus on the three types of writing emphasized in them—argument, informative/explanatory, and narrative. There are obviously other elements present in the Standards, but they all feed into developing these three primary types of writing.

And, as we pointed out in the previous section, although narrative does have a role in the Standards, evidence-based claims from text (also remember from the last chapter that text does not mean only the written word) clearly are considered essential. As David Coleman, one of the writers of the Standards, famously said, "As you grow up in this world, you realize people really don't give a shit about what you feel or what you think."[4] Of course, we don't recommend you share his comment with your students, though it may generate, as it does for us, a sad smile from your colleagues.

ARGUMENT

Argument is given great weight in the Standards. The idea is that students will first read a text or texts, examine the writer's explanations and points, and then—and only then—develop a claim that they will then back up with text-based evidence,[5] as well as acknowledge opposing positions and present counterarguments. The Standards place great stock in the importance of this kind of rational-based approach, which the writers of the Standards contrast with the emotional sway of "persuasion."[6] They say that persuasion also often relies on other less "logical" strategies like using the authority of the writer of the text or appealing to the audience's sense of identity or self-interest. Experience in producing evidence-based arguments, say the Standards, is what will truly prepare our students for college and career.

Based on our own experience, we believe that emotion—for good or bad—is a key element of how many arguments are made. It would be nice if completely rational thoughts all carried the day, but emotion rules how many things work in the world. And, as we've said before, we live in the world as it is, not as we might wish it to be. We do tell our students that logic should be the primary guide for most academic and professional writing. We also tell them, however, that emotion can have an important place in all writing arenas.

INFORMATIVE/EXPLANATORY

Argumentative essays are designed to convince the reader of a particular point of view. Informative/explanatory texts, on the other hand, are supposed to inform and explain. As Sargeant Joe Friday would say in the 1960s TV detective drama *Dragnet*, this kind of writing starts in a "Just the facts, ma'am" fashion and continues with an investigation to get to the bottom of things. In other words, these kinds of texts help readers *understand* how things work, why things happen, and what, in fact, did occur. Literary analyses, instructions, summaries, reports, and so forth are just a few examples of this kind of writing.[7] Both informative/explanatory writing, as well as argument essays, can be the result of research.

NARRATIVE

Narrative writing, as mentioned earlier, gets reduced by Common Core to 20% of student writing output when they get to high school, while argument and informative/explanatory both are increased to 40% of all writing.[8] Narratives can be memoirs, autobiographies, anecdotes, or real or imagined stories. They are avenues where students can develop skills to depict visual details, dialogue, and the personalities of different characters. Chicago high school teacher Ray Salazar makes an important point about how the Common Core has affected his teaching of narrative by suggesting that students need to "focus on making more meaning for the audience than for the writer." He goes on to say that he emphasizes "teaching students to communicate the significance of the experience to others after they understand the significance of the experience for themselves."[9]

WHAT DOES THIS MEAN FOR WRITING INSTRUCTION IN MY CLASSROOM IN GENERAL?

When we combine all the elements of the writing strands in the Common Core Standards, what might this mean for teachers of English language learners (ELLs)?

- Focus on the "Big Three" ideas in the Standards (argument, informative/explanatory, and narrative) and provide scaffolds such as allowing use of home language (for research and even initial writing) and technology support (see later in this chapter) and pay less attention to having them develop "flawless" writing with correct conventions and grammar. In other words, create "meaningful opportunities to communicate rather than mechanical exercises for text production."[10]

- As a corollary to the previous point, in addition to not being a "stickler" for perfect grammar and conventions, use the same guideline for citations. Provide students with one simple template to use when handwriting, and allow the use of automatic citation formatting tools when online.

- Recognize that ELLs will need modeling and guidance—more than many non-ELLs may require—before embarking on independent writing projects.

- Provide many sentence starters for students to use in their writing and graphic organizers to help support their planning.

- Look for opportunities to assign collaborative writing projects, or at least make them an option, so that ELLs can more easily access assistance from classmates.

- Regularly reinforce student use of metacognition (see Chapter 2) so they can monitor what they are doing well in writing, what challenges they are facing, and what learning strategies are helping them to most effectively work through those problems.

HOW CAN WRITING INSTRUCTION IN MY CLASSROOM SUPPORT ELL STUDENTS IN MEETING COMMON CORE STANDARDS?

What follows below is a list of instructional methods that can be used in multiple types of writing activities with ELLs.

MODELING

Researchers have found modeling to be an effective instructional strategy when teaching a variety of skills.[11] In the section on Read Alouds in Chapter 3, we share the importance of thinking aloud while reading in order to make our reading strategies "visible" to ELL students. Modeling our writing strategies is just as critical.

We often model various stages of the writing process for our students—planning/ outlining, drafting, revising, and editing. This isn't to say we stand at the overhead while writing an entire draft in front of students. Rather, we model writing a few sentences or a paragraph and share our thinking about the various choices we are making. We have also found it useful to share a sentence or paragraph we have written that contains mistakes or might be less than stellar and then ask our students to help us improve it. Engagement is always high during this activity as ELLs are eager to point out our failings! Modeling that writing is a process–where feedback from others is seen as helpful and not something to be feared–creates a classroom environment where students are more willing to take risks in their own writing. The upcoming section on Peer Review describes how we structure positive student feedback activities.

Model texts, also called mentor texts, are another critical part of writing instruction for ELLs. Before students write their own texts of a certain genre, they must first read and analyze texts of this genre. They need to study the features of a genre—the common patterns, language structures, and literary techniques that are used. This "study" helps them employ these critical language structures and elements into their own writing. For example, if we want our students to write their own argument texts, they must "study" the arguments of others—identifying and evaluating the claims, evidence, and rhetorical strategies being used to develop these arguments. In our experience, and as researchers have confirmed, the use of model texts as a tool for writing instruction can increase the quality of students' writing.[12]

However, the use of model texts, whether they are teacher-written, student-written, or written by professional writers, must be planned thoughtfully in order to reap their benefits. We don't want to simply throw a model text on the overhead, read it, and then turn students loose to try writing a similar text. We need to use model texts *throughout* the writing process if they are to be an effective tool. As veteran writing instructor Kelly Gallagher states, "We must teach students to imitate model texts before they write, as they write, and as they revise."[13] See the Tech Tools box for online sources of model texts, and see later sections in this chapter and the Lesson Plan on Argument Writing at the end of this chapter for more ideas on using model texts and modeling to improve student writing.

Tech Tools

Online Essay Models

There are many free models of student writing online for just about every genre imaginable. These can be used as mentor texts for students. You can access the best sources, as well as additional writing instructional resources, at the Best Websites for K–12 Writing Instruction/Reinforcement (http://larryferlazzo.edublogs.org/2008/01/11/the-best-websites-for-K-12-writing-instructionreinforcment/).

PLANNING AND ORGANIZING

We've discussed the value of making students aware of metacognitive strategies they can employ to improve their reading comprehension. It is also important to encourage students to use similar strategies to improve their writing. Just as readers monitor their comprehension while reading and make choices about which strategies to employ to help them better understand a text, writers also use metacognitive strategies such as planning, organizing, monitoring, and evaluating as they construct texts of their own. Teaching ELL students these critical language-learning strategies can make a difference in students' use of these strategies and in their writing proficiency.[14]

Of course, providing students with tools for planning and organizing their writing should be viewed as scaffolding that can gradually be removed as students gain writing proficiency. We never want them to internalize that formulaic writing is the way writing works. However, writing structures can be especially effective for ELLs if they are given supports that model the rhetorical patterns and features of academic writing. Gerald Graff and Cathy Birkenstein explain the value of using academic "templates" in their book *They Say, I Say: The Moves That Matter in Academic Writing* (which we frequently use with our higher-proficiency students):

> Critical thinking and writing go deeper than any set of linguistic formulas, requiring that you question assumptions, develop strong claims, offer supporting reasons and evidence, consider opposing arguments, and so on. But these deeper habits of thought cannot be put into practice unless you have a language for expressing them in clear, organized ways.[15]

In our experience, the use of graphic organizers is one of the best ways to help ELLs capture their thinking as they plan and organize their writing. In Chapter 3, we share ideas for using graphic organizers to support reading comprehension, specifically ones that represent the structure and discourse patterns of the text being read (i.e., argument-reasoning, problem-solution). Before students produce a longer piece of writing, we first have them use these types of graphic organizers to understand and analyze model texts. Then students use similar graphic organizers that reflect the structure of the text they will be writing to plan their ideas.

For example, as students prepare to write an argumentative text, we might give them a graphic organizer with a box at the top labeled "My Claim," with boxes underneath labeled "Evidence to Support My Claim" and another box labeled "Counterclaims." We might also give them an outline that follows the text's structure in which they can write their ideas and "see" how they might organize their writing. Less-advanced ELLs may need an outline that contains sentence starters or frames, while higher-proficiency students may not need an outline at all or can experiment with creating their own outlines.

We encourage students to monitor their thinking while they complete these organizers and ask themselves questions such as: Are there ideas I still don't understand? Do I need to find more information? Does my evidence support my claim? We might post these questions for students to answer in writing or in discussion with a partner.

Another way we support students as they plan and organize their writing is by providing them with paragraph structures, or writing frames, that they can use within longer pieces of writing. We describe two structures—the A-B-C format (Answer, Back it Up, Comment/Connect) and P-Q-C (make a Point, Quote from the text to support your point, make a Comment or Connection to your personal experience, another text, or some other knowledge)—in Chapter 3 as strategies to help students formulate higher-level responses to texts. Other variations might include—P-E-A (make a Point, provide Evidence, Analyze the evidence by connecting it to the point) and S-S-E (Summarize the issue, take a Stance, provide Evidence to support the stance). Students can also use these structures to assist them as they write arguments because they all represent some variation of making a point, providing evidence, and analyzing this evidence. Teachers can vary the sophistication of these structures by also providing sentence frames or by having students use the structure multiple times using different types of evidence (from a text, from personal experience, etc.) as support.

Teaching ELLs to deconstruct writing prompts is another way to support their planning and organizing processes. When selecting or constructing writing prompts for our students, we make sure they are well-written and that students can use the prompt itself as a tool for planning and organizing their writing. Accessible prompts list the key questions or steps that students will need to address in developing their response. We also consider three key points described in The National Writing Project's 2011 report, "Wise Eyes: Prompting for Meaningful Student Writing" by Mary Ann Smith and Sherry Swain (http://www.nwp.org/cs/public/download/nwp_file/15440/Wise_Eyes.pdf?x-r=pcfile_d, p. 3):

- The need for prompts to state a purpose and to specify or strongly imply an audience.

- The importance of authenticity: real-world credible topics.

- An emphasis on accessibility: age-appropriate tasks that are recognizable to students and offer a degree of choice.

As we described in our first book,[17] we teach our students a sequence for "attacking" a writing prompt that includes reading the prompt once all the way through, underlining unfamiliar words and using context clues to guess the meanings, rereading the prompt and circling key words (which tell them to do something and/or are repeated), numbering each "step" or question of the prompt, and then drawing boxes underneath the prompt (one for each numbered step) where they can brainstorm specific ideas to address each step. The lesson plan on argument writing at the end of this chapter contains an example of a writing prompt and describes strategies to help students use it to plan and organize their writing.

REVISION

As discussed above, it is ideal to teach students how to use metacognitive strategies such as organizing, monitoring, and evaluating to improve their writing. However, students (particularly adolescent ones) often have a way of reminding us we don't live in an "ideal" world. A classic example is demonstrated in a video clip of President Obama being interviewed by a middle school student.[18] As the president is explaining the importance of students revising their writing, the student interviewer cuts him off saying, "Yeah, I think you've pretty much covered everything about that question." We think that reaction "pretty much" sums up how many of our students feel about the revision process—they'd rather just move on!

So, how do we get our students to do something that they don't want to do because they may feel it's boring, hard, scary, time consuming, or a combination of these and other factors? The truth is, we don't—at least not all of the time. While revision is a critical part of the writing process and is highlighted as a way for students to strengthen their writing in the Common Core Standards, it isn't necessary or possible for students to revise every piece of writing they produce. Though it *is* possible to have students periodically practice revision in ways that don't feel rote, overwhelming, or meaningless.

One way we support the revision process with our ELL students is to help them understand what "revising" means in the first place. We point out that people are constantly "revising" their thinking and actions in life as they learn new things, work to clear up confusion, listen to the feedback of others, and for many other reasons. As writers, we are also constantly revising our thinking *while* we are writing, not just during an "assigned" time in between our rough draft and final draft. While students are drafting a writing piece we may have them pause when they are about halfway through and respond to questions like: "Which words or ideas am I feeling confused about? What can I do to figure them out? What do I need to learn more about before I continue writing?"

Experts often make the distinction between *revising* the content of writing and *editing* for grammar and word choice.[19] Some teachers have compared revision "to *fixing the car* and editing to *painting the car*."[20]

ELLs, in particular, often don't recognize this difference between revision and editing. They tend to focus on "correcting" surface-level issues in their writing such as grammar, spelling, and so forth. The writers of the Standards acknowledge that ELLs can achieve the standards without "manifesting native-like control of conventions and vocabulary."[21] We want to emphasize to students the higher importance of revising their ideas and organization rather than just fixing grammatical errors.

Another strategy to encourage revision is by having students revise just one section of a longer piece of writing. We might ask students to revise one or two paragraphs, especially concentrating on elements that are emphasized in our instruction—for example, revising one or two body paragraphs and focusing on introducing quotations in support of a claim and clearly explaining how the quotation supports the claim.

We've also found that students are more motivated when they can make their own choices about what to revise. Sometimes they choose which section of the text they would like to improve and work to revise just that section. At the end of the quarter or semester, we often ask students to choose their favorite or most interesting writing piece and revise it as part of their final.

Another way to enhance student motivation for revision is by providing authentic and meaningful situations where they see a need to revise. Teachers will get more bang for the buck when it comes to revision if students are writing for a real audience. Obviously when students write for authentic audiences and purposes, they pay more attention to what they are saying and how they say it. We have witnessed some of the best revision from our students when they are revising pieces that will be read by students in other classes, family members, the school administration, and even politicians. Also, when our students know that their writing will be posted online (for example, on our class blog), they spend more time on revision. Research confirms this, as well as the fact that it is easier for students to revise with technology. Look in the "Technology" section later in this chapter for more ideas on writing for an authentic audience and the use of technology for revision.

The suggestions above highlight ideas for encouraging students to revise on their own. In the next section, we will discuss peer revision and editing strategies.

PEER REVIEW AND COLLABORATIVE WRITING

Student collaboration is only mentioned in the writing standard related to using technology for developing and publishing writing, but that doesn't mean it can't be an important strategy to help meet the standards in this domain. In addition to assisting students develop the explicit academic knowledge listed in the Standards, collaborative writing has been found to be particularly helpful to ELLs in lowering anxiety and increasing self-confidence and motivation.[22]

Before we share some nontech ways to use collaboration in writing—apart from its more common usages in the classroom like think-write-pair-share—we want to remind readers of how we distinguish collaborative learning from cooperative learning in the previous chapter on reading, which we can apply to writing, as well.

In *collaborative* writing, students would do their own thinking and writing first and then connect with others to provide and receive feedback for improvement. Or, as is the case with the collaborative story-writing ideas we'll be discussing, there is explicit "space" made for students to first use their own intellectual abilities. Then, student interaction can follow so that the end "product" is one where everyone has contributed and is superior to what a student creates on his or her own.

This kind of *collaborative* learning contrasts with what is often called cooperative learning in classrooms. *Cooperative* learning for writing might involve forming student groups and giving them assignments like:

- Writing a story together by following a set of directions about its content, but providing little guidance about how to work together.
- Reading a chapter and having the group prepare a presentation on it (in writing and verbally), and each group member prepare a report on different individual sections without feedback from other group members.

- Deciding on a project-based learning and research strategies topic (see the section further on in this chapter) and having students divide up tasks, write their portion of the project, and reconvene only at the end to finalize their presentation.

Have we used cooperative learning in our classroom? Yes. Will we continue to use cooperative learning in our classroom? Yes. In our experience, it often takes more time to think through how collaboration might work in an assignment rather than cooperation and, as all teachers know, there's never enough time!

Do we use collaborative learning more than we use cooperative learning? Yes. Do students learn more when working collaboratively than when working cooperatively? In our experience, yes. Do we strive to do even more collaborative learning activities? Yes.

Are we human? Yes.

Peer Review. Peer review is one collaborative writing strategy that can assist students in achieving a number of the Common Core Standards, not least of which is the one stating that students will improve their writing by "revising, editing, rewriting, or trying a new approach." Research has shown that peer review, done well, results in improved student writing and learning about writing. Not least of these benefits has been increasing the ability of ELL students to self-edit and revise their future writing.[23]

We've tried many different methods of peer review—with an emphasis on the word "many." We've found that simpler is better, and have had the greatest success (success being defined as improved student writing and a positive classroom atmosphere) with two strategies. The first one requires minimal preparation, while the second is more involved. We have also found the second one to be a more beneficial learning experience all around. As always, teachers must balance which one they use and when they use it while considering other competing priorities.

The first peer-review strategy is a simple one for major student essays that follow a series of heavily scaffolded lessons involving teacher modeling, sharing multiple examples, using graphic organizers and much student practice. It's a matter of reviewing a Peer Review Sheet (Exhibit 4.2), which can easily be modified for any kind of essay (just keep it very, very simple) and modeling its use with an example essay from a previous year, one the teacher has written, or a paper retrieved off the Internet (see the Tech Tools box under the "Revision" section and see the Argument Writing Lesson Plan at the end of this chapter for an example of how to modify the Peer Review Sheet). Then, students are strategically divided into partners or groups of three (making sure that no group is composed entirely of less-advanced ELLs), exchange their papers, complete the checklist, discuss it with each other, and then writers make needed changes to their own draft.

EXHIBIT 4.2. Peer Review Sheet

This sheet should be stapled on top of your essay.

NAME OF WRITER:

NAME OF REVIEWER:

ESSAY CHECKLIST:

1. Does it have a title?

FIRST PARAGRAPH

2. Does it have a good hook?

3. Does it have a thesis statement communicating the main idea of the essay?

4. Does it have a sentence listing major topics the essay will cover?

BODY PARAGRAPHS:

1. Does each one have a topic sentence?

2. Does each one have good supporting details?

CONCLUSION:

1. Does it summarize the content that was covered in the essay?

2. Does it say why the essay topic is important?

The second peer-review strategy we have used successfully builds on educator/ author Ron Berger's approach to critique and feedback[24] that uses three key guidelines:

1. Be kind

2. Be specific

3. Be helpful

In our applied version of this approach (which we have gotten from both Mr. Berger and educator Andy Tharby[25]), we explain to a class that has just completed a draft of an essay (even a Beginner's version of one) that first we, the teachers, are going to talk about one student's essay—what they did well and what they could do better, and then students are going to do the same with the essays of their classmates. Students should see their essays taped on different parts of the classroom's walls as they enter the room. Each essay should have a number written on it.

We then review the sentence stems in the Peer Feedback Sentence Starters (Exhibit 4.3) and give all students copies of them (for Early Beginners, we narrow down the number of sentence starters used). Then, with one to three key elements we want to emphasize in mind, we put a draft of a student's essay that is a good model of these elements on the overhead (with his or her prior permission) and annotate it with a few of the sentence starters targeting these instructional points. An additional sheet we have sometimes shared is Brittany's Story (Exhibit 4.4), which was created by educator Katie Michaels Burke. It shows the impact that helpful peer feedback can have on a student's writing and can help generate a greater sense of seriousness and commitment by students to the process.

EXHIBIT 4.3. Peer Feedback Sentence Starters

KIND:

1. I really like the way you _____.

2. Excellent _____ throughout the essay.

3. The most successful thing about this was _____.

4. I enjoyed reading this because _____.

5. It was especially good when you _____.

SPECIFIC

6. In the first/second/third paragraph _____.

7. I think _____ is difficult to understand/could be explained better/could include more detail, etc.

8. Your sentence/paragraph about _____was _____ because _____.

HELPFUL

9. Think about adding a _____.

10. Think about taking away _____.

11. Have you thought about _____.

12. To improve your _____ try _____.

13. Perhaps you could _____.

Source: Republished (with slight modifications) with permission of Andy Tharby (https://reflectingenglish.wordpress .com/2014/03/27/adventures-with-gallery-critique/)

EXHIBIT 4.4. Brittany's Story

BRITTANY'S STORY BEFORE PEER CRITIQUE FEEDBACK:

Swim Josh Swim

"Can all you people stop splashing," I yelled with a nasty grin.

On a hot summer day, the heat burned on my face. I was in Bluegreen Resort.

"Brittany, can you teach me to swim?" my brother said.

But as he was paddling, he started to go under and started to drown. But he got better and better every time he tried. That's when he learned to swim, and he looked so proud and excited.

"Thank you Brittany," he said as he paddled and kicked all around the big pool.

As he was swimming he looked so funny but good at the same time. I thought to myself, "I did a really good job."

And I was so impressed, because he swim better than me now!

EDWARD'S FEEDBACK TO BRITTANY

I think you should describe more what you taught Josh. Also I think you should tell how old he is because people will be impressed that you were able to teach him.

BRITTANY'S STORY AFTER PEER CRITIQUE FEEDBACK

Swim Josh Swim

"Can all you people stop splashing," I yelled with a nasty grin.

On a hot summer day, the heat burned on my face. I was in Bluegreen Resort.

"Brittany, can you teach me to swim?" my **five year old brother said with his million dollar smile.**

So as I was teaching him to swim, he just kept that smile. So I can teach him well.

So first, I told him to, "kick his feet," and he kicked them hard, splashing people all around us with water. Then I told him to "paddle his hands," holding them over his head and moving back and forth. It reminded me of when I first learned to swim.

But as he was paddling, he started to go under and started to drown. **So I had to help him a little. I stayed in front of him and had him swim towards me.** But he got better and better every time he tried. That's when he learned to swim, and he looked so proud and excited.

"Thank you Brittany," he said as he paddled and kicked all around the big pool.

As he was swimming he looked so funny but good at the same time. I thought to myself, "I did a really good job."

And I was so impressed, because he swim better than me now!

Source: Created by Katie Michaels Burke. Originally appeared at "Unboxed" (http://www.hightechhigh.org/unboxed/issue9/introducing_peer_critique/). Reprinted with permission.

Next, students are given sticky notes and assigned a number. They will begin by going to the essay corresponding to their assigned number and be given 5 minutes (sometimes more, sometimes less, depending on the length of the essay) to write one kind, one specific, and one helpful comment on the sticky note (ideally, the size of the note is large enough to fit all three sentences). Students then sign it and stick it underneath the essay. Our model critique is left on the overhead and could be referred to by students to remember the one to three key points they should be noticing. At the end of 5 minutes, students move to repeat the procedure with the next numbered essay.

Instead of sticky notes, students can be given copies of the Writing Partnerwork—Peer Critique (Exhibit 4.5) sheet, also created by Katie Michaels Burke, to complete and then tape on the wall under each essay they review.

EXHIBIT 4.5. Writing Partnerwork—Peer Critique

Your Name: _____ **Partner's Name:** _____

DIRECTIONS: Listen to your partner read his or her story. Then give your feedback that is **KIND, SPECIFIC, and HELPFUL!**

WRITE ONE *kind* compliment and **ONE** *helpful and specific* **SUGGESTION**

To be kind, give a compliment using one of these prompts:

My favorite part of your story is _____ because _____.

OR

I really like your story because _____.

To be helpful, give your writer a suggestion and to be specific, tell the writer the part of the story where they can use your suggestion. Use one of the prompts below:

I think your story will be even better if you _____. A good place to do this is the part of your story when _____.

OR

I felt confused in the part when _____ because _____. I think it would be less confusing if you _____.

Source: Created by Katie Michaels Burke. Originally appeared at "Unboxed" (http://www.hightechhigh.org/unboxed/issue9/introducing_peer_critique/). Reprinted with permission.

We have students review anywhere between three and six essays, depending on available time and classroom energy. Students then collect their own essays with the sticky notes and highlight what feedback they decide is most helpful.

Finally, students write a quick reflection of the process answering these questions:

- *What is the most important thing you learned from reading and giving feedback to other students' essays?*

- *What is the most important thing you learned from reading the sticky notes students wrote about your essay?*

COLLABORATIVE WRITING

Collaborative storytelling that leads to writing can also include speaking, listening, and drawing. This section shares examples of what these kinds of activities can look like in the classroom.

Storytelling

In our last book, we described a fun and simple collaborative storytelling exercise.[26] We still like it and sometimes use it in the same way. However, we have also since revised it to reflect our new understanding of *collaboration* instead of *cooperation*, as well as enhanced the way it helps students learn the important elements in narrative writing, as described by Common Core: "Use narrative techniques, such as dialogue, pacing, description, reflection, and multiple plot lines, to develop experiences, events, and/or characters."[27]

In our new version, students work in pairs, instead of groups of three. We have found that a smaller number increases the chances that everybody is actively participating in the learning exercise, while still providing important collaborative opportunities that would be missed by working alone. Research has found that ELLs working in pairs (versus working alone) "produced shorter but better texts in terms of task fulfillment, grammatical accuracy, and complexity."[28]

First, we explain to the class that they are going to write a story with their partner and respond to questions (see below) that we are going to write on the overhead and read aloud. When we ask the question, though, students first have to be silent for 1 minute as they think about their response. After we say a minute is over, they will have 2 to 5 minutes (depending on the question) to share their answers and decide together which one they want to write down on the big easel paper each pair has in front of them. After they have answered each of our questions, they will have time the next day to write a simple version of their story (with illustrations), practice telling it, and then present it to another small group.

Sometimes we use this exercise as an introduction to a unit on stories and other times we use it during or after the unit as a reinforcement or review activity. If it is done as an introduction, the teacher may need to spend a short time modeling a response to each question and the exercise may take longer to complete.

Our previous version of this exercise did not include the individual "thinking time" and had fewer and more simplistic questions. Here is a list of ones we use, though we want to emphasize that we don't use all of them in one lesson because the number would be overwhelming. For example, sometimes we omit questions 7 and 8, and other times we don't cover 5 and 6. We wouldn't want this part of the lesson to take up more than one fast-paced full class period:

1. What is the setting? In other words, when and where does the story take place? Use the five senses—smell, touch, see, taste, feel—to describe it.

2. Who is the protagonist in the story? In other words, who is the main character? What does he or she look like?

3. Who is the antagonist in the story? In other words, who is the opponent of the protagonist? What does he or she look like?

4. What is the main problem in the story?

5. What is the protagonist's history? In other words, what has happened to him/her before that has led him/her to the problem in the story?

6. What is the antagonist's history? In other words, what has happened to him/her before that has led him/her to the problem in the story?

7. What is something the protagonist is thinking to him- or herself?

8. What is something the antagonist is thinking to him- or herself?

9. What is a dialogue the protagonist and antagonist have with each other?

10. What is one good thing that happens?

11. What is one bad thing that happens?

12. How does it end?

There are also many free online sites that are specifically designed for writers to create stories with others—some allow students and teachers to create "private" groups and some also allow the general public to also participate in writing the story (private ones obviously work better). At these sites, one person takes up the story where the other leaves off. We've used these sites (see the Tech Tools box) on occasion for follow-up homework to the in-class collaborative story assignment described earlier. For homework, partners can work together to write segments answering similar questions and then post the link to their creation in a class blog (we discuss blogs further on in this chapter).

Drawing and Writing

One fun way to do the collaborative storytelling activity we just described is to precede it with a collaborative drawing exercise. We've adapted this idea from ELL teacher Joe Budden.[29]

We begin by giving each student a legal size or 11″ × 14″ piece of paper and some colored pencils. We then tell students they will have 1 minute to draw whatever classroom appropriate image they want on the paper. At the end of 1 minute, they will pass their paper to the student next to them, who will also have 1 minute to add to the image. This can continue for 10 or 15 minutes. At the end of that time, the teacher can tell the last person that if their picture doesn't already show at least two people or animals, they should add those figures to the drawing.

The teacher then does the collaborative storytelling exercise previously described—with one difference. At the beginning of it, the paired students need to choose one of the pictures they are holding (each student will have the drawing they ended up with) and use that to help them answer the list of storytelling questions asked by the teacher. That drawing will be the illustration for their completed collaborative story.

Tech Tools

Online Collaborative Writing

The Best Sites for Collaborative Storytelling (http://larryferlazzo.edublogs.org/2010/ 12/29/the-best-sites-for-collaborative-storytelling/) lists our choices for the best free tools out there that are specifically designed for people to write stories together online.

If you're feeling more ambitious than we generally do, another potential collaborative storytelling structure is a "Choose Your Own Adventure" one, where the writer or writers create various options that readers can select at different points in the story. Though our ELL students love to read them, and there are many free tools available to create them, we have yet to find one that we can figure out how to use, much less teach to our students. Stories and tools can be found at The Best Places to Read and Write "Choose Your Own Adventure" Stories (http://larryferlazzo.edublogs.org/2009/05/ 02/the-best-places-to-read-write-choose-your-own-adventure-stories/).

MICRO-WRITING/QUICKWRITES

ELL students don't always have to produce long pieces of writing to increase their proficiency. Students can practice important writing skills, build critical thinking, and increase their confidence as writers by doing shorter bursts of writing. These shorter writing opportunities are called "micro-Writing" by some or are more well-known as "quickwrites," and are supported by the Common Core writing standards under "range of writing." The writers of the standards make it clear that students "must devote significant time and effort to writing, producing numerous pieces over short and extended time frames throughout the year."[30]

Here are some of the ways we use micro-writing/quickwrites in our classes:

- At the beginning of a lesson, we may ask students to write for a few minutes about a topic we will be studying that day in order to tap background knowledge and get students focused.

- During a lesson, we may post a prompt for students to answer, reflecting on what they've learned so far and what needs further study.

- At the end of a lesson, we may post a prompt that asks students to reflect on what they learned, how they learned it, and to set goals for future learning. See the section on learning logs in the Metacognition Mini-Lesson in Chapter 2, which contains examples of these types of reflective prompts.

- We have students respond to quickwrite prompts to explore their initial opinions on an issue or problem that they will be studying.

- Before reading a text with students, we select an important quote from the text and display it on the overhead. Then students write for a few minutes about the quote—what it means, how it might be connected to other texts we've read, what questions it brings to mind, and so forth.

- After teaching a challenging concept or vocabulary word, we ask students to write an explanation of it for someone who is younger or who doesn't know anything about the concept/word.

- We ask students to write to a question about a topic of study and to continue writing for a few minutes until we say stop. Then we tell students to choose an idea or important word from their writing and copy it on the next line of their paper. Students then write for a few more minutes about that idea/word. The process can be repeated as many times as student need and interest warrants.

- We often use quickwrites as a method of formative assessment—to check for student understanding in order to plan further instruction.

USING VISUALS

We discuss ways to use visuals in the previous chapter on reading, as we also continue to discuss in most of the upcoming chapters. They provide a rich resource to draw upon for teaching ELLs.

Though the next Tech Tools box provides links to multiple ways to use visuals in the classroom for reading, writing, speaking/listening, and language, we would like to highlight a few instructional strategies we've used that seem to particularly support the Common Core writing standards.

Instructions

Having ELLs create a list of instructions, ranging from explaining moves or plays from a sport they enjoy to a recipe for their favorite food (finishing that particular lesson with a tasting is always a crowd-pleaser!) is a good place for ELLs to start writing informative/explanatory texts. And accompanying such instructions with step-by-step images can be an aid to the writer and to the reader. There are even online tools like Tildee (http://www.tildee.com/) that provide scaffolded support where students can write a "tutorial" with supporting images from the Web or uploaded from their phone. Of course, if teachers want to emphasize speaking instead of writing with this kind of lesson, having students make a video tutorial would be another alternative.

Compare and Contrast

Students are required by the Common Core Standards to apply critical thinking as they compare and contrast the content and structures of various texts and other sources. We've found it to be important to introduce or review this concept with our ELL students since some have not learned it previously, and we think the easiest way to do this is through using photos and Venn diagrams.

We have typically found two photos that have a lot of similarities, along with some significant differences (see the Tech Tools box for how to easily find many examples). Then, along with providing lists of appropriate words to use (searching the Internet for "Compare and Contrast words" will bring you many printable examples), students can write a scaffolded essay. Again, of course, it's essential that a teacher model comes first.

After doing this with teacher-supplied images, having students take their own pictures and use them is an engaging next step.

What Is This Animal Thinking?

This activity fits under the last anchor standard for writing, which is sort of a grab bag saying students should have experience writing all sorts of things for all sorts of purposes. Obviously, not all writing done in a class is going to fit exactly under the umbrella of argument, informative/explanatory, or narrative, and there are lots of simple learning activities that can still provide effective language-learning opportunities to ELLs that lay outside these three "boxes." "What Is This Animal Thinking?" is one of these kinds of lessons, and we've found it to be particularly engaging and motivating for students to write.

It could be as simple as putting an image of an animal in an awkward (but safe) situation and asking students to write what they think the animal might be thinking, along with why he or she is thinking it (as always, teacher models are essential). Showing paintings and having students write what they believe characters in them are thinking is another option. To take it a step further, there are plenty of animal videos online that students could "dub" with their own dialogue, and plenty of examples to see as models. See the next Tech Tools box for online resources to help with all these activities.

We have found some ways to make this activity even more challenging. For example, the organization "Nature Is Speaking" (http://natureisspeaking.org/) has many videos of well-known actors and actresses "speaking" as endangered parts of our environment, like coral reefs and rainforests—as if they could talk and share their thoughts and feelings. We've had students use them as models for creating their own similar videos speaking as an endangered animal after conducting research.

Tech Tools
Online Resources to Support Using Visuals in Writing

There are a great number of free online resources to support using visuals in teaching and learning writing. They include:

The Best Ways to Use Photos in Lessons (http://larryferlazzo.edublogs.org/2010/ 06/27/the-best-ways-to-use-photos-in-lessons/), which shares many additional instructional ideas for teaching ELLs, apart from the four we talked about in the Using Visuals section.

The Best Resources for Teaching/Learning about How to Write Compare/Contrast Essays (http://larryferlazzo.edublogs.org/2015/08/01/the-best-resources-for-teachinglearning-about-how-to-write-comparecontrast-essays/), which provides many images and ideas on how to introduce this concept to ELLs.

The Best Resources for Using "If This Animal or Image Could Talk" Lesson Idea in Class (http://larryferlazzo.edublogs.org/2015/08/01/the-best-resources-on-using-if-this-animal-or-image-could-talk-lesson-idea-in-class/), which contains many useful images and writing prompts to support this kind of exercise.

We discuss the Picture Word Inductive Model in the last chapter as a strategy to develop reading skills for Beginning ELLs. For ideas on how to expand its use for writing, visit the Best Ways to Modify the Picture Word Inductive Model for ELLs (http://larryferlazzo.edublogs.org/2013/11/07/the-best-ways-to-modify-the-picture-word-inductive-model-for-ells/).

TECHNOLOGY

The use of technology is explicitly highlighted throughout the Common Core Standards, including the writing strand. Of course, even when the words "technology" or "digital" aren't included in specific standards, tech can still be used to help students meet them, as we show throughout this book with our "Tech Tools" feature.

We should point out that the following anchor standard appears to give equal weight to both producing writing *and* interacting and collaborating with others:

- *Use technology, including the Internet, to produce and publish writing and to interact and collaborate with others.*

However, as students enter high school, there appears to be a subtle, though significant, shift in the language explaining how that anchor standard should be applied: the word "and" (which sometimes is replaced with the term "as well as" in pre–high school standards) is changed to an "or".

- *Use technology, including the Internet, to produce, publish, and update individual or shared writing products, taking advantage of technology's capacity to link to other information and to display information flexibly and dynamically.*[31]

- *Use technology, including the Internet, to produce, publish, and update individual or shared writing products in response to ongoing feedback, including new arguments or information.*[32]

We point this out not to denigrate the many positive opportunities available for online collaboration. Instead, we're making this distinction because online student collaboration might not always be logistically possible. In other words, if you are a high school teacher, yes, it is important for your students to write online. Since we're big believers in the benefits of student collaboration, especially for ELLs, it is also important to create many opportunities for collaboration. If some of the online tools we present here work for you to make that happen, please go for it! But, if your school has technology limitations as ours does, and you can't always provide access to online collaboration or if your students have limited access to technology at home, feel secure in the knowledge that you will not be the recipient of a thunderbolt from the Common Core Gods.

Extensive research finds that, when students write using technology (especially in secondary grades), they will write more, write better, and be more willing to make revisions to their text.[33,34] ELLs benefit from the same ease in writing and revision that computers offer non-ELLs, plus they can particularly benefit from learning through the "automatic" spell and grammar check offered in most word-processing programs, as well as the ability to quickly learn the meaning and pronunciation of new words. At the same time, we all need to caution our ELL students not to write their entire piece in their native language and then simply use Google Translate to turn it into English.

The next Tech Tools box will share *many* resources for using technology in writing instruction in the context of the Common Core. In addition, we'd like to highlight two specific technology activities we use with our ELLs to help them improve their writing and meet the Common Core Standards.

Writing for an "Authentic Audience." As we discussed in the Revision section, we have found that many students are more motivated when they are writing for an audience other than the teacher and classmates, and research bears that out.[35,36] We have applied this research successfully in two ways.

One, by having students take advantage of the huge number of online sites where they can engage a global audience by writing book reviews, commentaries on current events, and even create their own virtual books for children. Many of these sites are designed specifically for students to safely interact. For example, the *New York Times* Learning Network hosts a system where editors regularly ask questions and students respond (in fact, Larry writes a weekly post for *The Times* specifically designed for ELL students). A list of these "authentic audience" sites that we have curated can be found in the Tech Tools box.

Another strategy we have used is developing "sister class" relationships around the world, often with classes of students who are also learning English. We have generally kept these projects simple—each class studies the other's country and compiles questions, and then students from both classes write and videotape responses. There are many ways that teachers can connect with other classes to do these kinds of projects and ones that are more extensive. The Tech Tools box shares links where you can see many examples of projects from our ELD classes and free sites to learn about similarly minded classes throughout the world.

Interacting on Class Blogs. Online journals called blogs can be invaluable classroom tools. Though many teachers have students create their own individual blogs, we have found it easier to create one class blog where we list assignments and instructions, and then have students write and reply to each other in the comment sections. This kind of interaction can function as a high-tech version of the peer-editing activity discussed earlier, a forum where teachers and students ask and answer questions from each other, and even a place where parents can also be invited to participate.

If you are more ambitious than we are, you can also have students create their own blogs. There are even educator networks set up to get people from outside of your school to leave comments for your students so that an authentic audience can be generated. See the Tech Tools box for details.

Tech Tools
Resources for Using Technology to Support Student Writing

We referred to many online resources in the "Technology" section. Here they are:

The Best Places Where Students Can Write for an Authentic Audience (http://larry ferlazzo.edublogs.org/2009/04/01/the-best-places-where-students-can-write-for-an-authentic-audience/) contains links to sites where students can write book reviews, comments on current events, and so forth.

The Best Ways to Find Other Classes for Joint Online Projects (http://larryferlazzo .edublogs.org/2009/05/30/the-best-ways-to-find-other-classes-for-joint-online-projects/) provides links to many groups coordinating classes who want to connect with others around the world.

Links to the Joint Projects My ELL Geography Class Did with Classes around the World—Want to Join Us This Year? (http://larryferlazzo.edublogs.org/2015/08/ 01/links-to-the-joint-projects-my-ell-geography-class-did-with-classes-around-the-world-want-to-join-us-this-year/) shares examples of the different projects Larry's students have done with "sister classes."

Here are three links that will lead you to many resources about blogging, including links to Larry's class blogs:

The Best Sources for Advice on Student Blogging (http://larryferlazzo.edublogs.org/ 2008/12/26/the-best-sources-for-advice-on-student-blogging/)

Resources from All My Blogs (http://larryferlazzo.edublogs.org/2015/05/02/ resources-from-all-my-blogs-6/)

The Best Sources of Advice for Teachers (and Others!) on How to Be Better Bloggers (http://larryferlazzo.edublogs.org/2009/06/03/the-best-sources-of-advice-for-teachers-and-others-on-how-to-be-better-bloggers/)

Last, there are legal issues related to student privacy when they post their material online. They can be easily handled through conversations with, and signatures from, parents, and you can learn how at the Best Teacher Resources for Online Student Safety and Legal Issues (http://larryferlazzo.edublogs.org/2009/08/10/the-best-teacher-resources-for-online-student-safety-legal-issues/).

There are a number of online resources that support Common Core that we did *not* refer to in the previous section. Nevertheless, they could be very useful to teachers and students alike:

Three elements that are highlighted in the Common Core are research, the ability to evaluate the credibility of online and other sources, and plagiarism. There is not enough space for us to write at length about how we teach about those areas (though we talk more about research in the "Project-Based Learning" section). However, we can provide collections of sites accessible to ELLs that we use to reinforce what we do in the classroom on those issues:

The Best Resources for Learning Research and Citation Skills (http://larryferlazzo.edublogs.org/2009/09/24/the-best-resources-for-learning-research-citation-skills/)

The Best Online Resources to Teach about Plagiarism (http://larryferlazzo.edublogs.org/2009/09/21/the-best-online-resources-to-teach-about-plagiarism/)

The Best Tools for Teaching Information Literacy (http://larryferlazzo.edublogs.org/2015/07/28/the-best-tools-lessons-for-teaching-information-literacy-help-me-find-more/)

Here are three other resource lists that teachers and students can use to help meet Common Core's technology standards:

The Best Places Where Students Can Write Online (http://larryferlazzo.edublogs.org/2008/10/19/the-best-places-where-students-can-write-online/)

The Best Online Tools for Real-Time Collaboration (http://larryferlazzo.edublogs.org/2008/03/02/the-best-online-tools-for-real-time-collaboration/)

The Best Online Tools for Collaboration—*Not* in Real Time (http://larryferlazzo.edublogs.org/2008/04/10/the-best-online-tools-for-collaboration-not-in-real-time/)

GRAMMAR

Grammar obviously is a key component of writing. However, the Common Core Standards list it under "language," so we'll be covering grammatical concepts in Chapter 6 on language. Of course, as we've mentioned several times, most lessons that are taught in class incorporate elements of all four Common Core domains.

INDUCTIVE LEARNING

In both Chapters 2 and 3 we discuss the value of inductive learning, where students seek patterns and create rules as they categorize a series of examples, as opposed to deductive learning, where students are provided with concepts or rules and then asked to apply them. As we state in Chapter 2, this method of instruction is especially valuable for ELLs. Research suggests that learning a second language is directly linked to a person's ability to discern patterns[37] and that concepts learned through pattern identification are more easily transferable to new situations by students than knowledge learned in other ways.[38]

Teaching inductively can be especially effective in helping ELLs meet the Common Core Standards for writing. Our last book contains many examples of inductive learning through the use of text data sets,[39] and Chapters 2, 3, and 8 in this book contain examples of them.

We often use inductive learning to help our students do research and write about it, both of which are highlighted in the Common Core Standards. We employ the following steps to help students use the inductive process to develop research essays (adapted from our work with Kelly Young at Pebble Creek Literacy). For each step below, we also list an example of what it looks like in a unit that we teach to our Intermediate/Advanced students on Nelson Mandela. However, the following process could be used with any thematic or topic-based unit.

Here are the steps for using the inductive process to produce research writing:

1. Students first read multiple examples of text—called text data sets—which can consist of words, sentences, short passages of text, images, and so forth and make annotations and/or highlight new or important information.

   Example: Students read a data set organized into 25 numbered short paragraphs containing information about Nelson Mandela and South Africa.

2. Students reread the data set to categorize the examples based on the patterns, concepts, or rules they identify as they study them.

   Example: Students begin to look for patterns in the Mandela data set such as grouping the examples that provide information on Mandela's childhood into a category named "Childhood." Other categories include "Young Adulthood," "Prison," "Apartheid," and "Legacy."

3. Students then provide evidence to support why they have placed examples in certain categories.

   Example: Students choose one of the categories and write an explanation of their thinking using sentence frames such as "I put number _____ in this category because_____" or they can highlight the clue words that provide evidence for their category choice.

4. Students summarize the key information they've learned about each category by writing a paragraph about each, creating a list of bullet points for each, drawing a visual representation, and so forth.

   Example: Students create a poster that contains the name of each category in the Mandela data set. Underneath each category they list three to five key ideas along with a drawing that represents those ideas.

5. Students have now read the data set multiple times, resulting in a deeper understanding of the categories. The teacher asks students, either individually or as a class, to generate questions of further interest for each category.

   Example: Students reread the information on each category they created in Step 4 and write questions they are still wondering about in each category. For example, after reading the key information in the Prison category, a student wanted to know what happened to Mandela's children while he was in prison.

6. Students use the questions to guide them as they do further research online, using other texts provided by the teacher, from viewing videos, and so forth. Students use a graphic organizer to capture the answers to their questions, along with other new information for each category.

   Example: Students bring their Mandela questions to the computer lab and look for answers online, along with seeking other new information for each category. (A quick review of "credible" versus "noncredible" online sources may be necessary. See the previous Tech Tools Box for information literacy resources).

7. Students then take their original category notes along with the new information and write a paragraph with a topic sentence and supporting details and examples for each category.

   Example: Students write paragraphs on five or six categories from the Mandela data set. Each paragraph contains a topic sentence and supporting details from the data set and their online research.

8. Students convert their paragraphs into an essay by adding an introduction, transitions, and a conclusion. The teacher can model how to do this on the overhead and can provide sentence frames for less-advanced ELLs.

Example: Students use their category writing to produce a research-based informative essay on Nelson Mandela.

We encourage our students to use this process in other classes when they are asked to write research papers. Even if they don't have text examples to work with, they can still come up with categories to research and then follow a similar process to develop their writing.

In our experience, using the inductive process to support students as they write other types of essays can also be effective. In our first book, we shared an inductive lesson plan focusing on problem-solution writing. As part of this lesson, students were given the Problem Solution Features Data Set (Exhibit 4.6). After reading and annotating the data set, students worked to figure out the categories: Hooks, Thesis, Causes, Effects, Solutions (with the teacher having the option of giving the categories to less-advanced students). From there, students were asked to work in pairs to develop a list of common characteristics and language features for each category. This activity could be extended to include students reading models of problem-solution texts and adding examples from these model texts to their original categories.

EXHIBIT 4.6. Problem/Solution Features Data Set

1. Childhood obesity is a widespread problem that needs to be addressed immediately.

2. One of the main causes of childhood obesity is lack of healthy food choices.

3. When I've taken students on field trips, I've been amazed at all the junk food they eat. I once saw a student eat three whole bags of potato chips in one hour.

4. A real solution to the growing problem of childhood obesity is to motivate students to exercise and to eat healthy by participating in contests at school.

5. Another cause of childhood obesity is that children don't spend enough time outdoors getting exercise.

6. Another solution to childhood obesity is to serve only fresh, healthy foods at school.

7. Imagine if schools offered only fresh fruits and vegetables and other healthy foods to students. What would be the effect? Would the problem of childhood obesity be reduced?

8. In my opinion, childhood obesity is a growing problem that must be stopped.

9. My friend Juan eats fast food everyday on his way to school, and when he goes home he drinks a soda and eats a bag of Cheetos. He is always complaining that he is tired and doesn't feel like doing anything. Do you know anyone like this?

10. Childhood obesity can affect how children perform in school. If they are eating unhealthy foods and are overweight, then they may have less energy for their schoolwork.

11. Have children stopped eating healthy foods? Does junk food really taste better than fresh fruit? Is it easier to buy junk food?

12. A big problem facing my community is childhood obesity, and something must be done.

13. Childhood obesity can result in devastating health effects like diabetes or heart disease.

14. I believe the biggest problem facing my community is childhood obesity.

15. Childhood obesity is also caused by parents who model unhealthy eating habits for their children.

16. In order to reduce childhood obesity rates, we must educate both children and parents about the dangerous effects of being obese.

17. One effect of being overweight as a child is low self-esteem.

CATEGORIZED: HOOKS, THESIS, CAUSES, EFFECTS, SOLUTIONS (NOTE: THIS PAGE SHOULD NOT BE REPRODUCED FOR STUDENT USE.)

Hooks

3. When I've taken students on field trips, I've been amazed at all the junk food they eat. I once saw a student eat three whole bags of potato chips in one hour.

7. Imagine if schools served only fresh fruits and vegetables and other healthy foods to students. What would be the effect? Would the problem of childhood obesity be reduced?

9. My friend Juan eats fast food everyday on his way to school, and when he goes home he drinks a soda and eats a bag of Cheetos. He is always complaining that he is tired and doesn't feel like doing anything. Do you know anyone like this?

11. Have children stopped eating healthy foods? Does junk food really taste better than fresh fruit? Is it easier to buy junk food?

Thesis

8. In my opinion, childhood obesity is a growing problem that must be stopped.

1. Childhood obesity is a widespread problem that needs to be addressed immediately.

12. A big problem facing my community is childhood obesity, and something must be done.

14. I believe the biggest problem facing my community is childhood obesity.

Causes

2. One of the main causes of childhood obesity is lack of healthy food choices.

5. Another cause of childhood obesity is that children don't spend enough time outdoors getting exercise.

15. Childhood obesity is also caused by parents who model unhealthy eating habits for their children.

Effects

13. Childhood obesity can result in devastating health effects like diabetes or heart disease.

17. One effect of being overweight as a child is low self-esteem.

10. Childhood obesity can affect how children perform in school. If they are eating unhealthy foods and are overweight, then they may have less energy for their schoolwork.

Solutions

16. In order to reduce childhood obesity rates, we must educate both children and parents about the dangerous effects of being obese.

6. Another solution to childhood obesity is to serve only fresh, healthy foods at school.

4. A real solution to the growing problem of childhood obesity is to motivate students to exercise and to eat healthy by participating in contests at school.

Source: Originally appeared in *The ESL/ELL Teacher's Survival Guide* by Larry Ferlazzo and Katie Hull Sypnieski (San Francisco, CA: Jossey-Bass, 2012). This material is reproduced with permission of John Wiley & Sons, Inc.

We have used similar inductive lessons to scaffold other types of writing. We support students' argument writing by giving students a data set where they must identify claims and distinguish between different types of evidence. To build students' narrative writing skills we've used a data set containing examples of different narrative strategies such as dialogue, use of imagery, and point of view.

We have also used data sets to teach features of writing such as effective introductions. An example of a data set from our first book[40] that could be used to teach effective openings is the Types of Hooks Data Set. It features examples of different attention grabbers or "hooks" and contains the following categories: Critical Thinking Questions, Anecdotes and Observations, and Interesting Facts and Statistics.

The Punctuation Data Set (Exhibit 4.7) comes from an inductive lesson plan in Larry's book *Self-Driven Learning*[41] and is an example of using the inductive process to reinforce writing conventions. In this lesson, students are given the data set to read and have to come up with the categories of different punctuation marks (Question Mark, Period, Quotation Marks, etc.). They must show evidence of their thinking by highlighting the clues in each example they are using to justify their choices. Students then work in pairs to write a sentence for each category explaining the rule that governs its use. Finally, students come up with their own example sentences for each category that demonstrates the rule.

Another form of inductive learning we use with ELLs to improve their writing is known as *concept attainment*, or the use of examples and nonexamples. This strategy, originally developed by Jerome Bruner and his colleagues (http://jan.ucc .nau.edu/lsn/educator/edtech/learningtheorieswebsite/bruner.htm), involves the

EXHIBIT 4.7. Punctuation Data Set

1. The sky is so beautiful!

2. Lorena likes to sing.

3. "Please give me money," said Sia.

4. Marco has candy, a pencil, and books in his backpack.

5. Marco yelled, "Goal!"

6. How are you?

7. January, February, March, and April are months of the year.

8. "Please give me candy!" cried Hiram.

9. Did the car turn right or left?

10. Abi said, "You are the best teacher in the world."

11. Eduar kicked the soccer ball, ran to the goal, and fell down.

12. "I got an A on the test," said Francisco.

13. Is Mr. Ferlazzo handsome or ugly?

14. Mr. Ferlazzo went to the cabinet, got candy, and threw it to the students.

15. Duy is silly.

16. "I love this class!" yelled Ma.

17. Sunday, Monday, Tuesday, Wednesday, Thursday, Friday, and Saturday are the days of the week.

Source: Originally appeared in *Self-Driven Learning* by Larry Ferlazzo (New York, NY: Routledge, 2013). Reprinted with permission.

teacher identifying both "good"/"yes" and "bad"/"no" examples of the intended learning objective. As the teacher shares the "yes" and "no" examples with students, they are encouraged to develop the reasoning that supports why an example is a "yes" or a "no." This inductive learning strategy is a great way to teach multiple elements of writing including sentence structure, grammar, development, and organization. Recent research shows that when students studied examples of both well-written and poorly written texts, as opposed to just studying well-written examples, they produced higher-quality writing of their own, understood the assessment criteria for the writing on a deeper level, and were able to better assess their own writing and identify areas for improvement.[42]

We have found concept attainment works especially well to teach elements of argumentation to our ELLs. We use this process (showing "yes" and "no" examples and asking students to determine what makes them a "yes" or a "no") to help students write better claims and evidence. The teacher can do two separate concept attainment lessons—one on claims and one on evidence—where students study both good and bad examples of each and discover the characteristics of each. They use this understanding to later produce "good" examples of their own. The Concept Attainment Mini-Lesson on Claims and Evidence at the end of this chapter contains a detailed explanation of how this instructional strategy is applied to teaching argument. Chapter 6 also contains examples of using concept attainment with ELLs to teach grammar.

PROJECT-BASED LEARNING AND RESEARCH STRATEGIES

"Research" has its own section in the Common Core for writing, and includes three separate anchor standards. The end product of much of this research can lead to straightforward argument, informative/explanatory, and narrative essays, and we've discussed some ways to apply that process in previous sections.

Another instructional strategy that has been gaining popularity (http://edsource .org/2015/project-based-learning-on-the-rise-under-the-common-core/78851) in schools across the United States is called project-based learning (PBL). A variation is called problem-based learning and, though there are some differences, both (though not always) share many attributes—a challenge or "driving question" around an engaging topic; small groups researching to find evidence on which they will base their answers; a final "product" (essay, PowerPoint presentation, video, etc.) sharing their conclusions; and a culminating presentation.

A PBL assignment can take anywhere from a few days to a few weeks. Interestingly, even though the Standards themselves call for "short as well as more sustained research projects," the Standards' guidelines to publishers appear to emphasize shorter ones.[43]

ELLs can thrive in a well-structured PBL environment and, by well-structured, we mean one that has a high-interest topic; strategically balanced groups (containing students with mixed-English and academic experience); and with scaffolds in place, including clear guidelines for collaboration (as opposed to cooperation, which we discussed earlier). Our collaboration guidelines usually include allocating specific time for students who might be working on individual components of the overall project to bring their drafts to the entire group for critical, though supportive, feedback—more than one time and certainly well in advance of the final deadline.

Our project-based learning assignments with ELLs have included:

- Focusing on the question "What is a 'good' neighborhood?" Students first identify what criteria is most important in the kind of neighborhood where they would like to live. Then students tour (either by field trip or by projecting Google street view for the class) both their neighborhood and the richest neighborhood in town and rate them using a checklist of their criteria. After conducting and analyzing this research, they write an argument essay declaring which neighborhood they believe is better and why. Typically, at least 90% of our students choose their neighborhood because it meets many of the criteria they have decided are important to them, like accessibility to public transit, the availability of stores that sell ethnic food, and affordable housing that allows family members to live near each other. This lesson applies our perspective of looking at our students and families through the lens of assets instead of deficits. Sharing essays on our class blog for feedback from classmates is then followed by a group project where students design and present their "ideal" neighborhood. You can read the complete lesson plan in Larry's book, *Helping Students Motivate Themselves*.[44]

- Ending each school year with an inquiry project where self-selected student groups identify topics and driving questions of their choice (subject to teacher approval). Students create materials that reflect the most common literacy strategies we use during the year—text data sets, Read Alouds, clozes, sequencing activities where text is "cut up" and students have to reorder it in the correct sequence while explaining their reasoning[45]—that they will then use to teach another small group about their topic and question. You can read the complete lesson plan for this activity in Larry's book, *Helping Students Motivate Themselves*.[46] This kind of very open project-based learning activity has also been called "Genius Hour," and you can find related resources in the next Tech Tools box, along with other PBL links.

- Chapter 2 discusses evidence-based "what if?" history projects. We've also used a slightly modified question (we deleted the word "science," which was originally located immediately before the word "knowledge" in the first line of the prompt below) that was originally posed by *Science* magazine for a contest[47] for another "what if?" project:

You can travel back in time to share one piece of knowledge from today. Where do you go? Describe the date and place you choose, the information you share, and how it might change the course of history. (Assume that the people you visit will understand and believe you!)

This section is just the tip of the iceberg of project-based learning. Many more excellent resources can be found through the links in the Tech Tools box.

Tech Tools
Online Resources to Support Project-Based Learning

Here are three useful project-based learning resources:

Q&A Collections: Project-Based Learning (http://blogs.edweek.org/teachers/ classroom_qa_with_larry_ferlazzo/2015/08/q_a_collections_project-based_ learning.html) is a collection of Larry's Education Week Teacher columns that include contributions from the leading PBL experts in the world providing advice to teachers.

The Best Resources for Applying "Fed Ex Days" (also known as "Genius Hours") to Schools (http://larryferlazzo.edublogs.org/2012/05/28/the-best-resources-for-applying-fed-ex-days-to-schools/) provides links to examples of more flexible PBL activities that we and other teachers have done in schools.

The Best Sites for Cooperative Learning Ideas (http://larryferlazzo.edublogs.org/ 2010/04/02/the-best-sites-for-cooperative-learning-ideas/) contains a lot (and we mean a lot) of more detailed PBL resources.

Lesson Plans

The following three lessons demonstrate how to scaffold argument writing for Beginning, Intermediate, and Advanced ELLs.

MINI-LESSON ON ARGUMENT WRITING FOR EARLY BEGINNERS

One way to fit problem/solution writing into the Common Core Standards' argument category is by ensuring that students conclude their written pieces by choosing one of their possible solutions as the "best" one and supporting it with evidence.

When working with Beginners, teachers can use a process originally developed by Brazilian educator Paulo Freire and modified by the Peace Corps.[48] This process is designed to connect the challenges that students face in their lives outside of school with language and literacy instruction.

We discussed this "critical pedagogy" instructional strategy in our last book[49] and have since changed it—and made it better—by more solidly corresponding the lesson plan to the Common Core Standards. Our revised description of this mini-lesson originally appeared in *ASCD Educational Leadership*, and is appearing here in modified form with permission.[50] Though this particular lesson plan uses a short video clip to introduce the problem of hunger, the lesson sequence can be used for any problem within the experience of students and can also be opened with an image or a short accessible text illustrating that problem.

In fact, to make the lesson even more student-centered, we've often had students identify problems they'd like to study and contribute photos, text, or video clips that they've found to illustrate them.

CONCEPT ATTAINMENT MINI-LESSON ON CLAIMS AND EVIDENCE

This lesson is designed to be used with Intermediate through Advanced students, but could easily be modified for Beginners by simplifying the examples used in the figures. It demonstrates the inductive learning strategy of concept attainment, which we described in the section on Inductive earlier in this chapter. Elements of this lesson originally appeared in *ASCD Educational Leadership* and appear here in a modified, more detailed form with permission.[51] For this mini-lesson we chose a hot topic facing our school—whether to allow the use of smartphones as a resource in class. However, teachers could use any issue of interest to students when following the process outlined in this lesson. For another engaging way to introduce or reinforce the concepts of effective claims and evidence see the lesson plan at the end of Chapter 5. Also see the lesson plan at the end of Chapter 6, which demonstrates how to use concept attainment to teach grammar.

ARGUMENT WRITING LESSON PLAN FOR HIGH INTERMEDIATE/ADVANCED STUDENTS

The Argument Writing Lesson Plan is designed for High Intermediate/Advanced ELL students and is the second of a two-part lesson sequence. The first part of this lesson features a close reading of a text and can be found at the end of Chapter 3. This lesson focuses on how to scaffold student argument writing as they respond to a prompt based on the text used in Part One of the lesson sequence. Again, we have used both lessons as culminating activities after teaching the Social and Emotional Learning (SEL) lessons on growth mindset, self-control, and grit in Chapter 2, but teachers could use this two-part lesson sequence with a different text and related prompt of their choosing. This lesson also assumes that students have had some practice with writing claims and evidence. If your students need more practice with this, then doing the Mini-Lesson on Claims and Evidence prior to this lesson is a good option. In addition, the Mini-Lesson On Speaking and Argument in Chapter 5 can also be used.

The writing prompt in this lesson sequence requires students to go back to the text they studied during the close-reading lesson, summarize the author's claims, develop their own position in relation to the author's ideas, and support it with evidence. This format—reading an argument posed by someone else and responding by developing your own—is found throughout academic writing. Specifically, it is used on college placement tests (such as the ones in our state for the California State University and University of California systems), on the writing sections of the SAT and ACT, and on the Common Core writing assessments from Smarter Balanced. In addition, as Common Core itself points out, this ability is critical for students to be able to apply to their everyday lives because of our "information-rich society."[52] Providing ELLs with the strategies they need to join this type of academic discourse—being able to read, listen to, summarize, and evaluate the arguments of others and respond with their own well-supported arguments—is critical to their growth in English and as members of a global society.

Mini-Lesson on Argument Writing for Early Beginners

1. The teacher begins by having students create a word chart of problem/solution academic vocabulary, including such words as *problem, cause, effect, solution, evidence,* and *reason.* Students are instructed to translate these words into their home languages, illustrate their definitions, and make a list of common English synonyms.

2. Students are then shown a short video clip of the first scene in the film *Les Misérables*[53] in which the main character is arrested for stealing bread to feed his sister's hungry family. The English subtitles will reinforce the dialogue that the students are hearing.

3. Students are then asked to describe what they saw and are given small whiteboards where they can write their responses. They might write comments such as "in old city," "the man broke window," "he took food," "man run," and "police." The teacher should make a list of these responses for all students to view.

4. Next, the teacher will ask students to share what problem they thought the clip portrayed. The teacher can model this concept in various ways—for example, by saying, and adding the appropriate sound effects, "My stomach is growling. What is the problem?" Students then use the sentence starter, "The problem

is . . ." to write out their responses ("the family is hungry"). All student white-board responses are again copied by the teacher and displayed on the board.

5. The teacher then asks students to identify, among those phrases they initially used to describe what they saw, evidence that this was indeed the problem. The teacher might use as an example how the comment "in old city" didn't show evidence of the family being hungry, whereas "he took food" did. Student whiteboard responses are then shared again and copied on the front board or overhead.

6. The teacher then asks students what they thought *caused* the problem, using the sentence starter, "The problem is caused by . . ." The teacher might need to model the meaning of the word "cause" (even though it was pretaught at the beginning of the lesson) by saying he is tired and explaining that his exhaustion is caused by not getting enough sleep. Students might write such comments as "man not have job" and "the rich people don't help the poor people." Whiteboards are used to share responses and the teacher copies the answers in front.

7. Next, the teacher asks students what they thought were the *effects* of the problem. Again, the teacher might need to model the meaning of the word "effect" by playacting falling asleep at his desk to continue the lack of sleep example (humor is always a welcome lesson addition). Using the sentence starters, "One effect is . . ." and "A second effect is . . . ," students might write such responses as "the family gets sick" and "they die."

8. The teacher then asks students if they, their family members, or their friends have ever experienced a similar problem (or if they have seen or read about others experiencing it). Some might respond, "We know poor people in my country," "I see poor people," "I poor," or "I saw hungry people on TV."

9. The teacher then asks students to write down their solutions—how they responded to that problem or how they saw others respond to it—by drawing an illustration and/or using the sentence frame, "I (we, they) solved the problem by . . . ." One student might respond by writing, "I see a family poor in my country, and I help with food, money, and more." Students share their answers on the whiteboards while the teacher writes them down on the overhead.

10. The teacher next encourages students to talk about other ideas for how to respond, using the sentence starter, "One solution is . . ." Students might say, "give them jobs," "get help from government," and "ask people for help." Depending on the English level of students, they could be asked to read "How Can We Solve the Problem of Hunger?" (Exhibit 4.8) at this time and/or the

teacher could read it aloud. Students could make a list of solutions shared in the article and add them to the class list.

Note: In the past, we would have asked students to make a poster that described the problem and solutions both in words and images and then called it a day. However, in light of the Common Core standards, we do the following additional steps.

11. The teacher then reviews the sentences the class had written during the lesson and asks them to combine sentences of their choice into a paragraph. For example:

    The problem is hungry family. *The problem is caused by* man not having job. *One effect is* the family gets sick. *A second effect is* family die. *One solution is* give them jobs. *Another solution is* ask people for help.

12. Finally, the teacher asks students to add one more sentence to their paragraph, which will likely require extensive teacher modeling: "*I think the best solution is __ because __.*" A student might write, "I think the best solution is to learn a new job because he can get money." Students can then turn their paragraph into a poster, type it into a class blog, and/or provide audio narration to it.

EXHIBIT 4.8. "How Can We Solve the Problem of Hunger?"

There are 795 million hungry people in the world (1). Fifty million of them live in the United States (2). There are many ideas about things that can be done to help solve this problem:

- Help hungry people get better education so they can get higher-paying jobs (3).
- Give money to groups to feed hungry people (4).
- Help people grow their own food by giving them land and seeds (5).
- Get the government to give food to hungry people (6).
- Let more people know about the problem of hunger so they give money to help (7).
- Have the government train hungry people for better jobs.

1. https://www.wfp.org/hunger/stats

2. http://nationswell.com/6-ways-to-solve-hunger-in-america/

3. http://www.theguardian.com/global-development/2013/jun/08/eight-ways-solve-world-hunger

4. http://www.wikihow.com/Take-Action-to-End-World-Hunger

5. http://borgenproject.org/10-ways-stop-world-hunger/

6. http://www.bonappetit.com/entertaining-style/trends-news/article/good-food-advocate

---

Concept Attainment Mini-Lesson on Claims and Evidence

1. The teacher explains that today students will be using a strategy to help them improve their argument writing. She explains it is like a puzzle and students will be figuring it out by studying good and bad examples of claims. The good examples are labeled "Yes" and the bad examples are labeled "No." She tells students they will need to take out a piece of paper where they can take notes.

2. The teacher places the Concept Attainment Example: Claims (Exhibit 4.9) on the document camera/overhead. At first, everything is covered with a blank sheet of paper except for the "Yes" and "No" titles. The teacher reminds students to note their thinking on a piece of paper and tells them they will also have a chance to share their notes with a partner at different times throughout the process. She explains that as she uncovers each example, she wants students to identify why certain ones are under "Yes" and others are under "No."

3. The teacher shows students the first "Yes" example. She asks students to write down why they think it is a "Yes." Then she shows the first "No" example and asks students to write why they think it is a "No." After giving them a minute to write, she then uncovers the second "Yes" and "No" examples. She again asks them to write their reasoning and tells them to share their thinking with a partner. She then calls on pairs to share their ideas with the class. Students might say that the "Yes" examples are opinions and the "No" examples are facts. She writes the discoveries students are making on the board.

4. The teacher uncovers the third "Yes" and "No" examples and asks students what they notice about all the "Yes" examples, asking "How are they similar?" She asks students to write their ideas on their papers and then share their thinking with a partner. As she calls on pairs to share out, she writes any further ideas on the board. Students might say that the "Yes" examples are opinions that people can agree or disagree with or they have opinion words like "should" and "must." She then asks students the same question about the "No" examples, "How are

they similar?" Students might say that the "No" examples are just describing facts or how someone feels.

5. The teacher then asks students to review their notes and write a response to the following prompt: "What are the features of a good claim?" After giving students a few minutes to write and share with a partner, she calls on specific students that she has noticed are writing down important features of good claims—such as they are specific, debatable (that is, they have more than one side), and logical/well-reasoned.

6. Students can then practice writing their own "Yes" examples, either about the cell phone topic or a topic of their choice, and share them with a partner or with the class.

7. The teacher can then repeat this same process using the Concept Attainment Example: Evidence (Exhibit 4.10).

EXHIBIT 4.9. Concept Attainment Example: Claims

Yes	No
Smartphones are a valuable and necessary resource for students to use in the classroom.	
	Smartphones are not allowed in many schools.
Schools should not allow students to use cell phones in the classroom because it distracts from the learning process.	
	Many students have phones in their backpacks.
My school district must reconsider its ban on cell phones in the classroom and allow them to be used as learning tools.	
	I hate my math teacher because he always takes my phone away during class.

EXHIBIT 4.10. Concept Attainment Example: Evidence

Yes	No
Studies show that the use of smartphones to conduct research in the classroom can increase learning.	
	My friend likes to use his smartphone in class.
Expert teachers Larry Ferlazzo and Katie Hull state, "Allowing our students to access Google Translate on their cell phones increases their understanding of complex texts."	
	Letting students talk on their cell phones at lunch is a great way to help them have more fun at school.
According to one study, cell phones were not found to increase student learning when used as a student resource in the classroom.	
	What if students don't even have a smartphone?

Argument Writing Lesson Plan for High Intermediate/Advanced Students

Instructional Objectives

Students will:

- Learn how to break down and respond to a writing prompt.
- Write an essay in which they summarize the claims of an author, develop their own claim, and support it with evidence.
- Use peer review strategies to strengthen their writing.

Duration

Five to six 55-minute class periods

Common Core English Language Arts Standards

Reading

1. Read closely to determine what the text says explicitly and to make logical inferences from it; cite specific textual evidence when writing or speaking to support conclusions drawn from the text.
2. Determine central ideas or themes of a text and analyze their development; summarize the key supporting details and ideas.
3. Delineate and evaluate the argument and specific claims in a text, including the validity of the reasoning as well as the relevance and sufficiency of the evidence.

Writing

1. Write arguments to support claims in an analysis of substantive topics or texts using valid reasoning and relevant and sufficient evidence.
2. Produce clear and coherent writing in which the development, organization, and style are appropriate to task, purpose, and audience.
3. Develop and strengthen writing as needed by planning, revising, editing, rewriting, or trying a new approach.
4. Use technology, including the Internet, to produce and publish writing and to interact and collaborate with others.
5. Draw evidence from literary or informational texts to support analysis, reflection, and research.

Speaking and Listening

1. Prepare for and participate effectively in a range of conversations and collaborations with diverse partners, building on others' ideas and expressing their own clearly and persuasively.
2. Adapt speech to a variety of contexts and communicative tasks, demonstrating command of formal English when indicated or appropriate.

Language

1. Demonstrate command of the conventions of standard English grammar and usage when writing or speaking.

2. Demonstrate command of the conventions of standard English capitalization, punctuation, and spelling when writing.

3. Apply knowledge of language to understand how language functions in different contexts, to make effective choices for meaning or style, and to comprehend more fully when reading or listening.

4. Acquire and use accurately a range of general academic and domain-specific words and phrases sufficient for reading, writing, speaking, and listening at the college and career readiness level; demonstrate independence in gathering vocabulary knowledge when encountering an unknown term important to comprehension or expression.

Materials

- Overhead projector or document camera to display the teacher's copies of all figures below.
- Student copies of:

    Exhibits from the lesson sequence Investigating a Text Lesson Plan outlined in Part One at the end of Chapter 3: "'Intelligence Is Not Enough': Making the Case for Social and Emotional Learning in Schools" (Exhibit 3.11), Investigating a Text Note-Taking Sheet (Exhibit 3.12), and the Visual Summary Chart (Exhibit 3.13).

    New exhibits for this lesson: Writing Prompt (Exhibit 4.11), Writing Prompt Idea Organizer (Exhibit 4.12), Counterarguments (Exhibit 4.13), Peer Review Sheet for Argument Writing (Exhibit 4.14).

Procedure

Note: This lesson plan teaches students the process of writing an argument essay. In the high school writing standards, Common Core uses the words "claim," "opposing claim," and "counterclaim" (http://www.corestandards.org/ELA-Literacy/W/ 11–12/). However, in our opinion, the standards do not define these terms as clearly as we would hope to inform our teaching practice. We know that argumentation is a complex process, but we are attempting to make it more accessible for our ELLs and more comprehensible for ourselves as teachers of argument. A search on the internet for elements of argument will find many different terms. In this lesson plan, we use the terms "claim," "opposing argument," and "counterargument," which we have found work best for us and for *all* our students. The bottom line is that as we are teaching these elements, it is less important to focus on what they are called and more important that students learn how to apply them in their essays. We are strong believers in the famous quote of Nobel Prize winner Richard Feynman , who said "I learned very early the difference between knowing the name of something and knowing something" (http://www.haveabit.com/feynman/2).

First Day

1. The teacher asks students to take out their annotated/completed copies of the article "'Intelligence Is Not Enough': Making the Case for Social and Emotional Learning in Schools" (Exhibit 3.11), the Investigating a Text Note-Taking Sheet (Exhibit 3.12), and the Visual Summary Chart (Exhibit 3.13)—these are all located in Part One of this lesson sequence (Investigating a Text Lesson Plan) at the end of Chapter 3.

2. She tells students that they are going to be using what they've learned over the past few days while investigating the text to respond to a writing prompt.

3. The teacher distributes copies of the Writing Prompt (Exhibit 4.11) and asks students to reflect on what they've learned about how to "attack" a prompt—in other words, to figure out what it is asking them to do. The teacher calls on a few students to share their ideas and then leads students through the following process:

    • First, the teacher reads the prompt aloud to students.

    • The teacher reads it again and reminds students to underline any words that are unfamiliar and to use context clues to guess the meaning of the words.

    • The teacher asks students to share their guesses with a partner and then calls on pairs to share with the whole class. She confirms the students' guesses when correct and clarifies the meanings of words as needed. Because students have completed Part One of this lesson, they should be familiar with most of the words in the prompt. They may not know the word "extent" and might correctly guess, based on its context, that it means "how much." The teacher may also need to review that in the context of this prompt, the word "position" is referring to one's argument/claim/opinion.

    • The teacher instructs students to reread the prompt on their own and to circle key words that are repeated more than once and/or are telling them to do something. She also reminds them to write a number next to each place in the prompt where they are being asked to do something (like numbering steps in directions). The teacher circulates to check for understanding. Students will likely place a number 1 either at the very beginning of the prompt or by the phrase "what does the author claim," a number 2 by the phrase "To what extent do you agree," and a number 3 by the phrase "Write an essay which."

4. The teacher distributes the Writing Prompt Idea Organizer (Exhibit 4.12). This organizer adapts ideas from the book *They Say, I Say* by Graff and Birkenstein (2009) and applies them to prompt analysis. The teacher displays her own copy of this sheet on the document camera. She then explains to students that in much of college and career writing they will have to read or listen to someone else's ideas and then respond with their own ideas. She reminds students that while she is giving them this graphic organizer now, sometimes they won't be given one, and will have to make their own. They should pay attention to which features of the graphic organizer are most helpful to them.

5. She asks students to point to the first thing the prompt is asking them to do. Students will likely point to the first sentence of the prompt or may point to the first box (They Say) and the teacher can confirm that students first have to figure out what "They Say" or, in this prompt specifically, what the author claims about social and emotional learning in schools. She tells students they will now review their Visual Summary Chart and Investigating a Text Note-Taking Sheet from the last lesson in order to write some ideas for this first box.

6. As students review their charts and notes and start to write their ideas, the teacher circulates looking for good examples to quickly place under the document camera (after asking for the students' permission). The teacher reminds students that in this article the author makes several claims, but there is a main or overall claim (which can also be called a *thesis statement* or *position*). She writes these terms on the board and reminds students to use their highlighting (in Part One of this lesson, students highlighted the claims in one color and evidence in another) to assist them. She also directs them to look at Step 4 on their Investigating a Text Note-Taking Sheet from Part One of the lesson because they have already written about the author's main claim there.

7. The teacher calls on several students to share what they have written, noting similarities and addressing any differences. She then passes out a sticky note to each student, tells them to write their name on it, and asks them to answer the following question:

   a. What is the author's main claim about social and emotional learning in schools?

   b. How do I feel about the author's claim?

      Note: It is helpful to have sentence frames posted that model how students can respond to the different parts of the prompt. As students write their answers to the above questions, the teacher can direct them to sentence frames such as:

"The author claims _____."

"In the article _____, the author argues _____."

"According to the author, _____."

"In my opinion, _____."

"I think the author's claim is _____."

You can find many more examples by searching "They Say, I Say templates" or "argument writing sentence starters" online.

8. The teacher collects students' responses as their "exit ticket" and later checks that all students have correctly summarized the author's main claim (essentially that schools need to help students apply social and emotional learning skills in the classroom).

Second Day

1. The teacher opens the day's lesson by asking students to share with a partner what they remember from the previous day about the author's main claim and how they feel about it. She calls on a few pairs to share with the class.

2. The teacher asks students to take out their Writing Prompt Idea Organizer (Exhibit 4.12) along with their copy of the article. While displaying her own copy of the "Writing Prompt Idea Organizer" on the document camera, she explains that today students will be focusing on the "I Say" and the "Support to back up what I say" sections of the prompt.

3. The teacher reminds students they've explored their own feelings about the author's main claim in more general ways, but now will be more focused in their thinking. The teacher explains that students will reread the article, paying attention to the "smaller" claims and evidence used by the author to support her "big" or main claim. Students will pause after reading each claim (which is already highlighted in a certain color) and write whether they agree, disagree, or partially agree (maybe they agree with some but not all of the claims and supporting evidence). The teacher models this process for students with the first page—sharing her thinking and opinions (but reminding students it is okay for them to have different opinions).

4. Students read the article and write *agree, disagree,* or *partially agree* in the margin next to the claims and supporting evidence. The teacher circulates offering support as needed. If any students finish early, the teacher can encourage them

to write a few words in the margin about why they agree, disagree, or partially agree for each one.

5. The teacher gives students a minute to silently review their notes and think about some reasons why they agreed, disagreed, or partially agreed with the author's claims. The teacher then divides students into groups of three and tells them they will be "testing out" their ideas before they begin writing by talking with other students. She explains it is similar to trying on different outfits and asking your friends which one looks best. Students will share the claims they agree/disagree/partially agree with and explain why. The teacher can post sentence frames for students to use as they share their opinions such as:

- "I agree that _____ because _____."

- "I disagree with the claim that _____ because _____."

- "I agree with _____, but not with _____ because _____."

   She can also post question starters for students to use as they discuss their ideas such as:

- "Why do you believe that?"

- "Can you tell me more about _____?"

- "Could you please repeat that?"

   The teacher circulates as groups are talking to offer support and check for academic language use.

6. The teacher tells students since they have had a chance to discuss their opinions and hear ideas from others, they are ready to address the second part of the prompt and write what "I Say" (to what extent they agree with the author's claims). The teacher asks students to review with a partner what a strong claim looks like (this assumes that students have had practice examining claims, like in the Concept Attainment Mini-Lesson on Claims and Evidence). Students might say that a strong claim is specific and debatable (someone can agree or disagree with it). The teacher directs students to the second box on their "Writing Prompt Idea Organizer" (Exhibit 4.12), which she has displayed on the document camera, and tells them to write their claim using an "I Say" sentence frame or creating their own sentence. The teacher can model writing a specific, debatable claim and/or share some of the following student examples we've collected:

- "I agree that schools should teach students social and emotional learning skills because if they have these skills they will be able to learn better in the classroom."

- "I disagree that schools should help students learn about social and emotional skills because that is the job of the parents and the teachers should teach only school content."
- "I agree that it is important for schools to teach students how to cooperate, but I don't think that schools can or should teach things like self-control and grit."

7. Once students have written their claims, the teacher directs them to the third box on their Writing Prompt Idea Organizer. She explains that now they will need to find evidence or "Support to back up what I say." She asks students to underline the three places they can get their evidence from (they should underline the phrase "personal experience, observations, or reading, including this article"). She directs students to circle the word "or" and asks what the difference is between having the word "or" instead of the word "and." Students will likely say that it means they don't have to use all three types of evidence, but could use just one or two types. The teacher can explain that while this is true, students want to remember their goal is to support their claims as effectively as possible and that may mean using all three types of evidence. She then explains that she wants students to practice using evidence from at least two different sources and that is why she has added the last line to the prompt.

8. The teacher asks students to reflect on what they know about what effective evidence looks like and share their ideas with a partner . Depending upon if students have already been taught (and reviewed) the Concept Attainment Mini-Lesson on Claims and Evidence, they might say that effective evidence directly supports the claim, doesn't contradict the claim, is based on statistics or other facts, research, an observation, or personal experience that directly relates to the claim. The teacher can remind students that these categories of evidence can be found and used in effective arguments.

    Then, the teacher asks students to make a list of the types of evidence used in the article "Intelligence Is Not Enough" and reminds them to look at the evidence they have already highlighted. After a few minutes, she asks students to share out and records their ideas on the board. They should include: research experiments and studies, use of experts (like Angela Duckworth and Carol Dweck), statistics, and a quotation from a student (personal experience).

9. The teacher instructs students to begin jotting down in the "Support to back up what I say" section of their graphic organizer any evidence they might use to support their claim. They may use evidence they have just identified in the article as well as other evidence from their own experiences and other readings that

support their claim. The teacher circulates and offers assistance to students who may need more direct support.

10. The teacher asks students to turn in their "Writing Prompt Idea Organizer" and reviews them before the next day. She can identify students who may need additional models and instruction and can meet with those students during the warm-up activity the following day.

Third Day

1. The following warm-up prompt is posted for students to write a response to as soon as class begins:

   • What do you think the word counterargument means? Hint: "counter" means "against"

   • Why would it be important to include counterarguments in your essay?

   As students are responding to the prompt, the teacher passes back the Writing Prompt Idea Organizers and checks in with the students whom she identified the previous day as needing additional support.

2. After several minutes of writing time, she asks students to share their ideas with a partner and encourages them to "steal" any ideas they like and add them to their own papers. Students might say a counterargument is people who are against your ideas and that it can be good to say why they are wrong.

3. Then the teacher passes out the Counterarguments sheet (Exhibit 4.13) and, building on the ideas students have already shared, points out that if we want to make our own claim even stronger, we need to imagine what people who disagree with us might say—these are called "opposing arguments" or "counterclaims." Then we must think about how we would respond to these opposing arguments and develop what is called a "counterargument." The teacher can share the following research with students by paraphrasing it or posting the following quote and discussing it: "if we bring up opposing arguments, then shoot them down, not only is the audience more likely to be swayed, we also see a boost in our credibility" (Dean, 2010). She can then model this process of counter argumentation using one of the example student claims from earlier:

   • Claim: "I agree that schools should teach students social and emotional learning skills because if they have these skills they will be able to learn better in the classroom."

   • Opposing argument: "It isn't the responsibility of the school to teach kids these social and emotional learning skills. Parents should teach them."

- Counterargument: "It is correct that parents should teach these skills at home. However, it is even better for students if both schools and parents reinforce these skills."

   Note: We have found it helpful when first introducing the words *claim* or *argument*, *counterclaim* or *opposing argument*, and *counterargument* to use gestures to demonstrate the meanings. One way we've done this is by using a "thumbs up" to represent my claim or argument, using a "thumbs down" to represent opposing arguments, and then using our other hand to turn our "thumbs down" into a "thumbs up" to represent our counterargument.

4. Students work on completing the Counterarguments sheet while the teacher circulates and assists.

5. If there is time left, the teacher can ask students to share their work with one or two other students to check their thinking.

6. The teacher collects the Counterarguments sheets from students as they leave and reviews them before the next day to check for understanding. She also tells them that they will be writing a draft in class the following day using their graphic organizers to assist them.

Fourth–Fifth Day

1. The teacher welcomes students and asks them to take out their Writing Prompt Idea Organizer. She passes back the Counterarguments sheets to each student (she has written feedback on the sheets of students who seemed confused and will check in with them individually as soon as the rest of the class begins writing).

2. The teacher reminds students of all the college-level thinking and writing they have already done in response to this prompt. She also reminds students of the structures they have practiced when writing essays—introduction, body paragraphs, and a conclusion. Now they will be using their graphic organizers to help them as they write a draft of their essay responding to the prompt. The teacher displays the prompt on the document camera, passes out lined paper, and tells students it is time to write their draft and that she is confident that they will do a good job. If the teacher has not done extensive teaching on using quotations and paraphrasing, now would be a good time to do a mini-lesson.

   Note: The teacher may need to address any groaning or complaining with a statement like, "You aren't being graded on writing a perfect draft. I'm grading you on your effort and how you are applying the things you've learned in your writing. Are you going to make mistakes? *Yes!* Is that a good thing? *Yes!* It means you're learning!"

3. Depending on the level and the size of your class, students may need one or two periods to complete their drafts. The teacher can always give students the option of finishing their drafts for homework. If some students finish in class before others, they can start the peer review activity with another student who is finished or they can read their draft to the teacher.

Fifth–Sixth Day

1. Teacher greets students and praises the effort they have shown working on their drafts. She explains that now they will be helping each other improve their writing and thinking. She distributes the Peer Review Sheet for Argument Writing (Exhibit 4.14). Teachers also have the option of using any of the other peer review methods used earlier in this chapter.

2. Students exchange papers with a partner and complete the Peer Review Sheet for Argument Writing. The teacher circulates and occasionally shares examples of helpful student comments that she notices on the Peer Review Sheets by posting them on the document camera. The teacher may also want to have individual conferences with students who may need additional support.

3. As students finish reviewing each other's writing, the teacher encourages them to return to their desks and make any revisions suggested by their partner. The teacher will need to be actively circulating in order to offer additional revision support.

4. The teacher tells students that before they write their final draft, they must read their essay aloud to at least one other student in order to catch any grammatical mistakes or problems with sentence structure.

5. Students either handwrite or type a final version of their essay. The teacher collects the Peer Review Sheets and the student essays.

Assessment

- As we stated in the introduction to this lesson plan, the writing prompt in this lesson plan reflects what many college placement writing exams and college essay assignments look like. The rubric we've used with students comes from the

EAP placement test for the California State University system and can be found online at https://www.calstate.edu/eap/scoring_guides_and_rubrics.shtml or other versions can be found by searching "EAP rubric" online. We think it is important to note that we often modify this type of rubric to fit our students' needs. We tend to use three strands on the rubric most frequently—response to the topic, understanding and use of the passage, and organization, development, and support.

- The teacher can collect and review students' graphic organizers each day to check for understanding and to make any changes in instruction for the following day.

- The teacher can develop a different rubric appropriate for your class situation. Free online resources to both find premade rubrics and create your own can be found at the Best Rubric Sites (And A Beginning Discussion About Their Use) (http://larryferlazzo.edublogs.org/2010/09/18/the-best-rubric-sites-and-a-beginning-discussion-about-their-use/).

Possible Extensions and Modifications

- Teachers can decide to have their students type and post their essays on a class blog. Students can then read and respond to their classmates' writing. See the "Tech Tools: Resources for Using Technology to Support Student Writing" earlier in this chapter for information on setting up and using class blogs.

EXHIBIT 4.11. Writing Prompt

In the article "'Intelligence Is Not Enough': Making the Case for Social and Emotional Learning in Schools" what does the author claim about teaching social and emotional skills in schools? To what extent do you agree with her claims? Write an essay which answers both of these questions and be sure to support your position with evidence from your personal experience, observations, or reading, including this article. You must use evidence from at least two different sources for this essay.

EXHIBIT 4.12. Writing Prompt Idea Organizer

Writing Prompt: In the article "'Intelligence Is Not Enough': Making the Case for Social and Emotional Learning in Schools" what does the author claim about teaching social and emotional skills in schools? To what extent do you agree with her claims? Write an essay which answers both of these questions and be sure to support your position with evidence from your personal experience, observations, or reading including this article. You must use evidence from at least two different sources for this essay.

"They say" — In the article "'Intelligence Is Not Enough': Making the Case for Social and Emotional Learning in Schools" what does the author claim about teaching social and emotional skills in schools?
"I Say" — To what extent do you agree with her claims?
Support to back up what I say — Support your position with evidence from your personal experience, observations, or reading including this article. You must use evidence from at least two different sources for this essay.

Source: Based on the work of Gerald Graff and Cathy Birkenstein *"They Say, I Say: The Moves That Matter in Academic Writing,"* 2009, New York, NY: W.W. Norton & Company.

EXHIBIT 4.13. Counterarguments

You can make your argument essay stronger by thinking about possible arguments against your claim and then (1) stating why these arguments are wrong, or (2) acknowledging that they are true, but your claim is still stronger in some way. This is called "counterargumentation."

Claim = my main point (I Say)

Opposing arguments = reasons why someone might disagree with my claim (They Say)

Counterarguments = why these reasons are wrong or why your claim is stronger (I Say)

Use the sentence frames below to help you develop your thinking and make your argument essay stronger.

My Claim: (write your claim on this line)

_____

Counterarguments:

Some people may argue that_____
_____.

However, _____
_____.

Others may claim _____
_____.

But, I would argue that _____
_____.

EXHIBIT 4.14. Peer Review Sheet for Argument Writing

This sheet should be stapled on top of your essay.

NAME OF WRITER:

NAME OF REVIEWER:

ESSAY CHECKLIST:

1. Does the writer introduce the topic at the beginning of the essay and provide background for the reader?

2. Does the writer summarize what the author claims about social and emotional learning in schools?

   Does the writer include the full title of the article and the author's name?

3. Does the writer state his or her claim (to what extent does he or she agree with the author)?

4. Is the writer's claim specific and debatable?

   If not, what suggestions can you give the writer to improve his/her claim?

5. Does the writer use good evidence to support his/her claim?

   Which paragraphs need more evidence?

6. Does the writer explain how the evidence connects to his/her claim?

   Which paragraphs need more explanation?

7. Does the writer address opposing arguments and provide counterarguments?

8. Does the writer conclude the essay by summarizing his or her claim?

Does the writer explain why this topic is important?

For downloadable versions of the lesson plans and Tech Tools boxes found in this chapter, go to the "Downloads" section of this book's web page at www.wiley.com/go/navccss.

CHAPTER FIVE

Speaking and Listening

You learn to speak by speaking.[1]

—*Francis de Sales*

What Does the Common Core Say about Speaking and Listening?

The Common Core Standards for speaking and listening (Exhibit 5.1) pay equal weight to listening/interactive conversation and to straightforward public speaking. Strangely, even though the title of this section of the Standards is "Speaking and Listening," the Standards themselves are listed in the reverse order. In the first half, there is an emphasis on listening and being able to evaluate the reasoning and evidence of other people's points of view, while at the same time being able to articulate one's own position keeping that criteria in mind (the elements of argument arise again!). In the second half, the Standards want students to acquire the needed skills to make a good presentation, utilize technology appropriately to support their message, and develop good judgment about when it is appropriate and when it might not be necessary to use formal English.

Key Elements of the Speaking and Listening Standards

As described in the summary, the speaking and listening standards are split in half—three under the subtitle of "Comprehension and Collaboration" and three under "Presentation of Knowledge and Ideas." The most important points are not as obvious in this domain as they are in the reading and writing ones, which might

EXHIBIT 5.1. English Language Arts College and Career Readiness Anchor Standards for Speaking and Listening

Comprehension and Collaboration

CCSS.ELA-Literacy.CCRA.SL.1

Prepare for and participate effectively in a range of conversations and collaborations with diverse partners, building on others' ideas and expressing their own clearly and persuasively.

CCSS.ELA-Literacy.CCRA.SL.2

Integrate and evaluate information presented in diverse media and formats, including visually, quantitatively, and orally.

CCSS.ELA-Literacy.CCRA.SL.3

Evaluate a speaker's point of view, reasoning, and use of evidence and rhetoric.

Presentation of Knowledge and Ideas

CCSS.ELA-Literacy.CCRA.SL.4

Present information, findings, and supporting evidence such that listeners can follow the line of reasoning and the organization, development, and style are appropriate to task, purpose, and audience.

CCSS.ELA-Literacy.CCRA.SL.5

Make strategic use of digital media and visual displays of data to express information and enhance understanding of presentations.

CCSS.ELA-Literacy.CCRA.SL.6

Adapt speech to a variety of contexts and communicative tasks, demonstrating command of formal English when indicated or appropriate.

be because they are shorter. Therefore, we'll share a brief analysis of each of the individual speaking and listening anchor standards here.

COMPREHENSION AND COLLABORATION

The Standards emphasize the need to prepare well for academic conversation, which could range from a think-pair-share to reading a lengthy text or doing substantial research on a topic. The first standard makes a particular point often missed in any kind of discussion—that it's important to listen to what others say and build upon it instead of just using the time when others speak as an inconvenient time to wait before you get to talk. During Larry's community organizing career, organizers often referred to this process as one of moving from *opinion* to *judgment*. In other words, the conclusions you reach on your own are an opinion; while the conclusions you reach after listening and discussing with others show judgment.

The second standard focuses on the need to evaluate information presented in multiple media formats (see our resources on Information Literacy in Chapter 4) and being prepared to articulate what was learned from them. Since this standard is in the section focusing on listening and discussing, we assume that the primary purpose of this standard is for use in oral conversation. But it seems to us that a fair assumption can be made that it's also meant for integrating information into presentations (and others have reached the same conclusion[2]).

The third standard is about what educator Dave Stuart Jr. calls "productive skepticism."[3] In other words, being able to apply many of the strategies needed in close reading a text to "close listening" to what someone—another student, a teacher, a public speaker—might be saying. We need to consider what their self-interests might be and evaluate their evidence. We discussed how Common Core distinguishes logical *argument* from more emotional *persuasion* in Chapter 4. Just as the elements of argument are expected in academic and professional writing, the same holds true in academic and professional discussion.

PRESENTATION OF KNOWLEDGE AND IDEAS

It's public speaking time! That's the focus of the Standards in this section, starting with the fourth one in the speaking/listening domain. This standard says that students should have the ability to make an effective and well-organized presentation. It should fulfill the purpose of the assignment, be well reasoned and be done appropriately with the audience in mind.

The fifth standard in the speaking/listening domain (and the second one in this "Presentation" section) simply wants students to be able to use technology to enhance understanding of presentations. This is an important point, and one that we often make to students: Consider how digital media will help an audience understand what you are trying to say, and don't just use it to make your presentation look pretty.

The last standard is a particularly challenging one for ELLs because it says that students need to "adapt" their speech in presentations for a variety of situations and, in particular, says that students need to "[demonstrate] command of formal English when indicated or appropriate." ELLs can certainly develop an understanding of when it's appropriate to use informal and more formal styles of talking and much of the vocabulary for both. However, the idea of demonstrating "command" of formal English is going to be a tough hill to climb for many, if not most. It is important here to say—again—what Common Core states about ELLs: "Teachers should recognize that it is possible to achieve the standards for reading and literature, writing & research, language development and speaking & listening without manifesting native-like control of conventions and vocabulary."[4]

WHAT DOES THIS MEAN FOR SPEAKING AND LISTENING INSTRUCTION IN MY CLASSROOM IN GENERAL?

When we combine all the elements of the speaking and listening strands in the Common Core Standards, then, what might it mean for teachers of ELLs?

We would suggest that it means to:

- Create a classroom environment where students (1) feel safe responding to conversations where they understand the gist but not necessarily all the spoken words *and* (2) don't feel hesitant in asking the meaning of what they consider a key word in order to comprehend a comment.

- Provide sentence-starters for students to use in small group and classroom discussions.

- Provide scaffolds, including graphic organizers and "speaking frames" for classroom presentations.

- Start with short and simple student discussions and presentations and gradually move to longer and more complex ones.

- If at all possible, create opportunities for students to first present in a small group prior to speaking to the entire class. This kind of "rehearsal" can be a confidence booster for ELLs and non-ELLs alike and ultimately result in a much better presentation. No matter how many times teachers will ask students to practice outside of class, some will choose not to do so or may not have access to an audience that can provide helpful feedback.

- Do not assume that students have experience with and are comfortable using technology tools in presentations. Identify the most simple tools available and train students in their use or, if some are already familiar with them, have those students act as peer tutors.

- Use the ELL accessible information literacy resources shared in Chapter 4.

HOW CAN SPEAKING AND LISTENING INSTRUCTION IN MY CLASSROOM SUPPORT ELL STUDENTS IN MEETING COMMON CORE STANDARDS?

Of course, as we've stated before, as teachers we don't keep reading, writing, speaking, listening, and language completely separate from each other in classroom learning activities. Though many of the instructional strategies and lesson plans we've already shared include speaking and listening components, here are some that particularly emphasize that domain and that we have found to be effective with our ELL students.

Class Discussions

Discussions, both in small groups and in ones engaging the entire class, provide key opportunities for assisting ELLs to develop their speaking and active listening skills.

WHAT IS NEEDED TO SET THE STAGE FOR SUCCESSFUL CLASSROOM DISCUSSIONS?

Before we share some specific strategies to accomplish this task in the context of classroom discussions, we'd like to highlight two concepts that we feel are important to be in both the back (and in the front) of teacher's minds when planning these speaking and listening opportunities (and, in fact, probably when planning just about *all* learning activities of any kind):

Classroom Environment: Educator Elizabeth A. City[5] has identified four key factors needed to create an atmosphere that will increase the odds of successful student discussions taking place in the classroom. The first, and most important, is feeling *safe* in sharing ideas and not having to fear being attacked for saying them (or, particularly for ELLs, how they are said). The second is ensuring that the speaking/listening task is not too hard and not too easy—it must provide a just-right *challenge* to as many as possible. *Authentic participation*, according to City, is another factor, one where students are taking the discussion task seriously and responding to each other's ideas. In other words, they are not speaking to hear themselves talk or, on the other end, staying completely silent. Student ownership is the final, and most instructionally difficult factor—where teachers need to create scaffolds/models and provide support in order to be more of the "guide on the side" rather than a "sage on the stage."

"Never Do for Others What They Can Do for Themselves": This is the famous "Iron Rule" developed by legendary organizer Saul Alinsky and one that

Larry learned and applied in his community organizing career. Language researcher Jeff Zwiers has his own term for violating it in the classroom with ELLs—"linguistic enabling," which he describes as happening:

> "when teachers use behaviors that do not push students to reach higher levels of learning and language development."[7]

Scaffolds and support are critical for ELLs, particularly in the context of Common Core. At the same time, we teachers must use our judgment to consider which scaffolds are needed and when. In addition, we need to encourage our students to use their metacognitive abilities to consider these same issues (see the section on metacognition in Chapter 2). And we must have a plan (and/or enlist students in creating one) about when those scaffolds will be taken away because they are no longer necessary.[8] Our students will generally be in social, academic and professional situations where those kinds of scaffolds will not be available, and it's our responsibility to prepare them for those times as best we can, which includes helping them develop their own desire to want to reduce their reliance on these supports.

HOW DO WE SET THE STAGE FOR SUCCESSFUL CLASSROOM DISCUSSIONS?

So, now that we've identified these two prerequisites for healthy classroom discussions—environment and the "Iron Rule"—what are specific actions we can take to ensure they happen in our classrooms?

One learning activity we've used effectively in our ELL classes to help build elements of a positive classroom environment for discussions is a shortened version of the "Are You a Good Listener or Bad Listener?" lesson plan found in Larry's book, *Self-Driven Learning*.[9] First, we tell the students that we are going to have a short lesson on listening. We then ask students to write down three to five things they like and know a lot about, and take a few minutes to jot down as many things as they can think of about those topics. Next, we explain that they are going to work with a partner. Once they go to their partner, one of them is going to talk for a few minutes about the things they wrote down, and their partner is going to show as many examples as they can think of demonstrating how a *bad* listener would act (the teacher should model a funny example). After a few minutes, the teacher tells students to stop, writes "Bad Listener" on the overhead, and invites students to share examples of inappropriate listener behavior (the teacher can make sure the list includes actions like not looking at the speaker, laughing at the speaker, talking to other people instead of paying attention to the speaker, etc.).

Next, the teacher tells students it's time for the other partner to talk but, this time, their partner has to be a *good* listener. Afterwards, the teacher elicits a list of qualities of a good listener (the teacher can make sure the list includes actions like facing the person, looking in their eyes, leaning forward to show interest, asking questions to learn more information, asking for clarification or repetition if the listener didn't understand something, etc.).

Though this activity doesn't touch on *all* the factors needed for a positive classroom environment, it does identify many of them and can be referred to as part of the preparations for any future small or large classroom discussion.

An obvious way to help create more student-centered discussions is to ensure that our ELLs are well-prepared prior to their beginning those conversations—a feeling of competence (in other words, feeling that one has the ability to be successful at accomplishing a task) is a key element of intrinsic motivation.[10] By ensuring that students have had time to read and comprehend a text, think and jot ideas down about a question, and/or practice sentence starters, ELLs' feelings of competence can be strengthened. And when you feel like you know how to do something, you are more likely to want to do it—even when the teacher isn't in your section of the classroom! Another action we've taken to make conversations more student-centered is a strategy we share in the "Introduction to Literal and Interpretive Questions" section found in Chapter 2—we look for opportunities to ask students to lead small discussion groups and help prepare them to facilitate conversations.

The challenge of "linguistic enabling" is real, and one with no easy answers, especially if you want, as we do, to not just have the class be teacher-driven with minimal student "buy-in." One way we address this challenge is by providing a few key sentence frames for students to use prior to discussions instead of a long laundry list. This way, students will be more likely to remember the frames and become more comfortable using them. An even better strategy is to first assign the small group discussion task and then elicit from students which sentence/question starters they think would be most appropriate for that kind of activity. Another way is by giving students a sheet of sentence starters/frames, having students use them for awhile, and then encouraging them to turn the paper upside down so they can't see the frames (but they are still available if needed). An additional strategy we've used to promote independence is by introducing the idea of the "Iron Rule" when students are doing some of the regular goal-setting exercises we discuss in Chapter 2. We encourage students to include a goal of reducing specific scaffolding if and when they feel they can do so.

Now, keeping these factors in mind, here are more specific classroom discussion strategies.

READ/WRITE/THINK-PAIR-SHARE

This classroom staple is one of our favorite instructional strategies for all students, including ELLs. The teacher poses a question, or gives students an assignment related to a reading text, and then tells students they have a few minutes to think and/or write about it. Then, after reminding students about the attributes of a good listener, which, ideally, are listed on the wall following the lesson described earlier in this chapter (and should include guidelines like students facing each other, leaning forward, not being distracted by or talking to other groups, etc.), students can be given a few sentence/question starters (see Exhibit 5.2 in this chapter) or, even better, the class is asked which sentence/question starters they think would be most appropriate to use for that discussion topic. In our experience, no matter how often we have used this process earlier, it always helps to take a short moment to review "ground rules" first. In fact, preparing a couple of students to role-play a discussion now and then in front of the class can also be a great way to model appropriate behavior. Students then break into pairs or groups of three to discuss the topic.

The discussion time can vary between 1 and 10 minutes, depending on the learning task, and students should feel comfortable modifying their answers based on what others say in their group, including feedback on their original thinking/ writing.

Teachers should circulate throughout the room during that time, helping students who need more support, monitoring that the discussion guidelines are being followed, and identifying students who are making comments that the entire class would benefit from hearing at a later time.

GROUP PROJECT ROUND-ROBIN

There are many opportunities to have student groups prepare easel-size posters highlighting key points from a text that is read in class. In Chapter 3, we discuss a "3-2-1" strategy for these kinds of written reports. One to way to emphasize *collaboration* in this kind of group work is to first have students individually identify the three most important points in the text, choose a quotation they liked, draw a visual representation of what they read, and explain how they could apply something they learned from it to another aspect of their lives. Then, they meet in a small group to share their individual work and decide which answers are best to put on their group poster.

Instead of having groups present in front to the entire class, another option is presenting in a "round-robin" or "speed-dating" style (groups facing each other, and when one group is done, every group in one of the lines moves to the next group while the other line remains where they are), using the following specific process for their discussion.

First, we give students a shorter sentence-starter list than the one found in Sentence/Question Starters for Meaningful Conversation in the Classroom (Exhibit 5.2), generally just showing three of the sections (we often use "Clarifying," "Agreeing," and "Disagreeing" questions, though we regularly "switch them up," too).

EXHIBIT 5.2. Sentence/Question Starters for Meaningful Conversation in the Classroom

Stating an Opinion

I think _____ because _____.

I believe _____ because _____.

It seems to me that _____.

Based on my experience, I think _____.

Inviting

What do you think, _____?

I'd be interested in hearing what _____ has to say.

I think we should hear from people who have not spoken yet. What do you think, _____?

We haven't heard from _____ yet.

Clarifying

Could you summarize your position in one sentence?

Is it your position that _____?

To be clear, are you saying that _____?

I'm confused when you say _____. Can you elaborate?

What do you mean by _____?

What makes you think that?

Could you be more specific about _____?

Could you repeat what you said about _____?

Paraphrasing

Put another way, you're saying _____.

So you're saying that _____?

Is it fair to say that you believe _____?

I hear you saying that _____.

In other words, I hear you saying _____.

Agreeing

I agree with _____ because _____.

_____'s point about _____ was important because_____.

The evidence for _____ is overwhelming when you consider that_____.

_____ and I are coming from the same position.

Despite disagreeing about _____, I agree with _____ that _____.

Disagreeing

I see it differently because _____.

The evidence I've seen suggests something different. For example, _____.

Some of that is fact, but some of it is opinion as well. For example, _____.

I agree that _____, but we also have to consider that _____.

We see _____ differently.

That's a good point, but _____.

Building On/Connecting

_____ mentioned that _____.

Yes, and furthermore, I believe _____.

The author's claim that _____ is interesting because _____.

Adding to what _____ said, I think _____.

My answer is similar to _____'s because _____.

Summarizing

Overall, what I'm trying to say is _____.

My whole point in one sentence is _____.

More than anything else, I believe that _____.

Justifying

What is your evidence for that statement?

Why do you believe that?

Can you give me an example?

I think the most convincing reason is _____.

My evidence is _____.

I believe _____ because _____.

One example of _____ is _____.

Source: Reprinted with permission from TeachThought (with a number of modifications and additions). Retrieved from http://www.teachthought.com/learning/sentence-stems-higher-level-conversation-classroom/

Students use them to guide their discussions with each group, with a group "leader" responsible for ensuring that everyone in their group is asking and answering questions. The teacher is the timer, and shows flexibility in both speeding it up and slowing it down depending on how the conversations are going.

These are the steps in the discussion:

1. First minute: each group silently reads and reviews the other group's poster.

2. Second minute: one group asks clarifying questions from the sentence-starter sheet.

3. Third minute: the other group asks clarifying questions from the sheet.

4. Fourth minute: one group uses the agreeing stems.

5. Fifth minute: the other group uses the agreeing stems.

6. Sixth minute: one group uses the disagreeing stems if they do, indeed, disagree with something.

7. Seventh minute: the other group uses the disagreeing stems—again, if they do, indeed, disagree with something.

Students then switch to discuss with another group at least another three or four times. In addition, we ask students to keep in mind which poster they like the best (and why), and which disagreement they found most interesting.

After "speed-dating," students meet in their groups for a few minutes to discuss their favorite poster and which disagreement they found most interesting, and each group then gives a *very* short report (see the "Mini-Presentations" section for guidelines on reporting-out from small groups).

This activity has always proven to be an excellent high-energy speaking/listening activity that certainly meets Common Core Standards. Unsurprisingly, it can also often be somewhat chaotic—though not in a bad way.

CHAT STATIONS

Educator Jennifer Gonzalez from the organization Cult of Pedagogy has described the idea of simple chat stations,[11] which are very adaptable to ELLs.

Here's how we apply her idea:

First, we give students a list of six questions, typically related to or about a text. Students are given 10 to 15 minutes to write their responses. Those questions are also taped individually around the room—in other words, in "chat stations." Station One lists the first question, Station Two lists the second question, and so on.

Then, students are told that they are going to be divided into groups of three to six (depending on the size of the class and the number of questions). They are also given a list of some sentence/question/answer starters. They are assigned a starting "station," and have a certain number of minutes to share and discuss their answers to the posted question at that station using the assigned sentence starters (and others of their choice). The group then comes to a consensus answer supported by evidence. Teachers can provide each group with a simple form to use to write down their group response. In addition, each group has to draw (and sign their number, which is the station at which they began) a very simple image on the sheet that contains the question at each station. This picture must represent their group response to the question. In other words, when they leave each station, the group will take their answer sheet with them but leave a picture behind.

After a certain amount of time, the teacher tells the groups to switch to the next station and repeat the process until each group has visited each station.

At that point, we've tried different next steps, including:

- Having each group prepare a very short report of their answers, ensuring that each member has a role, and having them present to another group.

- Calling on a specific person from each group to share one answer with the entire class.

- Having groups quickly rotate again to each station and decide on a group vote for the best picture drawn for each question, with the caveat that they can't vote for their own drawing.

- Combining the third option with either the first or second one.

GROUP PREDICTIONS

Sometimes prior to reading a text, we type out between six and ten sentences from the text. Then, we will give one sentence to each student, with two to five students receiving the same one. We explain that their job is to individually read it and make a prediction for what they believe happens in the full text and why. Then, students with the same sentence get into a small group and discuss their predictions using the sentence/question/answer starters from the "Stating an Opinion," "Agreeing," and "Disagreeing" sections in Exhibit 5.2 and come to a consensus about what they believe is the best prediction and why.

Students then make a simple poster that they present to the class in the round-robin activity described earlier in this chapter or each group can briefly present to the whole class. After hearing each group's sentence and their predictions based on them, students—either individually or as a group—can make a list of what they think are the best overall predictions that they can revisit after reading the text.

SENTENCE STEMS

Sentence/question/answer starters can be a boon to ELLs as long as they are used within reason (have students practice a few at the time) and are not used by students as a constant "crutch" that inhibits independence (see the first section of the Classroom Discussions topic to review ways to avoid this problem).

"Sentence/Question Starters for Meaningful Conversation in the Classroom" (Exhibit 5.2) is a list of the frames we use regularly in our classrooms.

Listening Strategies

We described earlier how teaching students what active listening looks like—and what it doesn't look like—helps to build a positive classroom environment for discussion. As teachers of ELLs, we know that our students need to develop their listening skills in English as they progress in other domains and in order to meet the Standards. It is also important to share with our students *how* being an active listener can benefit *them*. We explore this idea with our students by sharing research showing that listening in the workplace is seen as one of the most important traits in leaders and among colleagues.[12,13] We also prompt our students to think and write about how active listening can benefit them "here and now" with common student answers being that they will be able to learn English more quickly, can help their families, and will have better relationships with friends.

Asking students to reflect on the benefits of active listening is crucial to creating motivation for them to practice this skill, but what does this "practice" look like for ELLs in our classroom?

METACOGNITIVE LISTENING

This process is a precursor to directly applying many of the speaking and listening standards. Before ELLs can critically listen and evaluate content, they first must be able to understand what the content says. As we discussed in Chapter 2, metacognitive skills have been identified by the writers of the Standards as a critical skill for students to have in order to be successful in acquiring the academic knowledge listed in the Standards. We can use instructional strategies that promote both metacognition and listening skills to help our students move themselves from where they are now to where they want to be in the future.

While we emphasize to students that they are constantly employing their listening skills in their daily lives, we also set up listening practice sessions where students have an opportunity to learn, use, and evaluate different listening strategies. When students are practicing their listening skills, it is important for them to pay attention to the metacognitive processes they are using and to try out new ones. According to professor Larry Vandergrift, a researcher on listening and second language learning, students can increase their listening comprehension skills and will have more control over their learning processes when they know how to "analyze the requirements of a listening task, activate the appropriate listening processes required, make appropriate predictions, monitor their comprehension, and evaluate the success of their approach."[14] In other words, ELLs will make more progress if they are aware of how listening processes work and apply them in their own listening. We remind our students that they may already use many of these listening strategies in their home language automatically. We go on to tell them that these practice activities are designed to help them develop this automaticity in English because they are easy to forget when you have to work so hard just to understand what the words mean.

Before our students start a listening practice activity, we give them a Listening Practice Sheet (Exhibit 5.3) to help make them more aware of different listening strategies. These listening tasks can use a variety of "texts" such as podcasts, speeches, videos, dialogues, TED Talks, news reports, and so forth. The first time we give students this sheet, we model our own listening strategies while filling it out.

We start by writing the title of the listening text on the board and telling students what type of text it is (for example, we might have students listen to a podcast titled "The Beauty and Danger of Climbing Mt. Everest"). We then ask them to write anything they already know about the title and the type of text—if they know anything about them—in the first section on the Listening Practice Sheet. For example, they might say that Mt. Everest is a big mountain and that podcasts are like the radio. Students share their writing with a partner or in a small group to generate more ideas. Then, based on this knowledge, students write their predictions on the Listening Practice Sheet about the content of the text and about how this content will be delivered. For example, students might predict that the podcast will be about how climbing Everest is amazing because of the view, but is also dangerous because of avalanches and other hazards. They might also predict that the podcast will include descriptive words to help listeners create a picture in their minds because podcasts

EXHIBIT 5.3. Listening Practice Sheet

Title of listening "text": _____

Type of "text": _____

1. Before Listening: *What do I already know? What predictions can I make?*

2. While Listening: *What strategies can I use to help me understand what I'm listening to?*

3. After Listening: *Which strategies helped me the most? What will I do next time?*

don't contain pictures. Students share these predictions with a partner and add any new ones they get from their partner.

We then direct students to the second section on the Listening Practice Sheet and ask them to list any strategies they think might be particularly helpful to understand this "text" while they are listening to it. We often remind our students that many of the reading strategies they use to help them understand written texts can also be useful while they are working to comprehend a "listening text." Students might list strategies such as summarizing, using context clues to guess word meanings, asking questions, visualizing, and so forth. It is obviously difficult to use these strategies when listening to a "text" as a class and only hearing it once. Taking students to the computer lab with headphones can be a good way to have students practice these strategies on their own because they can pause and "relisten" as needed. If the teacher is playing a "text" for the whole class either on speakers or on a screen, it is important that he or she pause it and replay it when students ask so that they can utilize these strategies.

After the listening practice task is finished, we have students reflect on which strategies were most helpful and what was particularly difficult so they can target improvement the next time. We direct students to write these reflections on the third section of the Listening Practice Sheet and then to share them with each other.

This type of listening practice focuses on helping students "see" what are often invisible listening strategies. The emphasis in this type of practice is less about the content that students are learning and is more about teaching students how to listen. However, we often do focus students' listening skills on acquiring new content, which we will discuss next. It is all a question of balance—before students engage in a listening activity to learn new content, we often first ask them to review which listening strategies might be most helpful to their learning.

LISTENING FOR CONTENT

When preparing our ELLs to listen in order to reinforce or learn new content, we have found it helpful for them to follow the same thinking processes described above—tap prior knowledge, consider the purpose and features of the type of listening "text," and to make predictions based on all of this information. As students listen to the "text," it is also helpful if they have a graphic organizer to capture and organize the new information they are hearing.

In Chapter 4, we discuss how students can read and categorize a text data set and then seek out more information to add to these categories. One of the ways students can look for new information is by listening to videos, podcasts, news reports, and so forth, related to the topic. Listening with "categories in mind" helps students to focus on relevant details and to listen for key words.

Another strategy we use to help students process new content while listening—whether it is to add to a data set or for another reason—is to have them draw a combination of images and words to represent the key ideas from a listening text. For example, while watching a newscast about a recent earthquake in Nepal, we instructed students to listen for and take notes on key ideas to answer: Who? What? Where? When? Why? How? Then, after seeing examples displayed by the teacher, they used their notes to create a simple infographic representing this key information. Students can be creative and design charts, diagrams, graphs, and so forth. For our purposes, we also consider a comic strip to be a helpful infographic for students. In other words, any combination of a drawing and words that accurately summarizes the listening content can build student comprehension. Oftentimes we have our students draw their infographics on a piece of paper, but other times we have them use the computer to create them. See the Tech Tools box below for online resources on creating infographics.

One way we move our ELLs toward meeting Common Core Standards during these listening activities is by asking them to evaluate the credibility of the source (in this case, a listening text). For example, we might have students evaluate why a podcast produced by NPR might be more credible than one produced by a fifth-grader in Oregon. After listening to a speech from a political figure, we might have students list which of the politician's claims are believable and which are not and for what reasons. See the section in Chapter 6 on ethos, logos, and pathos for more ideas on teaching students this type of critical thinking.

It is also important to remind our students, especially ELLs, that they can access the listening strategies they use in our class (which tends to contain more student-talk versus teacher-talk) when they are in other classes that might be more lecture-based. For example, if a teacher is lecturing and students are required to take notes, students could quickly create a graphic organizer based on the categories of study or divide their paper into sections of Who? What? When? Where? Why? How?

Tech Tools

Infographic Resources

We've collected resources containing models of infographics and listing easy online tools that students can use to create them. They include:

The Best Resources for Creating Infographics (http://larryferlazzo.edublogs.org/2011/01/11/the-best-resources-for-creating-infographics/)

A Collection of "The Best . . ." Lists on Infographics (http://larryferlazzo.edublogs.org/2011/04/09/a-collection-of-the-best-lists-on-infographics/)

The Best Ways to Make Comic Strips Online (http://larryferlazzo.edublogs.org/2008/06/04/the-best-ways-to-make-comic-strips-online/)

Listening to Presentations

We have highlighted the importance of creating a positive classroom environment for class discussions and the same goes for class presentations done by students. We encourage our students to be active listeners during class presentations for two reasons: (a) It helps the students who are giving the presentations to feel supported, and (b) It helps the student audience to stay focused and to better comprehend what is being said.

We have found one of the best ways to encourage active listening during presentations is to make sure every student has a "job to do" while they are listening. Sometimes that job might be making a list of questions to ask the presenters, taking notes on key ideas, noting any new learnings, and so forth.

We also have students anonymously evaluate both the content of the presentation and the speaker's delivery. Students fill out a form where they comment on the speaker's points and the evidence backing them and list two things they liked and one helpful suggestion for improvement. Other times we ask students to fold a piece of paper into four boxes and label them (1) What I Learned, (2) What I'm Wondering, (3) My favorite part of this presentation was . . . , and (4) One way to make this presentation even better is . . .

Several times a year we have outside speakers present in our classroom for different school events such as Career Day or college presentations. Other times we host speakers related to a class topic of study—such as having volunteers from an organization which helps girls rescued from sex trafficking come while we are studying a unit on human trafficking. We tell our students to write down any questions that come to mind while they are listening to the presenter. Then, after the speaker is finished, we have students form small groups and spend a few minutes comparing their questions and deciding on which two or three would be best to ask the speaker. We have groups then take turns asking the presenter the questions and all students take notes on the answers. The next day, students can compare what they heard and add any information they may have missed. This allows students time to process all of the information they heard and apply it to future reading, writing, and speaking on the topic.

There are other ways to keep students actively processing as they listen to presentations such as using a K-W-L chart or having students work with a partner after a presentation to paraphrase the key points and their evidence. The key for us is that these exercises need to involve students thinking about *what* is being said and thinking about *how* it is being said so they can apply these learnings to their own presentations.

DICTATION

As stated in the beginning of this chapter, the Common Core Standards for Speaking and Listening require students to "integrate and evaluate" information presented to them in multiple ways. Processing information in an auditory manner is especially challenging for many ELLs who are attempting to process both information in a new language and new content in that language. In our experience, one of the most successful strategies for helping ELLs increase their language and content proficiency is through dictation activities. Research has shown that dictation not only increases student engagement, but also enhances listening comprehension in English.[15] Dictation also allows ELLs a chance to practice their listening skills in a low-stress environment because the listening text is repeated and students can make revisions.

Dictation can be done in numerous ways, but, to put it simply, the teacher reads a short text aloud, often one that students are familiar with or on a familiar topic. Then, after students have heard it once, the teacher reads it again and students jot down keywords and phrases. The teacher reads it a third time and students write down any additional notes. Then students work in partners or small groups to compare their notes and develop an accurate reconstruction of the text (one that might not be the exact wording, but does represent the meaning correctly). Finally, the teacher reads the text again and students judge how well they did.

One of the great things about dictation is that it can be varied in so many engaging ways:

- Students can work in partners and take turns "dictating" a text or part of a text to each other.

- The teacher can do "picture dictation" by describing a picture (that is hidden from students) and having the students draw the picture as they listen to the teacher's words.

- Students can take turns doing picture dictation with each other and afterward can write sentences about their picture.

- Students can play a version of "Simon Says" by writing down a series of actions and then "dictating" them to a partner who has to quickly act them out (i.e., hop on your left foot then turn around and walk five steps).

Tech Tools

Listening Resources

There is a wealth of free online resources that can assist ELLs with their listening skills, including accessible podcasts, audio of famous speeches, dictation exercises, and interactive tools specifically designed for those learning English.

We have collected links to those sites at the Best Listening Sites for English Language Learners (http://larryferlazzo.edublogs.org/2008/05/28/the-best-listening-sites-for-english-language-learners/). You can also find more ideas for listening lessons at the same post.

We'd also like to highlight the StoryCorps website and free app (http://storycorps .org/) as an exceptional listening (and speaking) resource. Not only does it provide a nearly endless supply of short, accessible, and engaging audio stories and videos, its app is a wonderful tool for students to use to interview others, particularly family members. The app provides suggested questions, and the final interview is automatically uploaded to StoryCorps and the Library of Congress.

Giving Presentations

The speaking and listening standards call for students to develop and present information in an organized, well-reasoned manner. Students must consider the task, purpose, and audience as well as use technology in strategic ways to enhance their presentations. Along with all of this, they must also "adapt" their speech to a variety of contexts, and when "indicated or appropriate" demonstrate a command of formal English. So how do we prepare ELLs to meet these standards, which are challenging enough for our non-ELL students?

MINI-PRESENTATIONS

First, we start small. We often have our ELLs develop and deliver short presentations so they can practice their presentation skills with a less overwhelming task.

Many people have heard the expression "elevator pitch"—the ability to clearly and succinctly define something (a product, a service, a process, etc.) and its value—in the amount of time it takes to go up or down a few floors in an elevator. While this may not be the most accessible metaphor for students, it is an expression they will likely need to know at some point in their professional lives and they can understand it if the teacher offers an explanation accompanied by a poor drawing of an elevator on the board! Once students understand its meaning, they can practice writing and delivering "elevator pitches" for many different learning activities.

For example, students can give an elevator pitch to the class or a small group recommending a favorite book by quickly summarizing the book's content (what it's about) as well as its value (reasons why someone would want to read it). Another variation of this strategy is after reading a text (an article, a short story, a poem, etc.) as a class, students can work together in pairs to develop and deliver an "elevator pitch" summarizing the text and why it would be important for other students to read. Students could also create an elevator pitch for the most important word they learned during a lesson and why it is a valuable word to know. These "pitches," which can last anywhere from 30 seconds to a couple of minutes, require students to consider their audience and their purpose as they come up with the best way to explain a concept, word, or a text and its value.

Doing short presentations, like the ones described above, can boost ELL students' confidence while also providing valuable speaking and listening practice. Another simple way we incorporate short presentations into our classes is by having students share their completed work in front of the class. We often have our Beginning students use My Storybook (https://www.mystorybook.com) to create free online and printable books. Students can use this online tool to write, draw, and add pictures from the Web to create a book on any topic. During a unit on animals, we had our Beginners create an A–Z Animal Book by researching online, summarizing key information about each animal in their own words and adding pictures. They then selected information on three to five animals in their book and prepared a brief presentation using the class computer and projector. They displayed the pictures in their book as they shared interesting facts about each animal.

Another type of mini-presentation is when students "report out" after working in a small group. It provides another chance for students to practice speaking in front of the class and for the audience to actively listen. We call it the "1-minute report":

1. Once students have completed a group activity (such as sharing their individual answers to a question and then coming to a consensus about the "best answer"), the teacher says "You have 3 minutes to prepare your 1-minute reports."

2. Students immediately begin rehearsing what they will say in their report to the class. It should be a summary of what their group has learned or produced during the group activity (such as explaining the "best answer" from the group and why they feel that it is the best) and must not be longer than a minute, though it can be shorter. Every student sees value in rehearsing what they will say during these 1-minute reports because the teacher randomly selects someone from each group to be the "reporter."

3. The teacher refocuses the class and begins the 1-minute report process by pointing to a group and calling on a "reporter." The reporter stands and gives the 1-minute report for that group. Depending upon the goals and time limitations of the lesson, the teacher could choose to have students take notes on each group's report or could call on a couple of different students after each report and have them share something they learned or heard during the report.

The key in using these short presentations to build students' confidence and English speaking skills is to make them a regular part of the class routine, but not make them feel "routine" by doing the same thing every time.

PRESENTING TO SMALL GROUPS

Another way we make presentations less overwhelming for ELLs is by having them practice these skills in small group settings. We often use the well-known "jigsaw" strategy to have our students practice preparing and presenting information to their peers in a low-anxiety setting.

We first pass out either different sections of a text or different texts altogether to groups of students. All the students with the first section of the text or text number one are assigned to "expert" group one, all the students with section two or text number two become expert group two, and so on. Before going to their expert groups, however, students first read the text on their own, making notes, highlighting key ideas, and so forth. Students can be given a graphic organizer to record key ideas, questions, and unfamiliar words.

Then students meet in their expert groups to share their learnings and to help each other prepare to teach their peers about this section of the text. It can be helpful for teachers to provide oral and written directions such as, "Each presenter must make a small poster containing a summary (one to two sentences) of the text, identifying one key word and explaining what it means and why it's important, asking a question they are still wondering about the text, and drawing an image to represent one of the key concepts in the text." After students have prepared their presentations, they can practice them with a person from their expert group. We often tell students to practice once while looking at their notes and then to turn them over and practice again without looking.

Once students have rehearsed they are ready to move to "teaching groups," groups composed of one member from each "expert" group. Students then take turns giving their presentations. The teacher reminds students that they are presenting, they should try to not just *read* from their notes but instead *talk* while glancing when necessary at the notes. The other students in the group can record the key ideas presented about each section of the text. The teacher could have students make a graphic organizer for this activity or give them one. Once everyone has had an opportunity to present, the teacher can post some reflection questions for students to respond to such as:

- What did you like most about doing this activity? Why?
- What was most difficult about this activity? Why?
- What will you do differently the next time we do this activity? Why?

Do we follow every one of these steps each time we have students give presentations?

No.

Do we offer our students enough opportunities to practice giving presentations?

No.

Sometimes students are tired, sometimes we are tired, sometimes we have time constraints, sometimes there are classroom management issues. Sometimes our students are facing challenges in their personal lives that make it difficult for them to focus or to be the focus of attention during a presentation.

Do we push ourselves to maintain positive energy to teach and do we encourage our students to have positive energy to learn?

Yes.

Do we try to increase speaking opportunities for our students despite all of the many challenges and limitations we have in the classroom?

Yes.

It is important to remember that not every instructional strategy we describe in these chapters has to be done by our playbook in order for students to learn and grow from it.

Formal/Informal Language

The speaking and listening standards highlight the ability for students to know when and how to use informal and formal English. We describe activities to apply this skill to speaking and to writing in the next chapter "Language."

Student Self-Evaluation

A key part in helping ELLs improve their speaking and listening skills while working to meet the Standards is to provide opportunities for them to evaluate their own skills and to set their own goals for improvement. In the "Listening" section above, we described how students can evaluate their own listening skills, specifically about which strategies work best, what is most difficult, and what changes they can make. We often ask students to similarly reflect on their speaking skills after participating in a group discussion or giving a presentation.

We also promote this type of "self-assessment" by having students record and evaluate their speaking using an online tool. Students can go to a site, such as English Central (http://www.englishcentral.com/videos), which allows students to record their speaking and then provides immediate feedback on their pronunciation (taking student accents into account). We have found our students enjoy being able to practice their speaking individually in a low-anxiety situation and receive instant feedback. There are many other tools students can use to record their speaking in order to evaluate their progress and set goals for future growth. See the Tech Tools box for a list of resources.

Tech Tools
Presentation and Speaking Resources

There are many online resources to supplement and reinforce the instructional presentation and speaking strategies we discuss in this chapter. We've collected the best ones at:

The Best Sources of Advice for Making Good Presentations (http://larryferlazzo .edublogs.org/2009/05/25/the-best-sources-of-advice-for-making-good- presentations/)

The Best Ways to Create Online Slideshows (http://larryferlazzo.edublogs.org/ 2008/05/06/the-best-ways-to-create-online-slideshows/)

The Best Sites to Practice Speaking English (http://larryferlazzo.edublogs.org/2008/ 03/17/the-best-sites-to-practice-speaking-english/)

The Best Websites for Learning English Pronunciation (http://larryferlazzo. edublogs.org/2008/03/31/the-best-websites-for-learning-english- pronunciation/)

Mini-Lesson on Speaking and Argument for ELL Upper Beginners and Intermediates

This lesson is adapted and modified (with permission) from one originally developed by Dave Stuart Jr., author of *A Non-Freaked-Out Guide to Teaching the Common Core*[16] and shared on his blog (http://www.davestuartjr.com/).

Note that, in this lesson, we use the terms that we feel are most effective in teaching our ELLs (and non-ELLs) the elements of argument. It might also be best to do this lesson near the beginning of the year when students don't know as much about their teacher or each other. The purpose of this lesson is to introduce, in a simple and fun way, the basic elements of argument. These concepts can then be built upon in later lessons on argument.

1. The teacher begins by telling the class three things about himself. For example, Larry might say that he loves his wife, enjoys playing basketball, and is a big fan of spicy food. He writes that list on the overhead, leaving a good amount of space between the sentences.

2. The teacher says he's going to turn each of those pieces of information into *claims*—ideas that are specific and debatable. For example, Larry might say that his wife is the most beautiful woman in the world, basketball is the best sport for people to play, and that nothing is better than spicy foods. He would write those under each of his original sentences, along with the word *claim*.

3. Then, the teacher asks students to develop three of their own claims about themselves and/or their interests. He gives students a minute or two to write them down, telling them to leave space between their sentences like he did and verbally share what they wrote with a partner. A few students can then share with the entire class.

4. Next, the teacher introduces the word *evidence* and explains that it is proof for your claim. Larry would write examples of evidence under each of his claims. For example, he might write (after the word evidence) that his wife had many other men who wanted to date her, that basketball is good for your heart because there is a lot of nonstop running, and that research shows that people who eat spicy foods tend to live longer.

5. The teacher then asks students to write down evidence under each of their claims, and then share what they wrote with a partner. Again, the teacher calls on a few different people to share their claims and evidence.

6. Next, the teacher says that not everybody is going to agree with our claims, despite the evidence we give. They will give an *opposing argument*. Larry would write "opposing argument" on the overhead and write that maybe other women had many more men who wanted to date them than his wife did, that soccer also has a lot of nonstop running, and that research also shows that spicy foods cause heartburn.

7. The teacher follows that up by asking students to write down opposing arguments after each of their claims and evidence. Students then share what they wrote with a different partner and a few share with the entire class.

8. Then, the teacher introduces the term *counterargument*. In other words, after you've given your claim, provided evidence, and heard an opposing argument, what are you going to say? Are you just going to say, "Yes, you're right and I was wrong"? The teacher can say that on occasion that's perfectly fine—we should be open to the idea that we may be wrong and might need to change our claim. Other times, however, we are still going to believe that we're right. In that case, we need to provide a *counterargument*.

   Larry would write "counterargument" on his sheet and write something like: he has done research and knows for a fact that there is not a woman alive who has had more men ask them out for a date than his wife has (as we've mentioned before, a little humor goes a long way in the classroom), that there are many more basketball courts than soccer fields, and that yes, you might get heartburn but there is medication you can take for that as long as you are alive.

9. Students then write their own counterarguments and share them with a partner, with a few sharing with the entire class.

10. The teacher then explains that all the things they did today—*claim, evidence, opposing argument, counterargument*—together make up what is called an *argument*. It means saying what you believe, backing it up with evidence, introducing a contrary opinion and either continuing to stand behind your claim with even more evidence or revising your claim based on the new information. The teacher can wrap it up by explaining that students will be writing and presenting many arguments over the course of the year and reminding students that they already use argument in their daily lives and will continue to do so.

For downloadable versions of the lesson plans and Tech Tools boxes found in this chapter, go to the "Downloads" section of this book's web page at www.wiley.com/go/navccss.

CHAPTER SIX

Language

Language is the dress of thought.

—Samuel Johnson[1]

What Does the Common Core Say About Language?

The Common Core Standards for Language (see Exhibit 6.1) emphasize knowing and using correct grammar, punctuation, spelling, and so forth. The high school standards are especially specific when it comes to grammar, and list terms that we hadn't seen since our linguistics courses ("absolute phrase, participial phrase"). The Standards also call for students to be able to use style guides (for example, APA or MLA). In addition, the language standards call for students to competently use various strategies to determine the meanings of words new to them, to understand the many nuances of language (such as figurative language) and to develop a wide-range of academic vocabulary.

Key Elements of the Language Standards

The six Common Core Standards for language are divided into three parts—"Conventions of Standard English," "Knowledge of Language," and "Vocabulary Acquisition and Use". Here is our interpretation of the most important points in each of these areas:

Conventions of Standard English

The two standards here, as applied to high school, assume that most basic language conventions have already been acquired in earlier grades[2] and suggest that it's time now for students to learn more complex and sophisticated ones.[3] Fortunately, another specific application of these standards to high school is that students

EXHIBIT 6.1. English Language Arts College and Career Readiness Anchor Standards for Language

Conventions of Standard English

CCSS.ELA-Literacy.CCRA.L.1

Demonstrate command of the conventions of standard English grammar and usage when writing or speaking.

CCSS.ELA-Literacy.CCRA.L.2

Demonstrate command of the conventions of standard English capitalization, punctuation, and spelling when writing.

Knowledge of Language

CCSS.ELA-Literacy.CCRA.L.3

Apply knowledge of language to understand how language functions in different contexts, to make effective choices for meaning or style, and to comprehend more fully when reading or listening.

Vocabulary Acquisition and Use

CCSS.ELA-Literacy.CCRA.L.4

Determine or clarify the meaning of unknown and multiple-meaning words and phrases by using context clues, analyzing meaningful word parts, and consulting general and specialized reference materials, as appropriate.

CCSS.ELA-Literacy.CCRA.L.5

Demonstrate understanding of figurative language, word relationships, and nuances in word meanings.

CCSS.ELA-Literacy.CCRA.L.6

Acquire and use accurately a range of general academic and domain-specific words and phrases sufficient for reading, writing, speaking, and listening at the college and career readiness level; demonstrate independence in gathering vocabulary knowledge when encountering an unknown term important to comprehension or expression.

should develop the ability to find answers to their questions on conventions independently.[4] As far as we're concerned, we place a much higher priority on the latter with our high school ELL students.

Knowledge of Language

Our interpretation of the one standard contained in this section is similar to the difference between language learning and language acquisition that we discuss in the first chapter. As applied here, the knowledge learned in the conventions section (and in the upcoming vocabulary one) is similar to language learning—you will theoretically know enough to complete a worksheet accurately. Now, in the knowledge of language section, as is the case with language acquisition, you have to apply that knowledge and use it to communicate effectively. In other words, how and when does context affect grammar and vocabulary usage in reading, writing, and listening? In addition, for high school, they throw in needing to know how to use style guides like APA and MLA.

Vocabulary Acquisition and Use

This section has three standards, more than the other two parts of the language standards. They state that students should be able to determine the meanings of new words through context clues, through knowledge of word roots or patterns, and through the ability to know where to look them up. The Standards also expect that students will learn about figurative language and figures of speech—in other words, some of the nuances in the English language. One nuance is the knowledge of idioms and, according to the Standards, this knowledge should be acquired in earlier grades. Obviously, many high school ELLs will need to learn them for the first time, and we assume that Common Core's flexibility towards ELLs will apply in this area, too. We will repeat (because it can't be repeated enough) once again, what Common Core says about ELLs: "Teachers should recognize that it is possible to achieve the standards for reading and literature, writing & research, language development and speaking & listening without manifesting native-like control of conventions and vocabulary."[5]

Finally, the Standards say that students should develop a college-level academic vocabulary and the knowledge of how to expand it further, including the ability to independently determine the meaning of new words.

WHAT DOES THIS MEAN FOR LANGUAGE INSTRUCTION IN MY CLASSROOM IN GENERAL?

When we combine all the elements of the language strands in the Common Core Standards, then, what might it mean for teachers of English language learners (ELLs)?

We would suggest that it means to:

- Remember that a perfect grasp of language conventions by ELLs is not required by Common Core in order to meet the Standards. Don't "drill-and-kill" with worksheets; instead, focus on supporting students to create meaning through higher-order thinking. In other words, if a student comes to you with a heartfelt story about their refugee journey to the United States, it's not a good time to pull out your red pen and give him/her a grammar lesson pointing out multiple written errors. In fact, it's probably never a good time to pull out your red pen and give anybody a grammar lesson that points out multiple written errors (see the "Grammar" section).

- Also recognize that the prior suggestion doesn't mean that some explicit instruction of grammar and conventions is unwarranted. As with anything, though, balance is key.

- Work hard at integrating grammar and vocabulary instruction with authentic reading and writing. Students are much more likely to learn, remember, and apply these new learnings when they can use—and benefit—from them right away. That doesn't rule out sometimes using grammar worksheets or word lists. It does mean, however, needing to make sure there's a reading or writing assignment coming up next where students will apply the knowledge gained from those worksheets or word lists.

- Try to learn the grammar rules from your students' home languages, as well as cognates, so you are prepared to highlight similarities and differences as part of your instructional "toolkit." What's the best way to learn those grammar rules? Ask your students!

- Gain an understanding of online resources available where your ELL students can practice grammar and acquire vocabulary in engaging and low-anxiety environments. Use your classroom time to introduce key grammar concepts and vocabulary in context and help students develop intrinsic motivation to acquire them. Then, if technology is available at school and/or at students' homes, these skills can be reinforced through online games and exercises (see the Tech Tools boxes on grammar and vocabulary later in this chapter).

- Look for everyday opportunities to quickly teach about nuances in language that might arise, whether it's an idiom said in a movie clip being watched for a different reason in class or when something happens at school that could be described using an example of figurative language.

HOW CAN LANGUAGE INSTRUCTION IN MY CLASSROOM SUPPORT ELL STUDENTS IN MEETING COMMON CORE STANDARDS?

As we state in earlier chapters, we integrate the teaching of reading, writing, speaking, listening, and language skills in our classroom. Many of the instructional strategies and lesson plans shared earlier include language components, but here are some that particularly emphasize this domain and that we have found to be effective with our ELL students.

GRAMMAR

The Standards for language call for students to "demonstrate command of the conventions of standard English grammar and usage when writing or speaking." It is difficult for English-only students to demonstrate a "command" of grammatical structures and obviously even more challenging for ELLs. The secondary language standards assume that students have already acquired many basic conventions of English grammar, but many ELLs are still in the process of learning or haven't ever learned these elements of English grammar and usage.

So, what does grammar instruction look like in our ELL classroom? First, we will explain what we *don't* do and then we will highlight some practices we *do* use. We will also share research related to both.

As we stated earlier, we don't use a "drill and kill" method of teaching grammar. When isolated language conventions are taught out of context by having students fill out worksheets or do grammar drills, it can be painful for both students and the teacher! Research indicates that "traditional grammar instruction," such as diagramming sentences or teaching specific grammar rules in isolation, isn't effective in improving students' writing skills. In fact, some studies have shown that the quality of student writing actually declined when they were directly taught grammar.[6]

However, this doesn't mean that we don't teach grammar at all. We know that our ELL students need explicit grammar instruction, but we believe, as much research confirms, that this instruction is most effective when grammar is taught in the context of meaningful academic work.[7] And, we have found that teaching inductively is one of the best ways to help our students learn and apply grammatical structures in an engaging and meaningful context.

Research confirms that teaching grammar inductively (having students practice grammar forms in context first and then discover the rules on their own) versus deductively (giving students grammar rules first and then having them apply the rules) can result in greater language learning in both the short- and long-term.[8] In our classroom, we often use the inductive teaching strategy of concept attainment to teach grammatical forms and usage.

In the Concept Attainment Mini-Lesson in Chapter 4, we describe how teachers can use this strategy to help students identify and create better claims and evidence by analyzing both "good" or "yes" and "bad" or "no" examples. We employ this same strategy to help students identify and then practice applying correct grammatical structures, spelling, and punctuation.

An example of this Concept Attainment strategy originally appeared in our article "Teaching Argument Writing to ELLs" in *ASCD Educational Leadership*, and appears here in modified form with permission.[9] First, we review written texts or drafts of essays produced by our students and identify common grammar and spelling errors to address. Then we put correct spelling or grammar usage of a particular rule under a column labeled "Yes" on the overhead and put incorrect usage under a "No" column (see Table 6.1). We then show students a "Yes" example and then a "No" example, with other similar examples covered by a blank piece of paper. We ask students why they believe each example is listed as a "yes" or a "no." We gradually uncover each sentence until students conclude what the common denominator is—in other words, what the "yes" examples have in common (in Table 6.1, it's correct subject-verb agreement), thus determining the error and its correction. Sometimes we use student writing (with names left off) to generate the "yes" and "no" examples. Other times we might create examples using a text students are currently reading.

After doing the concept attainment process, we might give students more "no" examples and have them correct them, turning them into "yes" examples, or have them create "yes" examples of their own. They could also go back to their drafts and look for "no" examples to fix. The key is that students can apply this new learning in a meaningful reading, writing, or speaking context.

ERROR CORRECTION

Other dos and don'ts in grammar instruction relate to error correction. This section, with some minor changes, also appeared in our previous book[10] and is reproduced with permission of John Wiley & Sons. It describes how we effectively use error correction as an opportunity to teach and learn and not as a source of embarrassment or stress. Also, see our Resilience Lesson plan in Chapter 2 for an example of how we use the inductive process to help students learn from their mistakes.

The issue of "error correction," particularly focused on grammar, can be a controversial topic in ESL/ELL circles.[11] A number of studies[12] suggest that correction—either through prompts that point out the error to a student and require an immediate attempt at a "repair" or through "recasts" when teachers

Table 6.1 Concept Attainment Example: Grammar

The teacher puts an example with correct spelling or grammar usage under a column labeled "Yes" on the overhead and an incorrect example under a "No" column and gradually uncovers each sentence until students determine what the sentences in the "Yes" column have in common. (The rows must be staggered to permit the teacher to uncover one example at a time.)

This figure shows examples with correct and incorrect subject-verb agreement.

Yes	No
Houses are cheap in our neighborhood.	
	Houses is cheap in our neighborhood.
The bus stop is close to my house.	
	The bus stop are close to my house.
The people in my neighborhood are from different cultures.	
	The people in my neighborhood is from different cultures.

rephrase correctly what the student said—can be a useful tool to assist language acquisition.

Other research, however, suggests the opposite—that overt grammar correction can actually be harmful to the English language learner. Some researchers[13] suggest that oral grammar correction interrupts communicative activities and can generate a negative reaction from students. These studies also point to similar hindrances resulting from correcting written grammatical errors, saying that it contributes to stress that inhibits language learning.[14]

These two points of view partially rely on varying perspectives on the difference between language "acquisition" and language "learning," which Chapter 1 describes. To "acquire" language, according to researcher/educator Stephen Krashen and many others who question the use of error correction, it is important to place a greater emphasis on communication rather than on the correct form. Professor Krashen would suggest that "learning" a language in schools can, instead, focus too much on the correct forms through grammar instruction and worksheets and not result in students actually being able to communicate effectively in the real world.[15]

We share the concerns of those who question the advantages of error correction. However, we still believe that error correction does have a place in the ESL classroom.

Regular use of concept attainment highlighting both correct and incorrect grammar usage as described above and using games to have students correct common grammar errors (for example, teachers could write examples of common writing errors on the board and have small student groups race to write them correctly) are two strategies we use regularly to effectively deal with error correction. We've also used an activity by Dave Dodgson, an English teacher in Turkey, where the teacher writes a paragraph incorporating several common mistakes made by students and then has them make corrections in small groups.[16]

In addition, instead of returning student-written papers where we point out numerous errors, teachers might emphasize several positive aspects of an essay and then only point out one type of error. We never simply hand back papers with written comments. Instead, we always have a private conversation—albeit a brief one—with the student. At times, instead of using this process or in addition to doing it, if we see a common error trend in the class (for example, subject-verb agreement), we might also do a short mini-lesson that provides more explicit instruction. We also might ask students as they begin a writing assignment to pay particular attention to their use of grammatical forms or conventions like verb tense or use of quotation marks to heighten their awareness and practice of those concepts. As we've stated earlier, we assess the content of their writing for meaning. In addition, we assess their use of grammar and conventions, but may choose to focus on only one or two grammar points at a time and offer feedback on them.

Tech Tools

Online Grammar Sites for Interactive Practice

There are many online sites that offer interactive exercises and games for grammar practice. We've collected the best ones and share them on the following two lists:

The Best Sites for Grammar Practice (http://larryferlazzo.edublogs.org/2008/12/07/the-best-sites-for-grammar-practice/)

The Best Beginner, Intermediate, and Advanced English Language Learner Sites (http://larryferlazzo.edublogs.org/2011/09/19/the-best-beginner-intermediate-advanced-english-language-learner-sites/)

FORMAL/INFORMAL LANGUAGE

The high school language standards require students to both understand how language functions and how to use language effectively in different contexts. The secondary speaking and listening standards identify similar abilities and further specify that students should demonstrate "a command of formal English when indicated or appropriate."

One way to help them meet these standards is to teach students about when and how to use both informal and formal English. We do this first by making students aware of how they already use informal and formal English in their writing and speaking. For example, we point out that one way they apply those differences is in their diction and organization when writing a text message to a friend versus writing an essay in their social studies class.

We also use the concept attainment strategy (see the earlier "Grammar" section for a more detailed explanation of this strategy) to reinforce the concepts of informal versus formal English. For example, we might include several "yes" examples representing formal, academic phrases such as "I have to disagree because . . ." and "Could you please repeat that?" and several "no" examples such as "You're hella wrong" and "Huh?" As we gradually uncover the "yes" and "no" examples, we prompt students to discover similarities and differences and then to come up with some "rules" or characteristics of formal and informal language—such as formal language sounds academic or professional while informal language seems more like slang.

Another way to help students identify the differences between formal and informal language—that incorporates speaking, listening, reading, and writing practice—is through the use of dialogues. Sometimes we give students sets of short dialogues that contain one speaker being too formal or too informal. Working in pairs, students have to identify the "inappropriate" language usage and then change it to fit with the dialogue. For example, in a dialogue between two friends about an upcoming party, the phrase "Might I trouble you to transport me to Maria's social gathering?" would be an inappropriate use of formal English. Students have fun identifying the "mistakes" and can then perform these revised dialogues or write new dialogues with examples of "inappropriate" language use.

We also reinforce the concept of informal and formal language usage when students are reading texts by having them identify whether writers are using a more formal or informal style and what the effect might be on the audience. We call attention to these different uses of language as students produce their own writing for different purposes—an informal tone may be more appropriate when doing a quickwrite in class, while a more formal style is needed when responding to an essay prompt on a district writing assessment.

The next section will focus on how we teach students a key part of formal English—academic vocabulary.

ACADEMIC VOCABULARY

The Standards call for students to "acquire and use accurately a range of general academic and domain specific words ... at the college and career readiness level." This is a challenge for ELLs, particularly those who enter the United States as teenagers—we're talking about learning a lot of words very quickly!

Before we talk about *how* to help ELLs learn these words, let's first discuss *what* words (according to Common Core) should be taught.

Academic vocabulary guidance from the Common Core relies on research that divides words into three categories, called Tier One, Tier Two, and Tier Three.[17] Tier One words are ones that are often used in oral conversation, such as *happy* or *school*, and the writers of the Standards assume that native English speakers have learned them in earlier grades. Though the Common Core writers say that "English language learners of any age will have to attend carefully to them,"[18] they are not counted as the "general academic vocabulary" highlighted in the language standards. We operate on the belief that the best way we can help our ELLs to "attend carefully to" this category of words is by teaching them!

Tier Two words *are* considered by Common Core as "general academic vocabulary." These are words that are more likely to appear in text than in oral conversation, and are usually the ones found in the lengthy online search results that come from an "academic vocabulary list" search query (you can also find links to our choices for the best ones in the Tech Tools box following this section). Tier Two words would be ones like *vary* and *accumulate*.

Tier Three words are the ones considered by Common Core to be "domain-specific." These are low-frequency words that might appear in textbooks or materials related to a specific subject, like *legislature* in a social studies class or *genre* in an English class.

STRATEGIES FOR VOCABULARY INSTRUCTION

Here are ways we teach words from *all* the Tiers in our ELL classrooms, including from Tier One. Of course, the Standards also want students to have the skills to determine the meaning of an unknown word. We describe these learning strategies in our reading chapter and we will share additional ones here.

Introducing General Academic Words

We have had success applying a *modified* version of the ESL vocabulary instruction model recommended by Robert Marzano and Debra Pickering.[19]

Their steps (without our modifications) can be summarized in this way:

1. Show and explain the new word (they recommend one to three new words each week).

2. Students then restate it in their home language.

3. Students write the word and a picture that represents it in their notebook.

4. Students do activities—immediately and in the future—to reinforce their understanding of the word (write sentences, categorize them, etc.).

5. Students talk to each other about the new word.

6. Students play games involving the new words they've learned.

Here is how we modify it in our ELL classes (a version of this description originally appeared in Edutopia,[20] and is reprinted with permission):

Each week our students learn new academic vocabulary that they list in a notebook. One way we identify these words is by consulting academic word lists that show key academic word knowledge by grade-level (see the following Tech Tools box for links to the best ones). Teaching these words using a modified version of the Marzano/Pickering sequence is one of the most popular lessons we facilitate. For 20 minutes three times each week, we divide Beginning and Intermediate students into groups determined by levels of English proficiency. (We support mixed groups as much as possible and are opposed to tracking by *ability*. In our multi-level class, we clarify that divisions—often fluid—are based on English proficiency, not intelligence).

Then with peer tutors, student teachers, bilingual aides or instructors alternating as they facilitate an activity with one group—while other students are doing something else—we discuss three or four new words each lesson. This "discussion" includes their meanings, connections to other words, visual images, and home language translations. We cover about 9 to 12 words each week, more than the number suggested by Marzano/Pickering, because we feel a sense of urgency, as our high school ELLs have a lot of words to learn in a short period of time. Other experts confirm that a number close to what we teach in a week is doable.[21] We've used different grade-level word lists depending on the English level of our students. However, when we distribute these word lists to our students, we are careful to remove the grade level from the title. Our learners don't need to be reminded how far away they are from English proficiency—they have multiple reminders of this challenge inside and outside our classroom each day already.

After the initial word "discussions" take place, we write down fun "question and answer frames" for each of the words:

"Do you believe that _____?" (Example: *Do you believe that Mr. Ferlazzo is a **fabulous** teacher?*)
"Yes, I believe _____" or "No, I do not believe _____."

We ask each student the question, and then they question each other in partners, adapting the "frames" to their own interests. Students write these words, definitions, and questions/answers in a vocabulary notebook. Then students review previously learned words with each other using their notebooks as a reference.

Some of the reinforcing activities that follow include games (see a section on them later in this chapter), asking students to use the words in short quickwrites, highlighting the newly learned words in texts we read as a class, and creating 15-second video presentations on the new words filmed with Instagram (see the Tech Tools box for more information).

Another follow-up exercise we do pushes students to "extend" their responses to demonstrate that they truly understand the meanings of the new words. For example, it is possible for a student to answer "Yes, I believe Mr. Ferlazzo is fabulous" without really understanding or remembering what the word "fabulous" means. So, by *extending* the answer frame by adding the word "because"—"Yes, I believe _____ because _____"—we are able to assess and challenge students on their comprehension.

In addition, we take advantage of opportunities to teach prefixes (for example "re" in "repeat") and cognates (words from two languages that share a common origin—between 30% and 40% of all English words have a cognate in Spanish[22]) so that students are able to apply this knowledge to determine word meanings independently.

There are a number of reasons why students enjoy doing this activity. One, they teach each other—both in their practice and by using prior knowledge to complete the question and answer frames. Two, we bring a spirit of fun to the lessons. For example, as we showed in the earlier example, we might begin by modeling, "Do you believe that Mr. Ferlazzo is a fabulous teacher?" to provoke laughter (and disagreement!). Students will subsequently develop their own questions that apply academic vocabulary to a similarly humorous topic. And third, students can easily quantify how much new knowledge they are learning each day—knowing they are making meaningful progress is essential for self-confidence (also known as the Progress Principle: http://progressprinciple.com/).

Tech Tools

Online Sites for Academic Vocabulary Practice, Word Lists, Video Word Presentations

There are many online sites that offer interactive exercises and games for academic vocabulary practice. We've collected the best ones in these lists, which also contain links to free academic word lists. In addition, we've included a list that contains many examples of student-made presentations of academic vocabulary and instructions on how to create them:

The Best Websites for Developing Academic English Skills and Vocabulary (http:// larryferlazzo.edublogs.org/2008/04/06/the-best-websites-for-developing-academic-english-skills-vocabulary/). This list contains links to word lists—we particularly like the ones created by the Berkeley public schools (www.berkeleyschools.net/wp-content/uploads/2013/05/BUSD_Academic_ Vocabulary.pdf).

The Best Sites Where ELLs Can Learn Vocabulary (http://larryferlazzo.edublogs.org/ 2009/07/15/the-best-sites-where-ells-can-learn-vocabulary/)

The Best Resources for Learning to Use the Video Apps "Vine" & Instagram (http:// larryferlazzo.edublogs.org/2013/02/18/the-best-resources-for-learning-to-use-the-video-app-twine/)

Introducing Domain-Specific (in This Case, Genre-Specific) Words

There are obviously other times we introduce new vocabulary words to students apart from the academic word activity previously described. One time could be prior to reading a class text that we know includes new and important words, and another could be when we are introducing a writing genre (like argument) where words like *claim*, *evidence*, and *opposing argument* need to be understood and potentially used in student writing.

In both cases, we introduce the words in advance, along with a word chart (see Table 6.2 for an example of one introduced prior to studying argument and preparing an argument essay). We lead students through a process of defining the words; writing related word forms, synonyms, or home language translations; and drawing a picture to represent the word meanings.

Table 6.2 Argument Word Chart

Word	Meaning	Related Words	Picture
Claim			
Evidence			
Credible (Credibility)			
Statistics			
Statement from Experts			
Personal Experience			
Opposing Argument			
Counterargument			
Audience			

Adapted from "Persuasive Word Chart," Ferlazzo & Hull Sypnieski, 2012, p. 133.

Before reading a class text, we distribute a word chart containing words students will encounter when reading the text and have them complete the process of defining the words as described in the previous paragraph. While they are reading the text, we often ask them to highlight these words in context. For example, a text on the Civil War might include words like "succession" and "abolition."

When introducing a writing genre, we also provide a word chart to be used in conjunction with a model text written in that genre and with their own writing. However, instead of highlighting the words in context, students highlight or label the concepts illustrated by the words. For example, if the class is learning about argument, after students have defined what the word "statistics" means, they might not actually see the word "statistics" in a text but will be able to label an example of a statistic being used as evidence.

When writing, we may ask students to include a certain number of new words in their essays or examples of the concepts represented by the words. For instance, if writing about the Civil War after reading a text or multiple texts, we might specify that they use at least five words from the word chart. If students are writing an argument piece, we might tell them that they need to include a "statement from an expert," "statistics," and "personal experience" as evidence supporting their claim.

Ethos/Logos/Pathos

We feel that the academic terms of ethos, logos, and pathos warrant a brief section of their own, especially in light of Common Core's emphasis on argument. We previously wrote about these concepts in our article "Teaching Argument Writing to ELLs" in *ASCD Educational Leadership* and we will discuss them again here in modified form with permission.[23]

Ethos, logos, and pathos, first classified by the well-known Greek philosopher Aristotle, represent three types of rhetorical strategies used by writers and speakers to form a persuasive argument. It is important for students to understand what these rhetorical devices are, and how writers and speakers use them to persuade their audiences. Students can then use these words and the concepts they represent to analyze the arguments of others and to write stronger arguments themselves. Therefore, early in the school year, we introduce our students to these three types of persuasive appeals: *ethos* (appealing to the reputation and credibility of the writer/speaker); *logos* (appealing to the audience's sense of logic, which may include use of reasoning, facts, and statistics); and *pathos* (appealing to the audience's emotions).

We help students to understand the basic meanings of these concepts by having them create visual representations of each word. For example, students can draw pictures of experts, such as doctors and scientists, to represent ethos; a graph or percentages to represent logos; and people with various expressions on their faces to illustrate pathos. The three types of appeals are usually represented as three points of a triangle, known as "The Rhetorical Triangle" or "Aristotelian Triad." However, we find it is easier for our students to understand a three-way Venn diagram to show how authors might use two rhetorical appeals to persuade readers or, to be really persuasive, a combination of all three. Many examples can be found online by searching "ethos, logos, pathos Venn diagram."

Once students understand what these three concepts mean, they are more prepared to identify the use of these persuasive strategies. We start by having students look at magazine advertisements to identify examples of ethos, logos, and pathos. Students then cut them out and choose the most persuasive ad (ideally, one that contains two or more types of appeals) to glue onto a piece of construction paper. Underneath the ad, they write a short paragraph explaining which types of appeals are being used and how they know this. For example, one student cut out an ad for face cream, which featured the statistic, "9 out of 10 women saw a decrease in wrinkles," as well as a photo of a woman laughing with her friends. Using the following sentence starters, the student wrote:

> *This advertisement is using pathos because* the woman feels young and happy with her friends. *It also uses logos because* it contains a statistic.

The teacher could also show TV commercials and have students work with partners or in small groups to identify the types of appeals being used and cite evidence to prove it.

We have found that introducing and reinforcing the academic terms *ethos*, *logos*, and *pathos*, even with Beginning and Low Intermediate students, creates a framework we can use throughout the year as students study the persuasive writing and speaking of others and as they produce their own.

Tech Tools
Persuasive Techniques

Here are links to two collections related to online resources for teaching persuasive techniques, including ethos, logos, and pathos:

The Best Online Resources for Helping Students Learn to Write Persuasive Essays (http://larryferlazzo.edublogs.org/2009/11/14/the-best-online-resources-for-helping-students-learn-to-write-persuasive-essays/) contains links to numerous resources on teaching students about elements of persuasion, including ethos, logos, and pathos.

The Best Sites to Learn about Advertising (http://larryferlazzo.edublogs.org/2009/07/19/the-best-sites-to-learn-about-advertising/) shares a list of resources for teachers and several engaging and accessible links for students to learn about persuasive techniques used in advertising.

Vocabulary Games

We're big fans of using games to reinforce learning. In fact, we devote an entire chapter to games in our previous book.[24] Due to space constraints, we haven't spent as much time on them in this book apart from a brief mention in the "Error Correction" section. However, we want to highlight a few here because playing games is the last stage in Robert Marzano and Debra Pickering's previously discussed vocabulary instructional model. You can also find links to ideas for many other games applicable to learning vocabulary, grammar, reading comprehension, and other areas in the Tech Tools: Online Grammar Sites for Interactive Practice box in this chapter.

One of the reasons we (and our students) like playing games and solving puzzles is because they have been found to cultivate the highest form of intrinsic motivation, also called "flow" by professor and researcher Mihaly Csikszentmihalyi.[25] Flow is what people feel when they are enjoying doing an activity so much that they are "being carried away in a current"[26] and lose track of time.

When playing vocabulary games (and, in fact, for most games), we prefer students to work in pairs or groups of three with small whiteboards. This kind of setup maximizes the odds of total class participation, allows us to be the judges of accuracy, and provides a great opportunity for formative assessment.

The first game is one of our own creation (though it's probably a safe bet that some other teacher somewhere has his or her own version). The other ones, surprisingly, are games we've seen on late-night television, principally Jimmy Fallon's *The Tonight Show*, and which we've adapted for the ELL Classroom. You can see videos of basic examples of each game by looking them up on *The Tonight Show*'s YouTube channel.

"Write a Sentence"

To play Write a Sentence, students are first divided into pairs composed of students from the same English "level" (in other words, if you have a combined Beginner and Intermediate class, a Beginner will be paired with a Beginner and an Intermediate with an Intermediate). Though this game can be played with a class entirely composed of one level, these instructions will describe how to play it with a mixed class that has two groups learning different academic vocabulary words.

Each group is given a small whiteboard, marker, and eraser, along with their academic language notebooks (where, as we described earlier, they keep track of the words they are learning).

Students are given 2 minutes to write a sentence correctly using academic words they have learned. For every word they use correctly, they receive one point. So, if they use three in one sentence, their team receives three points. They need to underline the academic words in their sentence, and assign a person to stand

and read it. Once they read it, the teacher determines which words are used correctly and awards the appropriate number of points. Afterwards, students are given another 2 minutes to develop a sentence using new academic words and assigning a new person to read them to the class.

We usually do four "rounds," and then students are given an opportunity to "bet" the points they have already won and can write two sentences using new words as a "finale."

"Word Blurt"

Word Blurt is a game played by Jimmy Fallon. We've adapted it for our classroom by, again, having students divided into pairs with whiteboards and their vocabulary notebooks.

The teacher calls out a word or phrase related to one of the academic vocabulary words that students have learned (or two words in case you have a combination Beginner and Intermediate class and they're learning different ones). Students then have 90 seconds to identify how the called-out word relates/connects in some way to one of their vocabulary words, and to explain the connection on their whiteboard. The teacher can post a sentence frame like:

_____ is connected to the word_____ because _____.

Students write it on their boards at the beginning of the game and have to change only what goes in the blanks during each round.

At the end of that time, students hold up their whiteboards and teachers determine who gets a point. For example, the teacher might call out "I think" and students would write

"I think" is connected to the word "opinion" because it is something you believe.

"Name It"

Name It is similar to the board game Catchphrase that has also been further popularized by Jimmy Fallon on *The Tonight Show*. In our adaptation, students again are in pairs with whiteboards and their vocabulary notebooks. The teacher explains that he is going to give clues to one of the words in the vocabulary notebook (without using the word), and that students will have 90 seconds (as in all games, teachers can adjust time limits up or down depending on the English level of their students) to guess the word. At the end of that time, students hold up their boards and the teacher determines which groups picked the right word. It's possible that students could guess a different word from their list that also makes sense based on the clues. An example might be giving multiple clues like "My wife is great. Football is the worst sport. Johnny is a good student", and then students could guess "opinion" or "claim."

Ideally, after the teacher has led the game a few times, students can be given a few minutes to identify words and come up with clues to share with the class. Students can then take turns leading the game.

Tech Tools
Online Sites for Learning Games

Here are links to three collections related to online learning games:

The Best Ideas for Using Games in the ESL/EFL/ELL Classroom (http://larryferlazzo .edublogs.org/2013/10/27/the-best-ideas-for-using-games-in-the-esleflell-classroom/) contains hundreds of game ideas for reinforcing multiple facets of ELL instruction.

A Collection of "The Best ..." Lists on Learning Games (http://larryferlazzo .edublogs.org/2010/08/28/a-collection-of-the-best-lists-on-games/) contains links to our choices for the best free online learning games accessible to ELLs.

The Best Ways to Create Online Tests (http://larryferlazzo.edublogs.org/2008/05/ 22/the-best-ways-to-create-online-tests/) shares links to tools that teachers can use for creating online tests, including many that can be used in a game-like environment.

High-Interest Academic Vocabulary Homework

A simple, and high-interest, weekly (sometimes every-other-week) strategy for vocabulary development is one for which we ask students to take pictures of words that are new to them—in books, signs, menus, and so forth—and text them to us. We then can easily create a slideshow of them (using any of a zillion free smartphone apps that are available) and share it with the class.

However, when it's time to show the slideshow, it's not a matter of the students sitting back while the teacher explains what the words mean. Instead, it's the responsibility of the student who took the picture to have figured out its meaning and teach it to the class.

More often than not, the words that are identified also appear in one of the future academic vocabulary lists we will be reviewing.

 For downloadable versions of the lesson plans and Tech Tools boxes found in this chapter, go to the "Downloads" section of this book's web page at www.wiley.com/go/navccss.

Mathematics

Wendy Jennings

The new Common Core State Standards for mathematics call for more in-depth focus on fewer mathematical strands with more emphasis on concepts over procedures, on problem solving over memorizing, on dialogue and collaboration over teacher-centered instruction, on "why" and "how" more than "what," and on the process as a whole rather than on singular steps.

The standards are divided into two sections: content and practices. The Standards for mathematical content outline the mathematics that students need to learn to be proficient, in other words, it is the "what." The Common Core Standards for Mathematical Practice (SMP) describes "how" mathematics should be performed. Specifically, the SMPs state that students should be able to:[1]

1. Make sense of problems and persevere in solving them

2. Reason abstractly and quantitatively

3. Construct viable arguments and critique the reasoning of others

4. Model with mathematics

5. Use tools strategically

6. Attend to precision

7. Look for and make use of structure

8. Look for and express regularity in repeated reasoning

For teachers of English language learners (ELLs), these new methods, through which math content is accessed, may create anxiety, frustration, and fear. How can students work through their problem solving and discuss their thinking when they are not yet proficient in English? How can students critique the reasoning of others or attend to precision when a shared language is not present? There are any number of additional challenges that educators who teach ELLs will face due to these new standards. This does not mean that ELLs will be unable to succeed in the Common Core; their teachers will just need a better understanding of how to differentiate their instruction.

Traditionally, mathematics education for ELLs involved simplifying the contexts of problems, focusing on procedural and scaffolded knowledge, and making mathematics relevant. It typically was not until these students were reclassified as English proficient that the content began to include a focus on critical thinking and complex problem solving. In other words, the level of rigor was more often based on a student's level of language proficiency. While many ELL math teachers have challenged this paradigm and have sought ways to incorporate more critical thinking activities with their ELLs, it is now required by the Common Core.

According to Anita Bright, a professor in Portland, Oregon, specializing in ELL education, all teachers of mathematics need to facilitate this new critical thinking since "the primary shift with the CCSS in mathematics is the new and unflinching emphasis on answering the question, 'Why?' "[2] Teachers of ELLs will need to simultaneously address the language needs of their students, especially as the mathematics standards are moving toward more conceptual fluency rather than the procedural fluency of old.[3] This chapter will address how to effectively respond to the challenges inherent in this transition.

Challenges with Traditional Mathematics and ELLs

ELLs come from a large variety of learning experiences, which could result in a mathematics class including beginning *and* advanced ELLs. The needs of these two student groups are vastly different. How can these needs be met in a single class so that no one student is bored or overwhelmed? How can the language needs be balanced with the mathematics goals so that students are able to complete grade level work and compete with native English speakers? Additionally, there are complexities involved with the roots of the nonnative languages. Latin root languages like Spanish have a bit of an advantage over Asian, Middle Eastern, and African languages, especially in mathematics and science as Latin plays such an important role in these subjects. How can you balance the Latin-based language needs with the non-Latin so that the needs of all students are met?

One linguistic challenge facing ELLs and their teachers is the direction in which text is read in a student's home language. For example, one day in my math class as I was helping a young Iraqi girl with her work, I discovered that she wrote her English numbers in a right to left fashion, opposite of how a native English speaker would. Students who read right to left or up to down might have more difficulty with how American mathematics is taught. For example, the order of operations, or PEMDAS, follows the traditional direction of Latin languages. A student who speaks Urdu or Farsi, however, will find this to be the opposite direction of how their native language is read. Teachers who understand this subtle difference can make teaching PEMDAS more equitable for those students.

Other differences include *how* numbers are written. For example, many Latin American countries use a crosshatch on a seven to distinguish it from a one and a nine is written with a hook at the bottom like the lowercase letter "g" so as not to be confused with a four.[4] Even notation involved in simple arithmetic operations, decimal places, factor trees, repeating decimals, and so on are subtly different between languages and cultures (see Exhibit 7.1).[5] Understanding the differences between not only U.S. mathematics notation and Latin American notation, but also between U.S. notation and the rest of the world, is essential to predicting common misunderstandings that can occur in an ELL mathematics class.

EXHIBIT 7.1. Mathematical Notation: Comparisons between the United States and Latin American Countries

NUMERALS

U.S.	Latin American Countries	Descriptions
1 and 7	1 and 7	In many Latin American countries, the crosshatch is drawn thru the 7 to distinguish it from the numeral 1.
8	8	The numeral 8 is often drawn from the bottom up.
4	4	The numeral 4 is sometimes drawn from the bottom up. Students may confuse the 4s and the 9s.
9	9	The numeral 9 may resemble a lowercase "g", particularly when written by Cuban students.

READING NUMBERS

U.S.	Latin American Countries	Descriptions
9,435,671	9.435.671	**READING NUMBERS FORM 1** • In the U.S. numbers are separated by groups of 3 (otherwise known as periods) and separated by commas. • In some Latin American countries, the point is used to separate such groups.
9,435,671	9 435 671	**READING NUMBERS FORM 2** • In some Latin American countries, a space is also used to separate groups of 3 and/or periods. This is especially true in Argentina.
9,435,671	9'435,671	**READING NUMBERS FORM 3** • As per the Secretaria de Educacion Publica of Mexico 1993, millions are separated by an apostrophe, and commas separate multiples of thousands.
9,435,671	9;435,671	**READING NUMBERS FORM 4** • The semicolon is also used in Mexico to separate the millions period from the thousands period.
−4	−4 or $\overline{4}$	**NEGATIVE NUMBERS** • In Mexico negative numbers may be written either of two ways- 1) As they are written in the U.S. with a preceding negative sign or 2) With a bar over the number. • The latter format may be confused as repeating decimal fraction.

U.S.	Latin American Countries	Descriptions
$.\overline{3}$ **0.333...**	**.3̂**	**REPEATING DECIMALS** • In the U.S. a repeating decimal is written with a bar over the digit that is repeating and/or the repeating digit(s) are shown followed by three dots. • Some books from Mexico indicate a repeating decimal with an arc rather than a line above the number.
4.56	**4,56**	**DECIMAL FRACTIONS** • The POINT located at the bottom is used to define a decimal fraction. • In the U.S. the point is used to separate the whole number from the fraction. • In some Latin American countries, the comma is used to separate the whole number from the fraction.

DIVISION OF FRACTIONS

U.S.	Latin American Countries	Descriptions
$\dfrac{3}{4} \div \dfrac{1}{8} =$ $\dfrac{3}{4} \times \dfrac{8}{1} = 6$	$\dfrac{3}{4} \div \dfrac{1}{8} =$ $\dfrac{24}{4} = 6$	• In the U.S. the most common procedure to divide fractions is to invert the second fraction and then multiply • In Mexico, students cross-multiply. The numerator of the first fraction is multiplied by the denominator of the 2nd fraction. That product is the numerator of the answer.

(continued)

U.S.	Latin American Countries	Descriptions
		Likewise, the denominator of the first fraction is multiplied by the numerator of the 2nd fraction and the product is the denominator of the answer. This is equivalent of multiplying the 1st fraction by the inverse of the 2nd fraction.

Source: From "Mathematical Notation Comparisons between U.S. and Latin American Countries" available from *TODOS: Mathematics for All,* NCTM, and *Beyond Good Teaching* and created by Noemi R. Lopez, *reprinted with permission.*

Standards for Mathematical Practice and ELLs

There are several excellent resources regarding teaching Common Core mathematics to ELLs. Stanford University's Understanding Language project has a dedicated web page to resources for ELL teachers. According to Judit Moschkovich, a contributing scholar to the Understanding Language project, there are four primary emphases required to accommodate ELLs within the CCSS:

1. balancing conceptual understanding and procedural fluency

2. maintaining high cognitive demand

3. developing beliefs [that mathematics should make sense and be useful in real life]

4. engaging students in mathematical practices[6]

In other words, she is suggesting that ELL mathematics for the Common Core be rigorous and relevant while also accommodating the linguistic needs of students. She suggests that this can be achieved by focusing on the eight Standards for Mathematical Practice (SMP). One example of focusing on the SMPs is through pattern recognition activities. Not only do pattern recognition exercises involve expressing regularity in repeated reasoning (SMP 8), but they can also involve reasoning abstractly and quantitatively (SMP 2), critiquing the reasoning of others (SMP 3), and any number of other practice standards. Functions as Patterns (Exhibit 7.2) is an example of an activity I do with my Integrated Mathematics 1 students involving differentiating between a linear pattern and an exponential pattern.

EXHIBIT 7.2. Functions as Patterns

Linear or Exponential?

A LINEAR pattern is created by the adding or subtracting of the same number to each y-value while an EXPONENTIAL pattern is created by multiplying or dividing the same number to each y-value.
Example: Which of the following is a linear pattern and which is exponential?

Ex. 1

X	y
−2	−7
−1	−4
0	−1
1	2
2	5

Because −7 + 3 = −4 and −4 + 3 = −1 and the others are created by adding 3, the pattern is linear because it is created by addition.

Ex. 2

X	y
−2	−7
−1	−14
0	−28
1	−56
2	−108

Because −7 × 2 = −14 and −14 × 2 = −28 and the others are created by multiplying by 2, the pattern is exponential because it is created by multiplication.

Determine which of the following are linear and which are exponential. Explain why.

1.

X	y
−2	10
−1	8
0	6
1	4
2	2

2.

X	y
−2	10
−1	5
0	2.5
1	1.25
2	0.625

3.

X	y
−2	$\frac{1}{3}$
−1	1
0	3
1	9
2	27

4.

X	y
−2	$\frac{1}{3}$
−1	$\frac{2}{3}$
0	1
1	$\frac{4}{3}$
2	$\frac{5}{3}$

Accommodations for this activity include modeling the first two examples and/or having students work on a single problem as a pair or group and then attempting a second problem individually. The principal SMPs used in this activity are constructing viable arguments as the students are asked to explain their reasoning (SMP 3), looking for and making use of structure since using a table of values is an important mathematical structure (SMP 7), and looking for and expressing regularity in repeated reasoning (SMP 8). It could even be argued that some abstract thought (SMP 2) and making sense of problems (SMP 1) are also being used in this activity. In any case, for those who prefer real contexts for pattern recognition, simple interest and compound interest using simple interest rates like 10% would also be appropriate. When adding context, however, teachers should be mindful not to add too much arithmetic complexity to the problem so that the main topic (differentiating between linear and exponential patterns) is lost.

To teach the concept of a linear function, the following stacking cups activity from Dan Meyer's blog[7] is hands-on, fun, and yields a linear function or pattern. Stacking Cups (Exhibit 7.3) and the Teacher Notes (Exhibit 7.4) contain the details for this activity.

EXHIBIT 7.3. Stacking Cups

1. The Question

How many Styrofoam cups would you have to stack to reach the top of your math teacher's head?

2. Make an Estimate

With your partner or group, come up with these ESTIMATES:

a. How many cups is too many? (Try to make it too big without being ridiculous.)

b. How many cups is too few? (Try to make it too small but not obvious.)

c. What is a good estimate? Why is it good?

One group member will share their estimates and the class will discuss the possibilities.

3. Get Materials

One person from each group will come to the front of the room and pick up cups, a ruler, scratch paper, and any other materials required to complete the activity.

4. Get a Graph and an Equation

Source: Modified from Dan Meyer's Blog, Linear Fun #2; Stacking Cups http://blog.mrmeyer.com/2008/linear-fun-2-stacking-cups/. Reprinted with permission.

EXHIBIT 7.4. Teacher Notes (not for distribution to students)

1. Let It Go

The rest largely runs itself. Just walk around, ask good questions, and correct faulty assumptions.

2. Good Questions

a. How many parts of the cup are there? Two.

b. Which part of the cup matters most over the long run? The lip. The base only counts once but you count the lip every time.

c. If I asked you to tell me how tall a stack of sixty cups would be, what would you do? Add the height of sixty lips to the height of the base.

d. If I asked you to go backwards and tell me how many cups are in a 200-centimeter-tall stack, what would you do? Subtract the height of the base and then divide by the height of the lip.

e. Does it matter if you round to the nearest centimeter? It definitely does.

3. Actually Stack Them

The team that comes closest receives fabulous cash and prizes (or a free homework assignment or bonus points or a sticker or just the knowledge that they ROCK!).

4. Extend It

a. Ask them the same question with a different cup. Maybe a red Solo cup.

b. Toss up this graphic.

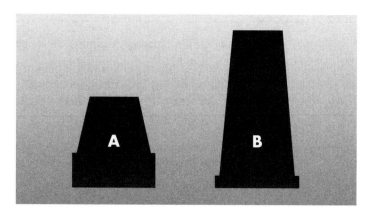

Have them measure the lip and base of each.

Ask them, "**Which will be taller after three cups?**" (A: Cup B.)

Ask them, "**Which will be taller after one hundred cups?**" (A: Cup A.)

And then ask them, "**How many cups does it take stack A to rise above stack B?**"

Source: Modified from Dan Meyer's Blog, Linear Fun #2; Stacking Cups http://blog.mrmeyer.com/2008/linear-fun-2-stacking-cups/. Reprinted with permission. Although Dan Meyer's activities are not designed specifically for ELLs, they can easily be made accessible and are a fun way of modeling with mathematics (SMP 4). His 3-Act Math page, which is hyperlinked to his blog and cited in the reference section, is a great resource for all mathematics teachers in the middle and upper grades.

Another fun activity that my ELL students enjoy involves the exploration of exponential functions using the Tower of Hanoi (pictured in Figure 7.1). Those of you who have seen *Rise of the Planet of the Apes* will recognize the Tower of Hanoi as the learning toy used by the chimpanzee to learn logical reasoning.

Because the Tower of Hanoi is a Hindu legend, this activity is particularly appropriate for ELLs because it connects diverse cultural constructs in terms of game theory and mythology in a mathematical context. In teams of two or three, students begin with one disk and record the minimum number of "moves" it takes to move that one disk to another pole. This is an activity that needs teams of at least two people because the students will begin to lose track of how many moves when working by themselves. Inexpensive towers are available online or at toy stores while paper versions, which use construction paper circles, can be downloaded from Web sources. Regardless, the number of disks versus the number of moves creates an exponential pattern.

There are only two rules in the game: only one disk can move at a time and a larger disk cannot be placed on top of a smaller disk. The Tower of Hanoi (Exhibit 7.5) is the lesson template that I use with my students. I begin with a round-robin reading

Figure 7.1 A Picture of the Tower of Hanoi

of the story at the top of the Tower of Hanoi worksheet followed by a modeling session of moving a one-disk tower and a two-disk tower. The story itself is more of a "hook," or attention getter, than an important part of the lesson. The students, however, enjoy how it connects to the puzzle.

Prior to the students reading the story aloud, I ask them to take out pencils and highlighters. I set a kitchen timer that is projected on the front board for 1 minute and ask students to read the story quietly to themselves for that 1 minute, highlighting parts that they feel are important to the task. Once that minute is over, I begin the round-robin portion, in which student volunteers read a sentence or two at a time until the story is complete. If I feel it is necessary, I may even reread it aloud a third time, pausing for discussion during the parts where the process of moving the disks and the "rules" are explained.

After this portion, I methodically model moving one- and two-disk scenarios (again using a document camera) and recording the number of moves so that all students, including Beginners, can understand how it works. We also discuss the concepts of a "minimum" number of moves and the best ways to determine what that minimum is. Once I am sure that the story and the rules are understood, I "let them go" and students begin to play the game. I circulate while the students work through the problems provided, assisting those who are still confused, correcting students who are "breaking the rules," and eavesdropping on what are hopefully productive discussions. While facilitating this activity, one common question to ask as a means of promoting metacognition is "How do you know that you have recorded the *minimum* number of moves?" The primary SMPs used are making sense of problems and persevering in solving them (SMP 1), modeling with mathematics (SMP 4), and looking for and expressing regularity in repeated reasoning (SMP 8).

EXHIBIT 7.5. The Tower of Hanoi

There is a legend of an Indian temple in Benares. At this temple, the priests were tasked with moving 64 very fragile disks of gold, each one a different size, from one part of the temple to another using three poles. At one end of the temple, all 64 disks are stacked on the first of these three poles in order with the largest on the bottom and the smallest on the top. In fact, the disks are so fragile that a larger disk can never be placed on top of a smaller disk because the larger one will break the smaller one. Also, the disks can only be moved one at a time to minimize the chance of dropping and breaking one. These priests believe that, through this moving of the disks, they will be able to predict the end of the world, . . . once all 64 disks have been moved and are stacked in order on the furthest the world will end, according to the legend.

This legend was popularized by a French mathematician, Edouard Lucas, in 1883. He referred to the three towers and the corresponding disks as the "Tower of Hanoi" or the "Temple of Brahma" after an actual temple in India. There is no evidence that this legend is anything more than a myth created by Lucas himself but the puzzle does yield some interesting mathematical patterns. This puzzle was even used in the 2011 movie "Rise of the Planet of the Apes" as an intelligence test for the chimpanzee Caesar, although no other use of this as a test of intelligence exists other than in this film.

Instructions/Rules:

1. Stack disks largest to smallest on "pole A."

2. Transfer all the disks from one "pole" to another.

3. You may move only one disk at a time.

4. You are trying to find the pattern that uses the smallest number of moves.

5. A large disk may not rest on a smaller one at any time.

Number of disks (x)	Number of moves (y)
1	1
2	
3	
4	
5	
6	

For this activity, begin with one disk and record how many moves are required to move it to a different pole.

Now, use two disks. Record how many moves are required to move two disks to another pole FOLLOWING THE RULES ABOVE.

Continue until all six have been moved and counted.

Record your results in the table.

When you are finished with the table, graph the results.

Use the table and the graph to determine the formula for this pattern.

(Hint: add 1 to the number of moves if needed to see pattern)

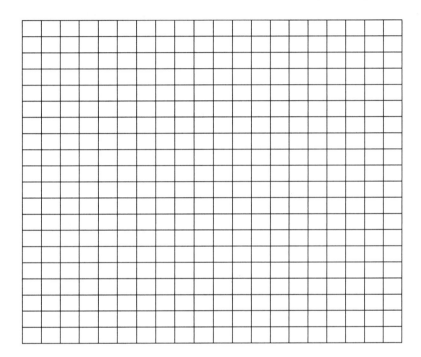

Promoting Discourse and Collaboration

One of the best ways to promote discourse and communication in ELL classrooms is the use of *sentence frames*. Sentence frames are scaffolded, partial phrases that allow students to participate in an academic discussion without fear of how to start or what to say. They help students use important academic vocabulary and concepts in a safe yet public way. This scaffold assists students to use English when connecting prior learning, new concepts, and the problem-solving techniques of revision and critique.[8]

The sentence frames themselves can even be tailored to differing levels of language acquisition so that Beginner ELLs are able to participate and learn along with more advanced ELLs. Sentence Frames (Exhibit 7.6) is an example of some of the sentence frames from Melanese, Chung, and Forbes.[8] These can be distributed to students and/or enlarged and posted on the classroom wall or even taped to individual student desks.

EXHIBIT 7.6. Sentence Frames

Language Functions and Sentence Frames

Function	Beginning	Intermediate/Advanced
Describing	A _____ has _____.	A _____ has _____ and _____.
Examples	An equilateral triangle has three congruent angles.	An equilateral triangle has three congruent angles and three congruent sides.
Comparing	A _____ has _____. A _____ has _____.	A _____ has _____, but _____ has _____. Although _____ and _____ are the same in that _____, they are different because _____.
Examples	An equilateral triangle has three congruent angles. An isosceles triangle has two congruent angles.	An equilateral triangle has three congruent angles, but an isosceles triangle has two congruent angles. Although an equilateral triangle and an isosceles triangle are the same in that they have three angles, they are different because an equilateral triangle has three congruent angles and an isosceles triangle has two congruent angles.
Categorizing	A _____ is a _____. It is _____, because _____.	A _____ is a _____, because _____ and _____.
Examples	A quadrilateral is a polygon. It is a polygon because it is closed.	A quadrilateral is a polygon because it is closed and has four straight sides.
Sequencing	First, _____. Next, _____.	First, _____ and then _____. After _____, _____. Before _____, _____.

Function	Beginning	Intermediate/Advanced
Examples	First, I measured the diameter. Next, I tried different ratios.	First, I measured the diameter and then I tried different ratios. After I measured the diameter, I tried different ratios. Before I tried different ratios, I measured the diameter.
Hypothesizing	If _____, then _____.	I know that for _____, the _____ is _____.
Examples	If the input value is 2, then the output value is 4	I know that for every input value of n, the output value is $2n$.
Predicting	_____ will _____.	I predict that _____ will _____. I predict that _____ will _____, because _____.
Examples	I will roll a 7.	I predict that I will roll a 7. I predict that I will roll a 7, because there are more number combinations that equal 7 than any other sum or number on the die.
Making Inferences	I can infer that _____. I think so because _____.	I can infer that _____, because I know _____.
Examples	I can infer that the number is a fraction. I think so because it is not an integer.	I can infer that the number is a fraction, because I know it is not an integer.
Drawing Conclusions	I think the _____ is _____.	I can conclude that _____. I can conclude that _____, because _____ and _____.
Examples	I think the function is $2n$.	I can conclude that the function is $2n$. I can conclude that the function is $2n$, because I multiplied the input value by 2 and the output value was 4.

(continued)

Function	Beginning	Intermediate/Advanced
Explaining Cause and Effect	The _____ is _____.	_____ because _____. Because _____ is _____, the _____ is _____. _____ caused _____ to _____.
Examples	The area of triangle #10 is 3.	The area of triangle #10 is 3 because if I enclose triangle #10 inside a rectangle, the area of that rectangle is 6. Because the area of triangle #10 is one half the area of the rectangle, the area of triangle #10 is 3. Enclosing triangle #10 inside a rectangle caused the area of triangle #10 to be one half the area of the rectangle.

Source: Melanese, Chung, & Forbes, 2011, pp. 176–177. Originally appeared in Supporting English Language Learners in Math Class: Grades V 6–8 (pp. 176–177) by Melanese, K., Chung, L. & Forbes, C; Sausalito, CA: Math Solutions. Reprinted with their permission.

Sentence frames are most effective when coupled with the appropriate teacher "talk moves."[9] Talk moves are questioning strategies or prompts that create more opportunities for students to process new information more completely and promote metacognition. The five main talk moves discussed by Chapin, O'Connor, and Anderson[9] are revoicing the student's own words to clarify (revoicing), asking the student to rephrase or restate the words of a peer (rephrasing/restating), asking the student to apply their own reasoning to the reasoning of a peer (asking for evidence or reasoning), prompting students to take the discussion further (adding on/elaborate), and using "wait time" to allow students time to think deeply rather than providing the answers for them. In terms of wait time and talk moves, the phrase "never answer a question that the students can answer themselves" seems appropriate. These talk moves are essential to the Common Core SMPs, primarily when asking students to critique the reasoning of others. Teacher Talk Moves (Exhibit 7.7) shows several examples of popular teacher talk moves, including four of the five from Chapin et al.,[9] along with the sentence frames students may find

EXHIBIT 7.7. Teacher Talk Moves

Talk Move	Teacher Talk	Student Talk
Revoicing	So what you're saying is_____. What I hear you saying is_____. Are you saying____?	Yes, that is what I said. No, I didn't say that. I want to clarify my idea. I said_____.
Say More/Elaborate	Can you say more about that? What do you mean by that?	I mean to say_____. An example is_____.
Rephrasing/Restating	Can you repeat what she/he said in your own words? Who can explain what she/he just said?	She/he said that_____.
Asking for Evidence or Reasoning	Why do you think that? What's your evidence? How does that idea compare to___'s example?	I think_____because_____. My evidence is_____.
Adding On/Elaborate	Would somebody like to add on? Does anyone have a connection to this idea?	I would like to add on to what___said. I connect to what was said because_____.
Applying Your Own Reasoning	Do you agree/disagree? Why? Do you support/oppose this idea?	I agree because_____. I disagree because_____.
Revising Your Thinking	Would you like to revise your thinking? I wonder if_____? What do you think about what she said? Why?	I want to change my idea because____. I want to revise my thinking. I think__. I think it might be false. I'm starting to wonder.

Source: A version of this figure originally appeared in *Classroom Discussions: Using Math Talk To Help Students Learn, Grades 1–6* 2003 Math Solutions. It has been modified by Justin Johnson at http://www.sentenceframes.com. It is reprinted here with permission.

appropriate when responding. These are from "Math Solutions" and have been modified by educator Justin Johnson.

Aside from sentence frames, there are other strategies to promote effective communication in an ELL classroom. In "think-pair-share" activities students are given a question, open-ended problem, or prompt, asked to think about a solution for a specific amount of time, and then asked to pair up to share their thoughts. This strategy not only supports constructing viable arguments and critiquing the reasoning of others (SMP 3), but also, depending on the prompt, may encompass making sense of problems (SMP 1) and reasoning abstractly and quantitatively (SMP 2). One way to ensure that both partner's share for an equal amount of time is to use an "As and Bs" approach where one student is "student A" and the other is "student B" and each speaks for 1 minute, and so forth.

Other communication strategies include the "heads together" activity, which is like a football huddle; a round robin or "toss the ball" approach, in which the student who is "it" answers and then chooses the next person to respond; or a random drawing, so students feel that "luck" determines who gets to talk rather than teacher preference.[11] Choral responses can also be effective although they do not necessarily promote independent thinking, rigor, or metacognition; they do, however, involve repetition and, perhaps, rephrasing, which are necessary strategies for ELL students.[8] Nonverbal responses can be equally effective. Many students genuinely enjoy using their arms to demonstrate angle definitions (like acute or obtuse) or using their fingers to show their solutions to mental mathematics problems.

A final note on promoting discourse and collaboration with ELLs relates to student grouping techniques. While random grouping can be effective for non-ELL classes, I find that this can sometimes be more stressful on ELLs and can, on occasion, cause some students to shut down. It may be appropriate to sometimes group Beginning ELLs with more advanced students while balancing this with other groups that are more homogeneous. While it may seem most advantageous to have more advanced English learners working with their less skilled peers, those advanced students also need opportunities to improve their own language and mathematics skills by working with others on their own level. A balance between the two is most effective.

Regardless, grouping decisions need to be made based on the cognitive demand of the task,[3] the social level of the students, the mathematical and linguistic goals of the lesson, and the mathematical and language skills of the students all the while promoting a safe and positive learning community within which the students can thrive.[8]

Additional Suggestions for Effective Teaching of ELLs in Common Core Math

Sylvia Celedon-Pattichis and Nora Ramirez (2012) in their book *Beyond Good Teaching*[3] recommend that teachers "highlight the distinctions between the meaning of terms used in math and the meaning of terms used in everyday life" (p. 24). As a way of meeting this suggestion, I often have students write a story using math words that also have meaning outside of mathematics. Typically, the nonmath meaning is similar to the meaning in mathematics so the discussion following these stories can assist students in remembering both the math and the nonmath meanings. In fact, if you consider mathematics vocabulary as a tool of math instruction, this activity and similar ones can be considered part of using tools strategically (SMP 5). Writing Assignment Instructions (Exhibit 7.8) is an example of a writing assignment for a general mathematics class, but it could be modified for use in other levels.

EXHIBIT 7.8. Writing Assignment Instructions

Choose at least 10 words from the word bank below to use in a creative writing story. Extra credit is given for more than 10 words.

The story can be about anything you would like; can be as simple as how you got to school this morning like "My sister drove the car in a line and we saw an accident at the intersection of Florin and 24th" or as complex as you would like. I have had great stories in the past about aliens, haunted houses, first dates, and mysterious school meals along with equally well-written ones about how to make a sandwich or put on make-up.

The story must be at least half a page long (or 100 words) but no more than two pages (or 500 words). PLEASE UNDERLINE THE VOCABULARY WORDS USED!

Word Bank

altitude	base	coordinate	degree
difference	edge	even	expression
domain	side	leg	solution
equality	minimum	intersection	mean
face	factor	function	inequality
median	negative	positive	odd
maximum	operation	order	range
value	absolute	rational	irrational
variable	coefficient	equivalent	term

Rules

1. Words can be used for their <u>math</u> meaning OR their <u>not-math</u> meaning. For example, you can say that "we played monopoly and I rolled an <u>odd</u> number" OR you can say that "I met an <u>odd</u> person."

2. Words CANNOT be used as proper names or titles. For example, do **not** talk about "~~Maximum Factor Street~~" or "~~Mrs. Variable.~~"

3. Do NOT list the words. For example, do **not** say "I went to math class today and learned about ~~domain, expression, even, minimum, negative, and variables.~~"

Stories will be graded by the number of words USED CORRECTLY in their sentences. Stories will NOT be graded for grammatical errors, only word meanings. Extra credit will be given for creativity and extra word use.

Another way to support ELLs in the mathematics classroom is by using graphic organizers. It can be more effective when vocabulary graphic organizers have students provide additional pieces of information and not just a traditional word and definition. The headers on my vocabulary organizers look like this:

Word	Book Definition	Definition in My Words	Picture or Example

I encourage Beginning ELLs to use translation dictionaries or cell phone apps that assist them in writing the definitions in their own words. Students can use these graphic organizers on most quizzes or exams and they keep them handy when working on activities and class problem solving. Through using these as common references, the students are better able to make sense of problems and persevere in solving them (SMP 1), along with constructing viable arguments (SMP 3).

There are other kinds of graphic organizers that I use for my ELL mathematics classes and many can be found online. The ones I find most useful include:

- The Frayer model, a popular vocabulary tool for vocabulary development that uses a graphic organizer to define, describe, model, and demonstrate that which is *not* encompassed by the definition (developed by Dorothy Frayer in 1969[10]), as shown in the Traditional Frayer Model Example (Exhibit 7.9).

EXHIBIT 7.9. Traditional Frayer Model Example

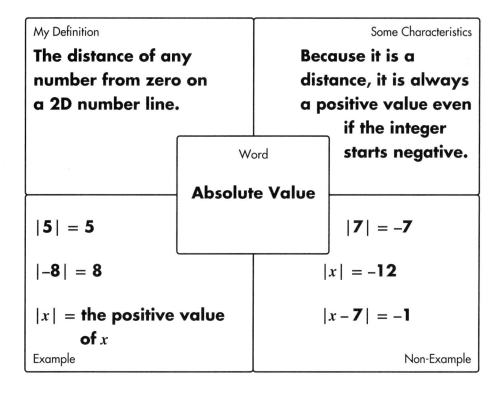

My Definition
The distance of any number from zero on a 2D number line.

Some Characteristics
Because it is a distance, it is always a positive value even if the integer starts negative.

Word
Absolute Value

$|5| = 5$

$|-8| = 8$

$|x| =$ **the positive value of** x

Example

$|7| = -7$

$|x| = -12$

$|x - 7| = -1$

Non-Example

Source: Adapted from the Frayer Model developed in 1969 by Dorothy Frayer.

- A modified Frayer model that also uses an image or picture for better understanding, as shown in the Modified Frayer Model Example (Exhibit 7.10).

- A Venn diagram to enhance similarities and differences in both vocabulary and solving techniques, as shown in the Venn Diagram Example (Exhibit 7.11).

- A description wheel to highlight examples, definitions, and misconceptions regarding math terms, as shown in the Wheel Graphic Organizer Example (Exhibit 7.12).

- A flow chart outlining the steps required to solve an equation, as shown in the Flow Chart Equation Solving Example (Exhibit 7.13).

- An equation solving tool similar to a flow chart that highlights the "undoing" of the order of operations required to solve an equation, as shown in Solving Using Graphic Visualization (Exhibit 7.14).

- A graphic organizer that, again, is similar to a flow chart but highlights the diversity of solving techniques for many mathematical concepts as shown in the Solving Options Graphic Organizer (Exhibit 7.15).

EXHIBIT 7.10. Modified Frayer Model Example

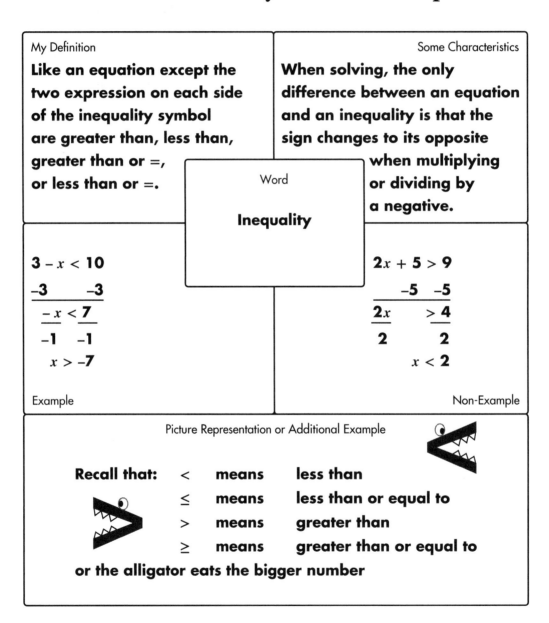

Source: The Modified Frayer Model is based on the model developed in 1969 by Frayer, Frayer and Klausmeier, the research of R. Marzano and D. Pickering, and the work done by countless educators.

EXHIBIT 7.11. Venn Diagram Example

Venn Diagram

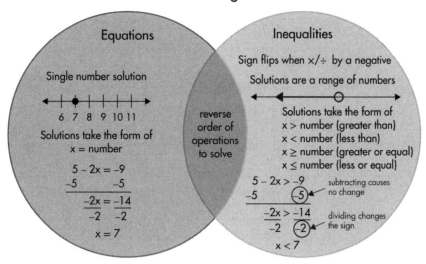

EXHIBIT 7.12. Wheel Graphic Organizer Example

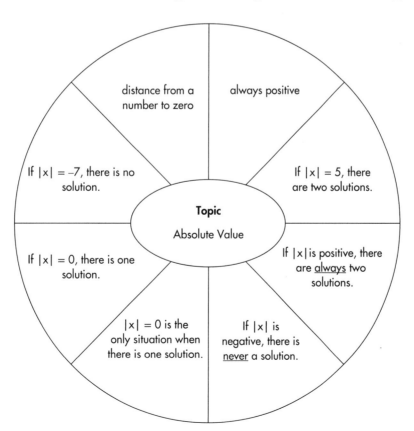

EXHIBIT 7.13. Flow Chart Equation Solving Example

$$3x - 5(x - 4) = 12$$

1. Distribute   −5 multiplies to both x and −4
$$3x - 5x + 20 = 12$$

2. Combine like terms   3x and −5x combine
$$- 2x + 20 = 12$$

3. Move numbers to one side   Subtract 20 from
$$- 2x = -8$$ both sides of =

4. Move variables with coefficients to other side
Already done

5. Divide by coefficient to finish solving
so x = 4

EXHIBIT 7.14. Solving Using Graphic Visualization

Start with x and build the variable expression on the top

Solve
8x + 5 = 29

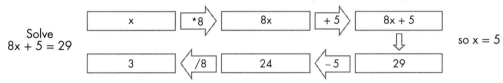

so x = 5

Undo the top steps to solve for x

EXHIBIT 7.15. Solving Options Graphic Organizer

Systems of Equations

Solve for x and y:
$$3x - y = 7$$
$$2x + y = 8$$

SUBSTITUTION

Step 1: Solve for one variable in one of the equations
2x + y = 8 (−2x both sides)
    y = −2x + 8
Step 2: Substitute for that variable into the other equation and solve
    3x − (−2x + 8) = 7
    3x + 2x − 8 = 7
    5x = 15 so   x = 3
Step 3: Using step 1, solve for the other variable.

ELIMINATION

Step 1: Line up equations so "like terms" and equals are above each other.
Step 2: Add equations and solve for remaining variable.
    3x − y = 7
    2x + y = 8
    ‾‾‾‾‾‾‾‾‾‾
    5x   = 15
    x = 3
Step 3: Pick ONE of the ORIGINAL equations and use Step 2 to solve for other variable.

GRAPHING

Step 1: Rewrite each equation so they read y = mx + b
    y = 3x − 7
    y = −2x + 8
Step 2: Graph the equations. Their intersection (where they cross) is the solution.

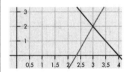

All methods of solving reach an answer of
(3, 2)

I choose the appropriate organizer based on the topic, the cognitive demand of the task, and the average language level of the class. The students find them more interesting than "taking notes" and are able to refer to them more easily on future assignments. Also, as mentioned previously, they assist greatly in helping ELLs meet the SMPs, primarily making sense of problems and persevering in solving them (SMP 1), along with constructing viable arguments (SMP 3).

In addition to graphic organizers, I also use more traditional manipulatives like algebra tiles. I find that some of these more traditional methods are still very useful for connecting mathematical concepts using tactile and visual stimuli rather than lectures and note taking. These also still fit within the SMPs because they are an example of using tools strategically (SMP 5) and sometimes are a way to model with mathematics (SMP 4). In fact, I teach lessons using these tools and then also make them available during other activities for student use. I have a bookshelf full of algebra tiles, toothpicks, blocks, colored pencils, graph paper, white paper, two-colored counters, and assorted other materials as well as six easel boards for group brainstorming, which students can access at any time.

Some final recommendations for accommodating ELLs include encouraging them to access their prior learning, teachers modifying the linguistic complexity of language and rephrasing math problems, guiding students to cross out the unnecessary vocabulary in word problems (or highlight the necessary ones), building knowledge from real-world examples, and using manipulatives intentionally.[6] It is also recommended that teachers use a metacognitive approach to both teaching content strands and language goals as ELLs benefit from reflecting on their own learning and progress much like traditional populations of students.[11]

Modifying a Lesson for ELLs

According to Melanese, Chung, and Forbes,[8] there are eight steps for modifying a lesson for ELLs. These are:

1. Identify a math goal.

2. Choose a language goal that serves the math goal.

3. Determine key vocabulary.

4. Design sentence frames according to proficiency levels.

5. Plan how to introduce academic language.

6. Build opportunities for talk.

7. Design a writing prompt to conclude the lesson.

8. Simplify the information using a lesson template (p. 189).

The section below contains a description of how a teacher would use these eight steps to develop an accessible math lesson plan for ELLs and is then followed by the lesson plan itself.

STEP 1: IDENTIFY A MATH GOAL

This lesson is from a set of workbooks for the Walch Integrated 1 mathematics curriculum.[12] The "Problem–Based Task" (found in Exhibits 7.17 & 7.18) requires students to work through a real-world prompt using collaboration and mathematical modeling skills. The prompt used for this lesson requires students to model using exponential functions. Hence, the primary math goal is to *model using exponential functions.*

STEP 2: CHOOSE A LANGUAGE GOAL THAT SERVES THE MATH GOAL

This is where the teacher decides how the students will share their thinking and what language structures they will need to do so. For this lesson, the students will need to *compare and contrast* two functions, *make predictions and inferences* from the data given, and generate valid *conclusions.* They may even need to *critique the reasoning* of others. Much of this mathematics vocabulary is provided within the SMPs but is also inherent in the sentence frames provided previously.

STEP 3: DETERMINE KEY VOCABULARY

The explicit vocabulary words that the students will need to use and understand are:

1. Mathematics primary vocabulary—*equation, function, exponential function, evaluate a function,* and *substitute.*

2. Mathematics secondary vocabulary—*principal, rate, interest.*

3. Other vocabulary—*savings, account, original, amount, deposit.*

STEP 4: DESIGN SENTENCE FRAMES ACCORDING TO PROFICIENCY LEVELS

The sentence frames that are most appropriate for this lesson involve those for comparing and contrasting. Beginning students should be provided with frames such as *"This account has _____ after _____"* or *"There is _____ more money in _____ than in _____."* Sentence frames for Intermediate and Advanced students could begin in a similar fashion but should require more elaboration and explanation. *"This account has _____ after _____ because _____ helps it _____ at a _____ _____"* would be one example.

STEP 5: PLAN HOW TO INTRODUCE ACADEMIC LANGUAGE

I provide 1–2 minutes of quiet, independent reading of the prompt followed by a discussion of key vocabulary. I have students use an *interactive notebook* with two different vocabulary sections: one for *math specific words* and one for more *general academic words*. Students note the meanings of the math words specifically used, like equation and rate, along with math words that are implied like exponential function. Words like amount, account, and deposit would be added to the general academic word section. See Vocabulary Notebook (Exhibit 7.16) for a model of what my students use.

EXHIBIT 7.16. Vocabulary Notebook

Left Side of the Page	Right Side of the Page
Math Words	General Academic Words
Word — Definition — Picture or Example	Word — Definition — Picture or Example

STEP 6: BUILD OPPORTUNITIES FOR TALK

Once the key *vocabulary is discussed and all preliminary questions are answered*, the students are expected to work in small groups on the provided problem. *Sentence frames are provided* and I circulate throughout using my talk moves to assist students who are hesitant to use their English, who are shy, or who are doing surface-level thinking rather than making deeper connections to the material. At the end of the lesson, *each group shares their solutions verbally* or through a written response.

STEP 7: DESIGN A WRITING PROMPT TO CONCLUDE THE LESSON

The writing prompt should be deep enough to get everyone thinking but simple enough so that Beginning ELLs can participate. A good writing prompt may be: "*Can you think of another situation that could be modeled by an exponential function? Explain.*"

If students struggled with the concept of an exponential function, however, a prompt such as *"How could the principal for Account A be changed so both accounts have the same amount after three years? Explain"* might be more accessible. If both are too difficult, using a "learning log" is often adequate where students are directed to *"Write down one thing you learned today and one thing you need to learn more about. Explain both."*

STEP 8: SIMPLIFY THE INFORMATION USING A LESSON TEMPLATE

One of the nice things about the Walch[12] curriculum is that it provides optional *coaching questions for students who need more scaffolding* throughout this task. These questions range from "What is the total amount in Austin's savings if he chooses Account A?" (p. U1–23) to "Who has more money at the end of the term?" With ELLs, creating more coaching questions may be necessary, such as "Which numbers represent the principals and what do they look like in the equation?" The following lesson plan also fulfills this "lesson template" guideline.

Modified Problem-Based Task Lesson Plan

Instructional Objectives

Mathematics Objective:

Students will:

- Be able to compare and contrast exponential functions in a real context.

Language Objective:

Students will:

- Be able to communicate their mathematical thinking about two different exponential functions through speaking and writing, which may include manipulatives and/or diagrams.

Duration

One 55-minute class period

Standards

CCSS Mathematics Content Standards

A-SSE.1 Interpret expressions that represent a quantity in terms of its context.

CCSS Mathematics Practice Standards

MP 1. Make sense of problems and persevere in solving them.

MP 2. Reason abstractly and quantitatively.

MP 3. Construct a viable argument and critique the reasoning of others.

MP 7. Look for and make use of structure.

Materials

- Copies of problem-based task for all students—Original Lesson Prompt (Exhibit 7.17) for Advanced ELLs or the Modified Lesson Prompt (Exhibit 7.18).

- notebooks, pens, calculators, and highlighters for all students.

Procedure

1. Hand out the problem-based task, either Original Lesson Prompt (Exhibit 7.17) or the Modified Lesson Prompt (Exhibit 7.18).

2. Provide students with 1 minute to read quietly, highlighting the "math parts" of the problem. Students may use dictionaries or translation apps to assist if necessary. If the class contains a majority of Beginning ELLs, 2 minutes may be more appropriate.

3. Discuss the prompt, both in terms of content and in terms of vocabulary, both mathematical and general academic words (5–10 minutes).

4. Have students get into groups (1 minute max).

5. In groups, students will decide on a strategy for how to solve the prompt (5 minutes).

6. While the teacher circulates, prompting and eavesdropping on conversations, students will work through the prompt together (15 minutes).

7. Students will either create a verbal presentation of their solution or a visual one, like a poster (10 minutes).

8. Students will share their solutions and discuss which arguments are "viable," or make sense, and which do not.

9. Activity ends with writing prompt.

Assessment

The assessment is the final presentation, whether verbal or visual, of the solution to the writing prompt.

Possible Extensions and Modifications

This activity can be made simpler by using easier percents, like 2 and 3. It can also be made more challenging by asking students questions such as, "What amount would need to be invested in Account A to have the same amount as Account B after 3 years?"

EXHIBIT 7.17. Original Lesson Prompt

Problem-Based Task 1.1.2: Searching for a Greater Savings

Austin plans to open a savings account. The amount of money in a savings account can be found using the equation $s = p \cdot (1 + r)^t$, where p is the principal, or the original amount deposited into account; r is the rate of interest; and t is the amount of time. Austin is considering two savings accounts. He will deposit $1,000.00 as the principal into either account. In Account A, the interest rate will be 0.015 per year for 5 years. In Account B, the interest rate will be 0.02 per year for 3 years. If he could, would it be wise for Austin to leave his money in the account that has less savings for an additional year? Explain your reasoning" (Hale et al., 2012, p. U1-22).

Source: Text from *CCSS Integrated Pathway: Mathematics I Teacher Resource* by Walch Education. Copyright 2012, 2014 by J. Weston Walch, Publisher. Used with permission. Further reproduction is prohibited.

EXHIBIT 7.18. Modified Lesson Prompt

Problem-Based Task 1.1.2: Searching for a Greater Savings

John *(the name Austin may be confusing if the students are also studying geography)* plans to open a savings account. This is an account at the bank that gives you interest for leaving your money with them. The amount of money in a savings account can be found using the equation $s = p \cdot (1 + r)^t$, where p is the principal, or the original amount deposited into account; r is the rate of interest given as a decimal and not a percent; and t is the amount of time in years. John is considering two different savings accounts. He will deposit $1,000.00 as the principal, or starting amount, into one of the accounts. In Account A (the name of the first account he looked at), the interest rate will be 0.015 per year for 5 years. In Account B (the name of the second account), the interest rate will be 0.02 per year for 3 years. If he could, would it be smart for John to leave his money in the account that has less savings (or the lower interest rate) for an extra year? Explain your reasoning.

NOTE: You may want to leave some ambiguity in the prompt, especially if there are higher-level students. Much of SMP 4, modeling with mathematics, requires students to identify missing information and make conjectures as to what that may mean. Then, test these conjectures to see if they make sense.

Tech Tools

Math Resources For English Language Learners

There are a number of free online math-related resources that are useful for teaching English Language Learners. We have collected some of the best at these two posts:

The Best Resources For Teaching Common Core Math To English Language Learners (http://larryferlazzo.edublogs.org/2014/11/22/the-best-resources-for-teaching-common-core-math-to-english-language-learners/)

All My Math-Related "The Best . . ." Lists In One Place (http://larryferlazzo.edublogs .org/2012/12/27/all-my-math-related-the-best-lists-in-one-place/)

For downloadable versions of the lesson plans and Tech Tools boxes found in this chapter, go to the "Downloads" section of this book's web page at www.wiley.com/go/navccss.

CHAPTER EIGHT

Social Studies

Elisabeth Johnson

The Common Core Standards encourage social studies teachers to utilize primary and secondary source documents to facilitate students' learning of analysis skills. Students practice these analysis skills as they read and then apply them to their writing. This chapter contains instructional strategies I use with English language learners (ELLs) to build these kinds of analytical skills and to make Common Core–aligned social studies content accessible. Each strategy is illustrated with an example from a unit on the Foundations of the Government in the United States using the primary sources of the Declaration of Independence and the Bill of Rights. The chapter ends with a lesson plan showing how these same strategies can be used while teaching about four types of government.

Chunking

If I started a lesson by giving students the Declaration of Independence without any supports, my ELL students could spend weeks combing through the text. At the end, I would probably see they had looked up every other word and written definitions, highlighted all over the place, and most likely would still have very little idea what the complex text was talking about. This would obviously be a waste of everyone's time. Instead, I give them small bits of information at a time, from multiple sources, as we move through our study of the Declaration of Independence and on to the Bill of Rights. This strategy is called chunking.[1]

The thinking behind "chunking" is that instead of overwhelming students, especially with a text that is very challenging, they review smaller pieces and work their way up to the larger picture. In this way teachers can assess students' understanding during the process, making changes and clarifying important points, before moving on to the next step. Chunking allows the teacher to more easily assess student comprehension and creates opportunities to celebrate small successes, giving students the confidence they need moving forward. Before introducing the actual primary source document, I give students small pieces of the Declaration of Independence in various forms. These include a music video, then a closer inspection of the lyrics, and, finally, short "chunks" of text from the actual Declaration of Independence.

"Close Viewing" or "Close Reading" a Video

We start our study of the Declaration of Independence by watching a music video called *Too Late to Apologize: A Declaration* (easily found online).[2] It is very important to have students "close-view" or "close-read" the video (see the "Use of Visuals" section in Chapter 3, which discusses close reading) in order to build comprehension. I have the students watch this video two or three times and follow along on copies of lyrics provided to them.

Watching video clips more than once allows ELLs to first gain basic comprehension, then look for the big ideas, and finally focus in on the details. Giving students the lyrics helps them to follow along and see the words, which is especially important for ELLs. When choosing video clips to watch, stick to short clips—longer videos can be overwhelming. Choose the videos you use in your classroom carefully and make sure they address the points you are teaching in an engaging way.

The music video *Too Late to Apologize: A Declaration* is just under three and a half minutes long. The first time students simply watch and follow along with their printed lyrics. After the second viewing, students share the main message of the video. Students can easily point out the "villain" of the video. Then, we may watch again and look through the lyrics to find why the men in the video are so angry at the "villain," whom I have identified as King George III of Great Britain. The close viewing of this music video gives the students the context they need to then begin to take a look at sections of the actual Declaration of Independence.

Inductive Learning

Generally, social studies textbooks give students a summary of the cause, effect, and details of events throughout history. These summaries are easily forgotten. However, teachers can help students more deeply understand and remember these historical events by using the inductive method (see Chapters 2, 3, and 4 for more background on inductive learning).

One of the best ways I have found to implement inductive learning with ELLs in my classroom is by using text data sets.

I first create context for the students through close reading the video. They can now identify the issues faced by the colonists and are more prepared to view the Declaration as a list of complaints. This process helps students to achieve the CCSS ELA–Literacy History/Social Studies Standard 2, which asks students to, at varying levels based on their grade, "Determine central ideas or themes of a text and analyze their development; summarize the key supporting details and ideas." Depending on the English level of your students, you might choose to give them the entire Declaration or break the list of complaints down into a Declaration of Independence Data Set (see Exhibit 8.1 for an example).

As the teacher, you get to choose how much of the primary source document you give to students. Perhaps you pull out only complaints that match those described in the music video and have students match the complaints from the song to those in that data set. Additionally, giving students both primary and secondary sources addresses the CCSS ELA–Literacy History/Social Studies Standard 9, as students are able to compare different texts on the same topic.

I would recommend using the data set instead of the actual Declaration with most ELLs. Students first read the data set independently or in pairs and circle words that they heard in the video or noticed in the lyrics. Then, students read each exemplar and highlight key ideas. Students can also write comments in the margins—a reaction or a question about the information. Students then categorize the exemplars. Depending on the level of your students you can give them all of the categories, some categories, or have them come up with the categories themselves. The categories can be flexible. For example, categories in the Declaration of Independence Data Set (Exhibit 8.1) could be different types of complaints (ones dealing with trade; ones dealing with soldiers/military; ones with issues related to justice).

EXHIBIT 8.1. Declaration of Independence Data Set

1. He has made judges dependent on his will alone, for the tenure of their offices, and the amount and payment of their salaries.

2. He has erected a multitude of new offices, and sent hither swarms of officers to harass our people, and eat out their substance.

3. For quartering large bodies of armed troops among us . . .

4. For protecting them, by a mock trial, from punishment for any murders which they should commit on the inhabitants of these States . . .

5. For cutting off our trade with all parts of the world . . .

6. For imposing taxes on us without our consent . . .

7. For depriving us in many cases, of the benefits of trial by jury . . .

8. For transporting us beyond seas to be tried for pretended offences . . .

9. He has plundered our seas, ravaged our coasts, burnt our towns, and destroyed the lives of our people.

10. He is at this time transporting large armies of foreign mercenaries to complete the works of death, desolation and tyranny, already begun with circumstances of cruelty scarcely paralleled in the most barbarous ages, and totally unworthy the head of a civilized nation.

Writing Scaffolds

Many social studies teachers may see that their students—ELL and non-ELL—don't automatically know how to write an argument, especially if they are not avid readers and writers or are new to the language. Scaffolds can help students build up to higher levels of writing.

Having students categorize the data set is one example of a helpful scaffolding activity. The exemplars in each category represent evidence. Students can use this evidence to support arguments that they write, as required in Standard 1 of the CCSS ELA–Literacy History/Social Studies Writing.[3]

Students can utilize an ABC structure to organize their writing (discussed in Chapter 3 in the section on "Read Alouds" and in Chapter 4 under "Planning and Organizing"). The students **A**nswer the question, **B**ack it up with evidence from the text, and **C**omment or provide an analysis or more personal perspective. This strategy is easy to adjust for different levels. For example, you would use sentence frames for an ELL Beginner, while a more advanced ELL might just need to be reminded of the ABC structure before writing. This assignment might look like:

> **Teacher question**: Why was the Declaration of Independence written?
> **Answer**: The Declaration was written because Great Britain was . . . (pick one of the complaints categories).

Back it up: In the Declaration, the writers describe how Great Britain ... (cite a specific piece of the text data set exemplar that specifies something Great Britain was doing that was unjust).

Comment: Great Britain caused difficulties for the colonists because ... (explain why the complaint against Great Britain was a problem for the colonists).

You can utilize this ABC strategy across social studies, and it works especially well with primary source documents including texts, pictures, and short video clips. In U.S. history, using pictures or short videos of sit-ins and marches during the Civil Rights era can lead up to the analysis of the text "Letter from Birmingham Jail" by Martin Luther King Jr. When studying the Holocaust in world history teachers can show pictures or short video clips of the concentration camps and then have students analyze "Hope, Despair and Memory" by Elie Wiesel. Both of these topics lend themselves well to writing activities where students are asked a question and then directed to respond using the ABC structure. Some possible Civil Rights questions might include: "What did Martin Luther King Jr. believe in?" or "Why was Martin Luther King Jr. in jail?" Holocaust-related questions could be "What was life like for the survivors of the Holocaust?" or "Why is it important to remember the Holocaust?"

Multiple Touches

When I want my students to really understand a concept(s), I give them the same information in multiple ways and have them read, write, and talk about that information in as many ways as possible. Sports analogies can be helpful in explaining why this idea works. I ask students to think about how many times Michael Jordan practiced shooting baskets or Lionel Messi practiced his shots on goal—to get good at something, you have to do it over and over again. The same is true with the information we want students to learn. They must read it, write it, and talk about it over and over again. The challenge is, "How do I get them to experience this repeated practice without it becoming boring?" Obviously, it's harder to get most students to reread text than it is to shoot multiple baskets.

When students learn about the Bill of Rights, they read, write, and talk about the material many times. They begin by watching very short video clips about each of the first 10 amendments. There are many options for short video clips that do this, but I use a free, online series by the Annenberg Classroom called "The Story of the

Bill of Rights."[4] While students watch the video, they note words that jump out at them for each of the 10 amendments. For example, they might write words like "religion, speech, freedom" for the first amendment. For Beginning ELLs, I add a photo analysis activity where students look at a visual representation of each amendment and describe what they see and how it might relate to the individual amendment. For example, I might show them a picture of a person speaking on a soapbox in a park to represent freedom of speech and ask them to describe what they see.

Next, I give students a paraphrased version of the Bill of Rights (search online for "paraphrased Bill of Rights" and you will find many options). The paraphrase can be modified for all levels of ELLs—simple one-sentence phrases for Beginner students and more complete paraphrases for Intermediate and Advanced ELLs. We then read through each of the paraphrased 10 amendments and students look for words they wrote from the video clips that connect to each of the paraphrased amendments.

Students now have enough context to match the paraphrases with the actual amendments from the Bill of Rights. I give the students the Bill of Rights as unnumbered, out of order statements. Their task is to match the actual amendment with the paraphrase. At this point, students have had multiple touches with the first 10 amendments and are now more prepared to write about them.

Graphic Organizer

The Bill of Rights Graphic Organizer (Table 8.1) helps students to organize and summarize their understanding of each amendment in a way that will help them remember the information in preparation for writing.

This organizer allows for students to work with the concepts multiple times, but in different ways to avoid boredom and the feeling of rote memorization. After students have created their graphic organizers the teacher can choose pieces from each student's organizer and create a "class organizer." Using this class organizer can become a daily activity. For example, teachers and students can create full page examples of the different visuals for each of the 10 amendments and spend a few minutes at the start of class displaying the visuals and having students write or tell which amendment the visual displayed refers to. The same could be done with the movements, key word, or main idea of the amendment. This repeated practice in different forms can be particularly helpful to ELLs.

This type of graphic organizer can be used with multiple social studies topics, including the reasons for the fall of Rome or the causes of World War I. This strategy would also work well with economics concepts like different market types. In government classes, this could be applied to learning and remembering different types of governments, which the following lesson plan describes.

Table 8.1 Bill of Rights Graphic Organizer

Amendment Number	Main Ideas	One- to Two- Word Summary	Visual	Movement
1	Freedom of speech, news, religion, protest, and complaining to the government	Five freedoms	(Here students draw a visual representation of the amendment.)	(Here students draw stick figures doing a movement that triggers the memory of this amendment. Of course, students should act out the movement, as well.)

Source: Graphic Organizer inspired by Kelly Young, Pebble Creek Labs.

Types of Government Lesson Plan

This lesson plan is designed for ELLs at the High Intermediate to Advanced level of English proficiency. It features all of the instructional strategies described earlier in this chapter and shows how they can be used to teach students about different types of government in an engaging and accessible way.

Types of Government Lesson Plan for High Intermediate and Advanced ELLs

Instructional Objectives

Students will:

1. Learn about the key elements of four basic types of governments—rule by none, rule by one, rule by a few, and rule by many.
2. Practice categorization

Duration

Three 55-minute lessons

Standards Addressed

Reading

1. Read closely to determine what the text says explicitly and to make logical inferences from it; cite specific textual evidence when writing or speaking to support conclusions drawn from the text.
2. Determine central ideas or themes of a text and analyze their development; summarize the key supporting details and ideas.
3. Determine the meaning of words and phrases as they are used in a text, including vocabulary describing political, social, or economic aspects of history/social science.

Materials

- Computer with Internet access, speakers, ability to project video for students.
- Types of Government Data Set (Exhibit 8.2), copies for each student and a teacher copy of Types of Government Data Set Answer Key (Exhibit 8.3).
- Types of Government Graphic Organizer (Table 8.2), copies for each student.

Procedure

Day 1

1. The teacher asks students to watch one video and write down key words and phrases about the different types of governments. Here are two possible videos: "Types of Government, Explained" (http://bit.ly/navccss12) and "Who Rules? Types of Government" (http://bit.ly/navccss13).

2. Students should watch the video at least twice. After the first viewing, students should meet in partners or small groups to share the words and phrases they wrote down and to work together in order to identify the different types of government. After the small group discussion, the teacher explains that while they watch it a second time, students should add more information about each type of government. After the second viewing, students meet again to share their notes and write a description of each type of government.

3. The teacher calls on different groups and asks each one to share their description of one type of government. The teacher writes student ideas on the whiteboard and consolidates them into four types—rule by none, rule by one, rule by a few, and rule by many.

Day 2

1. The teacher passes out the Types of Government Data Set (Exhibit 8.2). This data set is a collection of quotes about government from different famous people and philosophers throughout history. It can be modified to be shorter or simplified as needed.

2. The teacher instructs students to read the data set and highlight clue words in each exemplar that indicate evidence of the type of government. She also reminds them to refer to notes from the previous day, which may contain some of the clue words.

3. After students have completed the data set, the teacher tells them to review it again and use the clue words to help them label each exemplar with the name of one of these categories: One, Few, and Many. These are the main categories of government for the purposes of this lesson. Depending on the level of your students, you might model several or only one exemplar.

4. At the end of each page, students will share their categories and the evidence for their category placement with a partner.

5. The teacher then reviews the categorization of each exemplar with the entire class.

Day 3

1. Now that students have categorized the data set, they are ready to complete their graphic organizer. The teacher passes out the Types of Government Graphic Organizer (Table 8.2) to each student and has them work individually or in pairs to develop a one-sentence summary, one- to two-word main idea, visual, and physical movement for each type of government.

    The teacher should begin by modeling Rule by None (Anarchy), which isn't included in the data set, but is on the graphic organizer. For example, in the first column "Summary," the teacher might write "Rule by None means not having a government, people do what they want." In the column "One to Two Key Words," the teacher might write "no laws." In the "Visual" column, the teacher can draw something that represents government like a police badge or the White House and then draw a large "X" through it. In the final column, "Physical Movement," students might draw a stick figure with its arms held in the shape of an "X" to demonstrate the idea of no government. Of course, the teacher and students should act out the movement, as well.

2. After students have completed the graphic organizer, they can share them with partners or in small groups.

Assessment

1. The teacher asks students to write, using the ABC (answer, back it up, comment) strategy about the types of governments. The question can be as simple as "Which type of government do you think is the best and why?" or more complex, such as "What are the pros and cons of a government by few?" ELLs can be given sentence starters/frames for the writing, if needed. The teacher can also collect and review student data sets and completed graphic organizers.

Possible Extensions

1. Have students research a specific example in history of one or all of the government types and prepare a poster and/or PowerPoint for a class presentation.
2. Have students further research one of the types of government and write a letter or diary entry describing life under that type of rule.

EXHIBIT 8.2. Types of Government Data Set

1. "The stronger must dominate and not blend with the weaker, thus sacrificing his own greatness."

— Adolf Hitler

2. "Extremely wealthy families are hell-bent on destroying the democratic vision of a strong middle class which has made the United States the envy of the world. In its place they are determined to create an oligarchy in which a small number of families control the economic and political life of our country."

— Bernie Sanders

3. "The rich and powerful now have new means to further enrich and empower themselves at the cost of the poorer and weaker, we have a responsibility to protest."

— Nelson Mandela

4. "As all perfection and all strength are united in God, so all the power of individuals is united in the person of the [king]. What grandeur that a single man should embody so much!"

— King Louis XIV

5. "Any law which the people has not ratified in person is void; it is not law at all."

— Jean-Jacques Rousseau

6. "It is enough that the people know there was an election. The people who cast the votes decide nothing. The people who count the votes decide everything."

— Joseph Stalin

7. "I am the state [government]."

—King Louis XIV

8. "Surely every man will have advisers by his side, but the decision will be made by one man."

—Adolf Hitler

9. "A monarchy conducted with infinite wisdom and infinite benevolence is the most perfect of all possible governments."

—Ezra Stiles

10. "Educate and inform the whole mass of the people. . . . They are the only sure reliance for the preservation of our liberty."

—Thomas Jefferson

11. "We have learned from history we have reason to conclude that all peaceful beginnings of government have been laid in the consent of the people."

—John Locke

12. "Any constitution in which wealth confers the privileges of citizenship, whether the rulers are few or many, must be regarded as oligarchy."

—Aristotle

13. "There is danger from all men. The only maxim of a free government is to trust no man living with power to endanger the public liberty."

—John Adams

14. "The way to secure liberty is to place it in the people's hands, that is, to give them the power at all times to defend it in the legislature and in the courts of justice."

—Thomas Jefferson

15. "In a democracy, the people are sovereign."

—Montesquieu

16. "Men are equal; it is not birth but virtue that makes the difference."

—François-Marie Voltaire

EXHIBIT 8.3. Types of Government Data Set Answer Key

(NOT FOR DISTRIBUTION TO STUDENTS)

Rule by One: 1, 4, 6, 7, 8, 9
Rule by Few: 2, 3, 12
Rule by Many: 5, 10, 11, 13, 14, 15, 16

Table 8.2 Types of Government Graphic Organizer

Type of Government	Summary	One to Two Key Words	Visual	Physical Movement
Rule by None (Anarchy)				
Rule by One (Dictator, Monarchy)				
Rule by Few (Oligarchy)				
Rule by Many (Democracy, Republic)				

Tech Tools

Social Studies Resources for ELLs

There are many free social studies–related resources that are useful for teaching ELLs.

In fact, Larry has curated and collected over 400 categorized social studies lists that can be found under that category at "The Best Of" lists (http://larryferlazzo .edublogs.org/about/my-best-of-series/).

One of the most useful of those posts may be the "All-Time Best Social Studies Sites" (http://larryferlazzo.edublogs.org/2014/02/27/the-all-time-best-social-studies-sites/).

For downloadable versions of the lesson plans and Tech Tools boxes found in this chapter, go to the "Downloads" section of this book's web page at www.wiley.com/go/navccss.

CHAPTER NINE

Science

Caleb Cheung, Laura Prival, Claudio Vargas and Diana Vélez

The Common Core State Standards (CCSS) set the guidelines for English language arts (ELA) *and* for literacy in history/social studies, science, and technical subjects. The CCSS requires that students read, write, speak, listen, and use language effectively in these content areas from kindergarten to grade 12. In addition, the authors of the Next Generation Science Standards (NGSS) and the CCSS worked together to identify the following key literacy connections to the science content demands outlined in the NGSS:

> As the CCSS affirms, reading in science requires an appreciation of the norms and conventions of the discipline of science, including understanding the nature of evidence used, an attention to precision and detail, and the capacity to make and assess intricate arguments, synthesize complex information, and follow detailed procedures and accounts of events and concepts. Students also need to be able to gain knowledge from elaborate diagrams and data that convey information and illustrate scientific concepts. Likewise, writing and presenting information orally are key means for students to assert and defend claims in science, demonstrate what they know about a concept, and convey what they have experienced, imagined, thought, and learned.[1]

The Next Generation Science Standards (NGSS) provide tools and opportunities for significantly improving science learning for students, including English language learners (ELLs). Previous standards mainly emphasized what

EXHIBIT 9.1. The Three Dimensions of the Framework

Scientific and Engineering Practices

1. Asking questions (for science) and defining problems (for engineering)
2. Developing and using models
3. Planning and carrying out investigations
4. Analyzing and interpreting data
5. Using mathematics and computational thinking
6. Constructing explanations (for science) and designing solutions (for engineering)
7. Engaging in argument from evidence
8. Obtaining, evaluating, and communicating information

Crosscutting Concepts

1. Patterns
2. Cause and effect: Mechanism and explanation
3. Scale, proportion, and quantity
4. Systems and system models
5. Energy and matter: Flows, cycles, and conservation
6. Structure and function
7. Stability and change

Disciplinary Core Ideas

Physical Sciences
PS 1: Matter and its interactions
PS 2: Motion and stability: Forces and interactions
PS 3: Energy
PS 4: Waves and their applications in technologies for information transfer

Life Sciences
LS 1: From molecules to organisms: Structures and processes
LS 2: Ecosystems: Interactions, energy, and dynamics
LS 3: Heredity: Inheritance and variation of traits
LS 4: Biological evolution: Unity and diversity

Earth and Space Sciences
ESS 1: Earth's place in the universe
ESS 2: Earth's systems
ESS 3: Earth and human activity

Engineering, Technology, and the Applications of Science
ETS 1: Engineering design

students "knew." The NGSS focus on performance expectations, asking students to demonstrate and apply their new understanding.

Each performance expectation incorporates three dimensions: Science and Engineering Practices (SEP), Crosscutting Concepts (CCC), and Disciplinary Core Ideas (DCI) (Exhibit 9.1). The Science and Engineering Practices approximate the work and behaviors of scientists. Crosscutting Concepts identify major themes that cut across different science disciplines. The Disciplinary Core Ideas represent the key organizing concepts in four science domains.[2]

This three-dimensional approach is at the heart of NGSS. Each performance expectation at every grade level contains components from all three dimensions, requiring students to build deeper connections over time.

Equity and Access for All Students

As many states shift science instruction towards NGSS, it is imperative that educators look closely at whether equitable opportunities to learn and do science are available to all of our students. In Appendix D of the NGSS, "All Standards, All Students,"[3] the writers make the case that these new standards and expectations are intended for every child in each of our classrooms. This means that no student shall be denied the experience of actually doing and learning science. To achieve this, we must teach in equitable ways.

A student's opportunity to learn science can be examined in several ways: Are teachers prepared and given adequate class time to teach science? Are high-quality materials and curriculum available to all students and teachers throughout the school year? While these are crucial questions to consider in light of the heavy focus on ELA and math under NCLB, just increasing time spent on science instruction and placing science materials in classrooms are not enough to provide these expected equitable learning opportunities. The *quality* of science teaching and learning must also be examined. Are students coloring worksheets about science, copying concepts "learned" off the board, conducting "cookie-cutter" labs, or perhaps only experiencing science through textbooks or videos? Or are they truly engaged in the practices of science, as called for in the NGSS?

Equity, however, goes beyond making sure that all students have access to standards-aligned science instruction. To teach in an *equitable* way means that educators understand, value, and teach to the strengths, challenges, prior knowledge, and life experiences that each student brings to the classroom. It means holding high expectations for all students and believing that every student can succeed.

Science and Language

The three-dimensional teaching and learning aspect of the NGSS present both significant challenges and opportunities for ELLs. Providing equitable science instruction requires more than "sheltering" the science experience for ELLs in order to make the content comprehensible. Each and every student must have the opportunity to do the heavy lifting—to struggle with ideas and the means to express them. Although a student may not possess the language resources in English to express their thoughts, all students have a wealth of ideas and explanations to contribute to discussions and learning tasks. There needs to be a classroom culture of discourse, where all students can contribute to the conversation regardless of their "flawed" language. The NGSS were developed to ensure that all students, including ELLs, be afforded equitable opportunities to develop and share their own ideas, interact with the ideas of others, and arrive at a deeper understanding of science concepts as a result of rigorous meaning-making processes.

Many students in our state of California are ELLs or emergent bilinguals, and we consider their bilingual status to be a great asset that brings diversity and richness to our classrooms and will serve them well throughout their lives. There is a history in many urban districts of denying ELLs access to science learning opportunities due to extra time being spent on explicit language skills development—like grammar and vocabulary, often void of rich context and meaning making. Fortunately, many teachers know that language development can be best accomplished through content learning. We need language to access ideas, make meaning of investigations, and communicate observations and thinking.

Because of the focus on real-world materials and activities, not to mention the high-interest topics and potential for disciplinary language-rich discussions, science classes are ideal learning environments for English language development. Much of this work is supported by the new California English Language Development Standards (CA ELD). As stated in the CA ELD Standards, "A key goal of the CA ELD Standards is to support EL students to develop advanced proficiencies with academic English as they are also developing content knowledge across the disciplines."[4] This goal is also consistent with the English Language Proficiency Standards (ELPS) in other states such as Texas and New York, as well as the consortium of 36 states that have adopted the 2004 World-Class Instructional Design and Assessment (WIDA) ELP standards.

MAKING IT HAPPEN

Meeting the challenges of the NGSS requires identifying the language demands necessary for students to fully engage in the science and engineering practices—especially those that are highly language dependent and involve complex thinking processes such as argumentation, developing and using models, and constructing explanations. It is, therefore, necessary for all teachers of science to pay as much attention to language objectives as they do to content objectives when planning and implementing three-dimensional science instruction. In addition to answering the question, *What will students know?*, the learning objective should also answer questions about the language demands of the instruction, such as:

1. How will students be engaging in the science experience?

2. What are the language functions required when engaged in these practices? What vocabulary and language structures will students be using?

3. Where are students now in terms of these language functions? What are the expectations as a result of this instruction? What literacy supports will students need?

LANGUAGE OBJECTIVES FOR SCIENCE

Once the science and engineering practices for the lesson have been identified, the next step is to think about the language functions students will be using to engage in those practices. Knowing where students are and where you want them to be will inform the language objective.

The Scaffolds and Strategies That Support Student Engagement in the Science and Engineering Practices chart (Exhibit 9.2) provides examples of how to support ELLs with the language demands inherent in each of the science and engineering practices. These strategies and scaffolds can be used regularly to provide access for all students and/or as supports for ELLs to attain a higher level of language use. As with any scaffold, they should be used strategically on an "as needed" basis.

For example, in the following vignette, the teacher wants to move her students from sharing their own ideas to a higher level of discourse needed for engaging in argumentation. The language objective for her lesson on condensation is: *Students will build on and challenge each other's ideas in order to develop and use a model to explain why condensation forms on a cup of ice water. Scaffolds will include prompts for asking and answering questions in pairs, sentence frames (I agree with . . . because . . . .), and a pictorial to introduce key vocabulary (condensation, water vapor, condense).*

The main language objective in this example is for students to listen to—and build on—each other's ideas. Students will also be engaging in most of the other science and engineering practices as they interact with the phenomenon and with each other to come to a normative understanding of where condensation comes from. The teacher, therefore, will be attending to the language demands of planning an investigation, analyzing data, and so forth, to ensure access for all her students. However, her focus for this lesson is on argumentation and that is where she wants to

EXHIBIT 9.2. Scaffolds and Strategies That Support Student Engagement in the Science and Engineering Practices

NGSS Science and Engineering Practices	Corresponding Language Functions	Strategies and Scaffolds
Asking questions and defining problems	Inquire, identify, define	• Provide an engaging context that peaks student curiosity (discrepant event, interesting scenario, hands-on activity, relevant situation, authentic problem). • Keep class chart for student questions and/or students record questions in their science notebooks. • Sentence frames for oral and written discourse: *I wonder . . .* *What, where, when, and how?* *What would happen if . . . ?* *What causes . . . ? What are the effects of . . . ?* • Questions/Prompts: *What is the problem we are trying to solve? What are the criteria? What are the constraints?*
Developing and using models	Represent, predict, explain	• Model for students how to develop and use models to explain their thinking. • Regularly have students draw a model to use as an artifact for discussion. Encourage students to revise their models based on new information. Example: *Draw a model that explains how an electric circuit works.*

NGSS Science and Engineering Practices	Corresponding Language Functions	Strategies and Scaffolds
		• Sentence frames for small group/ one-on-one discussions: *What does your model show/predict/ explain? My model shows/ predicts/explains . . .* *What does . . . mean? What could you change in your model to make it better?*
Planning and carrying out investigations	Design, sequence, evaluate, describe, organize, compare, classify, draw, label	• Model the process for planning an investigation. Ask guiding questions: *What are you trying to find out? How could you find out . . . ? Is there another way? What materials will you need?* • Provide structures for sequencing procedures: *first, second, then, after.* • Teach a mini-lesson on ways to record and organize data in student science notebooks (e.g., T-charts, lists, technical drawings, labeling). • Introduce equipment and procedural words beforehand (*separate, pour, measure,* etc.) and post on a class Word Wall or chart with images. • After coming to a class or group consensus on a procedure for an investigation, document the steps on the board with illustrations so that all students have access to them. • Have students work in small groups. Encourage and make collaboration a focus.

(continued)

NGSS Science and Engineering Practices	Corresponding Language Functions	Strategies and Scaffolds

Analyzing and interpreting data	Compare, represent, classify, sequence, analyze	• Model ways of organizing data in class charts and student science notebooks (graphs, charts, Venn diagrams, graphic organizers).
		• Provide sentence frames for oral and written discourse:
		My data show . . .
		A pattern I see is . . .
		   . . . and . . . are similar because they both . . .
		   . . . and . . . are different because . . .

Using mathematics and computational thinking	Enumerate, measure	• Use opportunities in science to engage in math practices when appropriate. • Help students see the connections between what they are learning in math to how it is applied in science. *How did numbers and patterns help us understand what is going on?* *How does the quantitative data support your explanation?*
Constructing explanations and designing solutions	Infer, explain, provide evidence	• Teach a mini-lesson on language structures and norms for engaging in academic discussions. • Sentence frames: *Based on . . . , I think . . .* *I think . . . because . . .* *We think . . . is the best solution because . . .*

NGSS Science and Engineering Practices	Corresponding Language Functions	Strategies and Scaffolds
Engaging in argument from evidence	Discuss, persuade, synthesize, negotiate, suggest, critique, evaluate, reflect	• Provide norms and structures for students to discuss in pairs, small group, and whole class. • Model and discuss expectations for argumentation. • Sentence frames: *I claim . . . My evidence is . . .* *I agree/disagree with . . . because . . .* *What about . . . ?* *I used to think . . . but now I think . . .*
Obtaining, evaluating, and communicating information		• Reinforce vocabulary using pictorials (review key concepts by illustrating and labeling on chart paper in front of students). • Provide ample opportunities for students to talk, write, and read about their science experiences. • Use reading and multimedia to deepen students' understanding of the the phenomenon. • Model and provide scaffolds. (Use reading strategies such as: close reading, jigsaw, guided reading, graphic organizers, and visual literacy strategies.)

see her students grow in terms of their use of language. Just as the content objective should be focused on one idea for the lesson, the accompanying language objective should also be focused, attainable, and measurable in order to inform the next day's lesson.

Fifth-Grade Vignette: Where Does the Water Come From?

This vignette describes how a fifth-grade teacher enhanced her science lesson on condensation to (1) increase student engagement in three-dimensional learning and (2) attend to the demands and the opportunities for language development for her ELLs. However, the strategies demonstrated in this vignette can be applied to science lessons in any grade.

The focus of this lesson is: NGSS Performance Expectation 5-ESS2-1. Develop a model using an example to describe ways the geosphere, biosphere, hydrosphere, and/or atmosphere interact.[5]

BACKGROUND

Ms. Lopez's class is working on the Fifth-Grade NGSS DCI Earth Materials and Systems. She is beginning an investigation from the *FOSS (Full Option Science System) Earth and Sun Module* that will include the concepts of condensation, evaporation, the water cycle, and how these systems affect climate. Ms. Lopez's students' proficiency in English ranges from emerging, expanding, to bridging (Beginning, Intermediate, to Advanced). She also has one "newcomer" student whose family just moved to the United States from El Salvador a month ago.

ACTIVATING PRIOR KNOWLEDGE

Ms. Lopez starts every lesson with a prompt or short activity that will help students connect to something they've already experienced or think they know. Usually, she has students share their last science notebook entries with a partner to review what they learned the day before. However, this is the beginning of a new investigation and Ms. Lopez wants to know what ideas students have about the concept of condensation. She asks students to close their eyes and imagine what it looks like when it rains. She adds, *Think about the clouds and the air. What does the sky look like? What can you observe with your senses? Where do you think the rainwater comes from?* Ms. Lopez notices that Mario, her new student from El Salvador, still has his eyes open and is looking around. She points to a picture from the science resource book of a rainy day, closes her eyes and points to her temple, making a face that indicates she's thinking. When she opens her eyes, she sees that Mario is smiling and his eyes are now closed. (Ms. Lopez could have translated the instructions, but instead she is working on supporting Mario to employ learning strategies on his own when appropriate.)

After a minute of silent reflecting, Ms. Lopez tells students to open their eyes and share their ideas with their partners. (Ms. Lopez uses this strategy, *think-pair-share*, often. Students already know who their partners are and what the expectations are for their participation. In the beginning of the year, Ms. Lopez posted and had students practice using the sentence frames, *I observed...* and *I think... because...* to share their ideas.) Most students are naturally using the discussion structures; however, she points out the sentence frames to Mario and some of her emerging bilingual students to help them articulate their experiences with and knowledge about rain.

After a few minutes of partner discussion, Ms. Lopez asks students to share what their partner said to the whole group. (This strategy encourages students to listen attentively to their partner's ideas, instead of focusing only on their own thoughts.) Ms. Lopez uses *pick-a-stick* to call on three different students to share out. (Ms. Lopez finds that picking students' names randomly from a jar of sticks with their names on them increases student engagement and helps her to make sure she is not always calling on the first raised hand.)

From the sharing out and what Ms. Lopez was able to overhear in the partner talks, student understanding about condensation seems to be at a phenomenological level, for example, *Rain comes from clouds; when it's cloudy it rains,* and so forth. She also heard some ideas such as: *Clouds and rain are made by God.* She makes a mental note to research folklore and mythical stories from her students' cultures about rain to explore and discuss as a social studies and ELA connection (Ms. Lopez incorporates as many home-cultural connections as she can in her instruction to support student engagement and motivation).

SETTING THE CONTEXT

Ms. Lopez reminds students that scientists rely on evidence to support their explanations; therefore, today, they will be making observations and carrying out investigations in order to gather data that will help them explain where rainwater comes from. She explains, *I'm going to pour ice water into a cup on your tables and I want you to observe what happens.* (The desks in Ms. Lopez's room are in groups of four with students facing each other to allow collaborative interactions with materials and to encourage discussions.) She asks, *What do you notice?*

From their conversations, Ms. Lopez determines that all students have noticed the drops of water forming on the outside of the cup. Carolina seems very intrigued and asks, "How did the water get there?" Ms. Lopez smiles and says, "That is our focus question for today." She writes it on the board and, before she has to give the instructions, students have already pulled their science notebooks out of their desks. They find the next blank page and write the date and the focus question at the top of the page, *How did the water get onto the outside of the cup of ice water?* (Ms. Lopez has students write in their science notebooks before, during, and after every science investigation. The notebook gives students a place to record their observations and wrestle with new ideas, and allows each student to process and communicate information at their own level.)

ENGAGING IN THE PRACTICES: DEVELOPING AND USING MODELS

Ms. Lopez has been working with her students on the NGSS practice *developing and using models*. Students have made significant progress since the beginning of the year when they struggled with getting started or with trying to make the perfect drawing. Ms. Lopez asks students to make a model to explain where the water on the outside of the cup came from. She refers students to the class chart Key Elements of a Scientific Model (Exhibit 9.3) and reminds students to remember to include labels, arrows, and the science knowledge they have so far.

EXHIBIT 9.3. Key Elements of a Scientific Model

- Explains the phenomenon and helps us make predictions

- Involves cycles of evaluation and revision

- Consistent with observational data and established scientific ideas

Remember to use:

Arrows to show force and motion

Lines to label

After students have made their models in their notebooks, Ms. Lopez asks them to discuss their models with a partner. Ms. Lopez's language objective in this lesson is for students to move beyond sharing ideas to building on and critiquing the ideas of others. (This type of academic discourse is both a Common Core ELA speaking and listening standard and essential for the NGSS practice *Engaging in Argument from*

Evidence.) To accomplish this, Ms. Lopez wants students to practice active listening, so they can challenge each other's ideas. She writes prompts on the board and asks students to use them to ask and answer questions in their discussions. She explains, Partner A will ask Partner B, "How does your model explain where the water on the outside of the glass came from?" Partner B will answer, "My model shows . . ." Partner A can then ask a follow-up questions, such as, "What does this arrow mean?"

As students engage in the discussions, Ms. Lopez cruises through the room, checking in with students she knows may need additional prompting or modeling to engage in this sort of discourse. Ms. Lopez notices that Mario and a few of her more shy students are not talking, so she reassures them that it's okay to talk in Spanish. (At this point in the lesson, Ms. Lopez's priority is knowing what students are thinking and whether they can understand each other's ideas enough to question or challenge each other. She is confident that if students are able to engage at this level of discourse in their primary language they will transfer these skills to English with a little more practice.)

ENGAGING IN THE PRACTICES: PLANNING AND CARRYING OUT INVESTIGATIONS

Ms. Lopez asks students to share out their claims, and she lists them on the board. As she expected, students' ideas include: *Water leaks through the glass; Water moved over the top of the glass and dripped down the sides; The glass is sweating.* Fortunately, Carlos adds, "I think there is water in the air." Without acknowledging whether or not these ideas are scientifically accurate, Ms. Lopez asks students to discuss in their table groups how they could find more information to support or refute their claims.

Ms. Lopez goes from group to group asking questions and providing prompts to help students come up with an appropriate investigation. She points out the materials students can use in their investigation, and all the groups are eager to use the food coloring in the ice water to see if the colored water leaks through or over the top of the cup to the outside. Students write their plans in their notebooks. Ms. Lopez refers to a class chart on writing a procedure which includes sequence words like, *first, second, then, finally.* Students get to work making colored ice water and pouring it into another cup to see what happens. When they observe that the water on the outside is clear, there are exclamations and questions abound. As Ms. Lopez circulates through the groups, she asks students to record their results and questions they have in their notebooks. She observes some students have already made detailed drawings with labels, some are writing narratives, and others are making simple drawings with a few words.

Carlos asks if the same thing (water forming on the outside of the cup) happens with room temperature or warm water. Ms. Lopez suggests they find out and there is a flurry of further investigation. When students begin to make the connection that temperature is a factor, Ms. Lopez calls for attention and refers students to the list of claims they generated before the investigation. She asks, *Has anyone's thinking changed based on what we've observed in our investigations?* Many hands go up and Ms. Lopez goes through the list of claims, asking students to use hand signals to show if they agree, disagree, or are not sure for each one. (Using hand signals gives everyone an opportunity to communicate their ideas and gives Ms. Lopez a quick assessment of where her students are in their thinking.)

Ms. Lopez decides it's time to introduce some academic vocabulary. She draws a picture of the cup of ice water on chart paper and as she draws the droplets of water on the outside, she says, *The moisture you found on the outside of the cup is called condensation.* She writes the word *condensation* next to the droplets. *Condensation can mean making something shorter, like the condensed version of a long story; however, in science we use it to describe the liquid water that forms on a cold surface. Since we are scientists, I would like you to use the word condensation in your discussions and in your writing.* (Ms. Lopez is careful to introduce conceptually coded words like condensation *after* students have had sufficient hands-on experience with the concept. She strategically bridges their own language "drops, foggy" to the science word "condensation" so that they now have a schema to hang this idea onto).

ENGAGING IN THE PRACTICES: ENGAGING IN ARGUMENT FROM EVIDENCE

Referring back to the list of claims, Ms. Lopez says, *From your hand signals it seems we have some disagreement as to how the condensation formed on the ice water cups. Let's look at our data to see if we have evidence to support or refute some of our claims.* Ms. Lopez writes "Data" on the board and then calls on a "reporter" from each group to describe what their group observed. After compiling the list of observations, Ms. Lopez again focuses attention on the list of claims, *Now, let's look at the first claim, "The water leaked through the sides of the cup." Do you agree or disagree? What evidence do we have from our investigations that we've listed here as data that supports your idea? Talk in your small groups using these prompts: "I agree or disagree... My evidence is..."*

Ms. Lopez circulates listening in on the conversations. Earlier in the year she would have had to review the class norms for discussions but, at this point, students are naturally looking at the speaker, waiting their turn to speak, and being respectful. She pauses to listen in on one group of quieter students and encourages them to use the prompts for asking each other questions that are posted in the classroom. *Can you say more about...? Why do you think...?*

Ms. Lopez calls for attention and asks the reporters if their table groups have reached consensus. All the groups agree that the water did not leak through the cup based on the observation that the condensation on the cup of colored water was clear. Ms. Lopez wants to make sure all her students are making and can articulate the connection, that is, using reasoning to explain how the evidence connects to the claims, so she asks them to pair up and take turns convincing each other.

CROSSCUTTING CONCEPTS

Next, Ms. Lopez wants to bring in the idea of water vapor using NGSS crosscutting concepts, so she points out the observation students made that there was no condensation on the outside of the cup of warm water. She holds up the cold-water cup and the warm-water cup and asks students *What is different about the two systems and what might be causing the different results?* Ms. Lopez finds that using crosscutting concepts, such as *systems* and *cause and effect*, helps students deepen their understanding and provides a common vocabulary they can all use to help explain phenomena.

Carlos' hand shoots up: *I think the cold temperature causes the condensation.* Veronica adds, *I agree, because it's the only thing that is different in the two systems.* Carolina looks puzzled, *But why? How does the cold make condensation?* Ms. Lopez makes motions with her hands around the cups and asks, *What else might be in this system that we haven't mentioned? What is all around us?* Many students shout out, *Air! Yes*, explains Ms. Lopez, *air is part of the cup and water system. What did we learn about the composition of air (what is it made of)?* Students shout out *oxygen* and other gases and some refer back to their notebooks looking for information. Carolina lights up and exclaims, *Water vapor!* Ms. Lopez uses hand gestures as she explains that the liquid water on the outside of the cup came from the water vapor in the air. *Can you think of other examples where you've observed condensation?* From the silence and puzzled looks Ms. Lopez realizes students are not quite able to generalize the concept to their own experiences, so she asks them to take out their science textbooks to look at the photographs of foggy windows and mirrors, dew on the grass, breath on a cold day, low clouds, and so forth. The buzz returns to the room as students excitedly make personal connections.

Ms. Lopez then asks students to think about and share with a partner *What is the same about all the times and places when condensation occurs?* Most students are making the connection to the colder temperature. Ms. Lopez returns to the cup diagram and explains, *When water vapor comes in contact with a cold surface like the cup of ice water, it changes to a liquid. We say the water vapor condenses into droplets of liquid water.* Ms. Lopez adds the words *water vapor* and *condenses* to her diagram. *Tomorrow we'll investigate how this concept applies to rain.*

CLOSING

The science content objective for the vignette (develop a model to explain condensation on cold surfaces) provides the foundational knowledge and skills students will need to successfully execute the NGSS Performance Expectation 5-ESS2-1. To accomplish this, students will need lots of opportunities throughout the year to develop and use models to explain their thinking. The use of models is both a practice that students need to engage with in order to make meaning of their science experiences *and* an equitable means of communicating science thinking.

All students make their thinking visual when they develop a model, which then serves as an artifact for partner, small group, and whole class discussions—everyone has something to bring to the table.

Students also need many experiences in order to develop a deep and flexible understanding of how the crosscutting concept, *systems and systems models,* is applied in science and engineering. It will require many encounters across all disciplines for students to describe and explain phenomena in terms of a system, its components and their interactions. Providing a common and familiar vocabulary for making meaning in science supports a higher level of ELL participation.

The strategies described in the vignette illustrate the five areas that have been identified in the research literature where teachers can effectively support ELLs in language development at the same time they are learning science: (1) literacy strategies with all students, (2) language support strategies with ELLs, (3) discourse strategies with ELLs, (4) home language support, and (5) home-cultural connections.[6-8] By constructing our lessons with these in mind, we can move closer to ensuring that all students have access to high-quality, language-rich, NGSS-aligned science learning.

Tech Tools

Science Resources for English Language Learners

There are many free science-related resources that are useful for teaching English language learners.

In fact, Larry has curated and collected nearly one-hundred categorized science lists that can be found under that category at "The Best Of" lists (http://larryferlazzo .edublogs.org/about/my-best-of-series/).

One of the most useful of those posts may be "The All-Time Best Science Sites" (http://larryferlazzo.edublogs.org/2014/03/01/the-all-time-best-science-sites/).

Another particularly helpful post is "The Best Resources For Teaching The Next Generation Science Standards To English Language Learners" (http:// larryferlazzo.edublogs.org/2014/11/22/the-best-resources-for-teaching-the-next-generation-science-standards-to-english-language-learners/).

For downloadable versions of the Tech Tools boxes found in this chapter, go to the "Downloads" section of this book's web page at www.wiley.com/ go/navccss.

Notes

Introduction

1. Felton, E. (2015, May 28). Why are so many states replacing Common Core with carbon copies? *The Hechinger Report*. Retrieved from http://hechingerreport.org/why-are-so-many-states-replacing-common-core-with-carbon-copies/
2. Ferlazzo, L., & Hull Sypnieski, K. (2012). *The ESL/ELL teacher's survival guide: Ready-to-use strategies, tools, and activities for teaching all levels*. San Francisco, CA: Jossey-Bass.

Chapter 1 English Language Learners and the Common Core: An Overview

1. Kennedy, J. F. (1963, June 25). John F. Kennedy: Address in the Assembly Hall at the Paulskirche in Frankfurt. *The American Presidency Project*. Retrieved from http://www.presidency.ucsb.edu/ws/index.php?pid=9303
2. Ferlazzo, L., & Hull Sypnieski, K. (2012). *The ESL/ELL teacher's survival guide: Ready-to-use strategies, tools, and activities for teaching all levels*. San Francisco, CA: Jossey-Bass.
3. Ferlazzo, L., & Hull Sypnieski, K. (2012). *The ESL/ELL teacher's survival guide: Ready-to-use strategies, tools, and activities for teaching all levels* (p. 41). San Francisco, CA: Jossey-Bass.
4. Ruiz Soto, A. G., Hooker, S., & Batalova, J. (2015a, June). *States and districts with the highest number and share of English Language Learners*. Migration Policy Institute. Retrieved from http://www.migrationpolicy.org/research/states-and-districts-highest-number-and-share-english-language-learners
5. Flores, S. M., Batalova, J., & Fix, M. (2012, March). *The educational trajectories of English Language Learners in Texas*. Migration Policy Institute. Retrieved from http://www.migrationpolicy.org/research/educational-trajectories-english-language-learners-texas
6. Ruiz Soto, A. G., Hooker, S., & Batalova, J. (2015a, June). *States and districts with the highest number and share of English Language Learners*. Migration Policy Institute. Retrieved from

http://www.migrationpolicy.org/research/states-and-districts-highest-number-and-share-english-language-learners, p. 1.

7. Horsford, S. D., & Sampson, C. (n.d.). High ELL growth states: Expanding funding equity and opportunity for English Language Learners. *Voices in Urban Education*. Retrieved from http://vue.annenberginstitute.org/issues/37/high-ell-growth-states

8. Pitoniak, M. J., Young, J. W., Martiniello, M., King, T. C., Buteux, A., & Ginsburgh, M. (2009). Guidelines for the assessment of English-language learners. Princeton, NJ: ETS.

9. Santiago, D. A., Galdeano, E. C., & Taylor, M. (2015, January). *The condition of Latinos in education: 2015 factbook*. Excelencia in Education. Retrieved from http://www.edexcelencia.org/research/2015-factbook

10. Ruiz Soto, A. G., Hooker, S., & Batalova, J. (2015b, June). *Top languages spoken by English Learners nationally and by state*. Migration Policy Institute. Retrieved from http://www.migrationpolicy.org/research/top-languages-spoken-english-language-learners-nationally-and-state

11. U.S. Department of Education, Institute of Education Sciences, & National Center for Education Statistics. (n.d.). *The condition of education: Glossary*. Retrieved from http://nces.ed.gov/programs/coe/glossary.asp

12. U.S. Department of Education. (n.d.). *Title IX—General provisions*. Retrieved from http://www2.ed.gov/policy/elsec/leg/esea02/pg107.html

13. Baird, A. S. (2015, May 11). *Introducing the Dual Language Readers reader: Post #1*. EdCentral. Retrieved from http://www.edcentral.org/dllreader1/#_ftn1

14. National Council of Teachers of English. (2008). *English Language Learners*. Retrieved from http://www.ncte.org/library/NCTEFiles/Resources/PolicyResearch/ELLResearchBrief.pdf

15. California Department of Education. (n.d.). *Glossary of terms*. Retrieved from http://www.cde.ca.gov/ds/sd/cb/glossary.asp#eld

16. Tesol Direct. (n.d.). *What is TESOL?* Retrieved from https://www.tesol-direct.com/definition-of-tesol

17. http://www.ascd.org/publications/educational-leadership/mar07/vol64/num06/Focus-on-Adolescent-English-Language-Learners.aspx

18. Short, D.J., & Boyson, B.A. (2012). Helping newcomer students succeed in secondary school and beyond. Washington, DC: Center for Applied Linguistics.

19. National Education Association. (n.d.). *English Language Learners face unique challenges*. Retrieved from http://www.nea.org/assets/docs/HE/ELL_Policy_Brief_Fall_08_(2).pdf

20. Tamer, M. (2014, December 11). *The education of immigrant children*. Harvard Graduate School of Education. Retrieved from https://www.gse.harvard.edu/news/uk/14/12/education-immigrant-children

21. Hill, L. (2012, September). *California's English learner students*. Public Policy Institute of California. Retrieved from http://www.ppic.org/main/publication_quick.asp?i=1031

22. Long-term English learner. (n.d.). *The glossary of education reform*. Retrieved from http://edglossary.org/long-term-english-learner/

23. Menken, K., Kleyn, T., & Chae, N. (2012). Spotlight on "long-term English Language Learners": Characteristics and prior schooling experiences of an invisible popula-

tion. *International Multilingual Research Journal*, 6, 121–142. Retrieved from https:// katemenken.files.wordpress.com/2011/10/menken-kleyn-chae-2012-spotlight-on-e2809clong-term-english-language-learnerse2809d-imrj1.pdf

24. Olsen, L. (2010). *Reparable harm: Fulfilling the unkept promise of educational opportunity for California's long term English learners.* Californians Together. Retrieved from http:// www.niddk.nih.gov/health-information/health-topics/diagnostic-tests/thyroid-tests/ Pages/default.aspx#hcp

25. Menken, K., Kleyn, T., & Chae, N. (2012). Spotlight on "long-term English Language Learners": Characteristics and prior schooling experiences of an invisible population. *International Multilingual Research Journal*, 6, 121–142 (p. 122). Retrieved from https:// katemenken.files.wordpress.com/2011/10/menken-kleyn-chae-2012-spotlight-on-e2809clong-term-english-language-learnerse2809d-imrj1.pdf

26. Olsen, L. (2010). *Reparable harm: Fulfilling the unkept promise of educational opportunity for California's long term English learners* (p. 7). Californians Together. Retrieved from http:// www.niddk.nih.gov/health-information/health-topics/diagnostic-tests/thyroid-tests/ Pages/default.aspx#hcp

27. *California is the first state in the nation to define and identify English learners who after many years are struggling to succeed.* (2015, January 5). Californians Together. Retrieved from http://www.ciclt.net/sn/adm/editpage.aspx?ClientCode=calto&Filename=Website.txt

28. Olsen, L. (2010). *Reparable harm: Fulfilling the unkept promise of educational opportunity for California's long term English learners.* Californians Together. Retrieved from http:// www.niddk.nih.gov/health-information/health-topics/diagnostic-tests/thyroid-tests/ Pages/default.aspx#hcp

29. *AB-2193 Long term English learners.* (2011–2012). California Legislative Information. Retrieved from http://leginfo.legislature.ca.gov/faces/billNavClient.xhtml?bill_id= 201120120AB2193

30. *Reports.* (2014, December 17). Californians Together. Retrieved from http://www .californianstogether.org/reports/

31. Cummins, J. (1999). *BICS and CALP: Clarifying the distinction.* Educational Resources Information Clearinghouse No. ED438551. Retrieved from http://files.eric.ed.gov/ fulltext/ED438551.pdf

32. Scarcella, R. (2003, April). *Academic English: A conceptual framework.* University of California Linguistic Minority Research Institute. Retrieved from http://escholarship.org/uc/ item/6pd082d4#page-1

33. Krashen, S. D. (1982). *Principles and practice in second language acquisition* (p. 10). Oxford, UK: Pergamon Press. Retrieved from http://www.sdkrashen.com/content/books/ principles_and_practice.pdf

34. Goldenberg, C. (2008, Summer). Teaching English language learners: What the research does—and does not—say. *American Educator*. Retrieved from http://homepages .ucalgary.ca/~hroessin/documents/Goldenberg,_2008,_America_Ed_Summary_of_ research.pdf

35. *Common Core State Standards Initiative.* (n.d.). Retrieved from http://www.corestandards .org/about-the-standards/development-process/#timeline

36. *Common Core State Standards Initiative.* (n.d.). Retrieved from http://www.corestandards .org/about-the-standards/

37. American Federation of Teachers. (n.d.). *Frequently asked questions: FAQs about the Common Core standards*. Retrieved from http://www.aft.org/education/common-core/ frequently-asked-questions

38. National Education Association. (n.d.). *Our positions & actions*. Retrieved from http:// www.nea.org/home/56614.htm

39. Common Core or something else? A map of state academic standards. (2015, July 20). *Education Week*. Retrieved from http://www.edweek.org/ew/section/multimedia/map-states-academic-standards-common-core-or.html#.VZGEtDBpuQg.twitter

40. Felton, E. (2015, May 28). Why are so many states replacing Common Core with carbon copies? *The Hechinger Report*. Retrieved from http://hechingerreport.org/why-are-so-many-states-replacing-common-core-with-carbon-copies/

41. Common Core State Standards Initiative. (n.d.). *Read the standards*. Retrieved from http://www.corestandards.org/read-the-standards/

42. TESOL International Association. (2013, March). *Overview of the Common Core state standards initiatives for ELLs*. Alexandria, VA. Retrieved from http://www.tesol.org/docs/ advocacy/overview-of-common-core-state-standards-initiatives-for-ells-a-tesol-issue-brief-march-2013.pdf?sfvrsn=4

43. U.S. Department of Education. (2003, February). *Part II: Final non-regulatory guidance on the Title III state formula grant program – Standards, assessments, and accountability* (p. 10). Washington, DC: Author. Retrieved from http://www2.ed.gov/programs/nfdp/NRG1 .2.25.03.doc

44. U.S. Department of Education. (2007, May). *Assessment and accountability for recently arrived and former Limited English Proficient (LEP) students: Non-regulatory guidance*. Washington, DC: Author. Retrieved from https://www2.ed.gov/policy/elsec/guid/ lepguidance.doc

45. Klein, A. (2015, June 18). Waiver states seek leeway for English-learners' impact on school ratings. *Education Week*. Retrieved from http://blogs.edweek.org/edweek/ campaign-K-12/2015/06/nclb_waiver_states_seek_flexib.html

46. Klein, A. (2015, July 23). Seven states get NCLB waiver renewals, including opt-out friendly Oregon. *Education Week*. Retrieved from http://blogs.edweek.org/edweek/ campaign-k-12/2015/07/six_states_have_gotten_the.html

47. Mitchell, C. (2014, December 22). Federal officials grant Florida waiver on English-learner testing. *Education Week*. Retrieved from http://blogs.edweek.org/ edweek/learning-the-language/2014/12/feds_grant_florida_waiver_on_e.html

48. Ferlazzo, L. (2011, June 10). The best resources for learning about the "next generation" of state testing. *Larry Ferlazzo's websites of the day*. Retrieved from http:// larryferlazzo.edublogs.org/2011/06/10/the-best-resources-for-learning-about-the-next-generation-of-state-testing/

49. *PARCC accommodations for students with disabilities*. (n.d.). Retrieved from http:// osse.dc.gov/sites/default/files/dc/sites/osse/publication/attachments/PARCC %20Accommodations%20for%20Students%20with%20Disabilities.pdf

50. Smarter Balanced Assessment Consortium. (2015, June 1). *Smarter Balanced Assessment Consortium: Usability, accessibility, and accommodations guidelines*. Retrieved from http://www.smarterbalanced.org/wordpress/wp-content/uploads/2014/08/ SmarterBalanced_Guidelines.pdf

51. Council of Chief State School Officers. (2012). *Framework for English language proficiency development standards corresponding to the Common Core state standards and the Next Generation science standards* (p. ii). Washington, DC: Author. Retrieved from http://www.ccsso .org/Documents/2012/ELPD%20Framework%20Booklet-Final%20for%20web.pdf

52. Next Generation Science Standards. (n.d.). *Development process.* Retrieved from http:// www.nextgenscience.org/development-process

53. Council of Chief State School Officers. (2012). *Framework for English language proficiency development standards corresponding to the Common Core state standards and the Next Generation science standards* (p. 52). Washington, DC: Author. Retrieved from http://www.ccsso .org/Documents/2012/ELPD%20Framework%20Booklet-Final%20for%20web.pdf

54. WIDA. (2012). *English language development standards.* Retrieved from https://www.wida .us/standards/eld.aspx

55. Council of Chief State School Officers. (2014, April). *English language proficiency (ELP) standards.* Retrieved from http://www.elpa21.org/sites/default/files/Final%204_30 %20ELPA21%20Standards_1.pdf

56. California Department of Education. (n.d.). *English language development standards.* Retrieved from http://www.cde.ca.gov/sp/el/er/eldstandards.asp

57. California Department of Education. (n.d.). *SBE-adopted ELA/ELD framework chapters.* Retrieved from http://www.cde.ca.gov/ci/rl/cf/elaeldfrmwrksbeadopted.asp

58. California Department of Education. (n.d.). *SBE-adopted ELA/ELD framework chapters* (p. 17). Retrieved from http://www.cde.ca.gov/ci/rl/cf/elaeldfrmwrksbeadopted.asp

59. *New York State Bilingual Common Core Initiative: Progressions 2014–15.* (2014, October 7). EngageNY. Retrieved from https://www.engageny.org/resource/new-york-state-bilingual-common-core-initiative

60. *New York State Bilingual Common Core Initiative: Progressions 2014–15.* (2014, October 7). EngageNY. Retrieved from https://www.engageny.org/resource/new-york-state-bilingual-common-core-initiative

61. TESOL International Association. (2013, March). *Overview of the Common Core state standards initiatives for ELLs.* Alexandria, VA. Retrieved from http://www.tesol.org/docs/ advocacy/overview-of-common-core-state-standards-initiatives-for-ells-a-tesol-issue-brief-march-2013.pdf?sfvrsn=4

62. English Language Proficiency Assessment for the 21st Century. (n.d.). *ELPA21 deliverables.* Retrieved from http://www.elpa21.org/assessment-system/elpa21-deliverables

63. TESOL International Association. (2013, March). *Overview of the Common Core state standards initiatives for ELLs* (p. 6). Alexandria, VA. Retrieved from http://www.tesol.org/ docs/advocacy/overview-of-common-core-state-standards-initiatives-for-ells-a-tesol-issue-brief-march-2013.pdf?sfvrsn=4

64. California School Boards Association. (2014, April). *New assessment for English learner students from the CELDT to the ELPAC.* CSBA Governance Brief. Retrieved from https://www.csba.org/GovernanceAndPolicyResources/~/media/CSBA/Files/ GovernanceResources/GovernanceBriefs/201404_GB_ELPAC.ashx

65. *Spring 2015 NYSESLAT resources.* (2015, March 11). EngageNY. Retrieved from https:// www.engageny.org/resource/spring-2015-nyseslat-resources

66. *TELPAS resources.* (n.d.). Texas Education Agency (p. 64). Retrieved from http://tea.texas .gov/WorkArea/linkit.aspx?LinkIdentifier=id&ItemID=2147496942

67. Common Core State Standards Initiative. (n.d.). *Key shifts in English Language Arts*. Retrieved from http://www.corestandards.org/other-resources/key-shifts-in-english-language-arts

68. California Department of Education. (n.d.). English Language Arts (p. 12).

69. California Department of Education, 2014 (p. 30).

70. *English language standards. Anchor standards. College and career readiness anchor standards for reading*. (n.d.). Common Core State Standards Initiative. Retrieved from http://www.corestandards.org/ELA-Literacy/CCRA/R/

Chapter 2 Creating the Conditions for English Language Learners to Be Successful in the Common Core Standards

1. Teachers are like gardeners. (2010, August 19). *YouTube*. Retrieved from https://www.youtube.com/watch?v=aT_121H3kLY

2. Popova, M. (n.d.). Pioneering scientist Rachel Carson on wonder, parenting, and why it's more vital to feel than to know. *Brain Pickings*. Retrieved from http://www.brainpickings.org/index.php/2013/12/23/rachel-carson-on-wonder/

3. Kamenetz, A. (2015, May 28). Nonacademic skills are key to success. But what should we call them? *NPR*. Retrieved from http://www.npr.org/sections/ed/2015/05/28/404684712/non-academic-skills-are-key-to-success-but-what-should-we-call-them

4. *Common Core State Standards Initiative*. (n.d.). Retrieved from http://www.corestandards.org/about-the-standards/development-process/#timeline

5. Council of Chief State School Officers. (2013, February). *Knowledge, skills, and dispositions: The Innovation Lab Network state framework for college, career, and citizenship readiness, and implications for state policy*. Retrieved from http://www.ccsso.org/Documents/ILN%20Knowledge%20Skills%20and%20Dispositions%20CCR%20Framework%20February%202013.pdf

6. Council of Chief State School Officers. (2013, February). *Knowledge, skills, and dispositions: The Innovation Lab Network state framework for college, career, and citizenship readiness, and implications for state policy* (p. 5). Retrieved from http://www.ccsso.org/Documents/ILN%20Knowledge%20Skills%20and%20Dispositions%20CCR%20Framework%20February%202013.pdf

7. Ferlazzo, L. (2013, February 16). The best info on skills employers are looking for in job-seekers. *Larry Ferlazzo's websites of the day*. Retrieved from http://larryferlazzo.edublogs.org/2013/02/16/the-best-info-on-skills-employers-are-looking-for-in-job-seekers/

8. Achieve. (2012, December). *Understanding the skills in the Common Core State Standards* (p. 5). Retrieved from http://www.achieve.org/files/Understanding-Skills-CCSS.pdf

9. Dymnicki, A., Sambolt, M., & Kidron, Y. (2013, March). *Improving college and career readiness by incorporating social and emotional learning* (p. 9). Washington, DC: American Institutes for Research. Retrieved from http://www.ccrscenter.org/sites/default/files/Improving%20College%20and%20Career%20Readiness%20by%20Incorporating%20Social%20and%20Emotional%20Learning_0.pdf

10. Council of Chief State School Officers. (2013, February). *Knowledge, skills, and dispositions: The Innovation Lab Network state framework for college, career, and citizenship*

readiness, and implications for state policy (p. 10). Retrieved from http://www.ccsso.org/Documents/ILN%20Knowledge%20Skills%20and%20Dispositions%20CCR%20Framework%20February%202013.pdf

11. Ferlazzo, L. (2015, March 19). Creating the conditions for student motivation. *Edutopia*. Retrieved from http://www.edutopia.org/blog/creating-conditions-for-student-motivation-larry-ferlazzo

12. Ferlazzo, L., & Hull Sypnieski, K. (2012). *The ESL/ELL teacher's survival guide: Ready-to-use strategies, tools, and activities for teaching all levels* (p. 250). San Francisco, CA: Jossey-Bass.

13. *Setting goals: Who, why, how?* (n.d.). Harvard Initiative for Learning & Teaching (p. 1). Retrieved from http://hilt.harvard.edu/files/hilt/files/settinggoals.pdf

14. Moeller, A. J., Theiler, J. M., & Wu, C. (2012). Goal setting and student achievement: A longitudinal study. *The Modern Language Journal, 96*(ii), 153–169 (p. 163). Retrieved from http://communityconnectors.ohio.gov/Portals/0/pdfs/Moeller%20et%20al%20Goal%20Setting%20and%20Studnt%20Behavior.pdf

15. Coalition for Psychology in Schools and Education. (n.d.). *Top twenty principles from psychology for preK–12 teaching and learning* (p. 17). Washington, DC: American Psychological Association. Retrieved from http://www.apa.org/ed/schools/cpse/top-twenty-principles.pdf

16. Latham, G. P., Seijts, G., & Seijts, G. (2006, May/June). Learning goals or performance goals: Is it the journey or the destination? *Ivey Business Journal*. Retrieved from http://iveybusinessjournal.com/publication/learning-goals-or-performance-goals-is-it-the-journey-or-the-destination/

17. Latham, G. P., Seijts, G., & Seijts, G. (2006, May/June). Learning goals or performance goals: Is it the journey or the destination? *Ivey Business Journal*. Retrieved from http://iveybusinessjournal.com/publication/learning-goals-or-performance-goals-is-it-the-journey-or-the-destination/

18. *Setting goals: Who, why, how?* (n.d.). Harvard Initiative for Learning & Teaching (p. 3). Retrieved from http://hilt.harvard.edu/files/hilt/files/settinggoals.pdf

19. Davies, S. T. (2014, August 14). *A tiny, powerful idea: How to commit to your goals in the long-term*. Retrieved from http://www.samuelthomasdavies.com/how-to-commit-to-your-goals-in-the-long-term/

20. Ferlazzo, L., & Hull Sypnieski, K. (2012). *The ESL/ELL teacher's survival guide: Ready-to-use strategies, tools, and activities for teaching all levels* (p. 282). San Francisco, CA: Jossey-Bass.

21. Ferlazzo, L. (2011). *Helping students motivate themselves* (p. 7). New York, NY: Routledge.

22. Ferlazzo, L. (2013). *Self-driven learning: Teaching strategies for student motivation* (p. 10). New York, NY: Routledge.

23. Ferlazzo, L. (2015). *Building a community of self-motivated learners: Strategies to help students thrive in school and beyond* (p. 19). New York, NY: Routledge.

24. Locke, E. A., & Latham, G. P. (2006). New directions in goal-setting theory. *Current Directions in Psychological Science, 15*(5), 265–268 (p. 265).

25. Locke, E. A., & Latham, G. P. (2006). New directions in goal-setting theory. *Current Directions in Psychological Science, 15*(5), 265–268 (p. 266).

26. Morisano, D., Hirsh, J. B., Peterson, J. B., Pihl, R. O., & Shore, B. M. (2010). Setting, elaborating, and reflecting on personal goals improves academic performance. *Journal*

of Applied Psychology, 95(2), 255–264 (p. 263). Retrieved from http://selfauthoring.com/JAPcomplete.pdf

27. Zare, P. (2012). Language learning strategies among EFL/ESL learners: A review of literature. *International Journal of Humanities and Social Science, 2*(5), 162–169 (p. 164).

28. Lai, E. (2011, April). *Metacognition: A literature review. Research report* (p. 20). Retrieved from http://images.pearsonassessments.com/images/tmrs/Metacognition_Literature_Review_Final.pdf

29. Raoofil, S., Chan, S. H., Makundan, J., & Rashid, S. (2014). Metacognition and second/foreign language learning. *English Language Teaching, 7*(1), 36–49 (p. 40).

30. Raoofil, S., Chan, S. H., Makundan, J., & Rashid, S. (2014). Metacognition and second/foreign language learning. *English Language Teaching, 7*(1), 36–49 (p. 42).

31. Clegg, J. (n.d.). *Metacognition: An overview of its uses in language-learning* (p. 2). Retrieved from http://www.puglia.istruzione.it/portfolio_new/allegati/j_clegg_metacognition_an_ovwerview_of_its_uses_in_language-learning.pdf

32. Mevarech, Z., & Kramarski, B. (2014). *Critical maths for innovative societies: The role of metacognitive pedagogies* (p. 56). OECD Publishing. Retrieved from http://www.keepeek.com/Digital-Asset-Management/oecd/education/critical-maths-for-innovative-societies_9789264223561-en#

33. Ferlazzo, L. (2013). *Self-driven learning: Teaching strategies for student motivation* (p. 100). New York, NY: Routledge.

34. From Ferlazzo, L. (2013). *Self-driven learning: Teaching strategies for student motivation* (p. 100). New York, NY: Routledge.Reprinted with permission from Routledge.

35. Ferlazzo, L. (2013). *Self-driven learning: Teaching strategies for student motivation* (p. 106). New York, NY: Routledge.

36. *Teaching metacognition.* (n.d.). Geological Society of America. Retrieved from http://serc.carleton.edu/NAGTWorkshops/metacognition/teaching_metacognition.html

37. Pinard, L. (2013, May 23). *Bringing metacognition into the classroom.* Retrieved from http://reflectiveteachingreflectivelearning.com/2013/05/23/bringing-metacognition-into-the-classroom/

38. Price-Mitchell, M. (2015, April 7). Metacognition: Nurturing self-awareness in the classroom. *Edutopia.* Retrieved from http://www.edutopia.org/blog/8-pathways-metacognition-in-classroom-marilyn-price-mitchell

39. Fondas, N. (2014, May 15). Study: You really can "work smarter, not harder." *The Atlantic.* Retrieved from http://www.theatlantic.com/education/archive/2014/05/study-you-really-can-work-smarter-not-harder/370819/

40. Ferlazzo, L. (2013). *Self-driven learning: Teaching strategies for student motivation* (p. 98). New York, NY: Routledge.

41. Ferlazzo, L. (2010). *English language learners: Teaching strategies that work* (p. 64). Santa Barbara, CA: Linworth.

42. Shirkhani, S., & Fahim, M. (2011, May). *Enhancing critical thinking in foreign language learners* (p. 1091). Paper presented at the International Conference on Foreign Language Teaching and Applied Linguistics, Sarajevo.

43. Shirkhani, S., & Fahim, M. (2011). Enhancing critical thinking in foreign language learners. *Procedia—Social and Behavioral Sciences, 29*, 111–115.

44. *Picking up a second language is predicted by ability to learn patterns.* (2013, May 28). Association for Psychological Science. Retrieved from http://www.psychologicalscience.org/index.php/news/releases/picking-up-a-second-language-is-predicted-by-the-ability-to-learn-statistical-patterns.html

45. Sparks, S. D. (2015, June 18). Can sorting teach students to make better connections among subjects? *Education Week.* Retrieved from http://blogs.edweek.org/edweek/inside-school-research/2015/06/sorting_improves_science_transfer.html

46. Ferlazzo, L., & Hull Sypnieski, K. (2012). *The ESL/ELL teacher's survival guide: Ready-to-use strategies, tools, and activities for teaching all levels.* San Francisco, CA: Jossey-Bass.

47. Tarr, R. (2015, March 20). A Venn-tastic quiz format to ensure detailed Venn Diagrams. *Tarr's Toolbox.* Retrieved from http://www.classtools.net/blog/a-venn-tastic-way-to-ensure-plenty-of-detail-in-venn-diagrams/

48. Graff, G., & Birkenstein, C. (2009). *They say, I say: The moves that matter in academic writing.* New York, NY: W. W. Norton & Company.

49. Ferlazzo, L. (2011). *Helping students motivate themselves* (p. 142). New York, NY: Routledge.

50. Ferlazzo, L. (2013). *Self-driven learning: Teaching strategies for student motivation* (p. 109). New York, NY: Routledge.

51. Ferlazzo, L., & Hull Sypnieski, K. (2012). *The ESL/ELL teacher's survival guide: Ready-to-use strategies, tools, and activities for teaching all levels* (p. 46). San Francisco, CA: Jossey-Bass.

52. Step inside: Perceive, know about, care about. A routine for getting inside viewpoints. (n.d.). *Visible Thinking.* Harvard Project Zero. Retrieved from http://www.visiblethinkingpz.org/VisibleThinking_html_files/03_ThinkingRoutines/03g_CreativityRoutines/StepInside/StepInside_Routine.html

53. *Reflective Thinking: RT.* (n.d.). University of Hawaii. Retrieved from http://www.hawaii.edu/intlrel/pols382/Reflective%20Thinking%20-%20UH/reflection.html

54. Fondas, N. (2014, May 15). Study: You really can "work smarter, not harder." *The Atlantic.* Retrieved from http://www.theatlantic.com/education/archive/2014/05/study-you-really-can-work-smarter-not-harder/370819/

55. Mental rest and reflection boost learning, study suggests. (2014, October 20). *EurekAlert!* Retrieved from http://www.eurekalert.org/pub_releases/2014-10/uota-mra102014.php

56. Di Stefano, G., Gino, F., Pisano, G., & Staats, B. (2015, March 29). *Learning by thinking: Overcoming the bias for action through reflection.* Social Science Research Network. Retrieved from http://papers.ssrn.com/sol3/papers.cfm?abstract_id=2414478&download=yes

57. Robson, D. (2015, April 23). *A five-step guide to not being stupid.* BBC. Retrieved from http://www.bbc.com/future/story/20150422-how-not-to-be-stupid?ocid=global_future_rss

58. Ferlazzo, L. (2013). *Self-driven learning: Teaching strategies for student motivation* (p. 125). New York, NY: Routledge.

59. Goodwin, B., & Miller, K. (2013). Research says / Creativity requires a mix of skills. *Educational Leadership, 70*(5), 80–81, 83.

60. Iakovos, T. (2011). Critical and creative thinking in the English language classroom. *International Journal of Humanities and Social Science, 1*(8), 82–86.

61. Pearson Forward. (2011). *Thinking and academic success skills* (p. 2). A Pearson Forward overview paper. Retrieved from http://assets.pearsonschool.com/asset_mgr/current/201316/Thinking_and_Academic_Success_Skills_Overview.pdf

62. DeHaan, R. L. (2009). Teaching creativity and inventive problem solving in science. *CBE Life Sciences Education, 8*(3), 172–181.

63. Henderson, J. (2008). Developing students' creative skills for 21st century success. *Reading First, 50*(12). Retrieved from http://www.ascd.org/publications/newsletters/education-update/dec08/vol50/num12/Developing-Students%27-Creative-Skills-for-21st-Century-Success.aspx

64. Adams, C. (2013).Teachers urged to mix it up and use novelty to engage students. *Education Week.* Retrieved from http://blogs.edweek.org/edweek/college_bound/2013/11/teachers_urged_to_mix_it_up_and_use_novelty_in_class_to_engage_students.html

65. Association for Psychological Science. (2010, December 15). Positive mood allows human brain to think more creatively. *Science Daily.* Retrieved from http://www.sciencedaily.com/releases/2010/12/101215113253.htm

66. *Research summary—fostering creativity.* (n.d.). The Journey to Excellence, Education Scotland. Retrieved from http://www.journeytoexcellence.org.uk/resourcesandcpd/research/summaries/rsfosteringcreativity.asp

67. *Research summary—fostering creativity.* (n.d.). The Journey to Excellence, Education Scotland. Retrieved from http://www.journeytoexcellence.org.uk/resourcesandcpd/research/summaries/rsfosteringcreativity.asp

68. Iakovos, T. (2011). Critical and creative thinking in the English language classroom. *International Journal of Humanities and Social Science, 1*(8), 82–86.

69. Amabile, T., & Kramer, S. (2012, April 25). What doesn't motivate creativity can kill it. *Harvard Business Review.* Retrieved from https://hbr.org/2012/04/balancing-the-four-factors-tha-1/?utm_content=buffer994f7&utm_medium=social&utm_source=twitter.com&utm_campaign=buffer

70. Overdosing on incentives. (2014, February 25). *Minds for Science: Psychological Science at Work.* Retrieved from http://www.psychologicalscience.org/index.php/news/minds-business/overdosing-on-incentives.html#.UwzQMqxLKD8.twitter

71. Beghetto, R. A., & Kaufman, J. C. (2013). Fundamentals of creativity. *Educational Leadership, 70*(5), 10–15. Retrieved from http://www.ascd.org/publications/educational-leadership/feb13/vol70/num05/Fundamentals-of-Creativity.aspx

72. Beghetto, R. A., & Kaufman, J. C. (2013). Fundamentals of creativity. *Educational Leadership, 70*(5), 10–15. Retrieved from http://www.ascd.org/publications/educational-leadership/feb13/vol70/num05/Fundamentals-of-Creativity.aspx

73. Krulwich, R. (2012, March 5). Inside-out your mind. *NPR.* Retrieved from http://www.npr.org/sections/krulwich/2012/03/02/147825237/inside-out-your-mind?ft=1&f=1130

74. Maley, A., & Peachey, N. (Eds.). (2015). *Creativity in the English language classroom.* London, UK: British Council. Retrieved from http://englishagenda.britishcouncil.org/sites/ec/files/F004_ELT_Creativity_FINAL_v2%20WEB.pdf

75. Maley, A., & Peachey, N. (Eds.). (2015). *Creativity in the English language classroom* (p. 10). London, UK: British Council. Retrieved from http://englishagenda.britishcouncil.org/sites/ec/files/F004_ELT_Creativity_FINAL_v2%20WEB.pdf

76. Maley, A., & Peachey, N. (Eds.). (2015). *Creativity in the English language classroom* (p. 11). London, UK: British Council. Retrieved from http://englishagenda.britishcouncil.org/sites/ec/files/F004_ELT_Creativity_FINAL_v2%20WEB.pdf

77. Lai, E. R., & Viering, M. (2012, April). *Assessing 21st century skills: Integrating research findings* (p. 1). Vancouver, BC: National Council on Measurement in Education.

78. Lai, E. R., & Viering, M. (2012, April). *Assessing 21st century skills: Integrating research findings* (p. 13). Vancouver, BC: National Council on Measurement in Education.

79. Lai, E. R., & Viering, M. (2012, April). *Assessing 21st century skills: Integrating research findings* (p. 21). Vancouver, BC: National Council on Measurement in Education.

80. Raoofil, S., Tan, B. H., & Chan, S. H. (2012). Self-efficacy in second/foreign language learning contexts. *English Language Teaching, 5*(11), 60–73 (p. 66).

81. Fancsali, C., Jaffe-Walter, R., & Dessein, L. (2013, October 11). *Raikes Foundation: Student agency practices in middle shift learning networks* (p. 4). Columbia, MD: IMPAQ International. Retrieved from https://www.impaqint.com/sites/default/files/project-reports/Student%20Agency%20Practices%20in%20the%20Middle%20Shift%20Learning%20Networks_0.pdf

82. Fancsali, C., Jaffe-Walter, R., & Dessein, L. (2013, October 11). *Raikes Foundation: Student agency practices in middle shift learning networks* (p. 61). Columbia, MD: IMPAQ International. Retrieved from https://www.impaqint.com/sites/default/files/project-reports/Student%20Agency%20Practices%20in%20the%20Middle%20Shift%20Learning%20Networks_0.pdf

83. Hamblin, J. (2015, June 30). 100 percent is overrated. *The Atlantic.* Retrieved from http://www.theatlantic.com/education/archive/2015/06/the-s-word/397205

84. Starecheski, L. (2014, October 7). Why saying is believing—The science of self-talk. *NPR.* Retrieved from http://www.npr.org/sections/health-shots/2014/10/07/353292408/why-saying-is-believing-the-science-of-self-talk

85. Nagaoka, J., Farrington, C. A., Ehrlich, S. B., & Heath, R. D. (2015, June). *Foundations for young adult success: A developmental framework* (p. 43). Chicago: University of Chicago Consortium on Chicago School Research. Retrieved from http://ccsr.uchicago.edu/sites/default/files/publications/Wallace%20Report.pdf

86. Ferlazzo, L., & Hull Sypnieski, K. (2012). *The ESL/ELL teacher's survival guide: Ready-to-use strategies, tools, and activities for teaching all levels* (p. 152). San Francisco, CA: Jossey-Bass.

87. Sparks, S. D. (2015, March 31). 'Middle' students find success tutoring peers, in N.Y.C. study. *Education Week.* Retrieved from http://www.edweek.org/ew/articles/2015/04/01/middle-students-find-success-tutoring-peers-in.html?cmp=ENL-EU-NEWS2-RM

88. Ferlazzo, L. (2010). *English language learners: Teaching strategies that work* (p. 45). Santa Barbara, CA: Linworth.

89. Expecting to teach enhances learning, recall. (2014, August 8). *EurekAlert!* Retrieved from http://www.eurekalert.org/pub_releases/2014-08/wuis-ett080814.php

90. Toshalis, E., & Nakkula, M. J. (2012, April). *Motivation, engagement, and student voice* (p. 27). Jobs for the Future. Retrieved from http://studentsatthecenter.org/sites/scl .dl-dev.com/files/Motivation%20Engagement%20Student%20Voice_0.pdf

91. Stefanou, C. R., Perencevich, K. C., DiCintio, M., & Turner, J. C. (2004). Supporting autonomy in the classroom: Ways teachers encourage student decision making and ownership. *Educational Psychologist*, *39*(2), 97–110 (p. 101). Retrieved lwtype="spaced" from http://www.tandfonline.com/doi/abs/10.1207/s15326985ep3902_2?journal Code=hedp20

92. Marzano, R. J. (2011). Art & science of teaching / The perils and promises of discovery learning. *Educational Leadership*, *69*(1), 86–87. Retrieved from http://www .ascd.org/publications/educational-leadership/sept11/vol69/num01/The-Perils- and-Promises-of-Discovery-Learning.aspx

93. Freeman, S., Eddy, S. L., McDonough, M., Smith, M. K., Okoroafor, N., Jordt, H., & Wenderoth, M. P. (2014). Active learning increases student performance in science, engineering, and mathematics. *PNAS*, *111*(23), 8410–8415 (p. 8410). Retrieved from http://www.pnas.org/content/111/23/8410.full.pdf

94. Brown, H. D. (2007). *Principles of language learning and teaching* (5th ed., p. 105). White Plains, NY: Pearson Longman.

95. Ferlazzo, L. (2011). *Helping students motivate themselves* (p. 14). New York, NY: Routledge.

96. Ferlazzo, L. (2012, October 15). Response: Classroom strategies to foster a growth mindset. *Education Week*. Retrieved from http://blogs.edweek.org/teachers/ classroom_qa_with_larry_ferlazzo/2012/10/response_classroom_strategies_to_ foster_a_growth_mindset.html

97. Sparks, S. D. (2013, September 10). "Growth mindset" gaining traction as a school improvement strategy. *Education Week*. Retrieved from http://www.edweek.org/ew/ articles/2013/09/11/03mindset_ep.h33.html?qs=sparks+dweck

98. Bilingualism changes children's beliefs. (2015, January 13). *Science Daily*. Retrieved from http://www.sciencedaily.com/releases/2015/01/150113131919.htm

99. Byers-Heinlein, K., & Garcia, B. (2015, March). Bilingualism changes children's beliefs about what is innate. *Developmental Science*, *18*, 344–350 (p. 348). Retrieved from http://onlinelibrary.wiley.com/doi/10.1111/desc.12248/abstract

100. Spencer, N., Rowson, J., & Bamfield, L. (2014, March 1). *Everyone starts with an "A"* (p. 30). London, UK: RSA. Retrieved from https://www.thersa.org/discover/ publications-and-articles/reports/everyone-starts-with-an-a/

101. Yeager, D., Walton, G., & Cohen, G. L. (2013, February). Addressing achievement gaps with psychological interventions. *Kappan*, *94*(5), 62–65 (p. 62). Retrieved from https:// labs.la.utexas.edu/adrg/files/2013/12/PDK-Yeager-Walton-Cohen-2013.pdf

102. Yeager, D., Walton, G., & Cohen, G. L. (2013, February). Addressing achievement gaps with psychological interventions. *Kappan*, *94*(5), 62–65 (p. 63). Retrieved from https:// labs.la.utexas.edu/adrg/files/2013/12/PDK-Yeager-Walton-Cohen-2013.pdf

103. Ferlazzo, L. (2012, October 15). Response: Classroom strategies to foster a growth mindset. *Education Week*. Retrieved from http://blogs.edweek.org/teachers/ classroom_qa_with_larry_ferlazzo/2012/10/response_classroom_strategies_to_ foster_a_growth_mindset.html

104. Hammond, Z. (2015). *Culturally responsive teaching and the brain: Promoting authentic engagement and rigor among culturally and linguistically diverse students*. Thousand Oaks, CA: Corwin.

105. Ferlazzo, L. (2015, July 8). "Culturally responsive teaching": An interview with Zaretta Hammond. *Education Week*. Retrieved from http://blogs.edweek.org/teachers/ classroom_qa_with_larry_ferlazzo/2015/07/culturally_responsive_teaching_an_ interview_with_zaretta_hammond.html?qs=zaretta+hammond

106. *What is grit?* (2013, October 16). YouTube. Retrieved from https://www.youtube.com/ watch?v=Rkoe1e2KZJs

107. Spencer, N., Rowson, J., & Bamfield, L. (2014, March 1). *Everyone starts with an "A"* (p. 30). London, UK: RSA. Retrieved from https://www.thersa.org/discover/ publications-and-articles/reports/everyone-starts-with-an-a/

108. Felicano, R. (2015, May 12). *Introduction to growth mindset*. Retrieved from https://www .mindsetkit.org/practices/7SThZAFHExkJ3Bfk

109. Kirsten R., 2015. Retrieved from https://www.mindsetkit.org/practices/qdMc9BAp BJITA0fi

110. DiSalvo, D. (2014, September 18). Brains get a performance boost from believing effort trumps genetics. *Time*. Retrieved from http://time.com/3398960/brains-performance-boost-effort/

111. Ferlazzo, L. (2011). *Helping students motivate themselves* (p. 71). New York, NY: Routledge.

112. Gutman, L. M., & Schoon, I. (2013, November 21). *The impact of non-cognitive skills on outcomes for young people* (p. 3). London, UK: Institute of Education, University of London. Retrieved from https://educationendowmentfoundation.org.uk/uploads/ pdf/Non-cognitive_skills_literature_review_2.pdf

113. Adapted from zerosophy.com, http://zerosophy.com/tag/discipline-self-control/

114. Duckworth, A., & Gross, J. J. (2014). Self-control and grit: Related but separate determinants of success. *Current Directions in Psychological Science, 23*(5), 319–325 (p. 321).

115. Garcia, E. (2014, December 2). *The need to address noncognitive skills in the education policy agenda*. Economic Policy Institute. Retrieved from http://www.epi.org/publication/ the-need-to-address-noncognitive-skills-in-the-education-policy-agenda/?utm_ content=buffer022a3&utm_medium=social&utm_source=twitter.com&utm_ campaign=buffer

116. Association for Psychological Science. (2015, April 14). Childhood self-control linked to enhanced job prospects throughout life. *ScienceDaily*. Retrieved from http://www .sciencedaily.com/releases/2015/04/150414130403.htm

117. Stromberg, J. (2014, September 24). *7 things marshmallows teach us about self-control*. Vox Media. Retrieved from http://www.vox.com/2014/9/24/6833469/marshmallow-test-self-control

118. Ferlazzo, L., & Hull Sypnieski, K. (2012). *The ESL/ELL teacher's survival guide: Ready-to-use strategies, tools, and activities for teaching all levels* (p. 271). San Francisco, CA: Jossey-Bass.

119. Ferlazzo, L. (2011). *Helping students motivate themselves*. New York, NY: Routledge.

120. Ferlazzo, L. (2013). *Self-driven learning: Teaching strategies for student motivation* (p. 10). New York, NY: Routledge.

121. Ferlazzo, L. (2015). *Building a community of self-motivated learners: Strategies to help students thrive in school and beyond.* New York, NY: Routledge.

122. Marshall, M. (2012). *Discipline without stress.* Los Alamitos, CA: Piper Press.

123. Porath, C. (2015, June 19). No time to be nice at work. *New York Times.* Retrieved from http://www.nytimes.com/2015/06/21/opinion/sunday/is-your-boss-mean.html?smid=tw-share&_r=0

124. Farrington, C. A., Roderick, M., Allensworth, E., Nagaoka, J., Keyes, T. S., Johnson, D. W., & Beechum, N. O. (2012, June). *Teaching adolescents to become learners: The role of noncognitive factors in shaping school performance: A critical literature review* (p. 26). Chicago, IL: The University of Chicago Consortium on Chicago School Research.

125. Farrington, C. A., Roderick, M., Allensworth, E., Nagaoka, J., Keyes, T. S., Johnson, D. W., & Beechum, N. O. (2012, June). *Teaching adolescents to become learners: The role of noncognitive factors in shaping school performance: A critical literature review* (p. 53). Chicago: The University of Chicago Consortium on Chicago School Research.

126. Spencer, N., Rowson, J., & Bamfield, L. (2014, March 1). *Everyone starts with an "A"* (p. 28). London, UK: RSA. Retrieved from https://www.thersa.org/discover/publications-and-articles/reports/everyone-starts-with-an-a/

127. Perkins-Gough, D. (2013). The significance of grit: A conversation with Angela Duckworth. *Educational Leadership, 71*(1), 14–20. Retrieved from http://www.ascd.org/publications/educational-leadership/sept13/vol71/num01/The-Significance-of-Grit@-A-Conversation-with-Angela-Lee-Duckworth.aspx

128. *What is grit?* (2013, October 16). YouTube. Retrieved from https://www.youtube.com/watch?v=Rkoe1e2KZJs

129. Duckworth, A., & Gross, J. J. (2014). Self-control and grit: Related but separate determinants of success. *Current Directions in Psychological Science, 23*(5), 319–325 (p. 320).

130. Farrington, C. A., Roderick, M., Allensworth, E., Nagaoka, J., Keyes, T. S., Johnson, D. W., & Beechum, N. O. (2012, June). *Teaching adolescents to become learners: The role of noncognitive factors in shaping school performance: A critical literature review* (p. 22). Chicago: The University of Chicago Consortium on Chicago School Research.

131. Strauss, V. (2012, March 14). Telling students it's ok to fail helps them succeed—Study. *The Washington Post.* Retrieved from http://www.washingtonpost.com/blogs/answer-sheet/post/telling-students-its-okay-to-fail-helps-them-succeed_study/2012/03/12/gIQAxTwxBS_blog.html?wprss=rss_answer-sheet

132. Spencer, N., Rowson, J., & Bamfield, L. (2014, March 1). *Everyone starts with an "A"* (p. 34). London, UK: RSA. Retrieved from https://www.thersa.org/discover/publications-and-articles/reports/everyone-starts-with-an-a/

133. Farrington, C. A., Roderick, M., Allensworth, E., Nagaoka, J., Keyes, T. S., Johnson, D. W., & Beechum, N. O. (2012, June). *Teaching adolescents to become learners: The role of noncognitive factors in shaping school performance: A critical literature review* (p. 7). Chicago, IL: The University of Chicago Consortium on Chicago School Research.

134. Farrington, C. A., Roderick, M., Allensworth, E., Nagaoka, J., Keyes, T. S., Johnson, D. W., & Beechum, N. O. (2012, June). *Teaching adolescents to become learners: The role of noncognitive factors in shaping school performance: A critical literature review* (p. 26). Chicago, IL: The University of Chicago Consortium on Chicago School Research.

135. Ferlazzo, L. (2015). *Building a community of self-motivated learners: Strategies to help students thrive in school and beyond* (p. 25). New York, NY: Routledge.

136. Ferlazzo, L. (2011). *Helping students motivate themselves* (p. 71). New York, NY: Routledge.

137. Ferlazzo, L. (2015). *Building a community of self-motivated learners: Strategies to help students thrive in school and beyond* (p. 44). New York, NY: Routledge.

138. Briceno, E. (2015, January 10). Mistakes are not all created equal. *Mindset Works.* Retrieved from http://community.mindsetworks.com/blog-page/home-blogs/entry/mistakes-are-not-all-created-equal

139. Ferlazzo, L. (2013). *Self-driven learning: Teaching strategies for student motivation* (p. 7). New York, NY: Routledge.

Chapter 3 Reading

1. Dr. Seuss. (1978). *I can read with my eyes shut.* New York, NY: Random House Books for Young Readers.

2. Achieve the Core. (n.d.). *Common Core state standards shifts.* Retrieved from http://achievethecore.org/content/upload/122113_Shifts.pdf

3. Brown, S. (n.d.). Simplifying text complexity. *Teaching Channel.* Retrieved from https://www.teachingchannel.org/videos/simplifying-text-complexity

4. Ferlazzo, L. (2014, November 18). Response: Teaching "close reading"—Part three. *Education Week.* Retrieved from http://blogs.edweek.org/teachers/classroom_qa_with_larry_ferlazzo/2014/11/response_teaching_close_reading_-_part_three.html

5. Parks, T. (2015, July 11). The key to rereading. *The New York Review of Books.* Retrieved from http://www.nybooks.com/blogs/nyrblog/2015/jul/11/rereading-unlocking-the-mind/

6. Shanahan, T. (2012–2013). The Common Core ate my baby and other urban legends. *Educational Leadership, 70*(4), 10–16. Retrieved from http://www.ascd.org/publications/educational-leadership/dec12/vol70/num04/The-Common-Core-Ate-My-Baby-and-Other-Urban-Legends.aspx

7. Achieve the Core. (n.d.). *Common Core state standards shifts.* Retrieved from http://achievethecore.org/content/upload/122113_Shifts.pdf

8. *Supplemental information for Appendix A of the Common Core state standards for English language arts and literacy: New research on text complexity.* (n.d.). Retrieved from http://www.corestandards.org/assets/E0813_Appendix_A_New_Research_on_Text_Complexity.pdf

9. *Supplemental information for Appendix A of the Common Core state standards for English language arts and literacy: New research on text complexity.* (n.d.). Retrieved from http://www.corestandards.org/assets/E0813_Appendix_A_New_Research_on_Text_Complexity.pdf

10. Common Core State Standards for English Language Arts & Literacy in History/Social Studies, Science, and Technical Subjects. (n.d.). *Appendix A: Research supporting key elements of the standards. Glossary of key terms* (p. 9). Retrieved from http://www.corestandards.org/assets/Appendix_A.pdf

11. Brown, S. (n.d.). Simplifying text complexity. *Teaching Channel.* Retrieved from https://www.teachingchannel.org/videos/simplifying-text-complexity

12. Hakuta, K., Butler, Y. G., & Witt, D. (2000). *How long does it take English learners to attain proficiency?* (Abstract). University of California Linguistic Minority Research Institute. Retrieved from http://www.usc.edu/dept/education/CMMR/FullText/ Hakuta_HOW_LONG_DOES_IT_TAKE.pdf

13. Shanahan, T. (2012–2013). The Common Core ate my baby and other urban legends. *Educational Leadership*, 70(4), 10–16. Retrieved from http://www.ascd.org/publications/ educational-leadership/dec12/vol70/num04/The-Common-Core-Ate-My-Baby-and-Other-Urban-Legends.aspx

14. Shanahan, T. (n.d.). Common Core: Close reading. *Scholastic*. Retrieved from http:// www.scholastic.com/teachers/article/common-core-close-reading-0

15. Gallagher, K. (2015, July 20). *#7: Close reading is like broccoli. It's good for you, but only in moderation*. Twitter. Retrieved from https://twitter.com/KellyGToGo/status/ 623122274938261504

16. Ferlazzo, L., & Hull Sypnieski, K. (2012). *The ESL/ELL teacher's survival guide: Ready-to-use strategies, tools, and activities for teaching all levels* (p. 125). San Francisco, CA: Jossey-Bass.

17. Ferlazzo, L. (2011, February 26). The best resources for documenting the effectiveness of free voluntary reading. *Larry Ferlazzo's websites of the day*. Retrieved from http://larryferlazzo.edublogs.org/2011/02/26/the-best-resources-documenting-the-effectiveness-of-free-voluntary-reading

18. Common Core State Standards for English Language Arts & Literacy in History/Social Studies, Science, and Technical Subjects. (n.d.). *Appendix A: Research supporting key elements of the standards. Glossary of key terms* (p. 9). Retrieved from http://www .corestandards.org/assets/Appendix_A.pdf

19. Ferlazzo, L. (2012, October 4). The best posts & articles about why book "leveling" is a bad idea. *Larry Ferlazzo's websites of the day*. Retrieved from http://larryferlazzo.edublogs .org/2012/10/04/the-best-posts-articles-about-why-book-leveling-is-a-bad-idea/

20. Klingner, J., Lesaux, N., Goetz, S., Cook, J., & Soltero-Gonzalez, L. (n.d.). *IRA Commission on RTI: Meeting the needs of culturally and linguistically diverse students* (p. 11). Retrieved from http://www.reading.org/Libraries/resources/RTIDiversity.pdf?sfvrsn=0

21. Ford, K. (2005). *Fostering literacy development in English language learners.* ¡Colorín Colorado! Retrieved from http://www.colorincolorado.org/article/12924/

22. DeBarger, A. H., Penuel, W. R., Harris, C. J., & Schank, P. (2010). Teaching routines to enhance collaboration using classroom network technology. In F. Pozzi & D. Persico (Eds.), *Techniques for fostering collaboration in online learning communities: Theoretical and practical perspectives* (pp. 224–244). Hershey, PA: IGI Global.

23. Gawande, A. (2007, December 10). The checklist. *The New Yorker*. Retrieved from http:// www.newyorker.com/magazine/2007/12/10/the-checklist

24. Franke, M. L., Kazemi, E., Kelley-Peterson, M., Hintz, A., Lampert, M., Ghousseni, H., & Chan, A. (n.d.). *Conceptualizing and using routines of practice in mathematics teaching to advance professional education* (PowerPoint). Retrieved from http://sitemaker.umich.edu/ ltp/files/tdg_practice_08.pdf

25. Willis, J. (2007). The neuroscience of joyful education. *Educational Leadership, 64.* Retrieved from https://www.psychologytoday.com/files/attachments/4141/the-neuroscience-joyful-education-judy-willis-md.pdf

26. Willis, J. (2005). Attention: To have and to hold. Add the science of learning to the art of teaching to enrich classroom instruction. *Voices from the Middle*. Retrieved from http://www.radteach.com/page1/page8/page9/page9.html

27. Shanahan, T. (2013, September 3). *CCCS and units of study: To theme or not to theme.* The Center for Development & Learning. Retrieved from http://www.cdl.org/articles/ccss-and-units-of-study-to-theme-or-not-to-theme/

28. Heritage, M., Walqui, A., & Linquanti, R. (2015). *English language learners and the new standards: Developing language, content knowledge, and analytical practices in the classroom* (p. 44). Cambridge, MA: Harvard Education Press.

29. Yglesias, M. (2015, June 25). What Justice Scalia's King v. Burwell dissent gets wrong about words and meaning. *Vox Policy & Politics*. Retrieved from http://www.vox.com/2015/6/25/8845697/scalia-king-burwell-dissent-semantic-holism

30. Wiggins, G. (2015, May 30). *On reading, Part 5: A key flaw in using the Gradual Release of Responsibility model.* Granted, and . . . thoughts on education by Grant Wiggins blog. Retrieved from https://grantwiggins.wordpress.com/2015/03/30/on-reading-part-5-a-key-flaw-in-using-the-gradual-release-of-responsibility-model

31. Shanahan, T. (2013, Fall). Letting the text take center stage: How the Common Core state standards will transform English language arts instruction. *American Educator*, 4–11, 43 (p. 7). Retrieved from http://www.aft.org/sites/default/files/periodicals/Shanahan.pdf

32. Shanahan, T. (2014, November 24). *Prior knowledge: Can we really level the playing field?* Washington, DC: Thomas Fordham Institute. Retrieved from http://edexcellence.net/articles/prior-knowledge-can-we-really-level-the-playing-field

33. Shanahan, T. (2013, Fall). Letting the text take center stage: How the Common Core state standards will transform English language arts instruction. *American Educator*, 4–11, 43 (p. 8). Retrieved from http://www.aft.org/sites/default/files/periodicals/Shanahan.pdf

34. Ferlazzo, L. (2008, October 3). The best multilingual & bilingual sites for math, social studies, & science. *Larry Ferlazzo's websites of the day*. Retrieved from http://larryferlazzo.edublogs.org/2008/10/03/the-best-multilingual-bilingual-sites-for-math-social-studies-science/

35. Bunch, G. C., Kibler, A., & Pimentel, S. (n.d.). *Realizing opportunities for English language learners in the Common Core English language arts and disciplinary literary standards* (p. 4). Stanford, CA: Stanford University. Retrieved from http://ell.stanford.edu/sites/default/files/pdf/academic-papers/01_Bunch_Kibler_Pimentel_RealizingOpp%20in%20ELA_FINAL_0.pdf

36. Bunch et al., (2008) (p. 9). Retrieved from http://ell.stanford.edu/sites/default/files/pdf/academic-papers/01_Bunch_Kibler_Pimentel_RealizingOpp%20in%20ELA_FINAL_0.pdf page 9.

37. Gardner, D., & Hansen, E. C. (2007). Effects of lexical simplification during unaided reading of English informational texts. *TESL Reporter, 40*(2), 27–59 (p. 32). Retrieved from https://journals.lib.byu.edu/spc/index.php/TESL/article/download/32316/30515

38. Ferlazzo, L., & Hull Sypnieski, K. (2012). *The ESL/ELL teacher's survival guide: Ready-to-use strategies, tools, and activities for teaching all levels* (pp. 75, 158). San Francisco, CA: Jossey-Bass.

39. Strangman, N., Vue, G., Hall, T., & Meyer, A. (2003). *Graphic organizers and implications for universal design for learning* (p. 5). Wakefield, MA: National Center on Accessing the General Curriculum. Retrieved from http://aem.cast.org/about/publications/2003/ncac-graphic-organizers-udl.html#.VlIJhL_KMQ8

40. Jiang, X., & Grabe, W. (2007). Graphic organizers in reading instruction: Research findings and issues. *Reading in a Foreign Language, 19*(7). Retrieved from http://nflrc.hawaii.edu/rfl/April2007/jiang/jiang.html

41. Common Core State Standards for English Language Arts & Literacy in History/Social Studies, Science, and Technical Subjects. (n.d.). *Appendix A: Research supporting key elements of the standards. Glossary of key terms* (p. 27). Retrieved from http://www.corestandards.org/assets/Appendix_A.pdf

42. Johnston, V. (2015). The power of the read aloud in the age of the Common Core. *The Open Communication Journal, 9*(Suppl. 1: M5), 34–38 (p. 37). Retrieved from http://benthamopen.com/contents/pdf/TOCOMMJ/TOCOMMJ-9-34.pdf

43. Sutherland, S. (2015, June 11). When we read, we recognize words as pictures and hear them spoken aloud. *Scientific American*. Retrieved from http://www.scientificamerican.com/article/when-we-read-we-recognize-words-as-pictures-and-hear-them-spoken-aloud/

44. *Think aloud strategy summary*. (n.d.). Pebble Creek Labs. Retrieved from http://pebblecreeklabs.com/instructional-strategies/think-aloud/182-think-aloud-strategy-summary.html

45. Wyner, G. (2014, August 1). To get fluent in a new language, think in pictures. *Wall Street Journal*. Retrieved from http://www.wsj.com/articles/to-get-fluent-in-a-new-language-think-in-pictures-1406938139

46. Ferlazzo, L., & Hull Sypnieski, K. (2012). *The ESL/ELL teacher's survival guide: Ready-to-use strategies, tools, and activities for teaching all levels* (p. 41). San Francisco, CA: Jossey-Bass.

47. Gonchar, M. (2015, February 27). 10 intriguing photographs to teach close reading and visual thinking skills. *The Learning Network: Teaching & Learning with the New York Times*. Retrieved from http://learning.blogs.nytimes.com/2015/02/27/10-intriguing-photographs-to-teach-close-reading-and-visual-thinking-skills/?_r=0

48. Bennett, C. M. (2013, October 3). Close reading Constable's "The hay wain" and Turner's "The fighting Temeraire." *Used Books in Class*. Retrieved from http://usedbooksinclass.com/2013/10/03/close-reading-constables-the-hay-wain-and-turners-the-fighting-temeraire/

49. Visser, M. (2007, October 29). The guardian commercial—Points of view. *YouTube*. Retrieved from https://www.youtube.com/watch?v=E3h-T3KQNxU

50. Priestman, C. (2014, August 27). A video game for Ferguson. *The Atlantic*. Retrieved from http://www.theatlantic.com/entertainment/archive/2014/08/a-video-game-for-ferguson/379110

51. Baker, F. (n.d.). *How framing affects our understanding.* Media Literacy Clearinghouse. Retrieved from http://www.frankwbaker.com/framing.htm

52. Baker, F. (2014, August 6). *How to close read the language of film.* Middle-Web. Retrieved from http://www.middleweb.com/16848/close-read-language-film/

53. Ferlazzo, L. (2015, July 13). "The reading strategies book": An interview with Jennifer Serravallo. *Education Week.* Retrieved from http://blogs.edweek.org/teachers/classroom_qa_with_larry_ferlazzo/2015/07/the_reading_strategies_book_an_interview_with_jennifer_serravallo.html

54. National Reading Panel. (2000). *Teaching children to read: An evidence-based assessment of the scientific research literature on reading and its implications for reading instruction* (p. 233). Retrieved from http://www.nichd.nih.gov/publications/pubs/nrp/documents/report.pdf

55. Marzano, R. J. (2010). The art and science of teaching/summarizing to comprehend. *Educational Leadership, 67*(6), 83–84 (p. 83). Retrieved from http://www.ascd.org/publications/educational-leadership/mar10/vol67/num06/Summarizing-to-Comprehend.aspx

56. National Reading Panel. (2000). *Teaching children to read: An evidence-based assessment of the scientific research literature on reading and its implications for reading instruction* (p. 92). Retrieved from http://www.nichd.nih.gov/publications/pubs/nrp/documents/report.pdf

57. Marzano, R. J. (2010). The art and science of teaching/summarizing to comprehend. *Educational Leadership, 67*(6), 83–84 (p. 83). Retrieved from http://www.ascd.org/publications/educational-leadership/mar10/vol67/num06/Summarizing-to-Comprehend.aspx

58. Moses, E. (2015, January 17). 3-2-1 and the Common Core writing book. *Cues from Ekuwah Moses* [Blog]. Retrieved from http://ekuwah.blogspot.com/2015/01/3-2-1-and-common-core-writing-book.html

59. National Reading Panel. (2000). *Teaching children to read: An evidence-based assessment of the scientific research literature on reading and its implications for reading instruction* (p. 488). Retrieved from http://www.nichd.nih.gov/publications/pubs/nrp/documents/report.pdf

60. Yopp, R. H., & Dreher, M. J. (1994). Effects of active comprehension instruction on attitudes and motivation in reading. *Reading Horizons, 34*(4), 288–302 (p. 298). Retrieved from http://scholarworks.wmich.edu/cgi/viewcontent.cgi?article=1459&context=reading_horizons

61. Rosenshine, B., Meister, C., & Chapman, S. (1996). Teaching students to generate questions: A review of the intervention studies. *Review of Educational Research, 66,* 181–221 (p. 183). Retrieved from http://k3hss.pwnet.org/instruction/virginia_tiered_system_supports/training/higher_ed/tch_students_generate_questions_review.pdf

62. Hill, J. D., & Flynn, K. (2008). Asking the right questions: Teachers' questions can build students' English language skills. *Journal of Staff Development, 29*(1), 46–52 (p. 51). Retrieved from http://wuhsd.org/cms/lib/CA01000258/Centricity/Domain/16/ELL_-_Asking_Right_Questions1.pdf

63. Paul, A. M. (2013). Predictions produce interest. *The Brilliant Report.* Retrieved from http://us2.campaign-archive2.com/?u=bc04df008d4705e4e77c2eb35&id=2362d24fc9

64. National Reading Panel. (2000). *Teaching children to read: An evidence-based assessment of the scientific research literature on reading and its implications for reading instruction* (p. 233). Retrieved from http://www.nichd.nih.gov/publications/pubs/nrp/documents/report.pdf

65. REL West Reference Desk Team. (2015, July). *Summary of information on collaborative vs. cooperative learning.* E-mail communication to Larry Ferlazzo.

66. Collaboration vs. cooperative learning. (n.d.). *Teaching Channel.* Retrieved from https://www.teachingchannel.org/videos/collaboration-vs-cooperative-learning-nea

67. Author's choices: Collaborating in close reading. (n.d.). *Teaching Channel.* Retrieved from https://www.teachingchannel.org/videos/analyzing-author-choices-nea

68. Collaboration vs. cooperative learning. (n.d.). *Teaching Channel.* Retrieved from https://www.teachingchannel.org/videos/collaboration-vs-cooperative-learning-nea

69. S. Boss, personal communication, June 29, 2015.

70. Carr, P. B., & Walton, G. M. (2014). Cues of working together fuel intrinsic motivation. *Journal of Experimental Social Psychology, 53,* 169–184 (p. 170). Retrieved from http://gregorywalton-stanford.weebly.com/uploads/4/9/4/4/49448111/carr_&_walton_2014.pdf

71. Minugh, K. (2007, November 14). Luther Burbank High's program to teach English targets not only students but their entire families. *Sacramento Bee.* B1. Retrieved from www.mokoia.school.nz/documents/esol_article.doc

72. Ferlazzo, L., & Hull Sypnieski, K. (2012). *The ESL/ELL teacher's survival guide: Ready-to-use strategies, tools, and activities for teaching all levels* (p. 43). San Francisco, CA: Jossey-Bass.

73. Lehman, C., & Roberts, K. (2013). *Falling in love with close reading: Lessons for analyzing texts—and life* (p. 7). Portsmouth, NH: Heinemann. Retrieved from http://www.heinemann.com/shared/onlineresources/E05084/WebSample_LehmanRoberts_FallingCloseReading.pdf?submissionGuid=2c81cf17-8c49-401b-a899-4ad9d3a033f7

74. Wiggins, G. (2015, May 31). On literacy and strategy, Part 6: My first cut at recommendations. *Granted, and . . . thoughts on education by Grant Wiggins* [Blog]. Retrieved from https://grantwiggins.wordpress.com/2015/03/31/on-literacy-and-strategy-part-6-my-first-cut-at-recommendations/

Chapter 4 Writing

1. Steinbeck, J. (1969, June 2). *New York Times.* Retrieved from https://en.wikiquote.org/wiki/Writing

2. Coleman, D., & Pimentel, S. (2012, April 12). *Revised publishers' criteria for the Common Core standards in English language arts and literacy, Grades 3–12* (p. 13). Retrieved from http://www.corestandards.org/assets/Publishers_Criteria_for_3-12.pdf

3. Common Core State Standards for English Language Arts & Literacy in History/Social Studies, Science, and Technical Subjects. (n.d.). *Appendix A: Research supporting key elements of the standards. Glossary of key terms* (p. 24). Retrieved from http://www.corestandards.org/assets/Appendix_A.pdf

4. Goldstein, D. (2012, May 17). *On David Coleman, "life writing," and the future of the American reading list.* Retrieved from http://www.danagoldstein.com/2012/05/on-david-coleman-life-writing-and-the-future-of-the-american-reading-list.html

5. Common Core State Standards for English Language Arts & Literacy in History/Social Studies, Science, and Technical Subjects. (n.d.). *Appendix A: Research supporting key elements of the standards. Glossary of key terms* (p. 23). Retrieved from http://www.corestandards.org/assets/Appendix_A.pdf

6. Common Core State Standards for English Language Arts & Literacy in History/Social Studies, Science, and Technical Subjects. (n.d.). *Appendix A: Research supporting key elements of the standards. Glossary of key terms* (p. 24). Retrieved from http://www.corestandards.org/assets/Appendix_A.pdf

7. Common Core State Standards for English Language Arts & Literacy in History/Social Studies, Science, and Technical Subjects. (n.d.). *Appendix A: Research supporting key elements of the standards. Glossary of key terms* (p. 23). Retrieved from http://www.corestandards.org/assets/Appendix_A.pdf

8. Coleman, D., & Pimentel, S. (2012, April 12). *Revised publishers' criteria for the Common Core standards in English language arts and literacy, Grades 3–12* (p. 13). Retrieved from http://www.corestandards.org/assets/Publishers_Criteria_for_3-12.pdf

9. Ferlazzo, L. (2013, September 29). Developing student writers by letting them talk. *Education Week.* Retrieved from http://blogs.edweek.org/teachers/classroom_qa_with_larry_ferlazzo/2013/09/developing_students_writers_by_letting_them_talk.html

10. Bunch, G. C., Kibler, A., & Pimentel, S. (n.d.). *Realizing opportunities for English language learners in the Common Core English language arts and disciplinary literary standards* (p. 6). Stanford University. Retrieved from http://ell.stanford.edu/sites/default/files/pdf/academic-papers/01_Bunch_Kibler_Pimentel_RealizingOpp%20in%20ELA_FINAL_0.pdf

11. Rosenshine, B. (2012, Spring). Principles of instruction: Research-based strategies that all teachers should know. *American Educator* (p. 15). Retrieved from http://www.aft.org/sites/default/files/periodicals/Rosenshine.pdf

12. Olinghouse, N. (2013). *The Common Core state standards and evidence-based educational practices: The case of writing* (p. 347). ResearchGate. Retrieved from http://www.researchgate.net/publication/258148583_The_Common_Core_State_Standards_and_evidence-based_educational_practices_The_case_of_writing

13. Gallagher, K. (2014). Making the most of mentor texts. *Educational Leadership, 71*(7), 28–33 (p. 28). Retrieved from http://www.ascd.org/publications/educational-leadership/apr14/vol71/num07/Making-the-Most-of-Mentor-Texts.aspx

14. Wei, J., Chen, J. C., & Adawu, A. (2014). Teaching ESL beginners metacognitive writing strategies through multimedia software. *The CATESOL Journal, 26*(1), 60–75 (p. 62).

Retrieved from http://www.catesoljournal.org/wp-content/uploads/2014/10/CJ26_wei.pdf

15. Graff, G., & Birkenstein, C. (2009). *They say, I say: The moves that matter in academic writing* (p. 2). New York: W. W. Norton & Company.

16. Smith, M. A., & Swain, S. (2011, Fall). *Wise eyes: Prompting for meaningful student writing* (p. 3). Berkeley: National Writing Project, University of California. Retrieved from http://www.nwp.org/cs/public/download/nwp_file/15440/Wise_Eyes.pdf?x-r=pcfile_d

17. Ferlazzo, L., & Hull Sypnieski, K. (2012). *The ESL/ELL teacher's survival guide: Ready-to-use strategies, tools, and activities for teaching all levels* (p. 196). San Francisco, CA: Jossey-Bass.

18. Gass, N. (2015, April 30). Sixth grader who cut off Barack Obama: "I was just nudging him to get on." *Politico*. Retrieved from http://www.politico.com/story/2015/04/6th-grader-cut-off-obama-interview-osman-yahya-117526.html

19. Witte, S. (2013). Preaching what we practice: A study of revision. *Journal of Curriculum and Instruction*, 6(2), 33–59 (p. 47). Retrieved from http://www.nwp.org/cs/public/download/nwp_file/17665/witte_preaching_what_we_practice.pdf?x-r=pcfile_d

20. Witte, S. (2013). Preaching what we practice: A study of revision. *Journal of Curriculum and Instruction*, 6(2), 33–59 (p. 40). Retrieved from http://www.nwp.org/cs/public/download/nwp_file/17665/witte_preaching_what_we_practice.pdf?x-r=pcfile_d

21. Common Core State Standards Initiative. (2010). *Application of Common Core state standards for English language learners* (p. 1). Retrieved from http://www.corestandards.org/assets/application-for-english-learners.pdf

22. Mulligan, C., & Garofalo, R. (2011). A collaborative writing approach: Methodology and student assessment. *The Language Teacher*, 35(3), 5–10 (p. 5). Retrieved from www.jalt-publications.org/files/pdf-article/art1_13.pdf

23. Mulligan, C., & Garofalo, R. (2011). A collaborative writing approach: Methodology and student assessment. *The Language Teacher*, 35(3), 5–10 (p. 6). Retrieved from www.jalt-publications.org/files/pdf-article/art1_13.pdf

24. *Models, critique, and descriptive feedback*. (2012). Expeditionary Learning. Retrieved from https://www.engageny.org/file/7431/download/8.models_critique_descriptive_feedback_toolkit_booklet_nti_0713.pdf

25. Tharby, A. (2014, March 27). Adventures with gallery critique. *Reflecting English*. Retrieved from https://reflectingenglish.wordpress.com/2014/03/27/adventures-with-gallery-critique

26. Ferlazzo, L., & Hull Sypnieski, K. (2012). *The ESL/ELL teacher's survival guide: Ready-to-use strategies, tools, and activities for teaching all levels* (p. 57). San Francisco, CA: Jossey-Bass.

27. Common Core State Standards Initiative. (n.d.). *English language arts standards. Writing. Grade 11–12. 3.b.* Retrieved from http://www.corestandards.org/ELA-Literacy/W/11-12/3/b

28. Storch, N. (2005). Collaborative writing: Product, process, and students' reflections. *Journal of Second Language Writing*, 14, 153–173 (p. 154). Retrieved from http://www.lrc.cornell.edu/events/past/2012-2013/papers12/storchstorch.pdf

29. Budden, J. (2008). *Chain drawings*. BBC: Teaching English. Retrieved from http://www.teachingenglish.org.uk/article/chain-drawings?utm_source=facebook&utm_medium=social&utm_campaign=bc-teachingenglish

30. Common Core State Standards Initiative. (n.d.). *English language arts standards. Anchor standards. College and career readiness anchor standards for writing.* Retrieved from http://www.corestandards.org/ELA-Literacy/CCRA/W/

31. Common Core State Standards Initiative. (n.d.). *English language arts standards. Writing. Grade 9–10. 6.* Retrieved from http://www.corestandards.org/ELA-Literacy/WHST/9-10/6

32. Common Core State Standards Initiative. (n.d.). *English language arts standards. Writing. Grade 11–12. 6.* Retrieved from http://www.corestandards.org/ELA-Literacy/W/11-12/6/

33. The Alliance for Excellent Education. (2006, October 9). *Writing next: Effective strategies to improve writing of adolescents in middle and high schools* (p. 17). Retrieved from http://all4ed.org/reports-factsheets/writing-next-effective-strategies-to-improve-writing-of-adolescents-in-middle-and-high-schools/

34. The effect of computers on student writing: What the research tells us. (2003). *ASCD Research Brief, 1*(7). Retrieved from http://www.ascd.org/publications/researchbrief/v1n07/toc.aspx

35. The Alliance for Excellent Education. (2006, October 9). *Writing next: Effective strategies to improve writing of adolescents in middle and high schools* (p. 19). Retrieved from http://all4ed.org/reports-factsheets/writing-next-effective-strategies-to-improve-writing-of-adolescents-in-middle-and-high-schools/

36. Bliss, J. (2010). *Authentic writing and the impact it has on student motivation* (p. 10). (Master's thesis). St. John Fisher College, Rochester, NY.

37. *Picking up a second language is predicted by ability to learn patterns.* (2013, May 28). Association for Psychological Science. Retrieved from http://www.psychologicalscience.org/index.php/news/releases/picking-up-a-second-language-is-predicted-by-the-ability-to-learn-statistical-patterns.html

38. Sparks, S. D. (2015, June 18). Can sorting teach students to make better connections among subjects? *Education Week.* Retrieved from http://blogs.edweek.org/edweek/inside-school-research/2015/06/sorting_improves_science_transfer.html

39. Ferlazzo, L., & Hull Sypnieski, K. (2012). *The ESL/ELL teacher's survival guide: Ready-to-use strategies, tools, and activities for teaching all levels* (p. 184). San Francisco, CA: Jossey-Bass.

40. Ferlazzo, L., & Hull Sypnieski, K. (2012). *The ESL/ELL teacher's survival guide: Ready-to-use strategies, tools, and activities for teaching all levels* (p. 167). San Francisco, CA: Jossey-Bass.

41. Ferlazzo, L. (2013). *Self-driven learning: Teaching strategies for student motivation* (p. 120). New York, NY: Routledge.

42. Lin-Siegler, X., Shaenfield, D., & Elder, A. D. (2015). Contrasting case instruction can improve self-assessment of writing. *Educational Technology Research and Development, 63*(4), 517–537. Retrieved from http://link.springer.com/article/10.1007%2Fs11423-015-9390-9

43. Coleman, D., & Pimentel, S. (2012, April 12). *Revised publishers' criteria for the Common Core standards in English language arts and literacy, Grades 3–12* (p. 12). Retrieved from http://www.corestandards.org/assets/Publishers_Criteria_for_3-12.pdf

44. Ferlazzo, L. (2011). *Helping students motivate themselves* (p. 155). New York, NY: Routledge.

45. Ferlazzo, L., & Hull Sypnieski, K. (2012). *The ESL/ELL teacher's survival guide: Ready-to-use strategies, tools, and activities for teaching all levels* (p. 199). San Francisco, CA: Jossey-Bass.

46. Ferlazzo, L. (2011). *Helping students motivate themselves* (p. 106). New York, NY: Routledge.

47. NextGen VOICES: Results. (2013). *Science, 5*. Retrieved from http://www.sciencemag.org/content/341/6141/28/suppl/DC1

48. Peace Corps. (1992). *Teaching English as a foreign language to large, multilevel classes* (p. 38). Washington, DC: Author.

49. Ferlazzo, L., & Hull Sypnieski, K. (2012). *The ESL/ELL teacher's survival guide: Ready-to-use strategies, tools, and activities for teaching all levels* (p. 45). San Francisco, CA: Jossey-Bass.

50. Ferlazzo, F., & Hull-Sypnieski, K. (2014). Teaching argument writing to ELLs. *ASCD Educational Leadership, 71*(7), 46–52. Retrieved from http://www.ascd.org/publications/educational-leadership/apr14/vol71/num07/Teaching-Argument-Writing-to-ELLs.aspx

51. Ferlazzo, F., & Hull-Sypnieski, K. (2014). Teaching argument writing to ELLs. *ASCD Educational Leadership, 71*(7), 46–52. Retrieved from http://www.ascd.org/publications/educational-leadership/apr14/vol71/num07/Teaching-Argument-Writing-to-ELLs.aspx

52. Common Core State Standards for English Language Arts & Literacy in History/Social Studies, Science, and Technical Subjects. (n.d.). *Appendix A: Research supporting key elements of the standards. Glossary of key terms* (p. 25). Retrieved from http://www.corestandards.org/assets/Appendix_A.pdf

53. Rosemont, N. (Producer) & Jordan, G. (Director) & Gay, J. (1978). *Les Misérables*. [TV movie].

Chapter 5 Speaking and Listening

1. Camus, J.-P. (1880). *The Spirit of Saint Francis de Sales* (Chapter 1, p. 3). Retrieved from https://en.wikiquote.org/wiki/Francis_de_Sales

2. Burke, J. (2013). *The Common Core companion: The standards decoded, grades 9–12* (p. 145). Thousand Oaks, CA: SAGE.

3. Stuart, Jr., D. (n.d.). *Common Core SL.CCR.3 explained*. Retrieved from http://www.davestuartjr.com/common-core-sl-ccr-3-explained/

4. *Application of Common Core state standards for English language learners*. (n.d.). (p. 1). Retrieved from http://www.corestandards.org/assets/application-for-english-learners.pdf

5. City, E. A. (2014). Talking to learn. *Educational Leadership, 72*(3), 10–16. Retrieved from http://www.ascd.org/publications/educational-leadership/nov14/vol72/num03/Talking-to-Learn.aspx

6. Holden, J., & Schmit, J. S. (Eds.). (2002). *Inquiry and the literacy text: Constructing discussions in the English classroom* (p. 47). Retrieved from http://files.eric.ed.gov/fulltext/ED471390.pdf

7. Zwiers, J. (2014). *Building academic language: Meeting Common Core standards across disciplines, grades 5–12* (p. 57). San Francisco, CA: Jossey-Bass.

8. Shubitz, S. (2015, August 5). *Don't put a scaffold in place without a plan to take it away.* Twitter. Retrieved from https://twitter.com/raisealithuman/status/628964662764261376

9. Ferlazzo, L. (2013). *Self-driven learning: Teaching strategies for student motivation* (p. 62). New York, NY: Routledge.

10. Ferlazzo, L. (2015, March 19). Creating the conditions for student motivation. *Edutopia*. Retrieved from http://www.edutopia.org/blog/creating-conditions-for-student-motivation-larry-ferlazzo

11. Gonzalez, J. (2013, October 24). *Students sitting around too much? Try chat stations.* Cult of Pedagogy. Retrieved from http://www.cultofpedagogy.com/chat-stations/

12. Charan, R. (2012, June 21). The discipline of learning. *Harvard Business Review*. Retrieved from https://hbr.org/2012/06/the-discipline-of-listening

13. Rodriguez, T. (2012, October 18). How to use your ears to influence people. *Scientific American*. Retrieved from http://www.scientificamerican.com/article/how-to-use-your-ears-to-influence-people

14. Vandergrift, L. (n.d.). Listening: Theory and practice in modern foreign language competence. *Academia*. Retrieved from http://www.academia.edu/5274292/Listening_theory_and_practice_in_modern_foreign_language_competence_Author

15. Kiany, G. R., & Shiramiry, E. (2002). The effect of frequent dictation on the listening comprehension ability of elementary EFL learners. *TESL Canada Journal, 20*(1), 57–63. Retrieved from http://www.teslcanadajournal.ca/index.php/tesl/article/view/938/757

16. Stuart, Jr., D. (2014). *A non-freaked-out guide to teaching the Common Core: Using the 32 literacy anchor standards to develop college- and career-ready students.* San Francisco, CA: Jossey-Bass.

17. Stuart, Jr., D. (n.d.). *A first day of school activity that teaches argument, which teaches thinking* (updated). Retrieved from http://www.davestuartjr.com/first-day-of-school-activity-argument/?utm_content=bufferadb2c&utm_medium=social&utm_source=twitter.com&utm_campaign=buffer

Chapter 6 Language

1. Samuel Johnson. (1781). Cowley. *Lives of the English Poets* (Vol. 1, p. 58). Oxford, UK: Oxford University Press.

2. Common Core State Standards Initiative. (n.d.). *English language arts standards. Anchor standards. College and career readiness anchor standards for writing.* Retrieved from http://www.corestandards.org/ELA-Literacy/CCRA/W/

3. Common Core State Standards Initiative. (n.d.). *English language arts standards. Writing. Grade 9–10. 6.* Retrieved from http://www.corestandards.org/ELA-Literacy/WHST/9-10/6

4. Common Core State Standards Initiative. (n.d.). *English language arts standards. Writing. Grade 11–12. 6.* Retrieved from http://www.corestandards.org/ELA-Literacy/W/11-12/6/

5. *Application of Common Core state standards for English language learners.* (n.d.). (p. 1).Retrieved from http://www.corestandards.org/assets/application-for-english-learners.pdf

6. (Three Lessons, 2014).

7. Bunch, G. C., Kibler, A., & Pimentel, S. (n.d.). *Realizing opportunities for English language learners in the Common Core English language arts and disciplinary literary standards* (p. 8). Stanford, CA: Stanford University. Retrieved from http://ell.stanford.edu/sites/default/files/pdf/academic-papers/01_Bunch_Kibler_Pimentel_RealizingOpp%20in%20ELA_FINAL_0.pdf

8. Haight, C. E., Herron, C., & Cole, S. P. (2007). The effects of deductive and guided inductive instructional approaches on the learning of grammar in the elementary foreign language college classroom. *Foreign Language Annals, 40*(2), 288–310.

9. Ferlazzo, F., & Hull-Sypnieski, K. (2014). Teaching argument writing to ELLs. *ASCD Educational Leadership, 71*(7), 46–52. Retrieved from http://www.ascd.org/publications/educational-leadership/apr14/vol71/num07/Teaching-Argument-Writing-to-ELLs.aspx

10. Ferlazzo, L., & Hull Sypnieski, K. (2012). *The ESL/ELL teacher's survival guide: Ready-to-use strategies, tools, and activities for teaching all levels* (p. 265). San Francisco, CA: Jossey-Bass.

11. Ferlazzo, L. (2011, September 4). But will Secretary Duncan listen to her? *Larry Ferlazzo's websites of the day.* Retrieved from http://larryferlazzo.edublogs.org/2011/09/04/but-will-secretary-duncan-listen-to-her/comment-page-1/

12. Goldenberg, C. (2013, Summer). Unlocking the research on English learners. What we know—and don't yet know—about effective instruction. *American Educator, 37*, 4–11 (p. 5). Retrieved from https://www.aft.org/sites/default/files/periodicals/Goldenberg.pdf

13. Truscott, J. (2005, Spring). The continuing problems of oral grammar correction. *The International Journal of Foreign Language Teaching, 1*(2), 17–22. Retrieved from http://www.tprstories.com/ijflt/IJFLTSpring05.pdf

14. Truscott, J. (1996). The case against grammar correction in L2 writing classes. *Language Learning, 46*(2), 327–369.

15. Krashen, S. D. (1982). *Principles and practice in second language acquisition.* Oxford, UK: Pergamon Press. Retrieved from http://www.sdkrashen.com/content/books/principles_and_practice.pdf

16. Dodgson, D. (2011, August 7). #RSCON3: Feeding back and moving forward. *Reflections of a teacher and learner.* Retrieved from http://www.davedodgson.com/2011/08/rscon3-feeding-back-and-moving-forward.html

17. Common Core State Standards for English Language Arts & Literacy in History/Social Studies, Science, and Technical Subjects. (n.d.). *Appendix A: Research supporting key elements of the standards. Glossary of key terms* (p. 33). Retrieved from http://www.corestandards.org/assets/Appendix_A.pdf

18. Common Core State Standards for English Language Arts & Literacy in History/Social Studies, Science, and Technical Subjects. (n.d.). *Appendix A: Research supporting key*

elements of the standards. Glossary of key terms (p. 33). Retrieved from http://www .corestandards.org/assets/Appendix_A.pdf

19. Marzano, R. J., & Pickering, D. J. (n.d.). *Building academic vocabulary teacher's manual.* Retrieved from https://docs.google.com/presentation/d/1NZzE_I_ jGiPjfBlmKVv7OvuP_jL-FlmSzZ9SVy_cmeg/edit#slide=id.i224

20. Ferlazzo, L. (2014, February 27). English-Language Learners and academic language. *Edutopia.* Retrieved from http://www.edutopia.org/blog/english-language-learners-academic-language-larry-ferlazzo

21. Lawrence, J. F., White, C., & Snow, C. E. (2010). The words students need. *Educational Leadership, 68*(2), 23–26. Retrieved from http://www.ascd.org/publications/ educational-leadership/oct10/vol68/num02/The-Words-Students-Need.aspx

22. Colorado, C. (2007). Using cognates to develop comprehension in English. *¡Colorín Colorado!* Retrieved from http://www.colorincolorado.org/educators/background/ cognates/

23. Ferlazzo, F., & Hull-Sypnieski, K. (2014). Teaching argument writing to ELLs. *ASCD Educational Leadership, 71*(7), 46–52. Retrieved from http://www.ascd.org/publications/ educational-leadership/apr14/vol71/num07/Teaching-Argument-Writing-to-ELLs .aspx

24. Ferlazzo, L., & Hull Sypnieski, K. (2012). *The ESL/ELL teacher's survival guide: Ready-to-use strategies, tools, and activities for teaching all levels* (p. 239). San Francisco, CA: Jossey-Bass.

25. Csikszentmihalyi, M. (1990). Literacy and intrinsic motivation. Daedalus, *119*(2), 115–140.

26. Csikszentmihalyi, M. (2008). *Flow.* HarperCollins e-books.

Chapter 7 Mathematics

1. Common Core State Standards Initiative. (n.d.) *Standards for mathematical practice.* Retrieved from http://www.corestandards.org/Math/Practice/

2. Fenner, D. S. (2013). *Common Core math for English Language Learners.* Retrieved from J. Carr, http://blog.colorincolorado.org/2013/03/28/common-core-math-for-english-language-learners/

3. Celedon-Pattichis, S., & Ramirez, N. G. (2012). *Beyond good teaching: Advancing mathematics education for ELLs.* Reston, VA: National Council of Teachers of Mathematics.

4. Lopez, N. R. (n.d.). Mathematical notation comparisons between U.S. and Latin American countries. In *TODOS: Mathematics for all.* Houston, TX: Harris County Department of Education.

5. Exhibit 7.1 is an excerpt from "Mathematical Notation Comparisons between U.S. and Latin American Countries" available from *TODOS: Mathematics for All, NCTM,* and *Beyond Good Teaching* and created by Noemi R. Lopez.

6. Moschkovich, J. (2012). Mathematics, the Common Core, and language: Recommendations for mathematics instruction for ELs aligned with the Common Core. Commissioned Papers on Language and Literacy Issues in the Common Core State Standards and Next Generation Science Standards, 94, 17–27.

7. Meyer, D. (2008, March 16). Linear fun #2: Stacking cups. *dy/dan* [Blog]. Retrieved from http://blog.mrmeyer.com/2008/linear-fun-2-stacking-cups/

8. Melanese, K., Chung, L. & Forbes, C. (2011). *Supporting English Language Learners in math class: Grades V 6–8.* Sausalito, CA: Math Solutions.

9. Chapin, S. H., O'Connor, C., & Anderson, N. C. (2003). *Classroom discussions: Using math talk to help students learn.* Sausalito, CA: Math Solutions.

10. Hidayah, T. (n.d.). Frayer Model and its significance for vocabulary achievement in classroom environment. Retrieved from https://www.academia.edu/4023338/Frayer_Model_and_Its_Significance_for_Vocabulary_Achievement_in_Classroom_Environment

11. Carr, J., Carroll, C., Cremer, S., Gale, M., Lagunoff, R., & Sexton, U. (2009). *Making mathematics accessible to English Learners.* San Francisco, CA: WestEd.

12. Hale, J., Lien, Z., Larkins, C., May, M., Sommer, S. N., Ackley, V.,. . . Tierney-Fife, P. (2012). *Common Core state standards Mathematics I: Integrated pathway* Portland, ME: J. Weston Walch.

Chapter 8 Social Studies

1. Marzano, R. J. (2012). 9. What do I typically do to chunk content into digestible bites? In R. J. Marzano *Becoming a reflective teacher* (p. 194).

2. T. J. and the Revo. (2010, June 19). *Too late to apologize: A declaration.* Soomo Publishing. Retrieved from https://www.youtube.com/watch?v=XQmz1X0_JiE

3. Common Core State Standards Initiative. (n.d.). *English language arts standards. Anchor standards. College and career readiness anchor standards for writing.* Retrieved from http://www.corestandards.org/ELA-Literacy/CCRA/W/

4. Annenberg Classroom. (n.d.). *The story of the Bill of Rights.* The Leonore Annenberg Institute for Civics. Retrieved from http://www.annenbergclassroom.org/page/the-story-of-the-bill-of-rights

Chapter 9 Science

1. National Research Council. (2013, May). Appendix M: Connections to the Common Core State Standards for Literacy in Science and Technical Subjects. *Next Generation Science Standards.* Retrieved from http://www.nextgenscience.org/sites/ngss/files/Appendix%20M%20Connections%20to%20the%20CCSS%20for%20Literacy_061213.pdf

2. National Research Council. (2013, April). How to read the Next Generation Science Standards (NGSS). *Next Generation Science Standards.* Retrieved from http://www.nextgenscience.org/sites/ngss/files/How%20to%20Read%20NGSS%20-%20Final%2008.19.13.pdf

3. National Research Council. (2013, April). Appendix D: All standards, all students. *Next Generation Science Standards.* Retrieved from http://www.nextgenscience.org/sites/ngss/files/Appendix%20D%20Diversity%20and%20Equity%20-%204.9.13.pdf

4. California Department of Education. (2012). Appendix B: The California English language development standards Part II: Learning about how English works. In English language development standards for California public schools: Kindergarten through grade twelve. Sacramento.

5. National Research Council. (2015, June). 5-ESS2-1: Earth's systems. *Next Generation Science Standards*. Retrieved from http://www.nextgenscience.org/sites/ngss/files/5-ESS2-1%20June%202015.pdf

6. Fathman, A. K., & Crowther, D. T. (Eds.). (2006). *Science for English language learners: K-12 classroom strategies*. Arlington, VA: National Science Teachers Association.

7. Lee, O., & Buxton, C. A. (2013). Integrating Science and English Proficiency for English Language Learners. *Theory Into Practice*, 52(1), 36–42.

8. Rosebery, A. S., & Warren, B. (Eds.). (2008). *Teaching science to English language learners: Building on students' strengths*. Arlington, VA: National Science Teachers Association.

Appendix

Accessing the Bonus Web Content

This book's companion web page features a number of additional resources for readers.

- Downloadable versions of all the lesson plans and Tech Tools boxes featured in this book, with live hyperlinks to the many web pages that are referenced
- Two bonus web chapters: "School Counselors and English Language Learners" by Leticia Gallardo and "Art and English Language Learners" by John Doolittle

To access these materials, go to the "Downloads" section of this book's web page at www.wiley.com/go/navccss.

Index